LEED LAB

Facility performance evaluations inform the long-term life of a building and do not end with design or construction. To this aim, Patricia Andrasik created LEED Lab, in collaboration with the US Green Building Council, an increasingly popular international interdisciplinary collegiate laboratory course, which utilizes campus buildings as demonstration sites to facilitate the green assessment of existing buildings. *LEED Lab: A Model for Sustainable Design Education* uses the LEED O+M building rating system to measure and achieve performance-driven campus facilities in which the readers work and operate.

The book explains in simple terms the theory, tasks, tools and techniques necessary for credit implementation and achievement, and includes case studies and exercises for practical application in each chapter. Readers will learn the conceptual scientific framework used to understand existing operational performance and how to quantify sustainable synergies, create green campus policies with administrators, and understand systems such as energy and water in a research-based application. The entire manual is accompanied by a vast online 'Teaching Toolkit' to provide helpful educational resources such as syllabi, lectures, examinations, assignments, Individual Student Progress Presentation (ISSP) templates, web resources, and much more.

An excellent guide for undergraduate or graduate students enrolled in LEED Lab or a similar campus building assessment course, as well as construction or architectural professionals and facility managers, this manual navigates the complexities of using a green building diagnostic tool such as LEED O+M towards greater environmental literacy.

Patricia Andrasik is an associate professor at the School of Architecture and Planning at The Catholic University of America (CUA) and a licensed architect in Washington, D.C. She was a Fulbright Scholar at the Slovak University of Technology while earning her Master of Architecture at the University of Oklahoma. She then taught as a visiting professor in Beirut prior to returning to the US to practice.

Informing design through performance metrics, and using performance metrics to inform building operations and maintenance, have become the foundations of her teaching and scholarly research, and internationally recognized by the publications/conferences of organizations including JNIBS, NBI, AASHE, ACSA, AIA/COTE, and others.

Andrasik has created several novel courses to promote environmental integration into architecture. She was awarded seed funding to integrate building performance analytics (BPA) into the design process for local and international architectural projects, and collaborated with Autodesk to run a pilot class for analytical plug-ins. In addition to co-authoring *Heating Cooling Lighting: Sustainable Design Strategies Towards Net Zero Design* (Fifth Edition, 2020), Andrasik co-founded BEE*now*, a non-profit organization inspiring NAAB-accredited schools to emphasize the teaching of low-energy design, and recently received the President's Award for the Advancement of Teaching at CUA.

LEED LAB
A MODEL FOR SUSTAINABLE DESIGN EDUCATION

PATRICIA ANDRASIK

First published 2022
by Routledge
52 Vanderbilt Avenue, New York, NY 10017

and by Routledge
2 Park Square, Milton Park, Abingdon, Oxon, OX14 4RN

Routledge is an imprint of the Taylor & Francis Group, an informa business

© 2022 Taylor & Francis

The right of Patricia Andrasik to be identified as author of this work has been asserted by her in accordance with sections 77 and 78 of the Copyright, Designs and Patents Act 1988.

All rights reserved. No part of this book may be reprinted or reproduced or utilised in any form or by any electronic, mechanical, or other means, now known or hereafter invented, including photocopying and recording, or in any information storage or retrieval system, without permission in writing from the publishers.

Trademark notice: Product or corporate names may be trademarks or registered trademarks, and are used only for identification and explanation without intent to infringe.

Library of Congress Cataloging-in-Publication Data
Names: Andrasik, Patricia, author.
Title: LEED lab : a model for sustainable design education / Patricia Andrasik.
Description: New York, NY : Routledge, 2021. | Includes bibliographical references and index.
Identifiers: LCCN 2020049732 (print) | LCCN 2020049733 (ebook) | ISBN 9781138326682 (hbk) | ISBN 9781138326699 (pbk) | ISBN 9780429449703 (ebk)
Subjects: LCSH: Leadership in Energy and Environmental Design Green Building Rating System—Study and teaching (Higher)—Activity programs. | Energy auditing—Study and teaching (Higher)—Activity programs. | Sustainable construction—Study and teaching (Higher)—Activity programs. | College buildings—Energy conservation—Study and teaching (Higher)—Activity programs.
Classification: LCC TH880.A64 20221 (print) | LCC TH880 (ebook) | DDC 720/.4720711—dc23
LC record available at https://lccn.loc.gov/2020049732
LC ebook record available at https://lccn.loc.gov/2020049733

ISBN: 978-1-138-32668-2 (hbk)
ISBN: 978-1-138-32669-9 (pbk)
ISBN: 978-0-429-44970-3 (ebk)

DOI: 10.4324/9780429449703

Typeset in Univers
by Apex CoVantage, LLC

Access the Support Material: http://www.routledge.com/9781138326699

This book is dedicated to my husband Dennis, for his unwavering support, editing assistance, patience and love. Also to my mother Maria, whose love provided the constant 'reminders' to develop it. Also, to my sons Cyril, and triplets Dominic, Benedict and Julian, who were born witnessing the beginning and the end of its long execution.

CONTENTS

LIST OF ILLUSTRATIONS	xi
FOREWORD	xv
PREFACE	xvii
ACKNOWLEDGEMENTS	xix

1	**INTRODUCTION**		**1**
	1.1	Facility Performance Evaluation in Architecture	1
	1.2	Sustainable Campus Building Assessment	4
	1.3	LEED Lab: Campus Assessment as a POE of Facility Performance	5
2	**METHODOLOGY**		**10**
	2.1	A System of Approach	10
	2.2	Action Research as a Theoretical Methodology	11
	2.3	The Three-Part Integrated Diagnostic Process	12
	2.4	A Critical Feedback Loop	14
	2.5	The Textbook Methodology	16
	2.6	Toolbox Teaching Guide	17
3	**PLATFORM**		**19**
	3.1	Collaboration	19
		3.1.1 Educators	19
		3.1.2 Students	20
		3.1.3 US Green Building Council	21
		3.1.4 Green Building Certification Institute	21
		3.1.5 Consultants	22
		3.1.6 Administration	23
		3.1.7 Staff	23
	3.2	Learning	24
		3.2.1 Learning Management Systems	24
	3.3	Certification	24
		3.3.1 Assessment Systems	25
4	**PHASE 1: FEASIBILITY**		**35**
	4.1	Goals	35
		4.1.1 Academic Research	36
		4.1.2 Expedited Certification	38
	4.2	Approach	38
		4.2.1 The Campus Assessment	42
		4.2.2 Policies	42
		4.2.3 Choosing a Facility	44
		4.2.4 Performance Period	44
		4.2.5 Recertification	44
	4.3	Timeline	46
		4.3.1 Strategies and Synergies	47
		4.3.2 Point Integration Diagram	52
5	**PHASE 2: IMPLEMENTATION**		**57**
	5.1	Transportation	61
	5.2	Comparison	61
		5.2.1 Green Globes for Existing Buildings (EB)	62

CONTENTS

	5.2.2	BREEAM In-Use	64
	5.2.3	Green Star Performance	64
	5.2.4	LEED Operations and Maintenance (O+M)	65
	5.2.5	Other Rating Systems	65
5.3	Alternative Transportation		68
	5.3.1	Sample Campus Alternative Transportation Plans	73
5.4	Case Study		74
5.5	Exercises		77

6 SITE — 79

6.1	Theory		79
6.2	Comparison		80
	6.2.1	Green Globes for Existing Buildings (EB)	80
	6.2.2	BREEAM In-Use	82
	6.2.3	Green Star Performance	82
	6.2.4	LEED Operations and Maintenance (O+M)	83
	6.2.5	Other Rating Systems	84
6.3	Credits		87
	6.3.1	Site Management	87
	6.3.2	Rainwater Management	91
	6.3.3	Light Pollution Reduction	94
6.4	Case Study		98
6.5	Exercises		103

7 WATER — 107

7.1	Theory		107
7.2	Comparison		108
	7.2.1	Green Globes for Existing Buildings (EB)	109
	7.2.2	BREEAM In-Use	110
	7.2.3	Green Star Performance	110
	7.2.4	LEED Operations and Maintenance (O+M)	111
	7.2.5	Other Rating Systems	112
7.3	Credits		115
	7.3.1	Indoor Water Use Reduction	115
	7.3.2	Building Level Water Metering	120
	7.3.3	Outdoor Water Use Reduction	122
	7.3.4	Cooling Tower Water Use	124
7.4	Case Study		127
7.5	Exercises		128

8 ENERGY — 133

8.1	Theory		133
8.2	Comparison		134
	8.2.1	Green Globes for Existing Buildings (EB)	136
	8.2.2	BREEAM In-Use	138
	8.2.3	Green Star Performance	138
	8.2.4	LEED Operations and Maintenance (O+M)	139
	8.2.5	Other Rating Systems	139
8.3	Credits		142
	8.3.1	Best Management Practices	142
	8.3.2	Minimum Energy Performance	160
	8.3.3	Energy Metering	170
	8.3.4	Refrigerant Management	174
	8.3.5	Commissioning	183
	8.3.6	Demand Response	189
	8.3.7	Renewable Energy and Carbon Offsets	199

CONTENTS

8.4	Case Study	204
8.5	Exercises	215

9 MATERIALS AND RESOURCES — 220
- 9.1 Theory — 220
- 9.2 Comparison — 222
  - 9.2.1 Green Globes for Existing Buildings (EB) — 222
  - 9.2.2 BREEAM In-Use — 223
  - 9.2.3 Green Star Performance — 225
  - 9.2.4 LEED Operations and Maintenance (O+M) — 225
  - 9.2.5 Other Rating Systems — 226
- 9.3 Credits — 230
  - 9.3.1 Ongoing Purchasing and Waste Policy — 230
  - 9.3.2 Facility Maintenance and Renovation — 234
- 9.4 Case Study — 240
- 9.5 Exercises — 242

10 INDOOR ATMOSPHERE — 245
- 10.1 Theory — 245
- 10.2 Comparison — 252
  - 10.2.1 Green Globes for Existing Buildings (EB) — 254
  - 10.2.2 BREEAM In-Use — 255
  - 10.2.3 Green Star Performance — 256
  - 10.2.4 LEED Operations and Maintenance (O+M) — 256
  - 10.2.5 Other Rating Systems — 257
- 10.3 Credits — 260
  - 10.3.1 Air Quality Performance — 260
  - 10.3.2 Smoke Control — 279
  - 10.3.3 Green Cleaning — 286
  - 10.3.4 Lighting — 292
  - 10.3.5 Pest Management — 298
  - 10.3.6 Occupant Comfort Survey — 299
- 10.4 Case Study — 302
- 10.5 Exercises — 304

11 PHASE 3: DOCUMENTATION — 309
- 11.1 Coordination — 309
  - 11.1.1 Recording — 309
  - 11.1.2 Delegation — 310
- 11.2 Gaps — 314
- 11.3 Submission — 314
- 11.4 Review — 316
- 11.5 Certification — 317
- 11.6 Closing — 317

INDEX — 318

ILLUSTRATIONS

Figures

1.1	US CO_2 emissions by sector	1
1.2	US cities participating in building benchmarking	2
1.3	2017 Higher Education Sustainability Staffing Report	4
1.4	The Catholic University of America students in University Central Plant	7
2.1	LEED Lab students design and build a rainwater cistern	11
2.2	Sagor's Action Research Cycle	12
2.3	A charrette between facilities management and LEED Lab students	13
2.4	Scenario where existing students have already started to work on credits in a LEED Lab course that extends for one year	15
2.5	Learning module icons	17
3.1	Global sustainable existing building sustainability assessment tools comparison	26
3.2	Comparison of rating systems	27
3.3	The ARC Platform website portal	31
4.1	Harvard University's sustainability plan	37
4.2	LEED O+M credits that are eligible for Master Site	40
4.3	Comparison of O+M assessment systems	41
4.4	Performance Periods by credit	46
4.5	Timeline of the history of LEED O+M	46
4.6	LEED O+M implementation diagram for The Catholic University of America	48
4.7	Various sustainability strategies one can utilize to create a synergy	51
4.8	An example of how strategies can synergize	51
4.9	Final point integration diagram	52
4.10	Initial point integration diagram	53
4.11	An example of a synergy diagram that includes LEED calculations	55
5.1	Various LEED Lab classroom scenarios	57
5.2	Individual Student Progress Presentation, ISPP overview	58
5.3	Student example of ISPP1 for the Light Pollution Reduction credit	59
5.4	Student example of ISPP2 for the Light Pollution Reduction credit	60
5.5	Global sustainable existing building sustainability assessment tools: comparison of Transportation credits	62
5.6	Allocation of Transportation credits in various global sustainability assessment systems for existing buildings	63
5.7	Transportation credit equations	71
5.8	Alternative Transportation: strategies for achievement	75
5.9	How can the Innovation credit help?	76
6.1	Global sustainable existing building sustainability assessment tools	80
6.2	Global sustainable existing building sustainability assessment tools	81
6.3	LEED O+M v4 Reference Guide: Site Management best practices	89
6.4	Two options for a municipal sewage system	92
6.5	Small storm hydrology method	93
6.6	Light trespass	95
6.7	Sustainable Sites credit: Light Pollution Reduction	97
6.8	The Catholic University of America Campus Master Plan, April 2012	100

ILLUSTRATIONS

6.9	Terrain elevation map of The Catholic University of America, Campus Master Plan, April 2012	101
6.10	The Catholic University of America Campus Master Plan, April 2012	102
6.11	The Catholic University of America, area of vegetation on campus	103
7.1	Global sustainable existing building sustainability assessment tools	108
7.2	Global sustainable existing building sustainability assessment tools	109
7.3	Water Efficiency Prerequisite, Indoor Water Use Reduction: Option 1	117
7.4	Water Efficiency Prerequisite, Indoor Water Use Reduction: faucet flow rate conversion	118
7.5	Building-level water metering: stainless steel pulse output water meter	121
7.6	Cooling tower at Opus Hall, The Catholic University of America	125
7.7	Typical low chemical water treatment system	125
7.8	Examples of biochar	128
7.9	CUA community garden plots ready for the admission of biochar	129
8.1	Annual global building CO_2 emissions by sector	134
8.2	Building-level energy metering: Energy and Atmosphere Prerequisite	135
8.3	Global sustainable existing building sustainability assessment tools for energy	136
8.4	Global sustainable existing building sustainability assessment tools: comparison for energy	137
8.5	Global assessment systems: North America based and internationally based	140
8.6	Existing building plan	144
8.7	Combined fuel end-use breakdown for the Crough School of Architecture and Planning	149
8.8	Energy Accounting Feedback Loop (EAFL)	150
8.9	Statement of Energy Performance for the Crough School of Architecture and Planning	153
8.10	LEED Lab students are introduced to the central plant by a staff operator	154
8.11	A Building Automation System (BAS) or Building Management System (BMS)	156
8.12	Energy and Facility Management Software (EFMS) for buildings	157
8.13	Energy and Facility Management Software (EFMS) for Buildings Feedback Loop	157
8.14	A utility submeter system in a building	161
8.15	Shark Meter diagram	162
8.16	Energy Star Portfolio Manager	164
8.17	Energy and Atmosphere Prerequisite: minimum energy performance diagram	165
8.18	Energy and Atmosphere Prerequisite: minimum energy performance calculations for district energy supply	169
8.19	Shares of major energy sources used in commercial buildings, 2012	171
8.20	The ozone layer	175
8.21	The physics of the refrigerant cycle	177
8.22	Diagram of how a refrigerant is processed in an air conditioner	177
8.23	Diagram of how refrigerant is processed in a heat pump	179
8.24	Equation from LEED O+M v4 Reference Guide for simple payback for equipment replacement or conversion	180
8.25	Resulting annual maintenance and refrigerant cost difference equation	180
8.26	Energy and Atmosphere credit: demand response and how it works	190
8.27	Renewable Energy Certificate	200
8.28	Energy and Atmosphere credit: renewable energy and carbon offsets equations	202
8.29	Minimum project requirement for the Crough School of Architecture and Planning, Item 6	205

ILLUSTRATIONS

8.30	Metering Management System at the Crough Center	205
8.31	Space types at the Crough Center	209
8.32	Sample Meter Certificate of Calibration	215
9.1	A sample of an LCA Report from the Revit plug-in TALLY	221
9.2	Global sustainable existing building sustainability assessment tools for materials	223
9.3	Global sustainable existing building sustainability assessment tools comparison for materials	224
9.4	Procurement and waste management policy map	231
9.5	Percentage of floor area appropriate for a particular rating system	234
9.6	Facility Maintenance and Renovation (FMR) Policy Prerequisite map	235
9.7	Environmental Purchasing Policy (EPP) for Facility Maintenance and Renovation (FMR) steps	236
9.8	Procurement and Waste Management Policy for the CUA Sustainability Plan	241
10.1	Health and comfort of the indoor environment	246
10.2	How to read a Psychrometric Chart, page 1	248
10.3	How to read a Psychrometric Chart, page 2	249
10.4	How to read a Psychrometric Chart, page 3	250
10.5	How to read a Psychrometric Chart, page 4	251
10.6	A Psychrometric Chart, a tool to help determine interior thermal comfort levels	252
10.7	Global sustainable existing building sustainability assessment tools for indoor air quality	253
10.8	Global sustainable existing building sustainability assessment tools: comparison for indoor air quality	254
10.9	MERV rating chart	262
10.10	Second-floor plan of the Edward M. Crough School of Architectural Studies	263
10.11	Close-up of Figure 10.10	264
10.12	Close-up of Figure 10.10	264
10.13	Measuring airflow tips and techniques chart	275
10.14	Location of designated smoking areas at The Catholic University of America	281
10.15	Image of example of non-smoking sign at OPUS Hall	283
10.16	US state and local Smoke-Free Restaurant and Bar Laws, 2002–2012	284
10.17	Types of solar glare: disability glare and discomfort glare	292
10.18	Cycle of luminance	296
10.19	Color Rendering Index (CRI) for different types of lamps	296
10.20	Sample results from occupant survey for the Crough School of Architecture and Planning	300
11.1	LEED Online Portal login page	310
11.2	LEED Online Portal registration page	311
11.3	iDOR home page	312
11.4	iDOR page for Materials and Resources credits	312
11.5	iDOR page for Policy and Tracking Sheet templates	313

Tables

7.1	Reduction of water use in flow fixtures	119
7.2	Flush and flow summary statistics	120
7.3	Innovation savings chart: the building operating plan for the Crough School of Architecture and Planning	130

ILLUSTRATIONS

8.1	Sample of an O+M plan	145
8.2	Combined fuel end-use breakdown for the Crough School of Architecture and Planning	149
8.3	Comparison of refrigerants: global warming potential and ozone depletion potential	175
8.4	List of utility companies in the United States	193
8.5	Daily energy use at the Crough School of Architecture and Planning	208
8.6	Preventive maintenance schedule for the Crough School of Architecture and Planning	211
8.7	Energy conservation measures for the Crough School of Architecture and Planning	213
10.1	AHU schedule 2013, pages 1–4	265
10.2	ASHRAE's standard 62.1 outdoor air rates, Table 6–1	272
10.3	Indoor Environmental Quality credit: interior lighting: strategies for lighting quality	294

Boxes

4.1	Campus assessment checklist	43
4.2	Building feasibility checklist	45
5.1	Sample commuting transportation survey	72
5.2	Transportation sustainability plan for The Catholic University of America	75
5.3	The missing links in The Catholic University of America's current transportation sustainability plan	76
7.1	Option 1: calculated water use tasks	116
7.2	Option 2: metered water use tasks	116
8.1	Energy sources on campus	171
8.2	Main tasks for renewable energy and carbon offsets	201
10.1	Green cleaning resources from the US Environmental Protection Agency (EPA)	288
10.2	Option 1: lighting control	293
10.3	Option 2: lighting strategies	295
10.4	Integrated pest management plan tasks	298

FOREWORD

At the US Green Building Council we have a strong vision of a sustainable built environment within this generation. Each and every day we work towards this vision to transform the places where we live, work, play, and, most importantly, learn. Education is a key component of market transformation and, for our vision to become a reality, we know that driving change in places of learning is imperative. To achieve this, we are laser focused on two key tactics for higher education: transforming campus existing buildings and infrastructure, and preparing students for twenty-first-century careers in sustainability.

Our colleges and universities are the very center of communities around the world and are responsible for educating the next generation of future leaders, professionals, consumers and global citizens. They also play a critical role in moving the needle on important global issues, such as climate change and sustainability. At USGBC, we know healthy, safe, inspiring and resource-efficient places for learning are vital in preparing the next generation for a world that is drastically changing.

We know that implementing green building policies and strategies can transform our higher education institutions in powerful ways and help faculty, staff and students seize interconnected opportunities. Green campuses reduce the environmental impact of buildings and grounds, have a positive effect on the wellbeing and health of community members, and create spaces that enhance learning. However, many colleges and universities are underfunded and lack the resources and staff needed to implement campus sustainability programs holistically.

We also know that today's generation of college students are more focused than ever on jobs, and that they are seeking jobs in sustainability at a rapidly increasing rate. And we know that regardless of their field or major, they should have a clear understanding of the relationships between the natural world, social equity and economic progress, so that upon graduation they can use their personal and professional platforms to create a world that allows both people and planet to thrive.

We also must ensure that what students are learning at the post-secondary level is what the industry or their future employers are looking for, or practical for preparing them to truly make a difference. The higher education sector must provide our college and university students with the employability skills needed for twenty-first-century career jobs post-graduation. It is clear to us that if we are going to prepare our students for graduation and help them achieve the competencies and skills that they need to be successful, we need to change higher education.

With the goals of transforming our existing campus facilities and preparing students to be ready for twenty-first-century careers, USGBC sought to develop a practical tool and pathway to meet both needs that delivers tangible results. LEED Lab, an innovative solution for integrating sustainable practices into daily campus operations and maintenance that is directly powered by students, is a critical part of our strategy. A multidisciplinary immersion course, LEED Lab utilizes the built environment to educate and prepare students to become green building leaders and sustainability focused citizens.

This book is an example of a curricular tool that will be utilized in helping to transform the classroom experience. LEED Lab provides students with direct hands-on learning grounded in the built environment. The course impacts go beyond one single academic term resulting in lasting sustainable changes to campus communities and affecting the lives of so many young people.

At USGBC, we say every story about a green building is a story about people and every story about a LEED building is a story about leaders. Professor Patricia Andrasik is living proof of this in action – the LEED Lab effort originated and has been successful thanks to a pilot course created and taught by her at The Catholic University of America (CUA). She has

FOREWORD

been successful in implementing LEED at the higher education level by utilizing students as a catalyst for transformational change. This book will inspire others to follow her example.

LEED Lab is the future of higher education, bringing together academics and operations to achieve unprecedented results. Together, we can equip and empower the next generation to achieve our vision for this world, leaving a legacy of sustainability behind for future generations and *definitively* changing this world for the better.

Mahesh Ramanujam
President and CEO, US Green Building Council

PREFACE

After years of simultaneously practicing architecture and teaching it, I recognized a significant gap between what architects were required to know in the ever-emerging and evolving field of sustainable design, and how this was being taught to our new generation of aspiring young professionals. It was quite different. I endeavored to design a new type of class to address this issue.

The heightened international focus on LEED and other green building assessments within colleges and universities drew a natural pairing of *learning* and *applying* learned knowledge. Academic curricula was a logical solution to bridge this divide; creating a course dedicated to applying learned knowledge to an actual building provided a platform for action research. It simultaneously provided students with an opportunity to become impact-catalysts on their own campuses.

LEED Lab is a novel approach to a student's understanding of sustainable design by evaluating existing buildings through green assessment. Culminating in improvements of operations, maintenance, efficiency, function, occupant health, and a reduction in using natural resources on actual campus facilities, the course offers institutional benefits to not only a student's learning, but also to faculty, staff, external trade and technical consultants, and of course, to the facility being assessed.

After ten years of teaching and developing LEED Lab, I began to observe certain unique issues within its implementation: the LEED O+M v4 Reference Guide was far too technical for the beginner taking the course; facilities personnel simply did not have a grasp of the extent of the systems which impacted theirs, thus saw sustainable operations in their building only within a narrow perspective; faculty were not knowledgeable of the way that green policies actually impacted the entire protocol of facilities staff. A different approach was warranted. Besides a few articles introducing LEED Lab, brochures explaining how to start LEED Lab at an institution, tips to facilitate the course, and websites with successful LEED Lab stories, there was no direction for actually running the course with its technical content.

This textbook serves as a resource for LEED Lab students, faculty and staff to navigate the complex process of green assessment through the LEED Operations and Maintenance (LEED O+M) rating system, and is designed to accompany the LEED O+M v4 Reference Guide. More specifically, it provides the insight for students in LEED Labs at universities across the world to gain the experience of performing various resource tracking, writing green policies, and collaborating with multiple realms of professionals on buildings immediately available to them on their respective campuses. Campus faculty and administrators likewise benefit from this publication by better comprehending the measures necessary for a thorough existing building evaluation of their facilities. Government, military or hospital personnel and other organizations interested in maintaining sustainable efficiency on their campuses can use it as well for internal technical training, to launch a LEED Lab course, or refer to it as a method of self-evaluating their built infrastructure.

A significant amount of research was dedicated to producing this publication. Resources used in this publication include foremost the LEED O+M v4 Reference Guide, and my extensive experience of teaching the course to interpret its contents into LEED Lab's scholastic platform. LEEDuser was also invaluable, as it provided existing templates and recommendations. Since the methodology underlying this publication may be universally adaptable to other rating systems, categories and metrics of the most frequently used O+M international rating systems such as Green Globes, CASBEE, DGNB and many more, were carefully evaluated and compared to provide a platform for LEED Labs and similar courses at universities around the world. The book also applies national and international, governmental, and local green non-profit and for-profit organizational recommendations and explains how they relate to credits. Manufacturer and trade websites are referenced to

PREFACE

help explain technical jargon, equipment and systems. The book also streamlines complex steps and technical procedures necessary to accomplish credits, and provides tools and techniques specific to LEED's curricular and campus implementation so that they are coherent to the novice.

It is my strong belief that architecture students particularly, but students of other disciplines generally, require a real-world venue of exploration for their technical knowledge prior to entering today's green competitive work force. It is no longer sufficient to understand what global warming means, or to advocate for energy reduction. Rather, understanding *how* a collection of refrigerant leaks in a majority of HVAC units on a campus contributes towards that warming, or *where* to facilitate methods of reducing EUI on campus, respectively, provides an emerging professional credibility in today's world of environmental alliance.

Issues which I encountered in my research and execution of this book include the frequency of updates to formal green assessment systems which reflect the rapid evolution of the sustainable building industry as a whole. It is nearly impossible to keep track of the daily changes to building energy codes and standards as they impact assessment – as evidenced by the amount of addenda to the LEED rating systems issued by the USGBC on a regular basis. In fact, as this publication was being written, the organization launched an updated beta version of the LEED O+M rating system! Fortunately, this book serves as a foundational guide for curricular application of green assessment, even if links, resources and metric thresholds continue to evolve.

The work which culminated in this publication is extensive but not conclusive. It has the possibility of branching into other scholastic and professional applications such as vocational training schools, military facilities, and various corporate campus applications. Its dynamic content which integrates many environmentally related disciplines, trades and professional organizations into a cohesive team through academic curricula makes it a premier instrument for market transformation in the green building industry.

ACKNOWLEDGEMENTS

The success of LEED Lab would not have been possible without the support of John Garvey, President of The Catholic University of America (CUA), and Randall Ott, former Dean of the School of Architecture and Planning, who supported the LEED O+M certification of our Crough Center for Architectural studies and encouraged my teaching and research which led to this publication.

I would like to thank the amazing Jaime Van Mourik, ORISE Science, Technology and Policy Fellow in the Building Technologies Office of the US Department of Energy, for her unwavering collaboration of the LEED Lab pilot, its promotion, and partnering with our institution towards many mutual sustainability goals. I'm also indebted to Roger Chang, Senior Engineer – and that of his staff at the DLR Group – who volunteered their time to help our research in mechanical system analysis, and to conduct our ASHRAE level 1 and II surveys as a contribution to higher educational learning. Much gratitude also goes to Brian Alexander, the former Director of Energy and Utilities Management at CUA, for procuring any equipment we needed to facilitate the course, and for learning with us the ways of LEEDing via a Lab at CUA!

Aligned with its launch, I would like to thank Chris Grech, former Director of the Master of Science in Sustainable Design (MSSD) program and former Associate Deans Ann Cederna and George Martin, who established the course and promoted LEED Lab's advancement long ago, without hesitation. Deserving of special mention is former Research Dean, Barry Yatt, who confidently promoted the course, and convinced me to write this textbook.

Those staff members who traversed semester after semester with my students, and who provided me with the practical knowledge necessary to produce this publication, I would like to recognize as well. Those people include: Debra Nauta-Rodriguez, University Architect and Associate Vice President for Facilities Planning and Management, and Alex Harry, Assistant Director of Campus Facilities and Sustainability Initiatives who continue to support the triad of learning between faculty, staff and students and without whom LEED Lab's continuing success would not exist. Also deserving of mention is Chris Vetick, former Assistant Director of Ground Maintenance along with Charles Lakey (Sports and Turf manager) and William Moore (Grounds Manger), who activated many of the ideas to the campus grounds which my students proposed; Clark Rodano our Master Electrician, who knew where each air handling unit existed and who provided me an introduction to the complex world of metering and tracking; Karen Kramer, Director of Facilities Administration and Services who provided many recommendations beneficial to understanding the reality of procurement and campus operations; Kelly Geishauser Assistant Director of Facilities Maintenance whose knowledge and 'back-of-house' access to each building on campus made our course and learning simply fun; and finally the most dedicated Glenda Flores, Assistant Director of Custodial Services who began to take seriously greening protocol from our very first charrette – our Green Cleaning Policy was easily achieved and active in advance of other universities due to Glenda's attention and initiatives.

There are many students who also deserve my appreciation. First, I would like to formally recognize those instrumental in completing this publication. Most notable is Elizabeth Meyers who, for one year, became the prime graphic designer for the diagrams in this publication and organizer of the side lessons. Also, Allison Davin who assisted in wrapping up the manuscript and making sure it was written well enough for any level of college student to understand. I would like to recognize Milan Glisić, who greatly assisted with the graphics of the comparisons, assembling the Teaching Toolbox, and gathering data about the myriad global rating systems. From the book's inception, I would like to recognize Vanessa Hostick who initially helped to assemble the entire Teaching Toolbox,

ACKNOWLEDGEMENTS

and Ana Paraon for her technical assistance in completing the Documentation Phase of our first LEED Lab so well that we had an actual certified project from which to learn and write about for this textbook. I also feel very obliged to Christine Gibney for her contribution of case studies from the LEED Lab class which she has been teaching at CUA this past year. Other students who contributed to this publication are Jazzmin Reid who assembled the book in preparation for its first draft, and the many wonderful students whose participation in the course taught me the most valuable knowledge necessary in order to write this book.

CHAPTER ONE

INTRODUCTION

1.1 Facility Performance Evaluation in Architecture

The US Energy Information Administration in 2016 wrote that the residential and commercial sectors used 40 percent of total US energy consumption in 2020.[1] In a combined building sector evaluation by Architecture 2030 (Side Lesson A: Architecture 2030) showing the great influence buildings have on energy use, greenhouse gas emissions, and economic use. Nearly half of all energy and over half of electricity globally is used to build and operate buildings[2] (Figure 1.1). In fact, two-thirds of the existing building area will still exist in 2050 and the renovations of those buildings will only impact a small number of the building stock each

Side Lesson A – 1.1: Architecture 2030 is a non-profit, educational institution established in 2002 in response to an increased awareness and concern for worldwide climate change. It created the 2030 Challenge in 2006 which has set a goal for zero emissions, and which has been adopted by numerous governmental and architectural firms, and also the American Institute of Architects (AIA) (see https://architecture2030.org/about/).

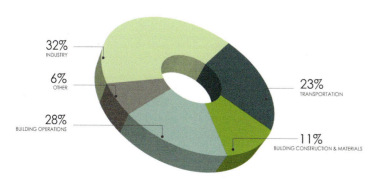

Fig 1.1 US CO_2 emissions by sector
Source: Derived from Architecture 2030 (https://architecture2030.org/buildings_problem_why/). Diagrammed by Elizabeth Meyers, 2019

DOI: 10.4324/9780429449703-1

INTRODUCTION

Side Lesson B – 1.1: Benchmarking is a familiar concept of tracking a building's water and energy consumption and comparing it to the buildings past performance and other buildings nationwide. It compares this consumption using a standard metric. This type of comparison inspires building owners to use energy efficiency upgrades (see www.energystar.gov/buildings/facility-owners-and-managers/existing-buildings/use-portfolio-manager).

year. Increased existing building energy efficiency renovations and the generation and procurement of renewable energy will be needed to hit emissions reduction targets set by the Paris Agreement.[3]

The high numbers attributed to energy consumption derive from existing buildings that have been benchmarked (Side Lesson B: Benchmarking). Mandatory energy benchmarking is rapidly proliferating in the US. The Institute for Market Research currently identifies areas as 'benchmarking,' 'going beyond benchmarking,' and adopting 'related policies' (to ensure that it occurs). In fact, at the end of 2016, 26 cities and 12 states had requirements for public building benchmarking. In mid-2019, these numbers increased to 31 cities and 18 states.[4] Following the lead of Washington and California, many of these states expanded their policies to include multifamily and commercial establishments (Figure 1.2).

In addition to the growing stock and an increase in energy mitigation requirements, buildings are being designed or redesigned concurrently to measure sustainable benefits in terms of their impact on human health, environment, and cost implications. Post Occupancy Evaluation (POE), also known as Facility Performance Evaluation (FPE), is defined by the National Institute of Building Sciences as a "continuous process of systematically

Fig 1.2 US cities participating in building benchmarking

Source: Derived from Institute for Market Transformation (www.buildingrating.org/graphic/us-citypolicies-building-benchmarking-transparency-and-beyond). Diagrammed by Elizabeth Meyers, 2019

evaluating the performance and/or effectiveness of one or more aspects of buildings in relation to issues such as accessibility, aesthetics, cost-effectiveness, functionality, productivity, safety and security, and sustainability."[5] This process improves the long-term usefulness of a building while decreasing operational costs and evaluating energy uses by continually collecting energy and design performance measurements.

Whereas once architects ended their relationships with buildings upon completion of construction, new roles encompass a broader range of FPE and verification services for the buildings they design. Z Smith, director of sustainability and building performance at Eskew+Dumez+Ripple, believes his firm and many others are starting to see post-occupancy research and engagement as a learning opportunity as well a marketing and business opportunity.[6] Firms like Perkins and Will have their own peer-reviewed research journal and ten labs which feature evaluations of select buildings they have designed. HKS offers building evaluations in conjunction with CADRE (Center for Advanced Design Research Exploration), a non-profit research group established by the firm that conducts intensive research projects focused on enhancing human and organizational wellbeing.[7] SmithGroup architect Greg Mella has been tracking their award-winning Brock Center's energy and water use beyond the 12-month period required by the Living Building Challenge (Side Lesson C: The Living Building Challenge), because maintaining net zero design, understanding building performance, and aspiring to net positive aligns with the goals of both his firm and his own knowledge.[8] According to a survey of sustainability leaders from 29 mid-size and large architecture firms in the United States and Canada, two-third currently conduct some type of facility evaluation.[9] Moreover, almost all respondents say they would like to complete POEs for a majority of their projects in the near future. The document also indicates that of all the clients who have requested or desired applying post-construction evaluation to their facilities, *the higher education industry demonstrated the most interest in an evaluation of the performance of their existing buildings*. This may be due to many factors: the high priority of enrollment, the deterioration of historic facilities on many campuses, a lack of personnel with the requisite experience, funding, skill or knowledge in how to track the performance, or the absence of a performance feedback mechanism.

Becoming aware of such simple practical measures via a performance evaluation should be learned in the foundational curricula of emerging building professionals. Buildings which students occupy daily as a part of their scholastic experience on campus benefit that institution and begin to foster a win-win cycle of analysis, documentation and feedback to fulfill new net zero and sustainability requirements of the building industry. Using campus facilities as educational tools has grown to be a popular trend among universities across the country.

Side Lesson C – 1.1: The Living Building Challenge is a set of performance standards created by the International Living Building Institute to ensure the construction of sustainable and green buildings (see https://living-future.org/basics/).

INTRODUCTION

1.2 Sustainable Campus Building Assessment

A three-prong focus of sustainable environments within scholarship, management, and the job force has emerged in higher education and has been growing for the past few decades. Scholarship of sustainability in academia was the first level of this focus as a formal topic and has impacted all three facets on campuses. The main catalyst of the succession was an institutional commitment to the cause of environmental concerns, evidenced by the increase of campus sustainability positions from the 1980s (Figure 1.3).

Many universities have established departments for campus sustainability which help to build relationships between the campus administration and the students in sustainability education. For example, Ball State University's greening of its campus is depicted in its "operational mantra of *celebrate, facilitate, anticipate* – – a conceptual structure by which to position momentary decisions in time and space while maintaining the vision of the long-term intent."[10] The university even established a unique interdisciplinary course in 1998, the Clustered Minors in Environmentally Sustainable Practices, which expanded the potential for environmental literacy among the undergraduate population. This endeavor, evident on many other university campuses, is typically headed by Sustainability Offices which report either directly to the Office of the President, to the Facilities Administration, or another related department.

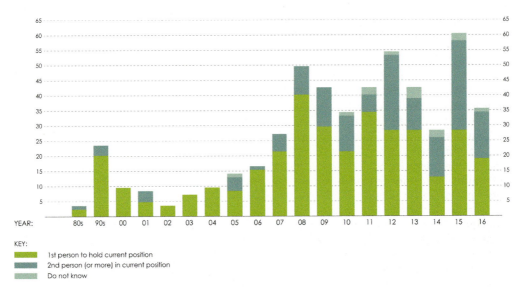

Fig 1.3 2017 Higher Education Sustainability Staffing Report, nature of position: year work began

Note: To provide insight into the history and recent growth of campus sustainability positions, respondents were asked to answer the question, "in what year did you begin working in higher education sustainability overall?"

Source: Derived from AASHE 2017 (www.aashe.org/wp-content/uploads/2017/09/AASHE-Staffing-Survey-Report-2017.pdf). Redrawn by Elizabeth Meyers, 2020

INTRODUCTION

As a response to the need of educating emerging architects in the skills they need to understand building performance evaluation, the School of Architecture and Planning at The Catholic University of America (CUA) created a similar cyclical platform of data gathering and dissemination. This was accomplished via a course intended to educate students and serve a vital role in cross-communicating with the Facilities Management Department. CUA did not have at the time, as many other colleges do, a sustainability officer to collect the efforts of the campus' environmental impacts.

LEED Lab was invented in 2011 at CUA as a pilot for the Center for Green Schools at the United States Green Building Council (USGBC) (Side Lesson D: The United States Green Building Council). Its syllabus, curriculum, administrative and interdisciplinary organization, and research methodology, premise, and findings were created and conducted independently by the author, to address educating students while providing facility personnel with information to help them analyze the environmental impacts of their facilities; buildings educate the students, who in turn educate the staff in new trends, tools, and methods of evaluation. Students are taught national building performance benchmarking mandates, performing simulations and tracking, the use of instruments (e.g., data-loggers, energy, and water meters), and how to craft environmental policies to serve as means of hands-on learning about sustainable potential and actual efficiencies. Experience gained through collaboration with facility managers, external engineering firms, NGOs, mechanical contractors, and students from other disciplines serves to disseminate that information and to generate a cycle of learning, functioning much like a POE.

Side Lesson D – 1.2: The United States Green Building Council, founded in 1993, is the premier professional organization dedicated to sustainable and green practices within the field of architecture (see www.usgbc.org/).

1.3 LEED Lab: Campus Assessment as a POE of Facility Performance

Being a broad catch-all designation, the POE and its scope of work can vary dramatically from project to project (by client interest and engagement, building typology, city, or region).[11] The basic composition of a POE is qualitative and quantitative data collection conducted with, for, and around occupied spaces in buildings. According to BuildingGreen.com, a full POE will contain data for the following four categories: energy and water performance, performance of the indoor environment (air quality, thermal comfort, acoustics, lighting, ventilation), usability of systems and spaces, occupant behavior).[12] Within these categories, the POE derives its information from three main sources: occupant feedback, bills and metrics, and measurements and readings.[13] There are a variety of POE methods of implementation available which focus on specific outcomes for these sources. For example, the DeMontfort method broadly covers the functional performance of the building, including energy use and potential savings, while the Post Occupancy Review of Building Engineering (PROBE) method relies on user satisfaction, productivity, and system development performance

INTRODUCTION

benchmarks.[14] Building walkthroughs have also been parts of various methods of POE (the DeMontfort method, Building User Studies [BUS] occupant survey and PROBE).[15] This was especially important for the CUA campus assessment since often-marginalized but key players of the facility (e.g., facility managers, administration, cleaning crews, building operators, and groundskeepers) had valuable information about the building processes, uses, and even misuses of the buildings. Through this method, perpetual environmental literacy would be injected into current facilities operations and usage and establish an ongoing record of success while educating students and staff symbiotically. Using a building assessment tool to conduct a POE on a campus facility was an approach that reaped multiple synergistic benefits towards achieving this goal.

Historically POEs have mostly been conducted using questionnaires, bills, and face to face interviews, although this is changing. Buildings are becoming more intelligent and responsive to user and environmental conditions simultaneously. Architectural firms like HKS have designed their own proprietary method for a POE called a functional performance evaluation (FPE); this extensively reviews a healthcare facility through quantitative and qualitative studies to gather and analyze subjective and objective data for a 12- to 16-week duration. Recently, numerous global building assessment systems have evolved in the past 20 years to expressly study the myriad technological and experiential aspects of existing buildings. These tools are able to function very logically in the POE since they can appropriately measure building performance quantitatively and qualitatively, while simultaneously documenting success in implementing environmental incentives.

The factors from a POE most beneficial in yielding the most efficient type of implementation on a campus were investigated and were considered to be an important factor to analyze within an existing green rating system such as LEED Operations and Maintenance (O+M). The certification process of LEED O+M was used in an academic setting to provide a platform for studying building diagnostics. LEED Lab therefore is an interdisciplinary laboratory which utilizes campus buildings as demonstration sites to facilitate a process of facility evaluation using an internationally recognized building assessment protocol. Students learn myriad sustainable facility activities: how to quantify sustainable synergies, create green campus policies with administrators, operate software to gauge metering and track various building systems including electricity, energy and water, and achieve performance-driven sustainable campus facilities (Figure 1.4).

Side Lesson E – 1.3: Green Building Certification Inc. (GCBI) is a certification and credentialing body within the green business and sustainability industry, providing third-party verifications of buildings for LEED and other credential systems (see https://gbci.org/).

First, the class creates a platform for direct student collaboration with USGBC, Green Business Certification Inc. (GBCI) (Side Lesson E: Green Business Certification Inc. (GCBI)), CUA Facilities and several other campus schools and departments. Next, experience gained from this course qualifies as a prerequisite for the LEED Green Associate (GA) and Accredited Professional (AP) examinations concurrently, meeting market demands for young professionals. For the LEED AP credentials, students will demonstrate how they contributed to the registered project through

Fig 1.4 The Catholic University of America students in University Central Plant
Source: Photo by Patricia Andrasik, 2017

active participation and continuous responsibility; the candidate for the exam will show how he has been exposed to the LEED process and has knowledge of the project.

The course also creates a platform to engage national building performance benchmarking codes; further, it creates a "continuous process of systematically evaluating the performance and/or effectiveness of one or more aspects of buildings in relation to issues" such as cost-effectiveness, functionality and sustainability.[16] Lastly, it creates a mechanism for student engagement and to drive sustainability efforts on campus that focus on the existing built environment. As students learn to organize and act as facilitators in charrettes and educate university administrators and operations staff members about policy revisions that embrace greater sustainability goals, their work will raise an awareness of inefficiencies on campus which will assist the college or university in its mission of greater sustainable stewardship.

The established rubrics of the LEED O+M rating system provide a universal set of criteria for gauging successful facilities, helpful for educating college students and professionals. The rating system has broad credit categories subdivided into 'credits' and 'prerequisites,' creating a hierarchy of different features, both necessary and optional, to be used at the onset of the evaluation. The credits have a set of points associated with them, and the accumulation of these points yields a level of achievement. LEED O+M certification is a goal, yet the research opportunities, learning outcomes, and knowledge gained from following the prescriptive FPE feasibility protocol are the primary reasons this rating system is appropriate for this course.

INTRODUCTION

Depending on where the student stands in the progress of the project, much of the research may be derived from a previous semester's research. A student in one semester of LEED Lab – e.g., the Feasibility Phase – gathers information about the feasibility of Building Level Water Metering, an optional credit for establishing a green building. When the student completes the course, their documentation is passed to the subsequent student assigned to that credit in another semester – the Documentation Phase. In such a case, navigating the details of the credit to understand if the documentation is comprehensive, correct and complete becomes the critical research task at hand. Various repositories of information to navigate the evaluation of the credit exist: National Reference Standards (e.g., ASHRAE, IESNA, etc.), the LEED O+M v4 Reference Guide, existing data and documentation which the university facilities department controls (e.g., sequence of operations for equipment, energy tracking logs, etc.), and forums where professionals discuss the credit's achievement (e.g., LEEDuser.com). The key to synthesizing all of this information is direct communication and discussion with the relevant parties, a cyclical interface of investigation involving peers, staff, and operations personnel, and diagnostic records. All of these propel LEED Lab's research basis.

Notes

1. "Frequently Asked Questions: How Much Energy is Consumed in U.S. Residential and Commercial Buildings?" US Energy Information Administration: Independent Statistics and Analysis, 2018. www.eia.gov/tools/faqs/faq.php?id=86&t=1
2. "Why the Building Sector? Buildings Generate Nearly 40% of Annual Global GHG Emissions," Architecture2030, 2018. http://architecture2030.org/buildings_problem_why/
3. Ibid.
4. "U.S. City Policies: Building Benchmarking, Transparency, and Beyond," BuildingRating: Sharing Transparency for a More Efficient Future, 2014. www.buildingrating.org/graphic/us-city-policies-building-benchmarking-transparency-and-beyond
5. Craig Zimring, Mahbub Rashid and Kevin Kampschroer, "Facility Performance Evaluation (FPE)," Whole Building Design Guide, 2016. www.wbdg.org/resources/facility-performance-evaluation-fpe
6. Paul Melton, "Why Post-Occupancy Review Is the Future of Design (And How It Can Serve You Now)," *Building Green* 24, no. 6 (2015): 1–16. www-buildinggreen-com.proxycu.wrlc.org/feature/why-post-occupancy-review-future-design-and-how-it-can-serve-you-now
7. "HKS Research," HKS (Harwood K. Smith), Inc., 2018. www.hksinc.com/hks-research/
8. Wanda Lau, "Lessons from a Living Builder: The Brock Environmental Center," *Architect Magazine*, June 2, 2016. www.architectmagazine.com/technology/lessons-from-a-living-building-the-brock-environmental-center_o
9. Julie Hiromoto, "Architect & Design Sustainable Design Leaders: Post Occupancy Evaluation Survey Report," Skidmore, Owings & Merrill LLP, May 13, 2015. www.som.com/ideas/research/post_occupancy_evaluation_survey_report
10. Robert J. Koester, James Eflin and John Vann, "Greening of the Campus: A Whole-systems Approach," *Journal of Cleaner Production* 14 (2006): 770.
11. Julie Hiromoto 2015, op. cit.
12. "Post-occupancy Evaluation," BuildingGreen, 2019. www.buildinggreen.com/post-occupancy-evaluation
13. Zafer Ozturk, Yusuf Arayici and Paul Coates, "Post Occupancy Evaluation (POE) in Residential Buildings Utilizing BIM and Sensing Devices: Salford Energy House Example," School of the Built Environment, University of Salford, 2012. http://usir.salford.ac.uk/20697/

14 Mel J. Barlex, "Guide to Post Occupancy Evaluation," University of Westminster and Higher Education Funding Council for England, 2006. www.smg.ac.uk/documents/POEBrochureFinal06.pdf

15 Zafer Ozturk, Yusuf Arayici and Paul Coates 2012, op. cit.

16 Craig Zimring, Mahbub Rashid and Kevin Kampschroer 2016, op. cit.

CHAPTER TWO

METHODOLOGY

2.1 A System of Approach

In any noteworthy scholarly accomplishment, a path, method and/or process is necessary to accomplish learning objectives and outcomes. LEED Lab is no exception. In 2014, the Crough Center was the first architecture school in the world to achieve LEED O+M certification and became the first curriculum-based, student-driven and completed LEED O+M certification in history because of its approach to achieving performance and pedagogical outcomes.

By creating a building performance process that monitors how efficiently a building meets the needs of thermal comfort, ventilation, energy, lighting, and many other performance variables, the LEED Lab course continuously optimizes building management and sustainable education at the same time. Synergistic evaluation of buildings between students, facility personnel, and faculty through one platform provides singular principles of action, which enable participation by all members in every stratum of the university community, as well as the community beyond.[1] The approach creates a high-caliber analytical achievement embedded within a methodology called action research.

Action research (Side Lesson A: Action Research) is a scientific approach utilizing research to solve an immediate condition, or a process for solving problems between teams. It has become an important part of a number of research programs, especially in the field of education,[2] because it discovers and describes problems and realities and addresses them through collaboration. It starts with the understanding that people hold deep knowledge about their lives and experiences and about their surroundings.[3] The need for practical outcomes, such as those which LEED Lab requires for its building assessment, places action research within a social context where the environment of the 'experiment' and the experiment itself interact, and in which values play a critical role.

Side Lesson A – 2.1: Action Research is a methodology developed by Kurt Lewin which uses critical reflection to link the process of taking action and doing research resulting in a transformation of the educational/learning process.

2.2 Action Research as a Theoretical Methodology

The LEED O+M rating system may facilitate the POE process but the aspect of multi-party interaction and participatory activities important to LEED Lab can be evaluated through action. These demand specific attention to how researchers (i.e., staff, consultants) engage with participants.[4] In LEED Lab, research occurs within the context of an occupied building through the cumulative information gained from students' diagnoses (Figure 2.1). However, it is critically dependent on communication with other parties, consultants, and facility personnel. These stakeholders are involved in the decisions which affect the operations and stability of their facilities beyond the LEED Lab course.

Originally coined in 1944 by Kurt Lewin as "comparative research on the conditions and effects of various forms of social action and research leading to social action,"[5] the purpose of the action research strategy has evolved to that of solving a particular problem and producing guidelines for best practice.[6] Leading scientists distinguish action research from basic research by asserting that the intention of the former is to solve an important problem for a client, and not simply to test features of a theory.[7] Researchers Jon Barton, John Stephens and Tim Haslett have created a normative set of criteria for use in the designing and assessing of action research and in so doing represent action research as a scientifically rigorous methodology.[8] LEED Lab identifies and utilizes four of their criteria:

1. Team processes that adopt multiple perspectives and pluralist values both as a hedge against fallible behavior and as a platform for ethical practice;
2. Logical processes that can be easily identified with abductive, deductive and inductive modes of inference;

Fig 2.1 LEED Lab students design and build a rainwater cistern as a part of pursuing water reduction credits, after it was discovered that there were many opportunities for creative stormwater management

Source: Photo by Patricia Andrasik, 2017

METHODOLOGY

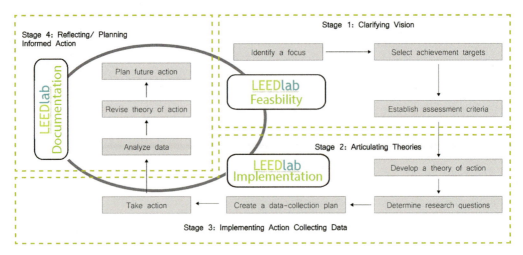

Fig 2.2 Sagor's Action Research Cycle underlying the critical phases of LEED Lab

Source: Derived from Sagor's Model: The Action Research Cycle, 2005. Diagrammed by Patricia Andrasik, 2021

3. Critical evaluation techniques that include single, double and triple loop learning, and monitoring processes within action research cycles that inform (minor) corrections that can be made and recorded;
4. The possibility of considering each stage in the recursive terms of action research.[9]

Dr. Richard Sagor, founder of the Institute for the Study of Inquiry in Education, proposed a specific and detailed process for identifying the action research sequence. This has been utilized as a theoretical underlay to describe how an integrated diagnostic process inherent to LEED Lab is organized within three phases – (1) Feasibility, (2) Implementation and (3) Documentation (Figure 2.2) – and executed through consecutive sets of semesters.[10]

2.3 The Three-Part Integrated Diagnostic Process

In a climate where the need for greener and more sustainable buildings puts pressure on both operational and capital budgets,[11] universities are often in a bind prioritizing between deferred maintenance and sustainable improvement costs. Choosing a particular campus building or opting to approach the campus as a whole initially and then identifying a focus building to assess is the first step of the course. The start of LEED Lab's assessment therefore begins with Phase 1 – Feasibility – and aligns with Sagor's first step in the action research cycle, clarifying a vision.[12]

Phase 1: Feasibility

The feasibility of which a building or buildings is to be assessed depends on several factors. First, does the building have

METHODOLOGY

established water, energy or any other metering? Are there policies guiding the operations of equipment and systems of the building? Are there mechanisms in place for ongoing maintenance? Who is responsible for these procedures within the university? These questions, related to understanding the baselines of the building, are easily navigated by LEED's establishment credits – required baseline measurements such as instituting a specific EUI (Side Lesson B: Energy Use Intensity (EUI)) for energy efficiency, creating a recycling program, establishing a minimal level of air quality in a building, or installing tracking meters.

In order to clarify a vision, a charrette (Side Lesson C: Charrette) should be scheduled in order to facilitate conversations and strategic planning for the facility being assessed. The charrette becomes the initial brainstorming session (Figure 2.3) and forum to test the students' knowledge of credits, to educate facility personnel, and to arrive at a set of assessment criteria defined by a Point Integration Diagram (PID) (Figures 4.9 and 4.10) (Side Lesson D: Point Integration Diagram, PID).

These various facets of feasibility – identifying a building (*identifying a focus*), learning about the existing equipment/policies already implemented (*selecting achievement targets*), and then using establishment credits and the PID (*establishing assessment criteria*) – ultimately as a part of *clarifying a vision* – formally follow this first quadrant of Sagor's cycle through the initial months of the course. The Feasibility Phase culminates with a check list offered by the USGBC to identify areas of required focus.

Phase 2: Implementation

Implementation is built around two quadrants of Sagor's cycle: *Articulating Theories* and *Implementing Action and Collecting*

Side Lesson B – 2.3: An Energy Use Intensity (EUI) is a standard metric used to express energy per square foot of a building. It allows you to compare buildings' energy usage based on their square foot. EUI for most buildings is expressed as energy per square foot per year. EUI is calculated dividing total energy consumption by the total of gross floor area. For example, if an office has an annual energy consumption of 250,000 kBTU and is 10,000 square feet. The EUI of this building would be 25 (see https://tinyurl.com/yv4m3wtd).

Side Lesson C – 2.3: Charrette: The term 'charrette' was first coined at the Ecole des Beaux-Arts in Paris in the nineteenth century. It is the French word for "cart." Nineteenth-century designers would use carts to carry items they needed and wanted to use a design collaboration session. Today the term is still being used for a design collaboration between a group of designers. The structure of a charrette depends on the individuals involved and the design problems. Charrettes are a good way of generating design options in a short amount of time (see Rob Roggema, "The Design Charrette," in The Design Charrette: Ways to Envision Sustainable Futures, ed. Rob Roggema (Dordrecht, Netherlands: Springer Netherlands, 2014, pp. 15–34)).

Fig 2.3 A charrette between facilities management and LEED Lab students
Source: Photo by Patricia Andrasik, 2017

METHODOLOGY

Side Lesson D – 2.3: A Point Integration Diagram (PID) is a visual depiction created during the Feasibility Phase of LEED Lab or other green assessments to establish the relationship between needed LEED (or other rating system) credits and strategies to obtain them. See Figures 4.9 and 4.10.

Side Lesson E – 2.3: Data Loggers, Water Sub-meters, and Anemometers: Data loggers are portable battery-powered devices that track lighting, relative humidity, electrical current, temperature, occupancy, and other variables, and which are capable of storing a multitude of data at any programmable frequency of easily understood data. Loggers may be USB, Web-based, wireless, or Bluetooth compatible. They are ideal for buildings that do not possess an EMS system, or as supplements for buildings with limited points of metering to optimize equipment operation. See Chapter 8, 'Energy'.

Water sub-meters are installed on current functioning water lines within a building and are read remotely via a wireless communication system. These meters give a breakdown of the total water usage within a building. See Chapter 7, 'Water'.

An anemometer is a device used to measure wind speed, pressure, and direction; either in a contained (air ducts) or an unconfined flow (atmospheric wind). To measure wind speed, the anemometer detects changes in the physical property of the fluid in the air. See Chapter 8, 'Energy'.

Data[13] (refer to Figure 2.2). Developing a *theory of action* involves answering questions such as: "How will the cited feasibility strategies be divided among students?"; "What Performance Periods are necessary for establishment?"; "Which tasks are required for tracking or analyzing strategies"; "Which equipment should be evaluated?"; "Which spaces warrant the greatest attention?"; "Which building functions have changed?" and so forth, in order to identify the ways in which the building evaluation will occur. Implementation is outlined in the "performance requirement" for each credit as identified in the LEED O+M v4 Reference Guide, followed by a "step-by-step guidance" that represents the *data collection plan*. The instruments which LEED Lab students use to collect data to verify credit completion include specialized software and instruments such as data loggers, water sub-meters, and anemometers (Side Lesson E: Data Loggers, Water Sub-meters, and Anemometers) in addition to many more which are addressed in detail throughout this publication, as noted in Figure 2.7.

"Tasks" sections help to identify processes; "Tools" help to identify instruments used to fulfill the processes of implementation; and "Techniques" indicate hints for successful credit accomplishment.

Phase 3: Documentation

Documentation is a phase which confirms the achievement of the tools and strategies used in Phase 2, the *Implementation* of the credit. This includes the creation of procedural, metric, and scheduling documents such as tracking sheets, templates, online calculators and third-party data platforms. In this phase, Sagor's *Reflecting and Planning Informed Action* occurs when collected data from Phase 2 is *analyzed* and processed. There may or may not be a *revised theory of action* once the credit is attempted (because it may be denied by USGBC), but there will always be a *planned future action* whether the plan is or is not to change anything.

The accuracy of tasks that occurred in Phase 2 is often called into question and re-evaluated in this phase. Much time dedication to organization, collection, and editing is also required for this phase, and typically it is most successful when a few students dedicated to a specific knowledge base input the analyzed data from Phase 2 to the LEED online platform. Measurable outcomes throughout the duration of the course are documented through Individual Student Progress Presentations, or ISPPs. ISPPs represent simple documentations of a student's credit progress which includes exploration, metrics and old vs new data obtained. The ISPP is presented to the entire class so that others may learn about credits which they were not assigned. The presentations also help the instructor understand the level of understanding and achievement of the student or team.

2.4 A Critical Feedback Loop

LEED Lab generates a critical feedback loop when Feasibility, Implementation, and Documentation of the building assessment

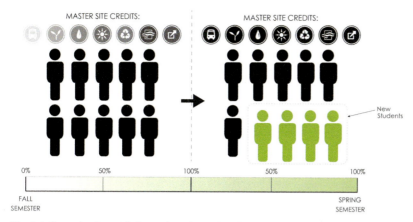

Fig 2.4 Scenario where existing students have already started to work on credits in a LEED Lab course that extends for one year

Note: There is a point where the transition between classes creates a slight learning curve as new members join and credit assignments are readjusted

Source: Diagrammed by Elizabeth Meyers, 2019

are fulfilled, regardless of how many credits are ultimately achieved. This occurs between classes (Figure 2.4), the building, campus and even a farther outreach to campuses around the world when schools disseminate their findings. It begins in class when students approach facility personnel to discuss the respective credits at the course's charrette. In this arrangement, the students are investigators while the facility personnel are resources, providing diagnostic information about the facility and operations. In this initial interaction, students convey the sustainability measures that are necessary to accomplish the credit and request information, data, policies or installation of tracking mechanisms to be instituted by the facility personnel; the facility personnel in turn provide the students with this necessary information.

When the facility personnel begin providing data to the students, they are engaging the case study of the building. The building may have the necessary tracking mechanisms and policies or it may not. Regardless, the information is disseminated between the metering infrastructure and the students/personnel collaboration engaging in the course. As the staff transfer information to the students, the students make decisions about which credits may be accomplished or not, and how. The accomplishment of certain credits thereafter impacts the entire campus, and certain questions need to be answered: Does the building inform certain campus operations or maintenance protocol? Are there policies created for the building which are required to be universally applied to the campus? Does a discovery in the system infrastructure recognize a correction to all campus building systems? As the campus begins to be impacted by one facility, such questions will likely mean providing the necessary information for other buildings, thereby creating a basis for subsequent LEED Lab courses.

External consultants, students, faculty and administration are all collaborators in this critical feedback loop, contributing to the success of the Lab by generating a dynamic learning effect back and forth between the buildings, and the campus as a whole. One of the most important factors to consider in establishing LEED Lab so that these collaborators work harmoniously is the organization of the class structure. Typically new students take the course each semester at most institutions. If a two-semester course is proposed, consideration for how new students will integrate will be important (Figure 2.6).

2.5 The Textbook Methodology

LEED Lab has been adopted within the past several years by over 44 colleges and universities globally.[14] This integrated and user-friendly educational text designed for academic use replaces myriad texts which dedicate only chapters to sustainable operations, building performance and/or sustainable facility management. Fortunately, the underlying principle of using an existing building green rating system for LEED Lab is not necessarily exclusive to LEED O+M (see Chapter 3.31 and the Comparisons in Chapters 5–10), yet is used in this textbook as a solid reference for application.

This book was designed to accompany the LEED O+M v4 Reference Guide as a means to usher students, faculty and staff through LEED Lab's goal of building assessment as an academic endeavor. However, it is not only for formal curricular application of the LEED Lab course, but may also serve as an instrument for accomplishing specific sustainability milestones for campus facilities beyond, or independent from, actual green building certification. It applies the LEED green rating system to a university curriculum. Based on the pilot course's content designed by author Patricia Andrasik, LEED Lab is at the cutting edge of sustainability education for students of architecture, facility management, and construction science. It is written for the undergraduate or graduate student enrolled in LEED Lab or a similar campus building assessment course. It can also be used by construction professionals, architects, facility managers, operations and maintenance (O+M) staff, as well as faculty interested in an integrated method of analyzing sustainability in existing campus buildings. It is primarily designed as the premiere textbook for the LEED Lab course for undergraduate and graduate use; however, it can also be used for vocational education and will also appeal to professional readership. It may also serve as a supplement to architectural, engineering, and facility management courses.

The book contains the subject matter in a traditional organization but includes numerous exercises for actual practice and has a supplementary online *Toolbox Teaching Guide*. It is organized for easy navigation. Chapter summaries introduce the main content to give the student a skeletal framework around which to build and retain content knowledge. The three-phase methodology (Feasibility, Implementation, Documentation) easily combines the critical steps of the building assessment within the curriculum. Readers will quickly gain experience navigating the complexity of credit category criteria required by LEED via several unique aids:

- *Side Lessons* to provide technical definitions in detail (identified in blue text in the margins).
- *Learning modules* for each category under the Phase 2 (Implementation) chapters to provide ease of navigation and reference through custom-designed icons as follows (Figure 2.5):

Fig 2.5 Learning module icons for Phase 2, Implementation

Source: Created by Patricia Andrasik, 2017

- **Theory** describes overall concepts and the big ideas behind a category's content or credit subchapter.
- **Tasks** describe specific steps which are unique to LEED Lab in order to implement the credit identified in text boxes.
- **Tools** describe the standards, instruments or certified methods to attain data.
- **Techniques** describe typical issues, challenges and handy recommendations to document the credit.
- **Partnering Credits** build upon prerequisites or other credits by having the same structure but higher benchmarks for attainment, or structures which synergize with them.
- **Case Studies** describe various applications of the ideas in the preceding chapters.
- **Comparisons** outline similar LEED categories within alternative O+M rating systems.
- **Exercises** provide scenarios from the Case Studies which the reader must address and for which solutions will be provided.

2.6 Toolbox Teaching Guide

The Toolbox provides a single-source online repository of current reference standards and links for green building certification in one convenient location. It has an extensive online repository of reference standards, forms and tracking sheets imperative to LEED O+M certification and critical to the Implementation and Documentation Phases. These include templates for tracking devices, forms, reference standards, software, calculators and external resources.

The Toolbox Teaching Guide provides instructors and staff direction in instruction via an online repository of modifiable syllabi for each phase, PowerPoint presentations, quiz and exam templates, Individual Student Progress Presentation (ISPP) templates, final project documentation templates and the final GBCI submission template.

Notes

1. Robert J. Koester, James Eflin and John Vann, "Greening of the Campus: A Whole-systems Approach," *Journal of Cleaner Production* 14 (2006): 770.
2. Michael Glassman, Gizem Erdem and Mitchell Bartholomew, "Action Research and its History as an Adult Education Movement for Social Change," *Adult Education Quarterly* 63, no. 3 (2013): 272–288.
3. Kyle Askins and Rachel Pain, "Contact Zones: Participation, Materiality, and the Messiness of Interaction," *Environment and Planning D: Society and Space* 29, no. 5 (2011): 803–831.
4. Andrea Wheeler and Masoud Malekzadeh, "Exploring the Use of New School Buildings through Post-occupancy Evaluation and Participatory Action," *Architectural Engineering and Design Management* 11, no. 6 (2014): 440–456.
5. Kurt Lewin, "Action Research and Minority Problems," *Journal of Social Issues* 2, no. 4 (1946): 34–46.
6. Martyn Denscombe, *Good Research Guide: For Small-Scale Social Research Projects*, 5th Edition (New York: Open University Press, 2014).
7. Chris Argyris, Robert Putnam and Diana McLain Smith, *Action Science*, Vol. 13 (San Francisco, CA: Jossey-Bass, 1985).
8. John Barton, John Stephens and Tim Haslett, "Action Research: Its Foundations in Open Systems Thinking and Relationship to the Scientific Method," *Systemic Practice and Action Research* 22, no. 6 (2009): 475–488.
9. Ibid.
10. Richard Sagor, *The Action Research Guidebook: A Four-Step Process for Educators and School Teams* (Thousand Oaks, CA: Corwin Press, 2005): 109–154.
11. Chris Hodges and Mark Sekula, *Sustainable Facility Management: The Facility Manager's Guide to Optimizing Building Performance* (Alexandria, VA: Vision Spots Publishing, 2013).
12. Richard Sagor 2005, op. cit.
13. Ibid.
14. "Bring Green Building Concepts to Life for Students through LEED Lab," US Green Building Council, 2019. www.usgbc.org/education/leed-lab?utm_source=usgbc-website&utm_medium=article&utm_campaign=education-resources

CHAPTER THREE

PLATFORM

3.1 Collaboration

The most important aspect of LEED Lab is its collective, interdisciplinary character. A variety of internal and external departments, schools, manufacturers and businesses are co-collaborators in the success of LEED Lab. Staff from these organizations will be involved in education about the sustainable potential of facilities and should be available during various analyses and data-gathering; they will also participate in the final presentations. *Planning* for the participants to engage with LEED Lab months in advance of its commencement is of paramount importance to its success! Identifying who they should be based on the prerequisites and credits the teams are pursuing, identifying at what project point they should participate, identifying any monetary compensation for their time, establishing tentative meeting times with them and other collaborators both outside of and within the course times sets the course in its most fruitful direction.

Since the course is a real-world experience in post occupancy and facility performance evaluation and building diagnostics, there are building systems and methods which students may not have access to as a result of inexperience, legality or lack of job certification. In these cases, facility staff, external contractors, and sub-contractors must be sought for their expertise to aid students. In this way, the course will reflect an actual architectural or facility management project, which is paramount to the unique learning experience which the LEED Lab course offers. General participants include educators, students, USGBC, GBCI, consultants, administration and staff.

3.1.1 Educators

LEED Lab is taught by a variety of educators. Although it was piloted by the author, a full-time faculty member, LEED Lab has become popular at universities led predominantly by part-time instructors and facilities staff. Although there are no formal guidelines for LEED Lab instructors, experience with O+M, tracking or any building performance endeavors is essential. Instructors who have not conducted an actual building performance evaluation or who have not been involved with LEED O+M certification will have much to learn prior to adopting the course at their institution. The more involvement with sustainable operations, the more expertise they possess to impart to students. From the launch of the pilot course, LEED Lab has generated many alumni, and these professionals have become prime candidates for hosting the course. The types of instructors may be broken down into the categories of faculty or staff.

University faculty are persons at an institution of higher education who have a common duty or obligation to teach. Among the academic ranks of faculty across the country there are few differences. Adjuncts, lecturers and/or instructors are typically part-time faculty associated with such an institution by contract instead of a full-time tenured position. Alumni of the course who themselves teach LEED Lab often do so while maintaining full-time employment elsewhere, providing mutually reinforcing benefits to both organizations they serve. The majority of LEED Lab instructors fall into this category.

Full-time faculty hold the title professor – assistant, associate, ordinary, distinguished or endowed – and are either tenured or candidates for tenure, and are fully affiliated with the institution. Faculty who have officially retired from the institution may possess the rank of 'emeritus' relieving the individual of any full-time responsibilities but also allowing the time to teach such a course.

University staff are defined as the group of individuals at a higher ed institution who do not have a requirement to teach, but are full-time personnel supporting the university in other capacities such as maintenance, security, administration, legal counsel and public relations. Staff follow regular business hours as opposed to faculty whose hours often vary. More recently, staff have been placed in offices of sustainability where teaching LEED Lab courses may become a job responsibility. Regardless of the position of the educator, it is recommended that they optimally possess a LEED O+M accreditation and/or some experience in certifying, and/or managing existing buildings.

3.1.2 Students

Students are the most important collaborators in the course. The pilot LEED Lab course at The Catholic University of America comprised architectural students. However, the following year, students from chemistry, politics, facility planning and engineering began to enroll and now regularly comprise an interdisciplinary cohort. At The Catholic University of America, its pilot institution, LEED Lab now regularly comprises this interdisciplinary mix. The array of students includes both undergraduate and graduate students, as well as doctoral students interested in incorporating their knowledge of building diagnostics into their advanced scholarly work. The same is true for the multitude of

LEED Labs across the globe: the mix of students varies per institution but often comprises those who are most interested in the practical application of their learned knowledge of sustainable operations and maintenance of facilities.

It is a hope that enrolled students are not the only participants in the course. Representative college and university groups of students and alumni from all disciplines should come together to learn and participate in these hands-on green building experiences on their own campuses. Should this be the case, LEED Lab then becomes a perpetual platform for the university community regardless of the semester. This student involvement engages young leaders through service and may be a good platform for the recruitment for future LEED Lab students.

When the course is not in session at any point during the year, student groups on campus can assist in the ongoing tracking and documentation of facilities. USGBC student groups and LEED Lab alumni are taught to understand the necessity of continuously monitoring equipment and processes even if the course has stopped meeting for the school year. At CUA, members of the USGBC Student Group and the university Green Club provided LEED Lab with current and accurate systems and policy documentation while the course was not in session. These students helped advocate for sustainable university practices and policies and facilitated green campus initiatives and activities, targeted by the previous semester's LEED Lab students as goals towards certification.

3.1.3 US Green Building Council

During the LEED Lab pilot course, USGBC's Center for Green Schools observed LEED Lab at CUA. The organization was involved in periodic meetings with the instructor about the progress and the needs of the class and participated once per semester in mid-semester charrettes (see Chapter 2.3). USGBC had a limited role in accomplishing specific technical tasks and activities with the course; since the course is an official vehicle for obtaining the LEED O+M designation, an intense role would create a conflict of interest in obtaining official LEED Certification. The course has since then evolved.

USGBC owns and uses the LEED Lab trademark and generates materials to be used in the course, and also markets LEED Lab globally. It partners with post-secondary institutions across the globe to offer LEED Lab on campus. As part of this collaboration USGBC provides tools, resources and staff support to equip instructors and students with the knowledge required to pursue the LEED O+M certification process.[1]

3.1.4 Green Building Certification Institute

The Green Building Certification Institute (GBCI), a subsidiary of USGBC, is the authority overseeing all certifications and accreditations and is involved in the certification review for all standard and LEED Lab projects equally. All LEED project teams – even those not officially a part of the LEED Lab course – can request calls with reviewers during the review process. Often in LEED

Lab, calls occur as a part of the semester's activities but culminate at the end of the semester when the students reach the milestone of formally submitting their projects to GBCI – either during the first review or at the final project review.

The added benefit of establishing a formal LEED Lab-registered building with USGBC is that the organization will provide a LEED Lab Coach who serves as liaison between LEED Lab and GBCI to provide technical assistance and support to instructors; this facilitates the creation of custom coursework and syllabi for any institution. For example, during the pilot course at CUA, the certification for the first building was divided into two separate certification reviews, spanning several semesters. In the first review, students submitted a partial completion of their credits to GBCI two weeks prior to the conclusion of the semester. On the final day of class, a virtual meeting connected the students with the GBCI reviewers, who scrutinized each credit that was submitted. Students were able to see the challenges and successes of accomplishing the credit milestones and actually competed to acquire the most 'points' for their work.

3.1.5 Consultants

In addition to students, educators, USGBC and GBCI, there is a need to involve specific representatives depending on the credits being pursued and how much experience in accomplishing these credits the institution already possesses. These individuals are consultants – contractors, sub-contractors and technicians – who possess the knowledge and skill of trades necessary to accomplish many of the tasks and calculations for various sustainable accomplishments. For example, if Master Site credits are being sought, the director or officer of campus landscaping will be involved with his or her crew of on-site staff and may solicit the expertise of civil and landscape engineers if the institution is not experienced with certain water and site conservation techniques.

Prerequisites become the most critical for external or internal professional support, and the actual credits take secondary priority. For example, the Energy Efficiency Best Management Practices credit requires, as a prerequisite, a diagnosis that includes a preliminary audit (ASHRAE Level I) of existing HVAC equipment and schedules which the building operator may not be familiar with. In that case, external consultation is required. A subsequent credit – Existing Building Commissioning Analysis – requires the operator to develop an energy audit plan following the requirements of ASHRAE Level 2, Energy Survey and Analysis, to evaluate efficiency opportunities (see Chapter 8, 'Energy'). The latter is not required for certification but requires a much more detailed evaluation of the mechanical systems – typically accomplished by an external engineering company. The former may not need a consultant and may be accomplished in-house pending the expertise of the operator and his or her staff.

During the certification of the Crough Center for Architectural Studies at The Catholic University of America, W.L. Gary, a mechanical contractor, volunteered to take outdoor air measurements of the HVAC fresh air intake, while the engineering firm

WRL volunteered to conduct both the ASHRAE Level 1 and Level 2 audits. Both firms interacted with the students, faculty, university administrators and facility personnel in order to achieve documentation of mechanical system operation and energy consumption rates and to facilitate a dynamic learning environment.

3.1.6 Administration

Any impactful work on or study of campus facilities requires the permission and participation of the university's administration. This includes the directors, vice presidents, attorneys and all associates who are in positions of decision-making for the institution. Often, these individuals are located within the office of sustainability or the facilities department, but they may even report directly to the president. A university's administrators are considered staff so their time commitments are allocated to the standard workday. Although these individuals may or may not directly attend the charrette or have an active role in the actual building diagnostics, their advice and direction is critical to the success of the course. Identifying these persons in relation to your sustainability goals and fostering a relationship that includes ongoing communication and education may be the difference in obtaining or not obtaining measurable outcomes on campus!

3.1.7 Staff

As indicated in Section 3.1.1, university staff are defined as a group of individuals at a higher education institution who do not have a requirement to teach but are often full-time personnel providing specialized support to the university in other capacities. Staff are fundamental to the daily operations of the institution, which in turn makes them fundamental to LEED Lab's success. They follow regular business hours which may render them unavailable for LEED Lab course meetings if the class is held in the evenings.

At CUA, several departments were co-collaborators in the success of LEED Lab. The Facilities Planning and Construction Department oversees building projects from inception through completion and has responsibilities that include planning, programming, budgeting and scheduling for the construction of new buildings as well as improvements to existing facilities. The Facilities Maintenance and Operations Department provides maintenance to buildings, grounds, fleet, and plumbing, electrical, and HVAC systems as integrated services enabling the efficient operation of the university. Staff from both departments committed to the delivery of professional quality support services, which enabled CUA LEED Lab students to simultaneously pursue scholarships and to research, facilitating sustainability advances to the university's infrastructure. Individuals from these departments became familiar faces to the students, teaching them valuable skills in their own disciplines while helping hone their project management skills.

Staff from these departments were involved in students' introductory education about the sustainable potential of CUA facilities, and all of them were available at different times – coordinated with the specific credit requirement in question – to be involved with various analyses and data-gathering. They also participated in the charrette and even the final presentation (see Chapter 2). A few of them single-handedly provided the necessary training and documentation which yielded in the obtainment of a LEED credit towards certification.

3.2 Learning

3.2.1 Learning Management Systems

Faculty at universities are responsible for delivering course content to students via the recommended mechanism at their respective institutions, but ultimately this is the instructor's choice. Instructors may choose to use their own methods (e.g., e.g., Excel spreadsheet for documenting grades, hand-outs with prescribed instructions for study) yet this all depends on institutional guidelines. Many institutions offer state-of-the-art tools to facilitate teaching and digital means of administering courses. These are called Learning Management Systems (LMSs) and many LEED Lab instructors opt to use these due to their expediency.

The LMS is a software application that automates the administration, tracking and reporting of training events.[2] The major applications are: the creation of assignments, quizzes, grading rubrics, and waiting lists; the uploading and managing of documents containing curriculum content; the delivery of that content via web-based interfaces; remote collaboration between students, teaching assistants, guests and instructors; and instant messaging, email discussion forums and the provision of a weighted grading roster.[3] In the academic arena, there are many LMSs. Some of the more popular platforms are Moodle, Brightspace, Sakai, Canvas, Google Classroom, Talent LMS, Docebo, Hubspot, Coggno, Oracle, Swiftwit, and Blackboard. Seventy-five percent of US colleges and universities in the United States use Blackboard.[4]

LEED Labs around the world have used myriad LMS platforms. For example, the University of California Merced uses Canvas, the Universidad Don Bosco in El Salvador and The Catholic University of America use Blackboard, and Agnes Scott College uses Wordpress. This alternative platform allows students to create digital portfolios to customize their education via posts and other progress tracking to critically analyze their knowledge. Students comment, monitor, and follow each other throughout the course while the instructor guides them in a focused way.

3.3 Certification

The university's strategic planning and platform about sustainability play a significant factor in the success of the course. However, the course as a learning tool should never be ignored as it is designed to instruct students towards comprehensively understanding building diagnostics. The relationship between the institutional heads and the instructors of LEED Lab must see to a balanced coordination in simultaneously meeting the needs of both the students and the institution via certification.

Official LEED certification of a building via LEED Lab may be an institutional goal, but the path by which the certification is gained is the actual learning tool. It is necessary to register for a project via the LEED online portal (Side Lesson A: LEED Online Portal) in order to establish a platform for realizing the synergistic benefits of the LEED rating system and categories. LEED Lab courses may become fully operational through payment of a registration fee, without officially or immediately becoming certified. The institution's goals take precedence over the course goals in this case. If the university has a goal of reaching a certain number of LEED certified existing buildings within a certain timeframe and is using the LEED Lab course for this purpose, then the course must be structured to follow this goal without compromising student learning. If the university's goals do not include expediency or even certification, then the course may be structured at a slower pace and acclimated more to learning objectives and research. For example, at CUA, LEED Lab was a transformative course – a bottom-up-approach where students became the catalysts for change, proliferating the action research impact on overall campus sustainability.

If the facility has been previously certified under LEED for Building Design and Construction (LEED BD+C) it may undergo a similar certification via LEED O+M. However, if the facility has previously been certified as LEED O+M, it would acquire 'recertification'. Recertification is the process of updating an existing O+M certified building and is required at a minimum of every five years to maintain O+M certification, otherwise the initial certification process begins once again.

Side Lesson A – 3.3: LEED Online Portal: In order to use the LEED online portal to register for a project, the user must create a USGBC account and login (see www.leedonline.com/).

3.3.1 Assessment Systems

Using an alternative rating system to implement LEED Lab is possible; there are myriad similar rating systems that may be used in this lab course. The variety of assessment systems may be compared to LEED in terms of their application to the LEED Lab course. Each rating system has a specific format which varies considerably in terms of measurement performance, scope, environmental criteria and overall requisite or optional 'points' for success (measured by achieving some type of milestone or point accrual). The commonality between all of the rating systems is the use of prerequisites and credits. Although weights vary between rating systems (Figure 3.1) the name of the course may require creative alteration if it should aspire to one of these alternatives to LEED!

Existing buildings detected and targeted by these systems are global, although opportunities of implementation are often local. For example, the climate particularities of certain regions, overall development, infrastructure, resources, and population density

PLATFORM

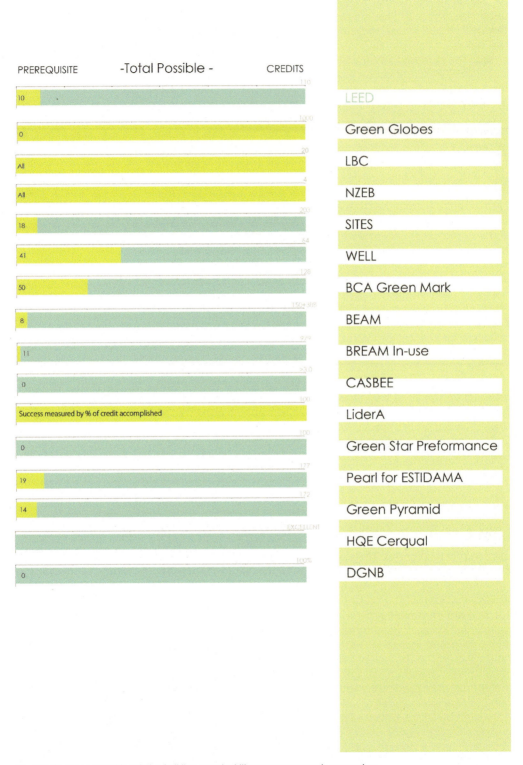

Fig 3.1 Global sustainable existing building sustainability assessment tools comparison
Source: Created by Milan Glisić, 2017

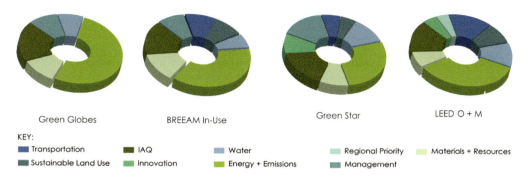

Fig 3.2 *Comparison of rating systems*
Source: *Created by Milan Glisić and Elizabeth Meyers, 2019*

play a significant role in the early stages of assessment and general applicability of the tools. When considering the *quantity* of buildings registered and global expanse however, the leaders are (in no specific hierarchy) Green Globes, BREEAM In-Use, Green Star and LEED O+M.

A closer look reveals Building Research Establishment Assessment Method (BREEAM), formed in the late 1980s as a rating system for new buildings, as the catalyst from where these and many others derived.[5] Its counterpart for existing buildings, BREEAM In-Use, was launched in 2009 and as of February 2017 has spanned over 117,515,680 sf of certified space within the UK, France, Finland, Lithuania, Poland, the Czech Republic, and other European countries.[6] Green Star Performance was launched as recently as 2013 yet is quickly gaining popularity in Australia and South America.[7] LEED O+M was launched in 2004 and was significantly revised in 2008 to focus on measured building performance and operational best management practices.[8] As of July 25, 2017 there were 1,687,206,989 sf and more than 2 billion (2,163,775,592) sf of LEED O+M certified space in the US and worldwide respectively.[9] All of these rating systems have similar categories for environmental criteria (Figure 3.2). Details regarding their processes for certification vary.

3.3.1.1 BREEAM In-Use

Like Green Globes EB, BREEAM In-Use checks and verifies a building's sustainable rating after occupancy and determines performance based upon the physical and management systems of the building. It is organized into three parts – Asset Performance, Building Management, and Occupier Management – each of which receives a rating from between a low "Acceptable" to a high "Outstanding" and which may be conducted sequentially with these three parts, or using only one of them. Asset performance relates to the way the building's form, fixtures and basic systems function. Building management is determined by how well the building is operated, and Occupier Management identifies the success of how users and services are administered. Categories of energy, water, materials and waste, health and well-being, pollution, transport, land use, innovation, and management[10] are evaluated within these parts via benchmarks unique to the type of category. Awards are given to facilities possessing a certain number of credits per category.

3.3.1.2 Green Globes EB

The publication *Green Globes for Existing Buildings* was developed in 2000 by ECD Energy and Environmental Canada, a company offering building environmental design and management tools.[11] *Green Globes for New Buildings Canada* followed shortly thereafter with the support of the Canadian Department of National Defence and the Department of Public Works and Government Services. In 2004, the system was adapted for the United States, where it is administered by Green Building Initiative (GBI), a Portland, Oregon based 501(c)3 and standards developer through the American National Standards Institute (ANSI). Since then, the assessments have undergone numerous periodic updates, the most recent being the updates to New Construction and Office Fit-ups modules based on the ANSI/GBI 01–2010: Green Building Assessment Protocol for Commercial Buildings. GBI acquired the global rights to Green Globes in 2017. The Green Globes brand and associated rating systems are administered in the United States by GBI and in Canada by its wholly owned, non-profit subsidiary, GB Initiative Canada.[12]

Green Globes EB (Existing Buildings) Certification comprises five steps. The first is to purchase and complete a Green Globes self-evaluation. This includes that the property managers, clients, owners, or certifying teams notify GBI that this self-evaluation (via an online survey) is complete and that the documentation supporting the responses is gathered. The second step is to hire a third-party assessor to perform the on-site assessment and issue a formal scheduling letter to the client and assessor. The third step involves working with a Green Globes assessor towards this aim. The final two steps are receiving the final report/score/rating and then requesting an official certification plaque.[13] The completion of the steps follow benchmarks within the categories of Energy, Water, Resources, Emissions, Indoor Environment, and Environmental Management.

3.3.1.3 Green Star Performance

Green Star Performance, developed by the Green Building Council of Australia, is used to determine the sustainable performance of buildings through the use of nine categories: management, indoor environment quality (IEQ), energy, transport, water, materials, land use and ecology, emissions, and innovation. Much like any other rating system, Green Star Performance requires several resources such as Submission Guidelines, Scorecard, Submission Templates, Calculators, Calculator Guides, and an online resource of technical questions to aid in the submission of credits; further, each category requires a specific rubric towards performance. There are calculators in particular, consisting of Excel spreadsheets containing instructions to determine if and how many points a building may be awarded for each credit.[14]

The process towards certification requires gathering resources, completing submission templates with supporting documentation, then submitting this information as a part of Round 1. The project is then assessed by the Australian construction-industry professionals Green Star Certified Assessors. If information is not complete or clear, the feedback will outline what should be addressed at the Round 2 submission.[15]

3.3.1.4 LEED O+M

LEED stands as the world's most widely used green building rating system in more than 162 countries and territories across the globe.[16] This fact, in addition to its universal accessibility and established partnership between USGBC and CUA, were the primary reasons LEED O+M became the vehicle for LEED Lab's curricular implementation.

There are two primary pathways within the LEED online portal to document the progress of a building's sustainability assessment, regardless of whether official certification is the goal: the traditional platform (LEED O+M rating system) and the performance platform (ARC) (Side Lesson B: ARC). Both are important to address because one builds upon the information of the other, loosely familiarizing students with algorithms of a process (traditional LEED path) before introducing them to a dashboard (performance path). For example, at North Carolina State University, LEED Lab instructor and Sustainability Program Coordinator Elizabeth Bowen found that while it is essential to measure performance in order to manage it, not everything that matters can be measured. The traditional path of progress for the O+M rating system at NC State supports better performance in ARC and also enhances the environment in valuable ways that support learning outcome for future designers.[17]

Side Lesson B – 3.3.1.4: ARC is the performance platform to assess a building. ARC analyzes performance for energy, water, waste, transportation, and human experience (see https://arcskoru.com/get-started-arc).

3.3.1.4.1 LEED Traditional Platform

There are benefits to the traditional platform over ARC. For one, the traditional platform requires *documentation* only during the Performance Period and not the entire year. This is helpful when budgets inhibit personnel or timing prevents students from monitoring ongoing performance metrics from semester to semester. This pathway is attractive as a course foundation due to its ability to navigate various depths within an organized platform of prerequisites and credits of the O+M rating system. These include Location and Transportation, Sustainable Sites, Water Efficiency, Energy and Atmosphere, Materials and Resources, Indoor Environmental Quality, Innovation, and Regional Priority. Falling short of achieving the prerequisite credits will not hurt the goals of the project at the initial stages of the traditional certification as much as they would under ARC, where they must be accomplished prior to implementation rather than accomplished throughout the entire duration of the traditional pathway.

Further, the traditional path allows for greater flexibility of transitioning from one rating system to another and a single-point registration. In the case of the release of a new rating system during the course of LEED Lab's Feasibility Phase, prerequisites of the new release should be accomplished due to the potential time it may take before the implementation of the newer release. It is also advisable to register for an O+M recertification of an existing building in a newer rating system if it is available. The registration for the traditional certification path requires an online launch of data at the onset of the project and allows the registrants to progress at their own pace throughout the building assessment.[18] Team members – select collaborators in the course – are invited via an email link from USGBC's LEED Online platform to participate in the project by the project administrator, a role which the website indicates as the instructor or staff person who guides the class through Implementation and Documentation, and sometimes Feasibility Phases. The instructor then has the capability to monitor progress for each credit after collaborators establish a password and log into the platform. How the instructor assigns credits to students, and how the students commence their work online during the Implementation and Documentation Phases is identified in Chapter 2.3.

3.3.1.4.2 LEED Performance Platform[19] (ARC)

ARC is a state-of-the-art user-friendly platform intended to help collect, manage and benchmark building data to improve sustainability performance, accomplished by tracking a building's incremental improvements through a performance score.[20] It was launched late 2016 by GBCI and designed for application to existing LEED-certified and non-certified buildings alike. LEED-certified buildings can use ARC to improve and benchmark with their peers everywhere as well as verify LEED performance on an annual basis to keep their certification up to date.[21] Buildings that are not certified can use this performance pathway to incrementally make sustainability improvements towards LEED O+M certification.

As with the example of NC State, a building can initially pursue a traditional LEED O+M certification and then apply ARC in the later stages of the process. Since prerequisites must be completed prior to utilizing ARC, this performance platform is most valuable when the basic prerequisites are accomplished and students in LEED Lab have gained an understanding of a credit's technical complexities as a learning goal. ARC is also a logical way to obtain recertification of an existing building since the team does not interfere with the traditional online protocol previously established. Instead, they engage with a cloud-based dashboard to enter data under five categories: *energy*, *water*, *waste*, *transportation* and *human experience* (Figure 3.3). Each category is described on the initial ARC dashboard with a comparison between the current and previous month's data, including year-to-date data.

To pursue this pathway, project teams must 1) register their project in ARC, 2) provide data and receive a Performance Score, and 3) complete all prerequisites within the traditional pathway.

PLATFORM

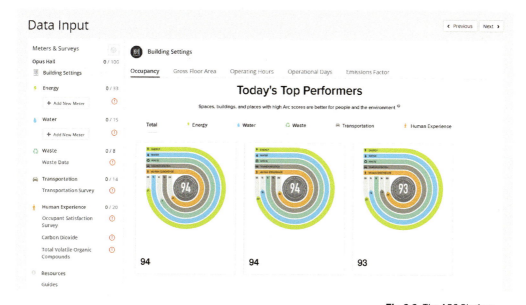

Fig 3.3 The ARC Platform website portal
Source: US Green Building Council

Specifically, projects achieve an optional 'Base Score' by pursuing LEED credits listed under LEED Credits for Base Score and submitting LEED forms on the traditional platform. The Base Score is directly derived from initial certification – a combination of previously earned credits – which translate up to 10 points in ARC and includes specific credits.[22] This Base Score contributes to ARC's Performance Score after GBCI reviews the credit documentation. After certification is granted, performance data and documentation are continually submitted to update LEED certification annually for a minimum of three years.[23]

The achievement of ARC categories uses vehicles different from the traditional path. For both the *energy* and *water* categories, utility bills can be input manually, or usage can be linked via the building's IP address directly to the project's Energy Star® portfolio (see Chapter 8, 'Energy') via ARC. Much like Energy Star®, the utility data in ARC is compared to a dataset of buildings to determine how many of the total possible points the building's performance earns.

The *waste* category uses two different metrics for ongoing waste and recycling values, plus the results of an annual waste audit. The ongoing diversion data is compared to a dataset of buildings to evaluate the diversion rate as well as the total amount of waste material the project is generating. ARC requires a compliant waste audit to achieve points. Much like the traditional pathway, the *transportation* category requires building occupants to be surveyed annually about how they typically travel to the building. ARC has integrated this survey into its online platform so occupants are simply sent a link to enable their transportation data to be automatically collected and analyzed within the ARC Platform. The *human experience* category

PLATFORM

Side Lesson C – 3.3.1.4: Volatile Organic Compounds (VOC): A VOC is an organic chemical emitted as a gas from material compositions such as plastics, paints, insulation and many other building and furnishing materials which negatively impacts a person's health (see www.epa.gov/indoor-air-quality-iaq/volatile-organic-compounds-impact-indoor-air-quality).

requires a more diverse set of data integrating various traditional pathway credits. For example, the same survey used for the *transportation* category doubles as a survey which assesses an occupant's thermal comfort – derived from the Indoor Environmental Quality (IEQ) category. The other metric for this category is building-wide testing for volatile organic compounds (VOC) (Side Lesson C: Volatile Organic Compounds, VOC) and CO_2 concentrations which must be conducted at least once annually. This is also derived from the traditional path IEQ credits along with very specific requirements as to how many readings are needed, the timeframe between readings, and the equipment used to take the readings.

The benefits of ARC over the traditional pathway include a more even and predictable internal time commitment and cost because categories are assessed each year rather than being consolidated once every five years. There are no prescriptive tasks required, like commissioning or energy auditing. Additionally, existing buildings can use ARC to earn LEED O+M certification and precertification in a much more expedient way now that ARC is open to all buildings, regardless of certification status.[24] Since the ARC score is performance based, increased or decreased performance translates quickly to the dynamic dashboard providing a clear visual impact of the project's progress or regression.

It is the combination of these two pathways that mark a successful LEED Lab, imbuing students with the necessary technical details required to accomplish credits traditionally and manually first before the dashboard is activated. A project team's ARC *performance score* determines the level of the (traditional pathway of) LEED certification awarded. Between the two pathways, certification levels remain consistent: performance score and certification levels are the same: 40–49 is Certified, 50–59 is Silver, 60–79 is Gold, and 80–100 is Platinum. The performance score generated through the ARC Platform does not replace a project's LEED certification level. It is an indicator of current performance.

Recently, ARC as an organization has started to issue "Performance Certifications" – recognitions of high-scoring facilities. This would afford the institution the ability to demonstrate and share performance with other parties through an unlimited number of certifications within one year (with a subscription).[25]

ARC is mentioned in *some* subsequent chapters within this textbook. However, it ultimately should be fully evaluated by the LEED Lab class at some point during the Feasibility Phase (see Chapter 5, 'Feasibility') in order to determine which performance factors from its platform will be used and/or applied to the building being assessed.

3.3.1.4.3 Resources

Accompanying any LEED Certification are a host of resources to improve understanding and increase success.

- LEEDUser is the preeminent online for-purchase reference tool for any credit completion. As the most widely used reference aid for any LEED certification, LEEDUser is operated by BuildingGreen, Inc. and comprises Q&A

blogs with various sustainability professionals who can answer questions about specific project details. USGBC and LEEDUser have joined to host public forum discussions within the USGBC LEED credit library.[26]

- USGBC LEED v4 Discussion Forums. The US Green Building Council hosts a monthly hour-long online discussion forum to focus on individual credits and also to address general questions about LEED project certifications. Led by a moderator and hosted by a panel of subject-matter experts, students can register for free and attend virtually.[27]
- LEED Project Credit Interpretation Rulings (CIR). The Project Credit Interpretation Ruling (CIR) process is a paid service offered by USGBC, meant to help LEED project teams obtain technical assistance from experts. Guidance on minimum project requirements (MPRs), prerequisites, and credits is available.[28]

Notes

1. "LEED Resources," US Green Building Council, 2018. www.usgbc.org/resources/
2. Ryann K. Ellis, *A Field Guide to Learning Management Systems* (American Society for Training and Development, 2009). http://web.csulb.edu/~arezaei/ETEC551/web/LMS_fieldguide_20091.pdf
3. Solomon A. David, *A Critical Understanding of Learning Management System*, n.d. www.academia.edu/3681177/A_Critical_Understanding_of_Learning_Management_System
4. Rip Empson, "Education Giant Blackboard Buys MyEdu to Help Refresh its Brand and Reanimate its User Experience," *TechCrunch*, January 16, 2014. https://techcrunch.com/2014/01/16/education-giant-blackboard-buys-myedu-to-help-refresh-its-brand-and-reanimate-its-user-experience/
5. Dot Doan, Ali Ghaffarianhoseini, Nicola Naismith and Tongrui Zhang. "A Critical Comparison of Green Building Rating Systems," *Building and Environment*, July 2017. www.researchgate.net/profile/Dat-Doan-2/publication/318302908_A_critical_comparison_of_green_building_rating_systems/links/5b3c19d4a6fdcc8506eecece/A-critical-comparison-of-green-building-rating-systems.pdf
6. S. Summerson, J. Atkins and A. Harries, *BREEAM In-Use: Driving Sustainability through Existing Buildings* (Watford: Building Research Establishment Ltd., n.d.). www.breeam.com/filelibrary/BREEAM%20In%20Use/KN5686---BREEAM-In-Use-White-Paper_dft2.pdf; "What is BREEAM In-Use?" Building Research Establishment Ltd., 2018. www.breeam.com/in-use
7. "The Operational Performance of Buildings," Green Building Council of Australia, 2018. www.gbca.org.au/green-star/green-star-performance-rating-tool-launch/
8. "LEED Facts," US Green Building Council, 2013. www.usgbc.org/articles/leed-facts
9. Communication between Jaime Van Mourik and Comm team at USGBC, 2017.
10. "BREEAM In-Use – Closing the Loop," BRSIA, 2009. www.bsria.co.uk/news/article/breeam-in-use-closing-the-loop/
11. "Certification Matters," Green Building Initiative: A Practical Approach to Green Building, 2018. www.thegbi.org/products/green-globes/history.shtml
12. "About Green Globes," Green Globes, 2018. www.greenglobes.com/about.asp
13. "Sensible Solutions to Reach Your Building's Potential," Green Building Initiative: A Practical Approach to Green Building, 2018. www.thegbi.org/green-globes-certification/how-to-certify/existing-buildings/
14. "The Operational Performance of Buildings" 2018, op cit.
15. "Guide on How to Prepare a Green Star Submission: May 2018," Green Building Council of Australia, 2018. https://gbca-web.s3.amazonaws.com/media/documents/green-star-submissions-290518.pdf
16. "USGBC Statistics," US Green Building Council, 2016. www.usgbc.org/articles/usgbc-statistics

17 "Arc Webinar Series," US Green Building Council, July 19, 2017, 12:00–1:00PM EST, North Carolina State Case Study. www.usgbc.org/event/arc-webinar-series
18 The specific steps recommended by USGBC prior to registering for ARC or the Traditional Platform are identified in USGBC's Welcome Packet (see www.centerforgreenschools.org/sites/default/files/resource-files/leed-lab-welcome-packet.pdf).
19 "Performance Score to LEED Certification," US Green Building Council, 2018. www.usgbc.org/buildingperformance
20 "Measure your Green Performance," ARC Skoru, 2018. http://arcskoru.com/
21 Nora Knox, "All about Arc: A Performance Platform Like No Other," US Green Building Council, 2016. www.usgbc.org/articles/all-about-arc-performance-platform-no-other
22 Jenna Lipscomb, "Arc: The Wave of Future for High Performance Building," Cadmus Group, 2018. www.cadmusgroup.com/articles/arc-wave-future-high-performance-buildings/:

- Building Exterior and Hardscape Management
- Integrated Pest Management, Erosion Control, and Landscape Management (one point)
- Site Development – Protect and Restore Open Space (one point)
- Stormwater Quantity Control (one point)
- Heat Island Reduction – Non-Roof (one point)
- Heat Island Reduction – Roof (one point)
- Light Pollution Reduction (one point)
- Enhanced Refrigerant Management (one point)
- Green Cleaning – Indoor Integrated Pest Management (one point)
- Controllability of Systems – Lighting (one point)
- Occupant Comfort – Thermal Comfort Monitoring (one point)
- Daylight and Views (one point)

23 "Performance Score to LEED Certification" 2018, op cit.

Projects that are currently pursuing LEED O+M standard path can also use ARC for performance data reporting. LEED O+M projects have two options to *maintain* their certification:

- Recertify using the credit-based approach in LEED Online;
- Recertify through the performance-based approach in ARC, i.e. ongoing certification.

For non-certified buildings that wish to achieve *initial* LEED O+M certification, the team can utilize the "Performance score to LEED certification" path. The initial certification must be achieved within three years of registration and maintained annually (see http://arcskoru.com/about). Nevertheless, projects pursuing LEED certification through "Performance Score to LEED Certification" need to achieve *all prerequisites* from the traditional LEED O+M: Existing Buildings v4 rating system and may receive up to ten points upon submission of further basic credit LEED documentation to GBCI for review (see www.usgbc.org/buildingperformance).

24 Jenna Lipscomb 2018, op. cit.
25 Chris Pyke, "Arc Performance Certificates," GBCI, 2019. www.gbci.org/arc-performance-certificates
26 "LEEDuser: The Essential Tool for any LEED Project," BuildingGreen, 2018. https://leeduser.buildinggreen.com/; "LEED Credit Library." www.usgbc.org/credits
27 "LEED v4 Discussion Forum," US Green Building Council, 2018. www.usgbc.org/event/leed-v4-discussion-forum-1. This link is to a portal on which users can sign up as a USGBC Community Member, required for participation.
28 "What is Project Credit Interpretation Ruling (CIR)?" US Green Building Council, 2018. www.usgbc.org/help/what-project-credit-interpretation-ruling-cir

CHAPTER FOUR

PHASE I: FEASIBILITY[1]

The purpose of starting your LEED Lab with the Feasibility Phase is to prepare the sequence of events leading up to the building assessment. It is necessary for the evaluation of your existing facilities, campus, and to identify the best candidate for the green building evaluation. It provides the time to set up a schedule for the remainder of the assessment, associated parties to tasks, and identifies staff, personnel, and even external consultants (if any) which will assist in a successful few semesters. While there is no specific step by step guideline to navigating this phase (unlike accomplishing credits in the Implementation Phase) there are recommendations to a fluid preparation utilizing checklists and procedures for a successful LEED Lab beginning.

4.1 Goals

There are primary goals of the course, and secondary goals of the project which function in tandem to deliver this integrated learning of the Feasibility Phase. The first primary goal includes creating a platform for direct student collaboration with the US Green Building Council (USGBC), Green Building Certification Institute (GBCI), and also a variety of campus groups and facilities departments. This provides an opportunity for students to work in tandem with the university tradesmen and personnel to identify buildings that require the most effort towards sustainable upgrades, and then to diagnose those facilities for sustainable potential – pioneering existing facility certification on the entire campus. At the close of the semester the students attain another goal of the course by gaining the required experience necessary to prepare for the LEED O+M professional credential exam. LEED Lab also meets the goals of industry by equipping students with the skills, knowledge and expertise needed to be effective communicators, project managers, critical thinkers, problem solvers, engaged leaders, and team players.

PHASE I: FEASIBILITY

Secondary goals are called Project goals and inherently stem from the Campus' overall initiatives, yet are specific to the building being certified. They involve building stakeholders who understand current facilities practices, such as the owner, building management staff, occupants, and vendors. Including them early in the process ensures that their interests are well represented.[2] The Feasibility Phase is the best time to identify project goals, and a charrette (see Chapter 2) is the best forum within this phase to discuss them.

Project goals include specific metrics which are identified and achieved through various credits of the LEED O+M rating system. For these goals to be identified, a fundamental alignment of Campus goals with Project goals is important. The team should look at traditional campus practices and management, considering the flow of materials, water, and energy through the building and site. It is also important to identify existing campus policies, practices, equipment, contracts, and budgets to set a baseline for improvement. For example, is there a campus-wide Social Responsibility Report (Side Lesson A: Social Responsibility Report) which may synergize with the project goals of specific LEED credits? How does the campus address indoor health – are there policies already set into place regularly monitoring health initiatives, travel considerations or workplace satisfaction which may be integrated as a project goal? Are there required annual metrics which should be reported to a local municipality or government such as global impact from waste, computing greenhouse gas emissions, or other calculations which identify the status of operations, such as the MIT Greenhouse Gas Emissions Inventory (Figure 4.1). Aligning project goals to existing ongoing campus operations is a logical step towards realizing both. The role LEED Lab plays in expediting the achievement of these goals depends on the *way* the LEED O+M certification process is intended to be applied.

Side Lesson A – 4.1: Social Responsibility Report: According to the Global Reporting Initiative, a Social Responsibility Report is a sustainability report on an organization's everyday impacts economically, environmentally, and socially (see shorturl.at/qCQZ8).

4.1.1 Academic Research

Since the university has no designated sustainability office or officer, LEED Lab was developed at CUA to be a course which would provide the platform for environmental literacy among all university parties. It was a necessary transformation; a bottom-up-approach where students became the catalysts for change, proliferated by faculty and staff as a new approach to integrative learning, empowered by a desire to employ creative methods of education while promulgating a greater awareness of energy, water conservation and other sustainability measures on campus. Thus, the role of LEED Lab at CUA is unique; the *quality* of scholarly research and analysis of buildings and knowledge gained by the students was more important at the institution than the *quantity* of buildings certified. Consequently, CUA's LEED Lab has evolved to attract students from a variety of disciplines. Politics, engineering, facility management and chemistry majors—from undergrads to Ph.D. candidates – have become key players in LEED Lab,

PHASE I: FEASIBILITY

Fig 4.1 Harvard University's sustainability plan

Note: 204,000 MTCO2e total emissions

Source: Derived from MIT Office of Sustainability, MIT Greenhouse Gas Emissions Inventory, 2018 main categories. Diagrammed by Elizabeth Meyers, 2020

| 37

in addition to the architectural students who led the pilot, enabling broad-reaching ideas, procedures, and methods of calculations as a facet of 'research'.[3]

4.1.2 Expedited Certification

The most common role of LEED Lab among campuses is to expedite Certification, while learning. Most universities have Sustainability Offices or the like, and have applied this course in tandem with their campus goals of LEED-certified building targets. These campuses may choose the performance pathway (see Chapter 3) which provides data across five categories – Energy, Water, Waste, Transportation, and Human Experience – in the ARC Platform to generate a performance score. In order to achieve certification, the project must achieve a minimum performance score, in addition to complying with all LEED O+M prerequisites. Projects choosing the traditional pathway will document the project within LEED Online and also must comply with all LEED O+M prerequisites. When deciding which pathway to pursue, consider how each option aligns with your Project goals. For example, the simplified performance testing requirements of the performance pathway allow for more self-directed work, whereas the traditional pathway may require additional training for students in areas such as the energy audit. In summary, the streamlined submittals of the performance pathway allow the course to move more swiftly through the certification process while the more prescriptive nature of the traditional pathway provides a step by step process for improving performance and fostering research opportunities.

4.2 Approach

The approach to realizing Project goals includes achieving Master Site (or 'campus') credits, initial building certification and/or may also include previously certified buildings. Projects previously certified under LEED O+M or BD+C, can update their certification using the performance score within the ARC Platform (see Chapter 3). No additional documentation of prerequisites is required! The approach to achieving initial building certification or Master Site *campus* LEED credits (sometimes referred to as 'Master Site Certification' although USGBC does not officially 'certify' campuses) is more involved. For LEED Lab, it is recommended that the team begins with a global view of the campus, thus pursuing Master Site credits. Many credits in LEED, such as those focused on purchasing, site maintenance, pest control, and waste management, can be implemented at the campus level because they can be quantified or assessed in aggregate, and are not unique to an individual building. This is the big idea behind Master Site credits. Achieving these type of credits means that any

> eligible LEED credits and prerequisites can be documented once for the entire area and development within a LEED campus boundary.

These campus credits are earned through a separate review in the Master Site. Once reviewed and earned in the Master Site, campus credits are available to LEED projects (both individual and group projects) associated with the same Master Site and located within that same LEED campus boundary.[4]

Which LEED credits qualify as Master Site credits? This is identified in the LEED O+M v4 Reference Guide under each credit's description. "Eligible" indicates that the specific credit may be documented at the 'Master Site' level. "Ineligible" means that every project within the campus boundary may earn the credit but each project must document compliance separately (Figure 4.2).[5] Since LEED Lab is originally based on the LEED O+M rating system, acquiring Master Site credits facilitates all future LEED O+M certification pursuits; once certain aggregate credits are earned via the Master Site, they apply to any campus building pursuing LEED O+M.

Master Site credits are planned in the same manner as individual building certification credits – during the Feasibility Phase of the LEED Lab course. They are also executed in the same manner (Feasibility, Implementation, and Documentation Phases), but typically *before* individual building certification, and often accomplished faster. Most LEED Labs can achieve these credits within a two, three or four-year process, but more ambitious project teams may be able to achieve them within a year.

During the Documentation Phase of the Master Site credits when data has been submitted to GBCI, the completed credits go through preliminary and final reviews. The preliminary review provides technical advice for credits that require additional work for achievement. Once the credit is revaluated per this feedback it is resubmitted for a final review which awards or denies the credit. The process of submitting and being awarded or denied credits is the same for individual building certification. In the latter, the final review contains the project's final score and certification level. Since Master Site credits are unable to earn an actual certification alone, the process ends with the award of the individual credits. Any decision of credit denial can be appealed if a team believes additional consideration is warranted. However to prevent or avoid the cost of a denial altogether, the team should supply a thorough resubmission of the credit prior to submitting their final review.

Individual building certification ends with one of four levels of certification, depending on the point thresholds achieved:

- Certified, 40–49 points
- Silver, 50–59 points
- Gold, 60–79 points
- Platinum, 80 points and above

If another O+M rating system is being applied in lieu of LEED O+M, credit and point awards would vary (Figure 4.3). These rating systems may or may not possess similar opportunities to accrue aggregate credits via a Master Site. Although Master

PHASE I: FEASIBILITY

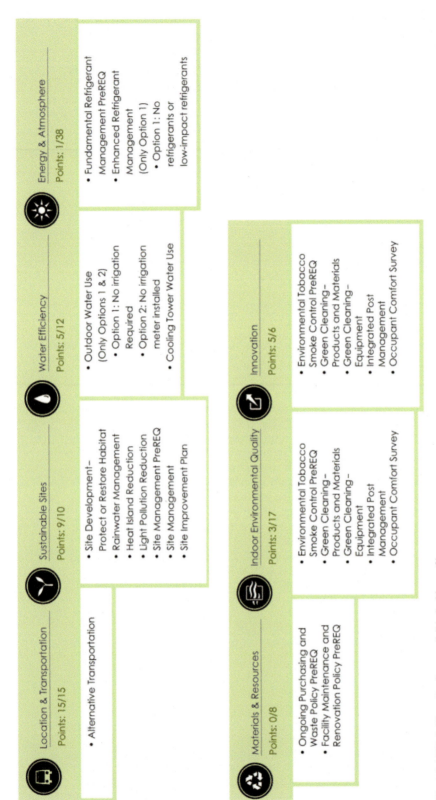

Fig 4.2 *LEED O+M credits that are eligible for Master Site*
Source: *Diagrammed by Elizabeth Meyers, 2019*

PHASE I: FEASIBILITY

Fig 4.3 *Comparison of O+M assessment systems*
Source: Diagrammed by Elizabeth Meyers, 2019

Site credits never amount to a certification independently, they certainly provide an easier route towards certifying a building despite the rating system used. Whether the campus is being assessed first and then initial building certification ensues (and/or re-assessing previous building certification) or only the building certification is being sought, the campus

| 41

assessment is a way to easily understand which credits to pursue in LEED Lab.

4.2.1 The Campus Assessment

Assessing your campus is a part of pursuing Master Site credits and building certification alike. It is particularly important for institutions that do not possess a protocol for green certification. Referring to USGBC's Campus Implementation Workbook,[6] we begin by identifying unique aspects of your campus. Many successful charrettes can justify that this exercise is best implemented *in advance* of your planning the charrette (Box 4.1).

- ☐ Identify your campus by its institutional name, then by its LEED campus boundary (e.g., whole campus, subset of related buildings). This is best accomplished via a site plan, often found on the campus' website.
- ☐ Next, establish the most important prerequisites of LEED by continuing to the Implementation Phase (see Chapter 5).

Refer to the respective chapters for details about what is required of successful implementation of these items.

4.2.2 Policies

Policies in LEED Lab exist to establish a protocol for successful sustainable strategy implementation. They are high-level rules or statements within the LEED rating system which commit the organization to an overarching course of action, empowering staff working at the operational level.[7] They serve as guides for sub-paths called "programs and/or plans" which are targeted at implementing those policies. For example, campus-wide smoking bans, chemical compositions for cleaning solutions and parking rules which reward low-emitting vehicles establish a clear path for accomplishing sustainability more detailed goals such as smoking allowed in designated areas of a certain building's exterior environment, cleaning methods for lavatories using specific solutions, and a lower parking rate for electric vehicles or a credit for biking to work – respectively. A policy is often required to precede many credits, while the program/plan is the field-level operational working document that lays out the series of steps required to meet that sustainability goal reliably in a given building or group of buildings – often identified in the form of a credit. A Site Management Policy for example is required to achieve LEED O+M certification. There is no option *not* to have this policy on your campus or for the building you are assessing. The Site Management credit is located hierarchically *below* this policy within this credit category, is poised as a plan to support the policy, and is an *option* for achievement. The "establishment period" is the time when building these policies are drafted, infrastructure is assessed, and programs or processes are put in place to enable ongoing performance

PHASE I: FEASIBILITY

Box 4.1 Campus assessment checklist

Identify your campus by its institutional name, then by its LEED campus boundary (e.g. whole campus, subset of related buildings).

This is best accomplished via a site plan, often found on the campus' website.

_____

Next, establish the most important prerequisites of LEED:
Minimum Energy Efficiency Performance requires each energy source to be metered at each building.

How is energy managed on your campus (purchased, central plant)?

_____

Any modifications needed to meet these requirements?

_____

See Chapter 8 for specific information about achieving this prerequisite.

Are there standard procedures campus-wide for the following items?

Purchasing: _____ Responsible Party: _____
(Chapter 9.3.1)

Waste Management: _____ Responsible Party: _____
(Chapter 9.3.2)

Building cleaning: _____ Responsible Party: _____
(Chapter 10.3.3)

Engineering/HVAC systems: _____ Responsible Party: _____
(Chapters 8 + 10 all credits)

Exterior maintenance: _____ Responsible Party: _____
(Chapters 9.3.2 + 10.3.3)

Pest management: _____ Responsible Party: _____
(Chapter 10.3.5)

Construction projects: _____ Responsible Party: _____
(Chapter 9.3.2)

Budget and financing: _____ Responsible Party: _____
(Chapter 4.2.4)

Refer to the respective Chapters for details about what is required of successful implementation of these items.

Source: Derived from USGBC Campus Implementation Workout. Redrawn by Elizabeth Meyers, 2020

measurement. This time is different from the better-known "Performance Period" (see Chapter 4.2.4) which is the continuous implementation of the strategies set during the establishment period.[8] Obtaining or evaluating existing policies, or writing new policies, often should occur at the same time as the campus assessment, but may extend even into the Implementation Phase at times.

4.2.3 Choosing a Facility

Perhaps the most exciting and equally challenging decision during the Feasibility Phase of LEED Lab is to select a facility on which to perform your assessment. The best approach for accomplishing this is to conduct a quick feasibility study of some of the possible buildings on campus to evaluate their ability to meet the major prerequisites for building-level metering, energy efficiency performance, minimum ventilation, and indoor water efficiency. This can be best accomplished shortly after or during the campus assessment and when policies are identified. Facilities on your campus which have been recently constructed, namely those possessing a LEED for New Construction certification, are good candidates because they already possess data about their performance. The checklist below will assist in the feasibility study (Box 4.2).

4.2.4 Performance Period

The LEED O+M certification, along with the process of many of the other existing building rating systems, is based largely on successful performance-based outcomes. These outcomes must be measured during a period of time that is common to all of the credits being pursued. The Performance Period is this consecutive duration of time during which the outcomes of credits and prerequisites is measured. There are several conditions to its establishment:

- ☐ It should be designated during the Feasibility Phase.
- ☐ It should reflect the most current operational activity prior to the certification submission.
- ☐ It should not contain any gaps.
- ☐ It should constitute a period of time longer than a full week.
- ☐ It should last at least three months.
- ☐ It should not last over 24 months.
- ☐ Credits being pursued within the Performance Period should conclude within 30 days of each other (Figure 4.4).

A helpful resource to help the LEED Lab class plan the Performance Period is provided by USGBC.[9]

4.2.5 Recertification

The LEED O+M for Building Operations and Maintenance rating system can be applied both to buildings seeking LEED certification for the first time and to projects previously certified under any version of the LEED Design and Construction rating systems. 'Initial certification' is considered any first-time application for LEED O+M certification. 'Recertification'

Box 4.2 Building feasibility checklist

Building Description (complete this form for each building on campus)

Building name: _____

Use: _____

Gross floor area: _____ Site area: _____

Operation hours: _____ No. of FTE occupants: _____

Major space types: _____

- Meters for each potable water source at the building level: List ALL energy types and meter numbers
  _____
  _____

- Meters for each energy source at the building level: List ALL energy types and meter numbers:
  _____
  _____

☐ Building is ENERGY STAR relatable
  If not, what benchmark can be used?_____

  Does it meet minimum efficient requirements? _____

☐ Efficient water fixtures (meet EPAact, UPC/IPC or Watersense)

☐ Ventilation rates meet ASHRAE Std 62.1

☐ HVAC equipment uses non-CFC refrigerants

☐ An ASHRAE Level 1 Walkthrough Analysis was/will be completed on

☐ Purchasing preference is given to sustainable products

☐ Green cleaning practices are used

☐ Staff and occupants are eager to participate

☐ Building is suited for LEED for Existing Buildings: O&M (complete a LEED checklist)

☐ Are changes necessary for this building to be eligible? _____
_____

Source: Derived from USGBC Campus Implementation Worksheet. Redrawn by Elizabeth Meyers, 2020

PHASE I: FEASIBILITY

Fig 4.4 *Performance Periods by credit*
Source: Derived from the USGBC Reference Guide. Diagrammed by Elizabeth Meyers, 2019

Fig 4.5 *Timeline of the history of LEED O + M*
Source: Derived from the Sustainable Investment Group. Diagrammed by Elizabeth Meyers, 2019

is the subsequent application(s) for certification after a project has received an initial certification under any version of LEED O+M,[10] of which there are many throughout history (Figure 4.5).

Projects require recertification within five years of their previous certification, but may be recertified as early as their one-year certification anniversary. In this case, their Performance Periods extend from the date of the previous certification to the date of the recertification application. The LEED O+M v4 Reference Guides recommends that,

> project teams continue to track building performance during the certification review process. Projects pursuing recertification are required to submit only performance documentation for review; they are not required to submit establishment documentation unless there have been major changes (e.g., major renovations, major addition, management turnover) that prompt review.[11]

4.3 Timeline

There is no required set of parameters for when the Feasibility, Implementation, or Documentation Phases of your project should start. Nor is there any set timeframe for the completion of credits, besides the requisite Performance Period. In this case, how do you organize your project to identify when it should begin and end? LEED Labs deploy the building assessment process at the onset of the semester, set a Performance Period, and then continue with the analysis until the award of the credits. All of this requires planning well in advance of initiating the class. That plan is described in a timeline.

Just as an architectural project requires a dedicated timeline for the design and construction of a building, the green assessment of a facility requires a carefully organized calendar of activities. A timeline for LEED Lab serves such a purpose (see Figure 4.6, spanning three pages). Although the graphic organization may vary, it should include the following:

- ☐ Feasibility, Implementation, and Documentation Phases
- ☐ Charrette/s
- ☐ Prerequisites
- ☐ Credits to be pursued based on The Campus Assessment
- ☐ Duration of various credits
- ☐ Timeline and LEED Lab Timing Chart
- ☐ Preliminary submission
- ☐ Preliminary review
- ☐ Credit update
- ☐ Secondary submission
- ☐ Final Award Certification

To accompany this timeline, The LEED Lab Timing Chart is a tool developed by USGBC which includes a credit breakdown for both a campus approach and a single building approach,[12] depending on the campus and project goals. It is a fine-tuning of the credit goals. Where the timeline provides an overarching view of the project, the Timing Chart should be modified per each class to include an additional column indicating the following:

- ☐ Credit assignments
- ☐ Student/s assigned to the credit
- ☐ Staff responsible for credit data
- ☐ Consultants responsible for credit data

The Timing Chart and timeline create the hierarchy of prerequisite and credit pursuit, are unique for each project, and are catalysts that help to achieve thoroughness of a sustainable assessment.

4.3.1 Strategies and Synergies

While prerequisites are not optional to pursue, credits should be weighed for their potential of achievement during The Site Assessment, the Charrette, while creating the timeline, or generally throughout the Feasibility Phase of LEED Lab. The situation often arises that one credit's potential may benefit or minimize the success of another credit. Where such circumstances arise, and they more often do, the concept of 'synergizing credits' assists in decision-making.

A sustainable strategy is one component of a building design or analysis which contributes towards a larger goal of reducing the environmental impact on that building. It is often a method, technique, or technology (Figure 4.7). In LEED Lab, a strategy is considered to be part of a credit since a credit is a specific method

PHASE I: FEASIBILITY

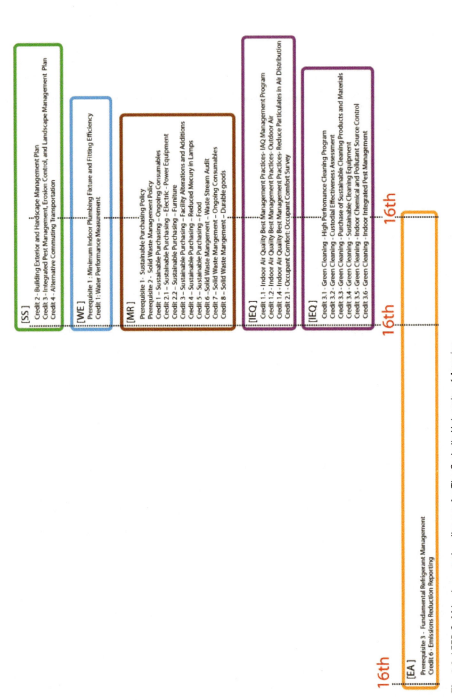

Fig 4.6 *LEED O+M implementation diagram for The Catholic University of America*
Source: *Created by Patricia Andrasik and Greg Wilke, 2012*

PHASE I: FEASIBILITY

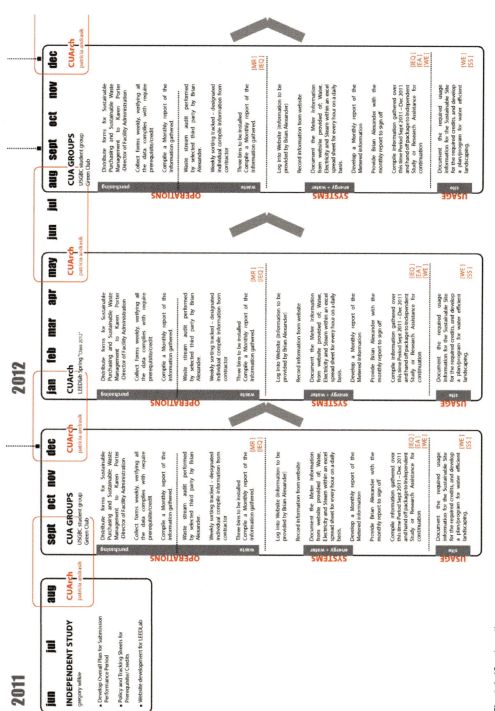

Fig 4.6 (Continued)

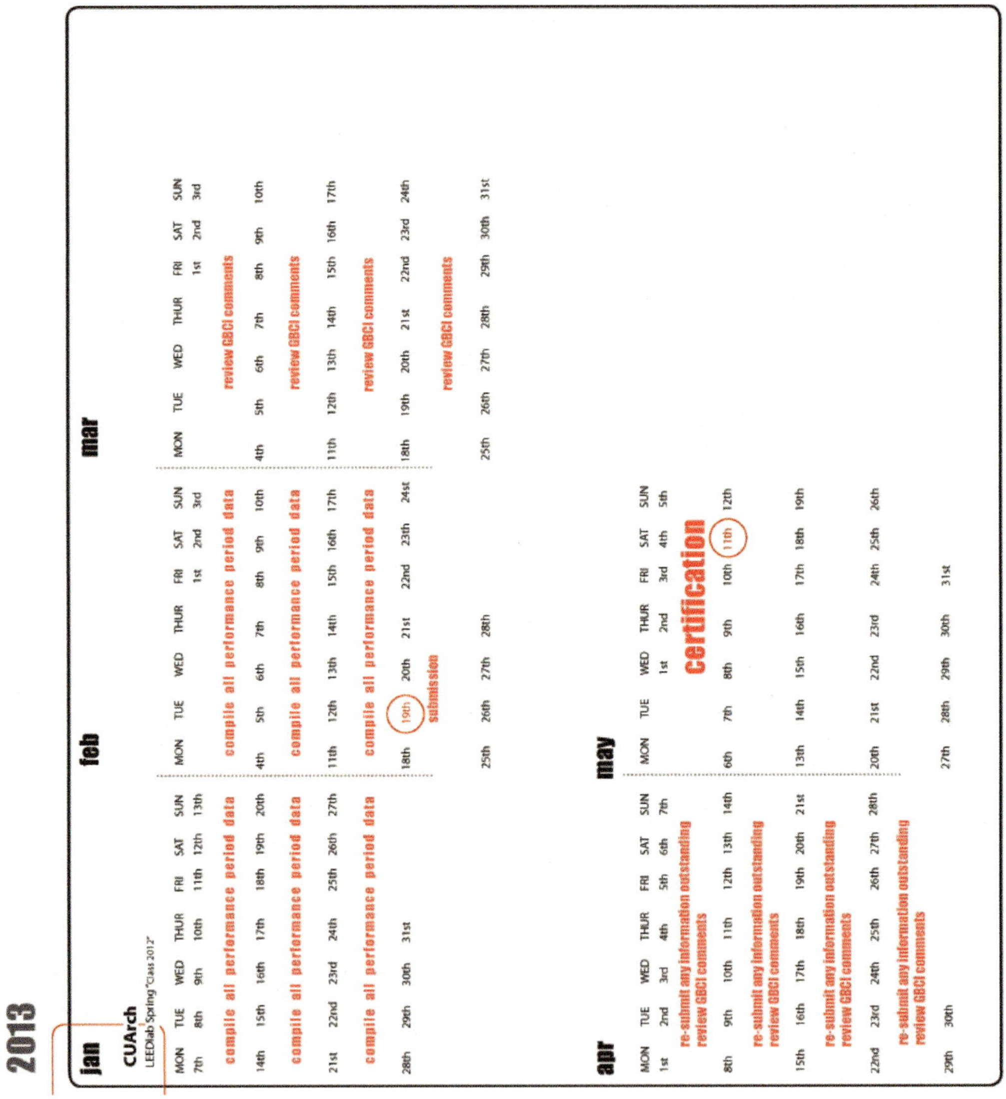

PHASE I: FEASIBILITY

2013

jan
CUArch
LEEDlab Spring °Class 2012°

MON	TUE	WED	THUR	FRI	SAT	SUN
7th	8th	9th	10th	11th	12th	13th
compile all performance period data						
14th	15th	16th	17th	18th	19th	20th
compile all performance period data						
21st	22nd	23rd	24th	25th	26th	27th
compile all performance period data						
28th	29th	30th	31st			

feb

MON	TUE	WED	THUR	FRI	SAT	SUN
				1st	2nd	3rd
compile all performance period data						
4th	5th	6th	7th	8th	9th	10th
compile all performance period data						
11th	12th	13th	14th	15th	16th	17th
compile all performance period data						
18th	19th	20th	21st	22nd	23rd	24th
submission						
25th	26th	27th	28th			

mar

MON	TUE	WED	THUR	FRI	SAT	SUN
				1st	2nd	3rd
review GBCI comments						
4th	5th	6th	7th	8th	9th	10th
review GBCI comments						
11th	12th	13th	14th	15th	16th	17th
review GBCI comments						
18th	19th	20th	21st	22nd	23rd	24th
review GBCI comments						
25th	26th	27th	28th	29th	30th	31st

apr

MON	TUE	WED	THUR	FRI	SAT	SUN
1st	2nd	3rd	4th	5th	6th	7th
re-submit any information outstanding / review GBCI comments						
8th	9th	10th	11th	12th	13th	14th
re-submit any information outstanding / review GBCI comments						
15th	16th	17th	18th	19th	20th	21st
re-submit any information outstanding / review GBCI comments						
22nd	23rd	24th	25th	26th	27th	28th
re-submit any information outstanding / review GBCI comments						
29th	30th					

may

MON	TUE	WED	THUR	FRI	SAT	SUN
		1st	2nd	3rd	4th	5th
6th	7th	8th	9th	10th	11th	12th
			certification			
13th	14th	15th	16th	17th	18th	19th
20th	21st	22nd	23rd	24th	25th	26th
27th	28th	29th	30th	31st		

Fig 4.6 (Continued)

PHASE I: FEASIBILITY

of assessing a sustainable aspect of a category. A sustainable synergy fuses together multiple sustainable strategies as symbiotic components of a sustainable system; if one strategy were to be removed, the strength of the design or analysis would be compromised. It is an integration of sustainable strategies which have a positive symbiotic performance outcome to reduce the environmental impact on the campus facilities (Figure 4.8).

An example of a synergy is the installation of a series of raingardens along the campus grounds – we can call this synergy "Raingarden Alley." Rainwater Management, Outdoor Water Use Reduction, Site Development – Protect or Restore Habitat, and Site Improvement Plan would be among the credit strategies which synergize. The raingardens would positively benefit the reduction of stormwater (calculated as required by the Rainwater Management credit), and exterior potable water (via the Outdoor Water Use credit calculations if adaptive or native species were planted in the rain gardens). The team would further

Fig 4.7 *Various sustainability strategies one can utilize to create a synergy*
Source: Diagrammed by Elizabeth Meyers, 2020

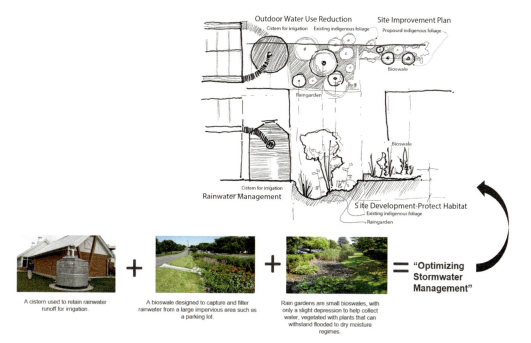

Fig 4.8 *An example of how strategies can synergize*
Source: Diagrammed by Patricia Andrasik, 2020

PHASE I: FEASIBILITY

increase the chances of obtaining the Site Development – Protect or Restore Habitat credit since the calculation for a specific amount of green space on the campus is a requirement for credit achievement. "Raingarden Alley" would also be a component to achieving the Site Improvement Plan if subsequent installations of rain gardens were planned for the future.

4.3.2 Point Integration Diagram

The Point Integration Diagram (PID) is a mechanism which graphically depicts the strategies and synergies by diagramming them. It can be defined as a graphic representation of individual credit categories and how they relate to each other; linking strategies to overall synergies. A PID is not unique to LEED Lab since it is a relevant tool for all green assessment yet may be designed specifically for the LEED Lab project to describe credit goals for the semester and the overall project. In order to complete the PID accurately, the credit and prerequisites must be evaluated first. On-site assessment can complete most of the work, but each credit should be fully investigated during the Feasibility Phase (Figure 4.9). The PID creates a clear graphic plan for campus and/or building assessment during the Feasibility Phase, and certainly should be presented at the Charrette since it may be informed or revised by feedback.

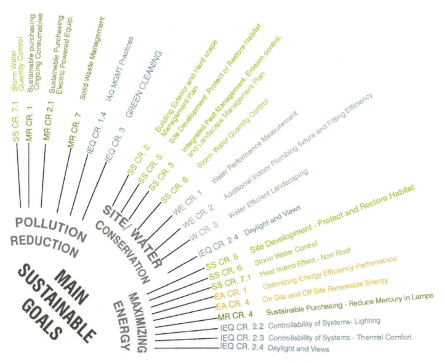

Fig 4.9 *Final point integration diagram from the LEED O+M certification for the Crough Center*

Note: The main goals were derived from initial charrettes between LEED Lab students, facility personnel, consultants and other members critical to the facility being evaluated. Three main goals were established as a result of these initial brainstorming sessions: Pollution Reduction, Site/Water Conservation and Maximizing Energy

Source: Created by Anthony Stofella, 2015

PHASE I: FEASIBILITY

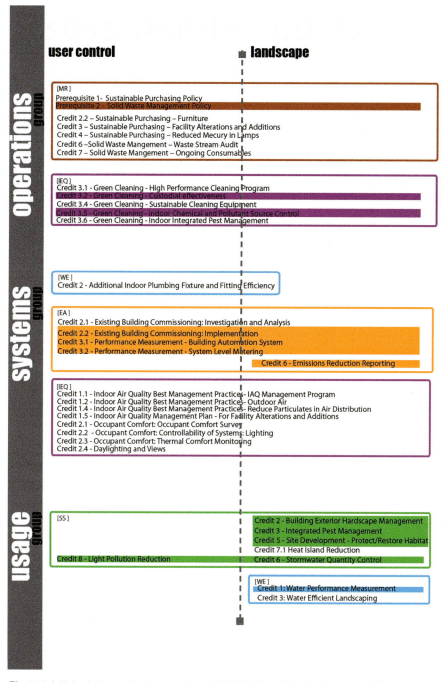

Fig 4.10 *Initial point integration diagram from the LEED O+M certification for the Crough Center*
Note: The main goals were derived from students in the initial LEED Lab course, prior to the initial charrette. In this diagram, colors are used to organize similar credit categories in both groupings for the purpose of the charrette groups and the topics of User Control (interior) and Landscape (exterior). Point Integration Diagrams are based on the decisions of the LEED Lab students and are not prescriptive in either their graphic appearance nor their content. They are simply used as a tool for clarifying information about goals. This diagram was eventually replaced with a diagram from a subsequent class which expresses new goals that include stakeholder input
Source: Created by Greg Wilke, 2014

PHASE I: FEASIBILITY

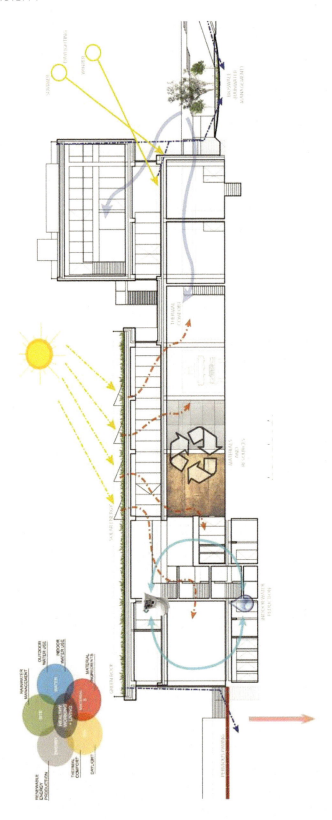

PHASE I: FEASIBILITY

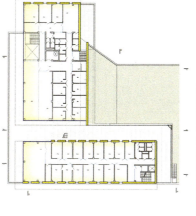

RENEWABLE ENERGY PRODUCTION (PV PANELS)

Total building annual energy cost = $27,846 x $5,366 = $33, 212

% RENEWABLE ENERGY = 41%

% renewable energy > 41% = 3 points

Sharp 250QCS Ballasted Roof System Pricing Examples

System size	50kW	75kW	100kW	250kW	500kW	1,000kW
System Area	3,846 sq. ft.	5,769 sq. ft.	7,692 sq. ft.	19,231 sq. ft.	38,462 sq. ft.	76,924 sq. ft.
List Price	$94,300	$138,990	$180,320	$442,750	$852,500	$1,705,000

- Sharp Solar Modules are Made in USA
- Qualifies as Buy American (AARA Compliant)
- Newest Sharp Solar Technologu

DAYLIGHT/ THERMAL COMFORT

Low-E glazing to North for indirect, natural light
Thick bearing walls to south provide shade and thermal mass

DAYLIGHT

Overhangs limit direct light entering building
Vericle louvers limit direct sunlight on third and fourth level

A firestation is a 24 hours building. The men who work at the Vilnius Fire Station work in 24-48 hour shifts during which they spend 24 hours living within the station followed by a 48 hour off period.

With this in mind, and thinking about the physical condition these men must be in to perform their jobs, it is important that architects provide for them a healthy space in which to work, live, and train.

Through a synergy of sustainable strategies we can provide this space for these men while also saving the company money and improving our envirnoment and it's future.

THERMAL COMFORT

Individual controls in single-occupant spaces
Multi-controls in multi-occupant spaces

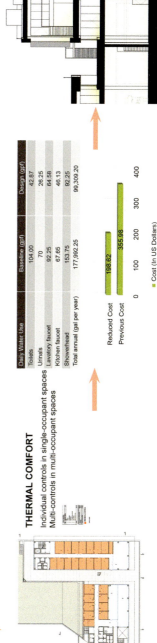

Fig 4.11 *An example of a synergy diagram that includes LEED calculations*

Source: Created by Chris Urban, 2013

| 55

PHASE I: FEASIBILITY

Once the Site Assessment, timeline, and PID have been completed (along with any other checklists recommended previously), and the charrette has occurred with a good repository of feedback, the plans to implement the requirements for all prerequisites and credits may commence. The project team is a step further to realizing the campus' sustainability goals, and is well-equipped to proceed to the Implementation Phase.

Notes

1. "LEED Lab," US Green Building Council, October 10, 2016. www.usgbc.org/leed-lab
2. US Green Building Council, "Getting Started," *Reference Guide for Building Operations and Maintenance* (Washington, DC: US Green Building Council, 2013): 12.
3. Patricia Andrasik, "LEED Lab in Action: Catholic University's LEED Lab Legacy," US Green Building Council, April 9, 2015. www.usgbc.org/articles/leed-lab-action-catholic-universitys-leed-lab-legacy
4. "LEED Campus Guidance," US Green Building Council, April 1, 2014, www.usgbc.org/resources/leed-campus-guidance
5. US Green Building Council 2013, 10, op. cit.
6. "Campus Implementation Workbook," USGBC, 2020, www.usgbc.org/sites/default/files/green-campus-workbook.pdf, 3.
7. "Policy, Program, and Plan Models for LEED for Existing Buildings: Operations & Maintenance," USGBC, June 14, 2010. www.usgbc.org/sites/default/files/EBOM%20Policy,%20Program,%20and%20Plan%20Model.pdf
8. US Green Building Council 2013, 10–13, op. cit.
9. See www.usgbc.org/resources/performance-periods-table-v2009
10. USGBC usually holds projects to the requirements of the most current rating system version available on the date the project registers for recertification.
11. US Green Building Council 2013, 10–13, op. cit.
12. "LEED Lab" 2016, op. cit.

CHAPTER FIVE

PHASE 2: IMPLEMENTATION

With the foundational work of the Feasibility Phase – assessing the campus, identifying the sought, understanding how prerequisites will be met, and basically organizing the map of the course for the next several semesters – the bulk of work in LEED Lab occurs in the Implementation Phase. This is the time when meters are installed or calibrated for tracking consumption. The phase should be planned to coincide with the start of the semester. The documents which have been produced in the Feasibility Phase should be made available to the students in the new course via one of the Learning Management Systems (see Chapter 3.2.1), which the course may have already been using for the Feasibility Phase. Although various methods exist for assigning credits – e.g., assigning a group of credits to a student, assigning one credit to one student, or group work on the entire bandwidth of credits and prerequisites pursued – (Figure 5.1) the way that Implementation is often accomplished most successfully in LEED Lab is through ISPPs.

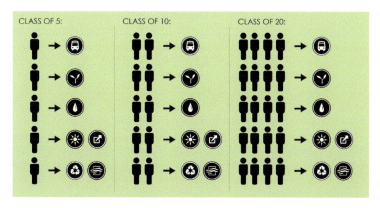

Fig 5.1 Various LEED Lab classroom scenarios
Source: Created by Patricia Andrasik and Elizabeth Meyers, 2019

DOI: 10.4324/9780429449703-5

PHASE 2: IMPLEMENTATION

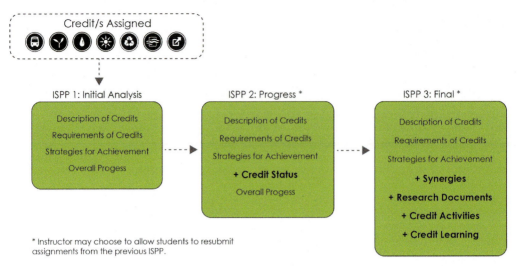

Fig 5.2 Individual Student Progress Presentation, ISPP overview
Source: Created by Patricia Andrasik and Elizabeth Meyers, 2019

As first introduced in Chapter 2, ISPPs are Individual Student Progress Presentations which indicate the level of progress a student or a group of students have made on their credit assignments. The information in the presentations is simply the data which that student has collected (up to the date of the ISPP presentation) about a credit's development. Is the credit a part of a prerequisite or policy that has yet to be enacted or applied? Does it require tracking from instruments which have not yet been installed? Can it be accomplished by the student alone, or will facility staff members or external consultants be called to assist? Such questions are answered an escalation of detail throughout the various levels of Individual Student Progress Presentations or ISPs (see Chapter 5 and Figure 5.2).

While ISPPs serve as the mechanism for identifying student progress within the LEED Lab semester/s, there are specific milestones within each credit which are identified in the LEED O+M v4 Reference Guide. These were written for the professional and not necessarily for the student. Therefore, the Theory, Tasks, Tools, and Techniques sections for each credit identified in the subsequent chapters – in addition to the exercises and case studies – serve as an abbreviated way for navigating this Implementation Phase with ease and clarity.

There are six major technical categories that LEED O+M uses. They are in order and abbreviated in this textbook: Transportation, Site, Water, Energy, Material, and Air Quality. The credits of Regional Priority and Innovation in Operations are also credit categories, but are not complex, fairly easy to accomplish and do not require any further guidance beyond the LEED O+M v4 Reference Guide. Let's begin with our first credit category, Transportation.

PHASE 2: IMPLEMENTATION

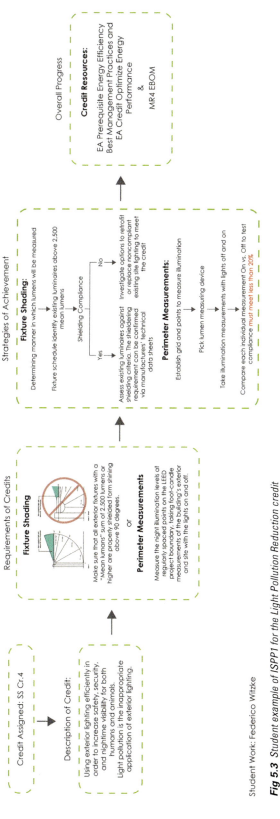

Student Work: Federico Witke

Fig 5.3 *Student example of ISPP1 for the Light Pollution Reduction credit*
Source: Created by Patricia Andrasik and Elizabeth Meyers, 2019. Student work by Federico Witke

| 59

PHASE 2: IMPLEMENTATION

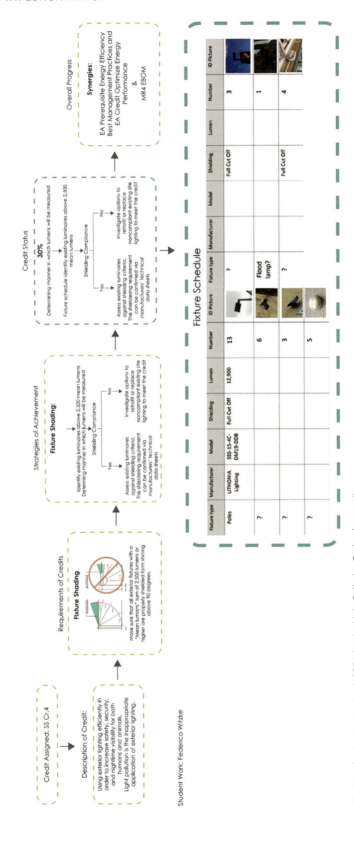

Fig 5.4 Student example of ISPP2 for the Light Pollution Reduction credit
Source: Created by Patricia Andrasik and Elizabeth Meyers, 2019. Student Work by Federico Witke

5.1 Transportation

Accountable for almost 30 percent of greenhouse gas emissions in 2017 according to the EPA,[1] the transportation sector includes cars, ships, and trains and uses over 90 percent of fossil fuel (Side Lesson A: Fossil Fuels). A significant portion of usage with respect to campuses comes from conventional commuting – to and from work, home, school, and daily activities. Much of this occurs using a single-occupancy vehicle running on gasoline. Disjoined transportation networks add to the attraction of using automobiles independently of other methods of transit. Land-use patterns and proximities of buildings with housing, retail, and other ancillary functions to the campus also contribute to the dependency on the car. The location of an existing building with respect to other buildings or amenities on campus, or its accessibility to modes of public or green transit, is therefore a key factor of sustainable assessment.

In the case of an existing campus building where changes in proximity to transit infrastructure are not typically met within the scope of the Performance Period, learning about the behavior of campus residents provides a good understanding of transit or vehicular usage. Additionally, providing incentives to carpool, use local public transportation, bike, or walk may be employed while studying the campus resident's behavior.

There are several ways incentives may be implemented at the campus level. For example, Transportation Demand Management (TDM) (Side Lesson B: Transportation Demand Management (TDM)) may be implemented on an administrative level during the analysis of this credit, and be tracked throughout the Performance Period. In combination with travel patterns, it will be helpful in developing policies which encourage alternative transportation and reduce overall dependence on unsustainable modes of transportation, thus decreasing fossil fuel. Although this category comprises only one credit, it has the potential to yield a significant amount of points, not only in the LEED O+M rating system but also in other global rating systems.

Side Lesson A – 5.1: Fossil Fuels are natural fuels created by the geologic process of anaerobic decomposition of ancient dead organisms buried in the earth. Examples of fossil fuels include coal, natural gas, and petroleum (see www.britannica.com/science/fossil-fuel)

Side Lesson B – 5.1: Transportation Demand Management (TDM) is a set of strategies used to increase a traveler's choices in regard to route, estimated time of arrival, and mode. This is to ensure that travelers have the most efficient, effective and reliable travel options (see https://ops.fhwa.dot.gov/plan4ops/trans_demand.htm).

5.2 Comparison

The majority of green rating systems around the world address transportation through an approach similar to LEED O+M: stimulating alternative modes of transportation yet with varying levels of significance within their overall rating categories (Figure 5.5) and their credit allocations (Figure 5.6). Regionally developed systems like BCA Green Mark focus on areas with high density and mature building stock, requiring certain options for alternative transportation or simply eliminating the use of vehicles with internal combustion engines using gasoline. Such regional factors impact the majority of rating systems.

What is common, or generally understood among the rating systems is that a location-efficient site well-connected to the larger context and close to amenities affording employment, retail, and services attracts businesses that want customer-access and the benefits of proximity to their employees, in addition to residents who want access to more jobs.[2]

PHASE 2: IMPLEMENTATION

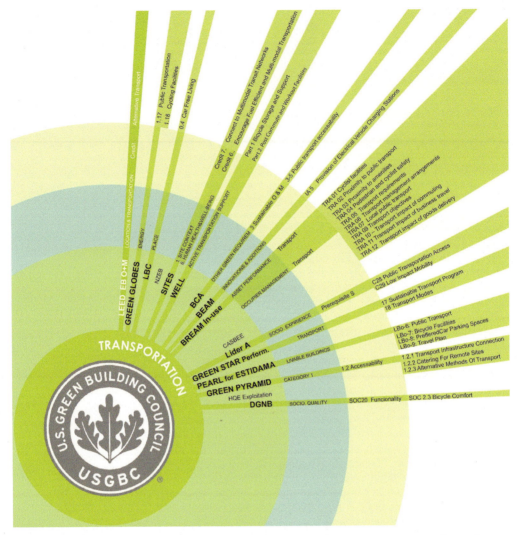

Fig 5.5 Global sustainable existing building sustainability assessment tools: comparison of Transportation credits
Source: Created by Milan Glisić, 2017

5.2.1 Green Globes for Existing Buildings (EB)

Originating from sustainability criteria developed by BREEAM, the Green Globes EB incorporates transportation in the Energy Environmental Assessment Area for Existing Buildings and allocates a total of 55 points, 45 for public transportation and 10 for cycling facilities, for a total of 55, or 5.5 percent of the total (points). The three-step path consists of an on-line survey, third-party on-site assessment of the Performance Period, and an accompanying post-assessment.

Unlike the separate category in LEED O+M, transportation in Green Globes EB is an integral part of the Energy Environmental Assessment Area.[3]

PHASE 2: IMPLEMENTATION

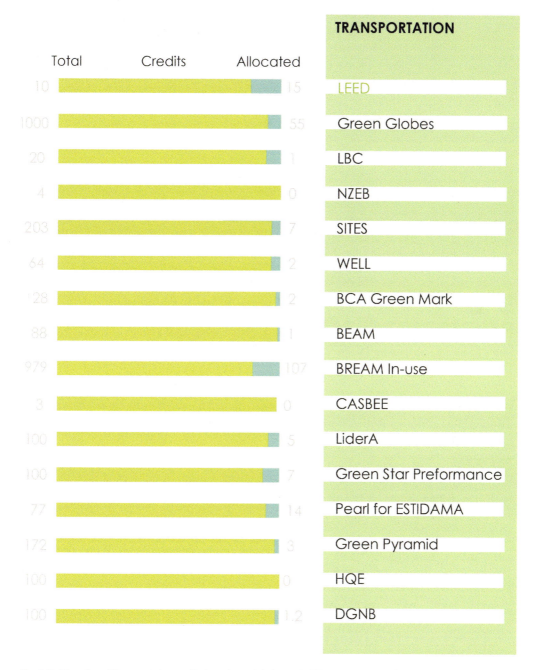

Fig 5.6 *Allocation of Transportation credits in various global sustainability assessment systems for existing buildings*
Source: Created by Milan Glisić, 2017

HOW?

The first step in the certification process includes completing an on-line survey related to all applicable areas. Next, data is collected during the Performance Period, similar to LEED O+M. This requires the team to provide links or schedules of public transport and as-built drawings related to cycling facilities.

| 63

PHASE 2: IMPLEMENTATION

Finally the sequence culminates with a post-assessment by a third-party. The total scoring applicable for the two subcategories related to transportation and applicable to final certification is the result of properly performing all three steps. Successfully performing all steps ensures the achievement of this Energy sub-category in the Green Globes EB rating system.

5.2.2 BREEAM In-Use

The primary aim of BREEAM In-Use is to mitigate the operational impacts of existing assets on the environment in a robust and cost-effective manner. A category dedicated to transport appears in the Asset Management and Occupier Management parts of the scheme, but not in Building Management. Transport under Asset Management offers 18 credits and Transport under Occupier Management offers 89, for a total of 107. This accounts for roughly 9.6 percent of all available credits.[4]

HOW?

As with the first part, the Asset Performance Category asks the assessors what provisions are available to cyclists and/or whether the asset is within walking distance of public transport networks which operate a frequent service. The aim is to encourage building users to cycle by ensuring adequate provision of cyclist facilities and/or to ensure appropriate public transport provision is available to building occupants. The different criteria are evaluated through evidence data in order to award weighted end-use on a 0–4/8 point scale without mandatory ones.

Unlike with other assessment categories within BREEAM In-Use, Transport is not assessed within Part 2, which covers Building Management.

Part 3 of this assessment system is concerned with Occupant Management and service use by the building users-occupants. Transport Management Arrangements under the same category awards up to 59 credits in order to encourage and award management targeted to reduce transport impact. This third part is supported by reports, surveys, and organizational policies at disposal of the occupants and pertaining to their transport options and objectives.

5.2.3 Green Star Performance

Green Star Performance, like LEED, treats transportation in a separate category. This rating system is also based on the assessment and benchmarking of a building's operations during a one-year Performance Period. There are two separate credits options – a Sustainable Transport Program (4) and a Transport Modes Survey (3) – with a total of 7 achievable points, about 6.4 percent of all available for this assessment system. The certification, once achieved, is valid for up to three years.

The Transport category rewards strategies and actions that discourage single occupant vehicle use and encourage the use of alternative transportation modes such as public transport, walking or cycling.[5]

PHASE 2: IMPLEMENTATION

HOW?

There are mandatory requirements, similar to LEED prerequisites, essential for points to be awarded, such as a 'Sustainable Transport Program' implemented for regular building occupants. Additional points are awarded where the Alternative Transportation Program also facilitates the use of alternative transportation by visitors to the premises.

Transportation or travel surveys (Side Lesson C: Travel Surveys) are used as a method of measurement for the use of alternative transportation modes; under the Transport Modes Survey credit, points are awarded where a transportation modes survey is undertaken to assess the transport use of a building's regular occupants throughout the Performance Period. Additional points are available upon benchmarking of those survey results through the Australian Bureau of Statistics census data for single-occupant vehicles.[6]

5.2.4 LEED Operations and Maintenance (O+M)

LEED O+M allocates 14 percent of all achievable points to an Alternative Transportation category, the most among the globally applied systems. There is no prerequisite and three options for Performance Period are given. This credit focuses on the transportation patterns of building occupants and determines how building occupants actually travel to and from the project. The credit takes a single, performance-based approach to evaluating a building's transportation characteristics.[7]

This category within the LEED assessment system endorses alternative transport and encourages the increase of alternative transportation use by occupants during the Performance Period and thereafter.

Side Lesson C – 5.2.3: Travel Surveys: A Travel Survey, also known as a travel behavior inventory or travel diary, documents the journey of the individual on a given day. Components of the survey include: end/start times, purpose of travel, mode of travel, and accompaniment. The survey also collects information about the person's demographic or socio-economic situation (see www.nrel.gov/transportation/secure-transportation-data/).

HOW?

The focus of this credit within LEED O+M is on transportation patterns. Regardless of which option is chosen by the project team, a transportation survey is required for attempting it. As a self-evaluation tool, this survey is the starting point for an adaptation of strategies convenient for each individual project. Following survey results, two further options are available: either an increase in the use of alternative transportation by occupants above the minimum 10 percent; or, if not achievable, the implementation of a long-term comprehensive alternative program.[8]

5.2.5 Other Rating Systems

Other regionally specific or localized rating systems also address transportation issues related to existing buildings and their occupants. The transport issues related to existing buildings operations and maintenance are treated differently in respect to the density of population, developed sites, climate, and environmental challenges. The relative weight of required and available credits, as well as the array of options, derives

PHASE 2: IMPLEMENTATION

from severity and longevity of transportation related to unique urban regions (Figure 5.6).

- **BCA Green Mark.** As a Singapore-based rating system, from its inception in 2005 BCA Green Mark intends to encourage the use of other green features which are innovative or/and have a positive environmental impact. BCA Green Mark incorporates the category of green transport under Section 1 – Sustainable Management, and 4 credits can be gained here: access to public transport (0.5), provision of a covered walkway (0.5), priority parking lots for hybrid and electric vehicles (1.5), and bicycle parking lots (1.5). The goal is to promote the use of public transportation or bicycles. It also includes requirements for adequate bicycle parking lots.[9]

- **BEAM Plus for Existing Buildings.** The urban density of Hong Kong is addressed through the Building Environmental Assessment Method (BEAM) rating system. Similar to BCA Green Mark, this assessment system incorporates transportation within the Innovations and Additions credit category.

  One bonus credit is available for providing quick charger(s) for electric vehicles (Side Lesson D: Quick Chargers for Electric Vehicles) for 50 percent of the total parking capacity of the site.[10]

- **CASBEE EB.** The Comprehensive Assessment System for Built Environment Efficiency (CASBEE) is an assessment tool used in Japan. The assessment standard within LR3 Off-Site Environment is concerned with GHG (greenhouse gas) emissions through promotion of public transportation use over driving by building users. Within LR3, Consideration of Global Warming (33.3 percent) and Consideration of Local Environment (33.3 percent) are relevant to transportation. Consideration of Local Environment is further broken down into Air Pollution, Heat Island Effect, and Load on Local Infrastructure, all of which relate to the emission of GHGs from transportation operations having to do with building operations or occupants.[11]

- **LiderA.** The Portugal-based rating system from its beginning in 2005 has considered the construction, operation, and decommissioning of built structures simultaneously. Thus, in the area of access for all, the quest for sustainability, according to LiderA, is based on the promotion of access to public transport (C28), promoting low impact mobility (C29), and inclusive solutions (C30), with a cumulative weight of up to 5 percent in the overall rating system.[12]

- **Pearl for ESTIDAMA (PORS).** The Pearl Operational Rating System is specifically designed for the climate of the Middle East and was developed by Abu Dhabi Urban Planning Council. Similar to LEED O+M, it intends to encourage the use of public transport by building occupants and visitors, minimize GHG emissions, and improve

Side Lesson D – 5.2.5: Quick Chargers for Electric Vehicles: At home, one can simply charge an electric vehicle with a plug to a power outlet. However, while out on the road, an electric vehicle requires a quick charging station in order to repower a vehicle. There are three main types of quick chargers in the United States: Tesla Superchargers, SAE Combined Charging System (CCS), and CHAdeMo. The type of quick charger depends on the brand and model of the electric car (see https://tinyurl.com/4ump6n98).

connectivity as well as encourage bicycle use, car sharing, and more fuel-efficient forms of personal transport.

In the Livable Outdoors subdivision (LBo) of the Livable Building (LB) section, a total of 8 credits are available for the inclusion of public transport (LBo6), bicycle spaces (LBo7), preferred car parking spaces (gas, hybrid, electric) (LBo8) and a travel plan to reduce commuting by car (LBo9). The submission of a narrative, photos and calculations according to the requirements is an essential part of submission for obtaining this rating.[13]

- **Green Pyramid.** Under the 1.2 Accessibility Category, Green Pyramid, a creation of the Egyptian Green Building Council, though predominantly focused on new constructions, also aims to minimize pollution and traffic congestion from car use and to conserve non-renewable energy by encouraging public and alternative transport.

  A credit point is obtainable for demonstrating a suitable connection with existing public transport systems. For demonstrating strategies to reduce reliance on private automobile use and encourage the use of greener methods of transport, one credit is achievable as well. These points are obtainable based upon documentary evidence.[14]

- **HQE Exploitation.** France's Green Building Council developed *Haute Qualité Environnementale* or High Quality Environmental Standard (HQE) Certification for Buildings in Operation (HQE Exploitation) in 2005. For this rating system transportation is an integral part of sustainable use and some credits are comparable to LEED and BREEAM. Similar to those systems, HQE places special emphasis on environmentally friendly modes of transport and a limitation on the number of parking spaces. In the HQE Sustainable Use scheme, Target 1 – Site has two subsections dedicated to addressing the problem of GHG emissions through advocating the use of public transport: 1) Analysis and management of methods of transport (30 possible points); 2) Measures taken by the user to limit the environmental impact of transport (eight possible points). Together, these total 38 of 321 points.[15]

- **DGNB In Use.** Existing or renovated buildings are considered in the Deutsche Gesellschaft für Nachhaltiges Bauen (DGNB) In Use scheme, developed by the German Sustainable Building Council in 2011. Of the six main criteria groups, only three can be used for the accreditation of an existing building: Ecological Quality, Economic Quality, Sociocultural and Functional Quality. The object of DGNB In Use is to develop and promote materials, means, and solutions for the operation of building processes to meet the criteria of sustainability. The consequences are important for the entire lifecycle of a building.

PHASE 2: IMPLEMENTATION

DGNB considers cycling as an essential part of an environmentally friendly individual transport scheme. The aim is therefore to demand and support the use of bicycles. An important prerequisite for this is a sufficient number of qualitatively appropriate bicycles on the ground floor. Convenience for cyclists can yield ten points. In addition, further components of accessibility can yield up to 20 points. Together, these offer 30 points out of the 540 for In-Use.[16]

The requirement Reference Guide lists a selection of possible and/or alternative forms of evidence. Regardless of which one of the documents is selected for submission, it must be supported extensively and plausibly. Two options are addressed: the number and quality of the storage facilities and option routes available for cyclists.

Similar to LEED O+M, assessment systems used worldwide are primarily focused on promoting and awarding the use of alternative transportation options, policies, and management. Some of these systems – German DGNB, Egyptian Green Pyramid – are concerned with the connectivity of existing building structures to the existing transport network and/or the ease of bicycle accessibility. BREEAM In-Use has several options to evaluate actual performance of existing assets and occupants in respect to transport modes and the frequency and availability of the options in current conditions. It is more oriented toward maximizing existing options. On the other hand, Pearl, a rating system customized for the climate and society of the United Arab Emirates and created by Abu Dhabi Planning Council, targets habitations and conditions in a dry and hot climate. Though the degree of restrictions may vary between systems, all of them consider the reduction of fossil fuels and GHG emission as their primary aim and reward the use of alternative modes of transit.

5.3 Alternative Transportation

(*Refer also to page 39 in the LEED O+M v4 Reference Guide*)

LEED O+M's attempt to address vehicles, as noted in the summary, follows nationally recognized standard systems by focusing on transportation patterns of building occupants. This category yields a significant amount of points in LEED (15), third only to Indoor Air Quality (17) and Energy (38). Whereas the rating system for new construction and some of the other national systems evaluate and reward features that building occupants may use such as proximity to transit stops, this credit identifies how current building occupants travel to and from the site. Consequently, the credit uses a single, performance-based approach to evaluate a building's transportation characteristics – a transportation survey.[17] Building managers can use survey results to understand how the building is performing in relation to transportation and the most effective programs for improving alternative transportation modes (Side Lesson E: Alternative Transportation).

There are three ways to achieve LEED O+M's Alternative Transportation credit, and all of them require the completion

Side Lesson E – 5.3.1: Alternative Transportation can be defined as other ways of commuting than driving. Examples of alternative transportation include: biking, public transportation, walking, and carpooling. These modes of transportation are highly suggested because it can help reduce air pollution (see www.highpointnc.gov/664/ Alternative-Transportation-Facts).

PHASE 2: IMPLEMENTATION

of this transportation survey which yields one point (Option 1). The survey should be a part of pursuing Master Site credits, expressly for the LEED Lab course. From this basis, subsequent points are earned if the institution demonstrates through calculations (Option 2) that transportation strategies yield a delta of at least 10 to 70 percent from a baseline using traditional vehicular transportation figures. If the institution offers an Alternative Transportation Program (Option 3) which includes education, support, and direct strategies, two points may be earned.

The ARC Platform is the easiest method of tracking the results of this credit. It applies a survey link that can be disseminated either via email or collecting responses via tablets. Twenty-five percent of the total occupants of and visitors to the building(s) must complete the survey by identifying their transportation modes and the distance traveled daily in order to quantify their respective carbon impacts. The final metric should obtain a minimum transportation score of 40, rating the Carbon dioxide equivalent emissions (CO_2e) (Side Lesson F: Carbon Dioxide Equivalent, (CO_2e)) against the score of other buildings globally.

If the survey results show that the minimum transportation score has not been realized, a team can follow Option 3 for two points and implement a comprehensive Alternative Transportation Program to reduce occupants' reliance on conventional commuting.[18]

Side Lesson F – 5.3.1: The Carbon Dioxide Equivalent (CO_2e) is a metric measure used to convert and compare different greenhouse gases as a common unit. CO_2e can also be noted as; CO_2eq, CO_2 equivalent, or CDE. CO_2e is used to help determine a type of greenhouse gases' global-warming potential (GWP) in comparison to other greenhouse gases. This measurement can also be used to help quantify greenhouse gases and their GWP. The quantity of greenhouse gases can be expressed as a CO_2e by multiplying GWP by the amount of greenhouse gases. CO_2e is a very helpful tool in comparing groups of greenhouse gases as a single unit. It is important to note that when comparing that each group contains the same greenhouse gases in each comparison so like-for-like comparisons are made (see https://tinyurl.com/v7nk88j4).

Tasks

There are two main tasks that are options to fulfill this entire credit. One uses the cloud-based ARC Platform and the other requires a series of decisions and documents which are a part of the manual administration. The tasks for each method of credit fulfillment is quite different, thus an itemized description is necessary.

1. Option 1. Transportation Survey (required for all options)

First, choose your survey instrument. Then follow the appropriate procedure below:

A. **ARC Platform**

- ☐ Create an account on the ARC Skoru website[19]
- ☐ Associate the LEED Lab project with the account if it does not automatically link to it.
- ☐ Launch and track the transportation survey. Follow the options for survey respondent sampling in the LEED O+M v4 Reference Guide.

B. **Manual Administration**[20]
(*Refer also to the LEED O+M v4 Reference Guide for equations*)

- ☐ Select survey instrument for regular building occupants and visitors (see Footnote 7). Note that these two should vary.
- ☐ Determine the type of survey and the medium of distribution.

PHASE 2: IMPLEMENTATION

- ☐ Develop a transportation survey to be distributed to both regular building occupants and visitors. Both must request information on a variety of transportation modes. Note in the Tools section various sample questions for the survey.
- ☐ Schedule survey: The time period over which the survey will measure travel and the dates it will be distributed should be within the Performance Period.
- ☐ Distribute survey(s).
- ☐ Analyze survey results for regular occupants (Figure 5.7):

    a. Ensure that the response rate meets or exceeds the minimum if random sampling is used.
    b. Calculate the number of alternative transportation trips using Equation 1.
    c. Calculate the number of carpool trips using Equation 2.
    d. Calculate the raw rate of alternative transportation using Equation 3: in this equation, account for regular occupants' absences because of vacation and sick leave.
    e. Determine the survey response rate using Equation 4.
    f. Extrapolate the responses to the entire population.
    g. Calculate the total alternative transportation trips using Equation 5.
    h. Calculate the alternative transportation rate using Equation 6.

- ☐ Analyze survey results for visitors

    a. Calculate visitors' number of alternative transportation trips using Equation 7.
    b. Calculate visitors' raw rate of alternative transportation using Equation 8.
    c. Calculate the overall alternative transportation rate using Equation 9.

2. Option 2. Alternative Transportation Rate[21] and Option 3

Alternative Transportation Plans are readily available for achievement once the survey has been completed and your LEED Lab team has assessed that your score is over 10 percent yielding three points. If fewer points are acquired, it is advisable to have a serious discussion with your facility personnel about your transportation strategies for the campus. An Alternative Transportation Plan in this case may be used to spur such initiatives.

Tools

There are several tools which can facilitate the components of successful credit completion. These tools assist the LEED Lab student to navigate what is a very complex series of steps in the LEED O+M v4 Reference Guide, to fulfill the requirements of what is only a one credit category!

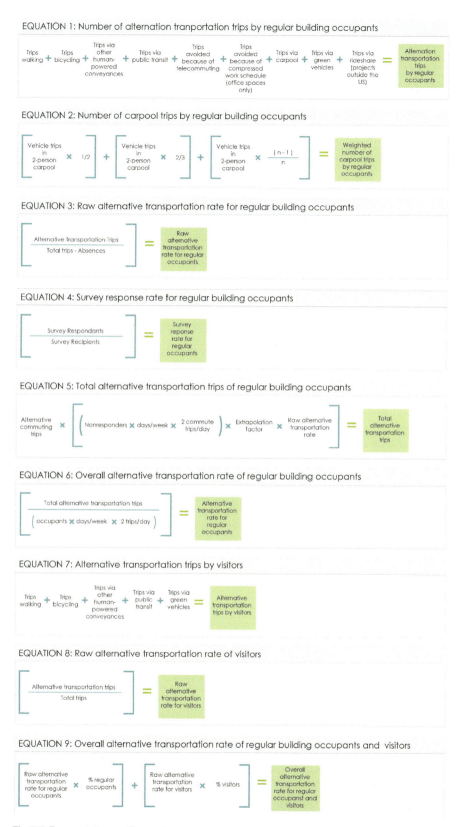

Fig 5.7 Transportation credit equations
Source: Derived from LEED O+M v4 Reference Guide. Diagrammed by Elizabeth Meyers, 2019

PHASE 2: IMPLEMENTATION

Box 5.1 Sample commuting transportation survey

<Project Building> is conducting a transportation survey to assess how building occupants commute to and from work. Your participation will help us evaluate use of alternative transportation and support our LEED certification efforts. Thank you for taking a few moments to complete the survey.

1. I live in the following zip code: _____

2. My average one-way commute distance in miles is: _____

3. Please indicate how you got to work each day during the week of **<insert 5-day survey period here>**. _____

If you used more than one mode of transportation, please indicate the mode used for the longest distance during your commute trip (i.e. if you took a train for ten miles and walked one mile, indicate that you used Light Rail).

	Mon	Tue	Wed	Thu	Fri
Commuter Rail					
Light Rail					
Bus					
Walk					
Bicycle					
Carpool / Vanpool					
Drive Alone					
Taxi					
Telecommute					
Compressed Workweek					
Out of Office					

4. If you drove to work, what is your vehicle's:

   Make_____

   Model_____

   Year_____

5. If you carpooled or vanpooled, indicate the total number of people in your vehicle each day:

	Mon	Tue	Wed	Thu	Fri
2					
3					
4					
5					
6					
7					
8					
9					
10					

PHASE 2: IMPLEMENTATION

6. Do you usually travel home using the same mode of transportation used to get to work?
_____

If "no," please briefly explain your mode of transportation used to return home from work below:
_____
_____
_____

7. Does your typical commuting pattern change significantly depending on the time of year? If so, please explain below (i.e. bike in the summer instead of bus).
_____
_____
_____

5.3.1 Sample Campus Alternative Transportation Plans

Many university campuses have dedicated webpages for alternative transportation. A few are listed here for reference:

- University of California, Los Angeles[22]
- George Mason University[23]
- North Carolina State University[24]

Calculations

The equations in the LEED O+M v4 Reference Guide provide the most detailed step by step instructions for calculating the total reduction in vehicular usage. The final equation establishes a "percentage reduction of commuting trips by the building's occupants and visitors" which is simply the delta between vehicular and alternative transportation modes.[25] The credit rewards you for an increased rate using alternative transportation.[26]

Techniques[27]

Although this is a one-credit category, its achievement can be complex if manual administration is pursued. Here are a few strategies which can facilitate ease of compliance:

- ☐ Note that for all options, the Transportation Survey is required.
- ☐ For a campus, this credit is absolutely worthwhile to pursue. However, don't be surprised if your project reviewer questions visitors who are coming from campus housing; it is expected that students do not require a vehicle when moving between their dormitories and class buildings.
- ☐ It is advised that the LEED Lab student pursue the ARC Platform particularly for the transportation survey and explain to the facility management personnel the value

PHASE 2: IMPLEMENTATION

of such a platform, not only for course use, but also for continuous tracking.

☐ Determine if facility personnel already track alternative transit use as part of a local or regional government program or a campus initiative.

☐ Is an existing Alternative Transportation Program providing information, infrastructure, or incentives to building occupants or facility personnel already?

☐ Could existing Alternative Transportation Programs be enhanced in a manner to increase the use of alternative commuting options – particularly during the Performance Period?

☐ Establish in advance *how* a university-wide transportation questionnaire can be administered via the LEED Lab course and ARC, or another platform, with a deadline which will allow for computation of results in a timely manner.

☐ Read the steps for conducting the survey very carefully from the LEED O+M v4 Reference Guide. The calculations can be tricky if not followed in their entirety. This is another reason the ARC Platform is the best route for this credit.

5.4 Case Study

The Edward M. Crough School of Architecture and Planning is located in an urban environment in Washington, DC. Transportation efforts in Washington DC are a key component of Clean Energy DC, focused on reducing greenhouse gas (GHG) emissions 50 percent by 2032 and achieving GHG neutral status by 2050. The goals of the supporting moveDC effort (Side Lesson G: MoveDC) focus on multimodal transportation by increasing public transit, biking and walking to a 75 percent share of trips, thus reducing vehicle use to only 25 percent.[28] The CUA campus is an active participant in this effort, and the CUA Sustainability Plan focuses on reducing single-vehicle ridership; actions include increasing electric vehicle charging stations, implementing a scooter and bicycle safety plan, and encouraging carpooling and ridesharing. The CUA Sustainability Plan targets a 55 percent alternative transportation rate for students and employees. The target aligns with moveDC goals.

A LEED Lab student analyzed LEED v4 requirements for alternative transportation and coordinated with the CUA Department of Transportation and Parking (Figure 5.8). He quickly realized the critical aspect of the transportation survey to achieve the credit. LEED v4 requires a transportation survey every five years as part of the Performance Period. CUA Transportation already conducts an annual survey so there were existing campus-wide processes available to align with LEED requirements.

The LEED Lab class was surprised at the robust plan for alternate transportation; it became evident that there were many alternatives on campus. However, many of these efforts were unknown to the CUA students. The students realized that this knowledge gap could result in unimpressive surveys because the CUA community was not aware of (or using) many of the resources in the transportation plan, as highlighted in Boxes 5.2 and 5.3.

Side Lesson G – 5.4: MoveDC is an effort led by the District's Department of Transportation (DDOT) to put a long-range multimodal transportation plan into motion. The transportation plan is a blueprint for how DC will support and adapt to the expected growth through 2040. The plan not only provides a reliable transportation system for tourists, commuters and residents, but also provides more and more transportation options for passing through the city (see https://movedc-dcgis.hub.arcgis.com/).

PHASE 2: IMPLEMENTATION

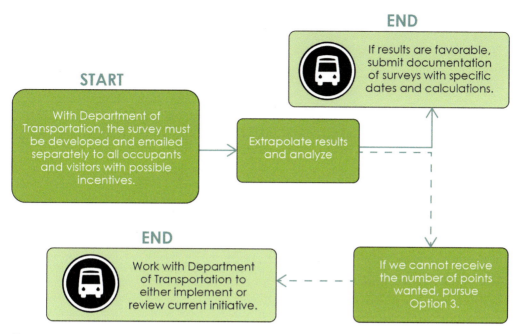

Fig 5.8 *Alternative Transportation: strategies for achievement*
Source: Derived from LEED O+M v4 Reference Guide. Diagrammed by Matthew Zernis and Elizabeth Meyers, 2020

Box 5.2 Transportation sustainability plan for The Catholic University of America

Action no	Action	Target date	Complete?
3.6.a	Create a reduction plan for on-campus parking	2020	Yes
3.6.b	Implement scooter and bicycle safety & adoption plan	2021	Yes
3.6.c	Encourage carpooling, vanpooling, and rideshare opportunities	2021	In progress
3.6.d	Execute long-term fleet low-emissions vehicle purchasing plan	2023	Forthcoming
3.6.e	Increase the number of electric vehicle charging stations by 25 percent	2021	Forthcoming
3.6.f	Do a feasibility analysis on additional transit benefits for The Catholic University community	2022	Forthcoming
3.6.g	Achieve a 55 percent alternative transportation rate for students and employees	2024+	Forthcoming

Source: Derived from LEED O+M v4 Reference Guide. Assessed by Matthew Zernis, 2020

PHASE 2: IMPLEMENTATION

> **Box 5.3 The missing links in The Catholic University of America's current transportation sustainability plan**
>
> - CUA has implemented many initiatives to decrease single-occupancy transit to campus, but this information is not known by all of the CUA community
> - Parking policy:
>   - Reduction of parking fees for carpool drivers while increasing parking fees for other drivers
>   - Impose limitations on parking permits issued
>   - Target access restrictions to commuter parking
> - Campus Shuttle
> - CityMotion App
> - TransitScreen
> - Install 338 new bike spaces (64 remain to be installed)
> - Two car share vehicle spaces
> - Fund and install 19-dock Capital Bikeshare station
> - Discounted membership for students
> - Provide information for non-automative travel visibly on Catholic University website and in student common areas
>
> Source: Created by Matthew Zernis, 2020

During the Eco-Charrette, the student outlined this shortfall and proposed ways to engage students by leveraging an Innovation credit focused on empowering occupants by using a holistic approach to the organizational, human, and physical environment (Figure 5.9).

Key elements of these suggestions focused on developing the knowledge of students and staff regarding existing initiatives. Enhanced knowledge of the initiatives should enable two positive results: first, more widespread knowledge of transportation

Fig 5.9 How can the Innovation credit help?

Source: Created by Stephanie Valdabrini and Christine Gibney, 2020

76

resources means students and staff will understand alternative ways to go back and forth from campus; second, a higher alternative transportation rate, required for obtaining the Alternative Transportation credit, can earn our team many points.

5.5 Exercises

The questions below are derived from the aforementioned case study. Questions testing knowledge of the breadth of tools, tasks and techniques are important for LEED Lab; the investigation required in answering these exercises helps students to approach their credit assignments from a synergistic perspective.

Questions testing knowledge and understanding of the breadth of Tools, Tasks, and Techniques are important for LEED Lab; the investigation required for answering these exercises relates to how students should be instructed in such an action research course.

Exercise Scenario 1

Identify three examples of how the Alternative Transportation credit supports CUA alternative transportation efforts and Washington DC's sustainability goals.

Exercise Scenario 2

Why should a campus issue a transportation survey annually instead of every five years?

Exercise Scenario 3

How do the initiatives in Box 5.3 reduce single-vehicle use?

Exercise Scenario 4

How many LEED points would CUA accrue upon achieving the 55 percent alternative transportation rate goal? What calculation considerations should be made for the students in this institution of higher learning?

Notes

1 "Sources of Greenhouse Gas Emissions," United States Environmental Protection Agency, 2020. www.epa.gov/ghgemissions/sources-greenhouse-gas-emissions
2 "Location and Green Building," US Environmental Protection Agency, 2018. www.epa.gov/smartgrowth/location-and-green-building
3 Green Building Initiative, *Green Globes® for Existing Buildings 2007 Technical Reference Manual, Version 1.21 December 2019* (Green Building Initiative, Inc., 2019): 16. www.thegbi.org/files/training_resources/Green_Globes_EB_2007_Technical_Reference_Manual.pdf
4 BREEAM, *BREEAM In-Use Technical Manual SD221 2.0:2015* (Watford: BRE Global Ltd, 2016): 122, 336.

PHASE 2: IMPLEMENTATION

https://tools.breeam.com/filelibrary/Technical%20Manuals/SD221_BIU_International_2015_Re-issue_V2.0.pdf

5   Green Building Council of Australia, "Sustainable Transport Program" and "Transport Modes Survey," *Green Star - Performance v1.2 - Initial Certification Submission Template r1.* www.gbca.org.au/greenstar-manager/resources/?filter-rating-tool=101&_ga=2.107716033.213355384.1592333897-29415128.1591753717

6   *Green Star – Performance Summary of Categories and Credits, Pilot* (Green Building Council of Australia, 2013): 26. www.gbca.org.au/uploads/203/4043/Green_Star-Performance_Summary_of_Categories_and_Credits.pdf

7   US Green Building Council, "Alternative Transportation," *Reference Guide for Building Operations and Maintenance* (Washington, DC: US Green Building Council, 2013): 39.

8   Ibid.

9   Singapore Building and Construction Authority, *BCA Green Mark GM ENRB: 2017: Technical Guide and Requirements* (Singapore: Building and Construction Authority, 2017): 7. www.bca.gov.sg/GreenMark/others/GM_NREB_V2.1.pdf

10 *BEAM Plus Existing Buildings Version 2.0 (2016.03): Comprehensive Scheme* (Hong Kong: Hong Kong Green Building Council, 2016): 184. www.beamsociety.org.hk/files/download/BEAM%20Plus%20Existing%20Buildings%20v2_0_Comprehensive%20Scheme.pdf

11 Thilo Ebert et al., *Green Building Certification Systems: Assessing Sustainability – International System Comparison – Economic Impact of Certifications* (Detail, 2013), 60. http://ebookcentral.proquest.com/lib/cua/detail.action?docID=1075570

12 Manuel Duarte Pinheiro, *LiderA: Voluntary System for the Sustainability of Built Environments: Working Version V2.00c1* (Lisbon: Manuel Duarte Pinheiro, 2011): 22–23. www.lidera.info/resources/_LiderA_V2.00c1%20sumario_ingles.pdf

13 *The Pearl Rating System for ESTIDAMA Emirate of Abu Dhabi, Pearl Building Rating System: Design & Construction, Version 1.0* (Abu Dhabi: Abu Dhabi Urban Planning Council, April 2010): 65–71. www.upc.gov.ae/-/media/files/estidama/docs/pbrs-version-10.ashx?la=ar-ae&hash=58A67F549081968086D016E8D3757366BF29B10F

14 The Egyptian Green Building Council, *The Green Pyramid Rating System First Edition – April 2011* (Egyptian Green Building Council, 2011): 10. www.eg.saint-gobain-glass.com/download/file/fid/1246

15 *Assessment Tool for the Environmental Performance of Buildings in Operation (EPB) Non Residential Buildings* (Paris: Cerway, 2017). www.behqe.com/documents/download/215

16 Thilo Ebert et al. 2013, 60, op. cit.

17 US Green Building Council 2013, 42, op. cit.

18 Ibid.

19 Website found here: https://arcskoru.com/

20 Ibid., 45.

21 Ibid.

22 www.sustain.ucla.edu/wp-content/uploads/STP-Report-FINAL-v3.pdf

23 http://transportation.gmu.edu/wp-content/uploads/GMU_FairfaxCampus_TransMgmtPlan_Final.pdf

24 https://transportation.ncsu.edu/wp-content/uploads/2019/01/18Transportation-Master-Plan.pdf

25 Ibid.

26 Calculations for a campus must factor in regular occupants (staff, faculty, personnel) and visitors. In LEED Lab visitors include the students and any other person who does not hold a steady full-time employment at the school. This includes visiting professors, lecturers and any other visiting person. This is different from K-12 schools because university students often occupy multiple facilities throughout the day while K-12 are typically housed in only one.

27 Dan Ackerstein, "EBOM-v4 LTc1: Alternative Transportation," BuildingGreen, 2018. https://leeduser.buildinggreen.com/credit/EBOM-v4/LTc1

28 "The District of Columbia's Multimodal Long-Range Transportation Plan," moveDC, 2014. http://wemovedc.org/resources/Final/Part%201_Strategic_Multimodal_Plan/Strategic_Multimodal_Plan.pdf, 13.

CHAPTER SIX

SITE

6.1 Theory

A United Nations study indicates that of the ecosystem services that have been assessed worldwide, about 60 percent are currently degraded or used unsustainably. The results are deforestation, soil erosion, a drop in water table levels, extinction of species, and rivers that no longer run to the sea.[1]

The building site in prospective or existing buildings is critical to addressing this global dilemma and it begins on the small scale of the individual building or campus. In addition to its effects upon the larger environment, the site is also a fundamental part of a building's functioning. People use the site for navigation to and from the building, enjoy the landscaping for activities or simply visual pleasure, and engage with the site as they navigate to their transportation destinations, among other uses. The site provides the building with direct benefits for thermal comfort and energy reduction depending on its material surfaces, and can assist in the retention of rainwater, diverting it from the municipal stormwater system. The site also may be redesigned to mitigate pollutants carried by oil, sediment, chemicals and fertilizers, which are usually directed to streams and rivers, harming aquatic ecosystems and species.[2]

How is site important to a college campus in particular? The applications of the theory behind it are clear: the ecological health of the entire campus site affects the sustainability of operations for each building as well as the overall well-being of each campus user. The landscaping systems relate to the irrigation systems, which in turn relate to the drainage systems meant to capture run-off water to prevent the flooding of property and buildings.

Sensitivity to the multitude of students, faculty and staff traversing the campus site must be considered in the application of landscape and exterior building treatment. Ease of navigation across the site, the site appeal, and the economy of stormwater management considering landscaping and foliage are also serious campus-specific site considerations. Variation within a campus relates to all of these, and the sustainable upgrading of these systems affects the overall sustainable character of the campus. Let's see how various green rating systems apply such site considerations to determine their sustainability success.

SITE

6.2 Comparison

All rating systems are equally focused on ensuring the degree in which activities undertaken on the site result in minimal impacts to the local environment. Activities, operations, and conditions of the site are measured for their installation and management practices. This may include a biodiversity plan, or otherwise sustaining the ecology of the site. Every rating system applies subcategories supporting major categories. Some are similar and some are quite distinct, relating to the region they address. The methods of achieving these sub-site strategies are also different between the rating systems. The most popular rating systems, and then shorter descriptions of other global rating systems compare the differences and similarities of these alternatives to LEED O+M (Figures 6.1 and 6.2).

6.2.1 Green Globes for Existing Buildings (EB)

The Green Globes EB program comprehensively assesses environmental impacts through a multi-point scale. Overall, the building must attain a minimum overall score of 35 percent

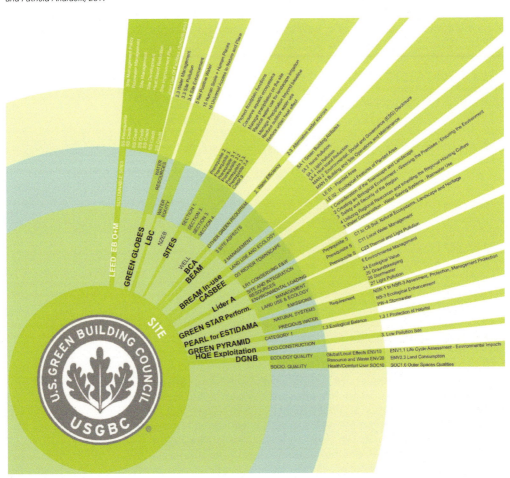

Fig 6.1 Global sustainable existing building sustainability assessment tools

Source: Created by Milan Glisić and Patricia Andrasik, 2017

80 |

SITE

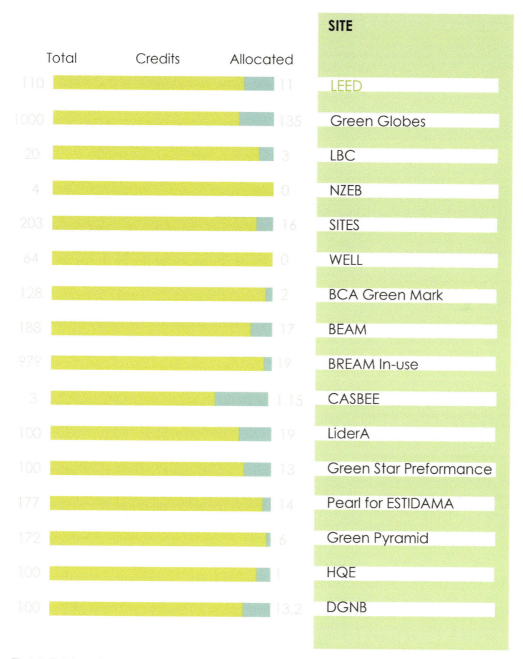

Fig 6.2 Global sustainable existing building sustainability assessment tools
Source: Created by Milan Glisić and Patricia Andrasik, 2017

to be certified. Site credits in total contribute 100 points or 10 percent of all available points in this system. The focus is under Environmental Assessment Areas of Water and Resources particularly on conservation, management, pollution, and enhancement.

| 81

HOW?

This system has four categories under the Environmental Management assessment area: Environmental Management System Documentation (30 points), Environmental Purchasing (25 points), Emergency Response (20 points), and Tenant Awareness (25 points). The process begins with an on-line survey and feedback followed by on-site third-party assessment. Unlike LEED O+M, this rating system does not have prerequisites. The assessor should be supplied with schedules of waste reduction work plans, site pollution enhancement and as-built drawings related to cycling facilities.[3]

6.2.2 BREEAM In-Use

BREEAM In-Use is focused on determining the level at which activities undertaken on the property site result in minimal impacts to the local environment. This assessment system was developed by Building Research Establishment Global (BRE Global) in 2009 and site impact and management are dealt with through a three-part assessment process – Asset Performance, Building Management, Occupier Management.

> Assets are assessed for the robustness of management practices relating to the presence of green areas on site, the implementation of a biodiversity plan, contribution to ecology or biodiversity enhancements, and other activities which reduce the impacts to the local environment.[4]

Unlike in LEED O+M, the site related areas are evaluated through several areas, pollution, land use and ecology, and management. There are a total of 19 credits which could contribute to overall rating in BREEAM In-Use, up to 9 percent, more or less equal to LEED O+M.

HOW?

Land Use and Ecology appears in all three parts of the assessment process. Within Asset Performance there are Planted Area (four credits) and Ecological Features of Planted Area (two credits). The aim is to measure and encourage planted areas within the asset's footprint that enhance the asset's site ecology. Occupier Management and Land Use and Ecology categories contain Ecology Reports (four credits), Biodiversity Action Plan (four credits), and External Landscaping Maintenance (two credits). Within Occupier Management there is the Ecology/Biodiversity Enhancement category (three credits).[5]

It is worth mentioning that BREEAM In-Use addresses many particularities related to light pollution and water management in all of its categories.

6.2.3 Green Star Performance

Similar to the BREEAM In-Use, Green Star Performance focuses on the site through two categories: Land Use and Ecology and Emissions. Within Land Use, Ecological Value (three points) and Groundskeeping Practices (three points) pertain to site. Within Ecology and Emissions, Stormwater (two points) pertain to site. About 5 percent of all achievable categories are related to sustainable site preservation, management, and enhancement within this rating system. Effective environmental management involves the identification, management and reduction of negative impacts to the environment that result from a building's operation. The Land Use and Ecology category assesses the approach taken to determining the ecological value of a site; the management and improvement of biodiversity through policies and management practices. Emissions credits even address the approach taken to manage and minimize emissions from stormwater.[6]

HOW?

The Green Star rating is determined by comparing the number of points achieved out of the total available points. Greenhouse gas emissions and potable water are typically some of the first environmental attributes (beyond statutory compliance) that are benchmarked in this system.

As a minimum, projects must be registered for Portfolio credits plus Greenhouse Gas Emissions and Potable Water to be eligible for Green Star – Performance using a portfolio approach.[7] The system applies, similarly to LEED O+M, the Performance Period for assessment of operations and credits. This is followed by 12 months of audits and may be applied for the subsequent recertification, valid for three years.

6.2.4 LEED Operations and Maintenance (O+M)

LEED O+M establishes the Site Management Policy as a prerequisite for projects aspiring to certification. There are many credits which can attribute up to 9 percent of overall available credits under LEED O+M. In that respect LEED O+M and BREEAM In-Use are similar in site assessment.

The Sustainable Site category combines traditional approaches with several new strategies. These include working with conservation organizations to target financial support for off-site habitat protection (Site Development – Protect or Restore Habitat credit), using low-impact development to handle a percentile storm event (Rainwater Management credit), using three-year aged SRI values for roofs and nonroof hardscape (Heat Island Reduction credit), and creating a five-year improvement plan for the project site (Site Improvement Plan credit).[8]

HOW?

There are several steps after meeting the Site Management Policy Prerequisite that include navigating other related and non-related credits. The majority of available credits under the category of Sustainable Sites are available through options focused on protection of natural habitat, aquifers, the prevention of heath and light pollution and are inclined toward long-term solutions. The team describes them through site plans and calculations for the submission and then they are awarded, denied or sent for resubmission. The method is similar for most all assessment systems measuring site conditions.

6.2.5 Other Rating Systems

The importance of site sustainability and environmental stress caused by existing buildings is well identified by the most propagated global assessment systems already noted (also identified in Chapter 3.3). These demonstrate that other assessment applications may be considered as a substitute rating system for LEED O+M for LEED Lab. Other rating systems also reflect this specificity to locale while maintaining a similar nomenclature of credits and points.

- **BCA Green Mark.** Singaporean BCA Green Mark allocates two of the total 128 available points of the Non-Residential Existing Building Criteria to the site and sustainable impact. The focus is on the use of alternative and suitable sources for non-potable uses: irrigation, washing, water features, cooling tower make-up water to reduce the use of potable water. The numerous options identify rainwater, graywater, air handling unit condensate. Points are awarded based on the percent reduction in potable water usage.[9]

- **BEAM Plus for Existing Buildings.** Hong Kong Green Building Council's (HKGBC) existing building rating system – called Building Environmental Assessment Method (BEAM) – is focused on sustainable and environmentally responsible building management. The Management and Site Aspects categories contain credits relating to site. Management 5, Building and Site Operation and Maintenance offers two credits. Within Site Aspects, there is Noise Pollution (two credits), Light Pollution (two credits), Heat Island Reduction (one credit plus two bonus), Green Roof (one bonus), and Barrier Free Access (three credits). Taken together, there are ten credits plus a few bonus credits available comprising 6.6 percent of the total credit weighting of this rating system.

    The assessment criteria in these categories focus on the location of the building, emissions from the site, microclimate enhancement to the surroundings and amenities provisions. The consideration of impacts on neighboring developments and various discharges and emissions from the site is also assessed.[10] The influence by existing buildings on the surrounding site is additionally tested in these categories. In fact, several bonus credits are available under Site Aspects and Management categories as well.

- **CASBEE EB.** Japan's Comprehensive Assessment System for Build Environment Efficiency (CASBEE) has various scales of evaluation incorporating site metrics from detached residences to cities. This category comprises over 38 percent of all the other categories in the rating system. Within CASBEE's Q3 section, several imperatives are outlined for the site: "creating a richer townscape and ecosystem"; "consideration of the cityscape and landscape"; "creating the biological environment"; "safety and security of the region"; and "utilizing regional resources and inheriting the regional housing culture."

- **LiderA.** As the major Portuguese green assessment system since 2005, LiderA encompasses different building types at various stages, including planning and design, construction and management[11] simultaneously. This rating system uses six categories that are subdivided into 22 'areas.' The Site and Integration category credits account for 14 percent of all categories. Its areas include soil, natural ecosystems, landscape and heritage and further break down into six subdivisions: Territorial valorization, Environmental Deployment Optimization, Ecological Valorization, Habitats Connection, Landscape Integration, Heritage Protection and Enhancement.[12] Light and noise pollution, water use and treatment on the site is evaluated as well, though under the Resources category. In order to be certified, the project must show good environmental performance, verified by existing documentation.

- **Pearl for ESTIDAMA (PORS).** Because of Abu Dhabi's limited annual rainfall, hot climate, and the significant energy embodied in potable water due to desalinization, water conservation is a priority for this rating system. As discussed in the April 2006 UAE Initial National Communication to the United Nations on climate change, it is a distinct possibility that the UAE will become even drier due to the effects of global warming.[13]

  The Pearl Operational Rating System (PORS) released in 2013 is an answer to those challenges and an alternative to LEED O+M in the United Arab Emirates. The Natural Systems category is most comparable to a Site category because it identifies environmental components of the site based on the Priority Habitats and Species. Also, it minimizes the demand for site resources, promotes soil protection/enhancement and ensures the long-term survival and management of landscaped or habitat areas.

  Up to two credits are available if the project demonstrates that a Natural Systems Design and Management Strategy has been prepared ensuring the long-term survival of the landscape within the site and promoting soil protection and enhancement, low maintenance requirements, and low demand for resources. Up to four points are available under the Precious Water category for stormwater management. The minimum required is a protocol for maintaining regular system checks and maintenance.[14]

- **Green Pyramid.** The Egypt Green Building Council's Green Pyramid Rating System (GPRS) currently only focuses on guidelines for new construction of buildings in Egypt,[15] so it would not adequately substitute for LEED Lab. It does however possess a site category called Ecological Balance, which aims to minimize the environmental impact on the site and its surroundings; to protect existing natural systems, such as fauna and flora (including wildlife corridors and seasonal uses), soil, hydrology and groundwater from damage and to promote biodiversity.[16]

- **HQE Exploitation.** As a counterpart to BREEAM In-Use and LEED O+M in France and recently in Brazil, *Haute Qualité Environnementale* or High Quality Environmental Standard (HQE) Certification for Buildings in Operation (HQE Exploitation) employs three certification areas for valuing the engagement of the owner, the manager and the building use.[17] An Eco-Construction Target is part of High Environmental Quality area and relates to the impact building may have on the immediate site, at the regional or local level. The first segment of this Target is the physical relationship of the buildings with its immediate environment. In order for a building to be certified, it must satisfy a number of fundamental prerequisites and justify current, built performance. There are three possible performance levels, which include establishing a Prerequisite, Performing and High Performing,

- **DGNB In Use.** The assessment categories Ecology Quality and Sociocultural Quality are integral parts of *Deutsche Gesellschaft für Nachhaltiges Bauen* (DGNB) In Use Scheme, developed by the German Sustainable Building Council in 2011. The application of those categories relates to the site of either an existing or renovated building. Within each category are assessment criterions that focus on the site. The aim of one of the criterions is to prevent further sprawl of the landscape. The aim of another evaluates the use of the building by the degree of hardscape preventing the seepage of rainwater. The quality of the site development and use is assessed by means of quantitative and qualitative sub criteria, focused on real estate aspects.

The majority of rating systems consider many site attributes. However, the overall weight that Site is allocated in each individual rating system is heavily related to local climate, availability of freshwater, management of urban storm water systems and preservation of existing ecosystems (Figure 6.2). LEED O+M has a broad approach, promotes collaboration with conservation organizations and supports off-site habitat protection and low-impact development. As with other categories, LEED O+M provides a clear path through mandatory prerequisites and possible credits which can apply to the global spectrum.

6.3 Credits

6.3.1 Site Management

(Refer also to pages 59 and 105 in the LEED O+M v4 Reference Guide)

Maintaining the outside of your facility is as important as maintaining the inside, which is why establishing a policy of exterior upkeep is a requirement of LEED O+M certification and a fundamental aspect of LEED Lab activities. A maintained project site should not only benefit human health, but also the sustenance of soil, water and other precious resources. Therefore, crafting a strong Site Management Policy will function as a performance baseline against which the campus facility personnel and the LEED Lab project team can begin to establish future success benchmarks. This is evidenced in subsequent credit categories. Understanding how a campus manages various aspects of its landscaping, painting, and site water consumption – to name only a few – leads to an understanding of which equipment is optimal for sustainable upgrading and which equipment already 'passes' as environmentally friendly. With a clear Site Management Policy, future issues can be better-addressed, a staff site protocol can be clearly outlined, and both the facilities and LEED Lab class teams are able to understand the full scope of what the campus grounds keeping tasks should entail.

Tasks

Generate a Site Maintenance Inventory that will help both the LEED Lab class and the facility personnel to understand existing protocol for exterior campus maintenance activities. Some activities may be sustainable from the onset, some may require further attention, tuning to best management practices, and some may not have been addressed at all!

1. Create a Site Maintenance Inventory Spreadsheet which includes the following:
    - ☐ The *functions* required for the campus' exterior activities.
    - ☐ The existing *equipment* for these activities.
    - ☐ The standard operating *procedures* of applying this equipment to fulfill the activities.
    - ☐ The *metrics* which dictate success of the activity.
    - ☐ The *schedule* of operations and assessments.
    - ☐ *Personnel* who are or will be designated to fulfill that activity.
    - ☐ Identify which activities hold *contracts* with external vendors.
    - ☐ Identify opportunities for improvement for each category in the Site Maintenance Inventory.

SITE

2. Write the Site Management Policy. Use the aforementioned Site Maintenance Inventory spreadsheet together with the Template link in the Tools section below. The narrative should further identify:[18]

   ☐ Goals of the document
   ☐ Quality assurance of activities
   ☐ Environmental harm reduction

3. Adoption of the Site Management Policy[19] by facility personnel, contractors/external personnel and LEED Lab students.

Tools

Specific tools are critical to learn as a part of accomplishing the tasks above. These are not provided in the LEED O+M v4 Reference Guide with respect to their application to LEED Lab. Since learning how to diagnose building performance is the main focus of LEED Lab as a research course, and the education gained by knowing what each tool accomplishes is advantageous to any participant, the following is an abbreviated list of resources to guide successful accomplishment of this prerequisite, specifically complied for LEED Lab:

- Site Management best practices can be found in (Figure 6.3) or on page 62 of the LEED O+M v4 Reference Guide.
- Site Management Policy Template[20]
- EPA Tools, Strategies and Lessons Learned from EPA Green Infrastructure Technical Assistance Projects December 2015 EPA 832-R-15–016.[21]

Techniques

A walkthrough with the campus site maintenance crew and groundskeepers will be enough for a thorough inventory of what constitutes the activity list indicated on the first task on the previous page. Ask questions! Here are some questions helpful in creating the policy:[22]

   ☐ What maintenance equipment is currently used onsite and when is it typically purchased? Are there opportunities for purchasing low-impact more sustainable equipment, substituting manual practices for electric or gas-power equipment?
   ☐ How are snow and ice removed on drives and walkways (if the climate requires this) and is there an opportunity to implement an "anti-icing" program?
   ☐ How is cleaning performed on the campus building exteriors and hardscape, and are there opportunities for using less environmentally harmful products?
   ☐ What is the protocol for facility personnel when erosion and sedimentation occur on the site?

SITE

Erosion & sedimentation control for on-going operations
- Keep debris, garbage, and organic waste out of storm drains through routine maintenance, such as pavement sweeping.
- Provide cigarette butt receptacles, empty them regularly, and sweep butts off ground frequently.
- Regularly inspect, clean, and repair rainwater infrastructure, including roof drains, gutters, and downspouts.
- Maintain healthy groundcover and vegetation to prevent erosion, especially in sloping areas, and restore any eroded soils by reestablishing vegetative cover, mulching, or adding stone aggregates.

Storage of materials and equipment
- Store materials and equipment according to manufacturers' recommendations.
- Ensure that products and equipment are properly contained and secured to prevent materials and fuels from leaking.
- Ventilate storage areas so that chemicals and equipment do not degrade indoor air quality.

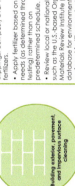

Irrigation Management
- Monitor irrigation systems regularly (at least every two weeks) during operating season for leaks, breaks, irregularities in water usage, and system time settings.
- Test operation of system components regularly during operating season.
- Monitor watering schedule regularly and adjust based on plant and soil conditions.
- Visually inspect landscaped areas for instances of under- or overapplication of irrigation water.
- Use high-efficiency irrigation systems, drip irrigation, and/or weather-based controllers.
- Install pressure sensors that respond to water pressure surges by closing mainline.
- Use weather forecasting data to optimize irrigation.
- Group plantings according to water requirements to optimize timing and quantity of irrigation.
- Turn off irrigation zones in areas where plants are established and require supplemental watering only during droughts.
- Replace plants that are inappropriate to ecoregion and/or natural habitat
- Convert cool-season lawns to warm-season grasses (which require less water in summer).

Fertilizer & herbicide use
- Test soil to establish soil type (classification and texture); contact extension service for information. Retest every other year for nutrient content and pH.
- Use no ammonia-based fertilizers, biosolid-based fertilizers formulated for continuous application, synthetic quick-release fertilizers, or weed-and-feed formulations.
- Use fertilizer derived from animal or vegetable matter, organic or natural fertilizer, and slow-release formulas.
- Prioritize use of organic waste generated on site (e.g., grass clippings, compost) over traditional fertilizers.
- Apply fertilizer based on plants' needs (as determined through soil testing) rather than on predetermined schedule.
- Review local or national sources, such as the U.S.-based Organic Materials Review Institute (OMRI) database for environmentally preferred fertilizer products that comply with USDA organic standards (omri.org).
- Control turf weeds by spot spraying only; use no blanket applications of herbicides.
- For performance metric in SS Credit Site Management, track percentage of environmentally preferred fertilizer used, by cost or quantity (units of weight or volume).

Invasive & exotic vegetation species management
- Develop list of regionally invasive and exotic vegetation and regularly monitor grounds for their presence.
- Engage local nursery, county extension agent, or other knowledgeable resource to identify invasive and exotic vegetation.
- Eradicate any invasive or exotic vegetation found on site through low-impact means.
- Work with neighboring properties to remove their invasive and exotic vegetation to prevent its spread to project site.

Building exterior, pavement, and impervious surface cleaning
- Use cleaning products that meet requirements of EQ Credit Green Cleaning Products and Materials.
- Optimize cleaning frequencies to conserve water and reduce emissions.
- Perform periodic power washing with water only to reduce chemical use.
- Use water-reclaiming power washers.
- Maximize use of manual cleaning strategies.
- Reduce gasoline-powered equipment to limit emissions and noise pollution.

Snow & Ice Removal
- Identify high-traffic areas (e.g., outdoor plazas) that can forgo treatment or require less deicer because traffic helps melt snow and ice.
- Consider developing drawings to show users or tenants areas not treated. Cone or mark off untreated areas before storms begin.
- Prewet pavement with granular or liquid deicers before storms to reduce total amount of product used.
- Consider using salt-free and environmentally preferred deicers (e.g., potassium acetate, potassium chloride, magnesium chloride, or calcium magnesium acetate CMA).
- Always plow or power sweep snow before applying deicer.
- Use vehicles with electronic spreader controls for more precise deicer application in terms of both quantity and location.
- Apply only enough deicer to loosen ice for plowing; do not use deicer to melt entire depth.
- Reduce idle time of snow removal vehicles.
- Use prewetted salt rather than dry salt when possible.
- Keep records of deicer use (dates applied, quantities used, area treated) and its effect for each snow event to optimize future deicer applications.
- Save leftover deicers for the next season, using safe storage techniques that fully contain the material.
- For the performance metric in SS Credit Site Management, track percentage of environmentally preferred deicer used, by cost or quantity (units of weight or volume), or track percentage reduction in area treated with calcium chloride or sodium chloride deicers, from baseline application area.

Maintenance Equipment
- Use low- or zero-emissions maintenance equipment.
- Replace gasoline-powered equipment (including pruning equipment) with electric, manual, or propane-powered equipment and strategies.
- Maintain and repair equipment according to manufacturers' recommendations.
- Reduce lawn areas to reduce dependence on powered equipment such as mowers, edgers, trimmers and blowers.
- Convert lawn to restored habitats, native or adapted plants, mulches, aggregates, or no-mow grasses.

Organic waste management
- Compost or mulch leaves and waste on site.
- Use mulching mowers on turf areas.
- Compost at off-site facility.

Fig 6.3 *LEED O+M v4 Reference Guide: Site Management best practices*

Source: *Derived from LEED O+M v4 Reference Guide. Diagrammed by Elizabeth Meyers, 2020*

| 89

SITE

 Partnering Credits

There are many synergistic credits which relate back to the Site Management Policy. For LEED Lab, the credits of Site Management, Site Development, Site Improvement and Heat Island are tightly associated with this prerequisite.

If the following questions may be answered affirmatively, the Site Management credit should be attempted:[23]

- ☐ Can manual or electric-powered equipment meet site maintenance needs?
- ☐ If no, does the equipment meet the threshold of 50 percent emissions reduction?
- ☐ The schedule of operations and any accompanying manufacturer's data for the equipment is already logged with the grounds personnel and they are regularly engaged with its performance tracking.

If the following questions may be answered affirmatively, the Site Development credit should be attempted:[24]

- ☐ The project has at least 20 percent of the site area/5,000 square feet minimum dedicated to native or adaptive vegetation and there are opportunities to expand this area.
- ☐ If the project does not have the minimal areas identified above, it is able to restore areas to these requirements during the Performance Period.
- ☐ Native and adaptive vegetation contributes to the project's goals for sustainable sites and water use reduction (this should be identified in the Site Improvement Plan); it improves the site's appearance, reduces or eliminates maintenance, and/or improves rainwater management.
- ☐ If the aforementioned conditions are unable to be met, there is an accredited land trust that you would be willing to support financially.

If the following questions may be answered affirmatively, the Site Improvement credit should be attempted:[25]

- ☐ The project team will be able to implement the no-cost and low-cost improvements that are identified in this credit.
- ☐ At least 5 percent of your site is currently vegetated, or the current vegetated area can be increased to 5 percent of the site before the Performance Period ends.
- ☐ Monitoring protocols for all site-related improvements are in place or can be in place during the Performance Period.
- ☐ Professionals specializing in hydrology, vegetation and soils are able to provide input to the facility personnel and LEED Lab students to facilitate creating a 5-year Site Improvement Plan.

If the following questions may be answered affirmatively, the Heat Island Reduction credit should be attempted:[26]

- ☐ The site provides underground parking or a parking garage.
- ☐ The existing roofing membrane complies with the Heat Island credit per its manufacturer's data.

SITE

- ☐ Regular roof cleaning occurs at a frequency of at least every three years and contributes towards maintaining SRI (Side Lesson A: Solar Reflectance Index (SRI)). Alternatively, roof cleaning to occur at this frequency is identified in the Site Management Policy and will begin during the Performance Period.
- ☐ High-reflectance paving exists on more than 50 percent of the site's hardscape.
- ☐ Regular cleaning of the exterior hardscape occurs at a frequency of at least every three years and contributes towards maintaining SRI. Alternatively, hardscape cleaning can be specified to occur at this frequency, shall be identified in the Site Management Policy, and will begin during the Performance Period.

6.3.2 Rainwater Management

(*Refer also to page 75 in the LEED O+M v4 Reference Guide*)

When water from rain or melted snow settles on rooftops and hardscape, it does not drain or percolate as in a natural environment. This is called a stormwater or (Side Lesson B: Stormwater) rainwater. In typical stormwater design, artificial drainage must be introduced. This often causes unmanaged water flow which has excess volume, is unable to shed, and drains slowly, creating a deterred timing of runoff ending in floods. Unfortunately, it also means that the water carries contaminants which requires another layer of design management for filtration.

This artificial drainage also often terminates in the municipal sewage system. In such a system, we can see that there may be a separation between sewage and rainwater or stormwater. In a combined system, both domestic and commercial sewage combine with stormwater and more energy is required to treat the water to tertiary standards of reuse. In a split system, less energy is required. Regardless of which type of engineering infrastructure is designed (Figure 6.4), it is an artificial disruption of natural hydrology.

The role of sustainable rainwater management is to duplicate an organic hydrological cycle. In natural landscapes, soil absorbs water. Plants also reduce it by improving infiltration through taking up water into their roots and intercepting precipitation as it falls.

How could such a design be successful on campuses which require significant attention to occupant use of the exterior? There are many strategies that have evolved throughout the years. For example, containing the water on site and reusing it for other purposes is one option. Another option is to re-create, through the physical materials, opportunities for percolation to replicate these natural systems. A third option is to leave the natural environment as is, designing around these natural systems. There are many ways architects and building owners can embrace natural drainage design – and a few are identified in this subchapter. Despite the method in which it is accomplished, credit is warranted and in LEED Lab it also must be well-researched and documented.

Side Lesson A – 6.3.1: The Solar Reflectance Index (SRI) is the measure of a material's ability to reflect and absorb solar heat. This measurement is determined by the temperature of a material when exposed to sunlight. For example, a black roof has aN SRI of 0 because it absorbs sunlight completely. While, a white roof has an SRI of 100 because it reflects sunlight. The lower the SRI a material has the hotter the material becomes when exposed to the sun (see https://heatisland.lbl.gov/).

Side Lesson B – 6.3.2: Stormwater is the surface water caused by heavy rainfall or snow. This definition includes water found in gutters, downpipes, drains, and surface water on roads, footpaths, driveways, and lawns. Stormwater is not the same as rainwater, which only refers to the water on the roof. The quality of rainwater is much higher than that of groundwater because the chances of pollutants such as soil, fertilizers and automobile oil are fewer (see www.nationalpolyindustries.com.au/2018/06/14/what-is-the-difference-between-stormwater-and-rainwater/).

SITE

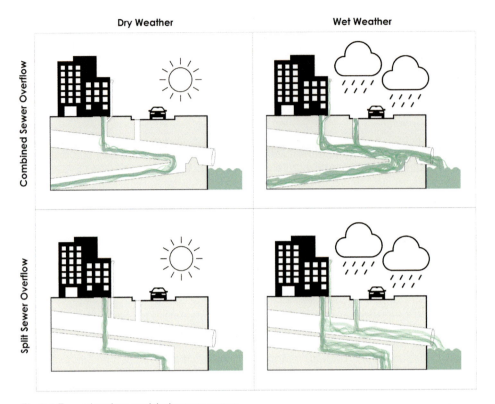

Fig 6.4 *Two options for a municipal sewage system*
Source: Derived from Sewer Equipment Co. Diagrammed by Elizabeth Meyers, 2020

Side Lesson C – 6.3.2: Low Impact Development (LID), is a land planning and engineering design approach to utilize stormwater as protection for water quality and aquatic habitat. The EPA uses the term "green infrastructure" as the management of wet weather flows through systems and practices that mimic the natural water cycle. LID and GI have the same goal of protecting, restoring and creating green spaces by using rainwater harvesting techniques, soil types and vegetation (see www.epa.gov/nps/urban-runoff-low-impact-development).

Tasks

There are several technical tasks which are required for this credit. Their benefits and calculations should be identified in the previous subchapter, Site Management Policy, for ease of availability, particularly if the campus does not have a standard documentation medium for recording successful rainwater management strategies. Considering the structure of LEED Lab, and its campus application, the following tasks should be followed (refer to the Tools section):

☐ Identify the historical rainfall quantities of the site for the past ten years.
☐ Indicate which existing stormwater and rainwater management strategies are able to capture and treat at least 25 percent of the impervious areas.
☐ For those existing stormwater and rainwater management strategies which do not meet the aforementioned requirements, create a process for expanding these in the Sustainability Improvement Plan (see Partnering Credit for Site Management Plan) which includes Low Impact Development (LID) (Side Lesson C: Low Impact Development (LID))[27] measures.
☐ Calculate the rainwater and stormwater using the strategies from the preceding task (see Tools section, US EPA Storm Water Management Model).

SITE

- Calculate the amount of runoff from impervious areas on site (see Tools section, Small Storm Hydrology Method).
- Indicate how the strategies will be annually inspected and recorded through a set schedule identified in the Site Management Policy. The tracking should begin during the Performance Period.

Tools

Specific tools help to achieve these tasks. Tools for rainwater/stormwater management simply require calculations and ideas! For the LEED Lab student, providing these calculators and examples helps to facilitate conversations between facility personnel and university administrators and gives students the confidence to recommend strategies which are actually implemented. A few of these include:

- ☐ NOAA Past Weather History, developed by the government to describe historical climate data.[28]
- ☐ US EPA Storm Water Management Model (SWMM)- Developed by the government to predict runoff quantity and quality.[29]
- ☐ Small Storm Hydrology Method (Figure 6.5). This is a simple manual step-by-step procedure of calculating large or small impervious site areas.
- ☐ National Menu of Best Management Practices (BMPs) for Stormwater www.epa.gov/npdes/national-menu-best-management-practices-bmps-stormwater

Fig 6.5 Small storm hydrology method

Source: Derived from USGBC. Diagrammed by Elizabeth Meyers, 2020

This method is used to estimate the runoff volume from small storms in urban and suburban areas. Runoff is the water that runs off smooth surfaces due to a rain, storm, or melted ice.

Small Impervious Areas:
An average dimension no greater than 24 feet (7.3) meters in any direction.
Examples include: roads without curbs, small parking lots without curbs, and sidewalks.

Large Impervious Areas:
An average dimension greater than 24 feet (7.3) meters in any direction.
Examples include: parking lots with curbs, roads with curbs, highways etc.

For each land use type, runoff volume is calculated based on land use area and land use coefficient using the following equation:

$$\text{Runoff Volume (ft}^3\text{)} = \left[\left(\frac{P}{12} \right) \times Rv \times A \right]$$

Small Storm Hydrology Method Runoff Coefficient

$$Rv = \left[0.05 + 0.009 \times I \right]$$

KEY:
- Rv Small Storm Hydrology Method Runoff Coefficient
- I   % of impervious area expressed as a whole number
- A   Area of Land Use (ft²)
- P   % rainfall depth (in)

| 93

SITE

- Examples
  - Description of LID Technologies: www.wbdg.org/resources/low-impact-development-technologies.
  - Case studies analyzing the economic benefits of low impact development and green infrastructure programs: www.epa.gov/sites/production/files/2015-10/documents/lid-gi-programs_report_8-6-13_combined.pdf

Techniques[30]

- ☐ Natural infiltration strategies in a high ratio of pervious to impervious surfaces may bring the project to compliance alone. Confirm these strategies first.
- ☐ Construction documents which demonstrate the capacity of existing rainwater collection systems such as cisterns, detention ponds, and bioswales already existing on site are sufficient for fulfilling this credit if they comply with the rainwater/stormwater mitigation quantities.
- ☐ Replacing existing non-native groundcover (Side Lesson D: Groundcovers) with indigenous foliage and swales which increase pervious filtration may be a cost-effective method for achieving this credit.
- ☐ This credit requires LEED Lab students and facility personnel to manage rainwater/stormwater runoff from the entire site, even if there are greenfields (Side Lesson E: Greenfield Land) within the project.

Side Lesson D – 6.3.2: Groundcovers are low-maintenance and low-lying plants that cover certain areas of the ground. They are used in landscape design not only for aesthetics, but to protect the top level of soil from drought and erosion. Examples of ground cover include: clover, alfalfa, ivy, gazania, ice plant, and ground-elder (see www.thespruce.com/groundcovers-are-low-lying-plants-2131058).

Side Lesson E – 6.3.2: Greenfield Land is undeveloped land in either a rural or urban area that can be left to evolve naturally or can be used for landscape land or agriculture. Typically, greenfields are considered for urban development (see www.gray.com/insights/greenfield-vs-brownfield-whats-better-for-your-manufacturing-facility/).

6.3.3 Light Pollution Reduction

(*Refer also to page 97 in the LEED O+M v4 Reference Guide*)

Light pollution is the extreme use of artificial light impacting the exterior environment, particularly at night. It has significant consequences for our globe, our health, wildlife and our university grounds. Although it is a necessary amenity on the campus since many people traverse its grounds, exterior light – inefficiently designed – wastes energy, harms human health, contributes towards habitat demise, and may be a safety hazard if it is used in excess.

Outdoor lighting in this country illuminating streets and parking lots consumes as much energy in an average year as New York City's total electricity needs for two years![31] The impact of large fields of illumination such as at a university is significant, thus mitigation can contribute towards energy savings not only for the institution but also the region and subsequently the world.

The top two critical issues with light pollution are its impact on the health of humans and on ecosystems. It is common scientific knowledge that artificial light at night has deadly effects on many creatures including amphibians, birds, mammals, insects and plants living around the light trespass (Side Lesson F: Light Trespass).[32] If light trespass occurs from the building into the environment, the environment into the building, or if it exists on the exterior and fixtures are not properly positioned, the ecology being illuminated at night suffers because nocturnal activity or rest becomes misaligned with the illuminance. In this case, the obliquing angle of the interior fixtures

Side Lesson F – 6.3.3: Light Trespass is when artificial light is present during the nighttime in an unwanted area that alters natural conditions. This is also considered as light pollution. An example of this is when an exterior night light illuminates an interior space (see www.lrc.rpi.edu/programs/nlpip/lightinganswers/lightpollution/lightTrespass.asp).

SITE

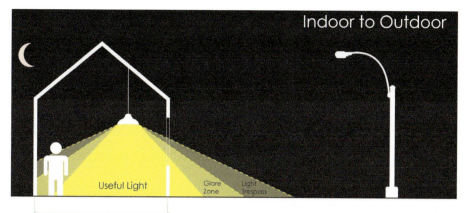

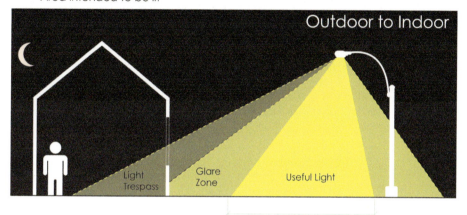

Fig 6.6 Light trespass
Source: Derived from Dark Skies Paonic. Diagrammed by Elizabeth Meyers, 2020

(Figure 6.6) and the overall fixture types and their placing must be revised in order to avoid ecosystem demise.

With respect to the cycle of human functions, light pollution disrupts circadian rhythms (Side Lesson G: Circadian Rhythm) and increases sleeping disorders. Nighttime exposure to artificial light suppresses physiological processes by fooling our bodies into the false perception that is it daytime. For example, when light trespasses into living quarters from the outside through windows and fenestration, an unnatural occurrence to sleeping patterns obscures our melatonin level (Side Lesson H: Melatonin) which helps induce sleep, support the immune system, and aid the functioning of the thyroid, pancreas, ovaries, testes and adrenal glands.[33]

On a campus, exterior lighting serves to direct the multitude of occupants, providing some aesthetic relief and a modicum of safety. However, a large range of bright, confusing groupings of lighting sources called clutter (Side Lesson I: Light Clutter) intended to provide safety sometimes creates glare (Side Lesson J: Glare) from poorly shielded outdoor lighting and becomes detrimental to the navigation it was designed to assist by decreasing

Side Lesson G – 6.3.3: Circadian Rhythm is the daily cycle of mental, physical, and behavioral changes to the body. Light is a good example of a circadian rhythm. The body naturally sleeps during the night, while awake during the day (see https://tinyurl.com/7ke458zu).

| 95

SITE

Side Lesson H – 6.3.3: Melatonin is a hormone that is released by the pineal gland during nighttime. It is referred to as the "Dracula of hormones" because it only comes out at night, usually switched on around 9 pm. At night, as melatonin levels rise in the bloodstream, alertness decreases. However, while it may be dark outside, bright lights may interfere with melatonin levels (see www.sleepfoundation.org/ melatonin).

Side Lesson I – 6.3.3: Light Clutter is the excessive placement of lighting that leads to improper illumination, confusion, and distraction. A good example of light clutter is the improper placement of street lights, which distracts the driver's attention. This issue is considered as a type of light pollution (see https:// tinyurl.com/nnuysvsa).

Side Lesson J – 6.3.3: Glare is a reduction in vision caused by excessive lighting and uncontrolled brightness. It can be uncomfortable and even disabling. Elderly people are more sensitive and prone to glare due to decrease in vision capability with age. Two types of glares are disability and discomfort. Disability glare is when too much lighting and brightness impairs the user by obstructing their field of view. Discomfort glare is when glare causes annoyance and pain to the user (see www.lrc.rpi.edu/programs/ nlpip/lightinganswers/ lightpollution/glare.asp).

vision and reducing contrast. This limits the ability to see potential dangers at night. As in other building types, light pollution not only gives an unhealthy and unnatural look to a campus, but also can cause an unpleasant effect upon the surrounding neighborhood. Although lighting is a key component to exterior circulation and is required on the college grounds, many decisions about the placement, type and quality of lighting selected can be assessed for sustainable resiliency at your institution. Specific tasks assist LEED Lab students to document this credit.

Tasks

All of the factors mentioned contribute towards light pollution and should be considered when pursuing this credit. However, the LEED Lab student is only required to document two primary methods of light reduction required for credit achievement. At this point, the scope of the project should have already been evaluated through charrettes and preliminary project preparation, so the student/s should have a grasp of whether or not the lighting documentation comprises the entire campus as an aggregate credit, or one facility as an individually certified building. Either way, documentation is accomplished through the following tasks:

1. If the first option – Fixture Shielding – is pursued, identify which lighting fixtures on campus have the greatest lumen levels (above 2,500 mean lamp lumens).[34]
   - ☐ Confirm via the manufacturer's data that the fixture shielding does not permit any vertical light trespass greater than 90 degrees.
   - ☐ For fixtures which do not meet this criteria, prepare a plan during the Performance Period to replace either the shielding or the fixtures.

Or

2. If the second option – Perimeter Measurements[35] – is pursued, identify at least eight measurement points around the project boundary, spaced at 100 ft intervals.
   - ☐ Use a light meter to take illumination measurements at these points with lights both on and off.
   - ☐ Compare the lights-on and lights-off measurements to ensure credit compliance if the lights-on illumination is no more than 20 percent of the lights-off illumination.

Tools

- **Light meter** (Side Lesson K: Light Meters). There are various sources for procuring a light meter if the facility personnel do not have one available.[36] Otherwise, searching for an 'ambient light meter' is the best way to begin procurement.
- **Procedure.** Besides the light meter, the only tools that would assist this credit accomplishment would be a diagram of the process for measuring the perimeter lighting (Figure 6.7).

SITE

Fig 6.7 *Sustainable Sites credit: Light Pollution Reduction*
Source: Derived from LEED O+M v4 Reference Guide. Diagrammed by Elizabeth Meyers, 2020

SITE

Side Lesson K – 6.3.3: Light Meters or lux meters are instruments used to quantity the amount of natural and artificial light. These meters help designers ensure optimal levels of light not only for human comfort but to monitor the efficiency from an environmental point of view. Light meters are used for routine efficiency audits and OSHA regulations (see www.instrumart.com/ categories/5639/light-meters).

Techniques[37]

Although this is a straight forward credit, the LEED Lab student should factor in research time for the following in order to facilitate credit compliance:

☐ Research if the project demands any client or code-initiated minimal light trespass at the LEED project boundary if Option 2 is being pursued. There may be a conflict between LEED and project requirements which should be exposed first.
☐ An assessment of fixtures requires a walk-through of the property with the facility personnel responsible for the grounds lighting. Schedule this walk-through prior to pursuing either credit option.
☐ A very easy way to meet this credit if you are close to achievement is to assess if exterior lighting levels can be lowered or if there are any excessive fixtures which can be removed.
☐ Identifying the existing shielded fixtures via a manufacturer's catalog or contact at the product distribution agency and/or literature provides a solid documentation of appropriate light distribution and shielding confirmation. Submit this as a part of your credit documentation.
☐ Confirming that the current lumen values of lamps exceed 2,500 lumens for all fixtures should be accomplished after the aforementioned manufacturer's shielding data is collected. Remember that there are two ways to accomplish this credit.

6.4 Case Study[38]

The Catholic University of America has an aggressive approach to landscaping and site work which includes many sustainable efficiency measures – as evidenced by its Site Management Policy and Site Improvement Plan. Strategies that would be implemented in the next five years include managing water runoff, soil compaction, and better documentation of onsite vegetation. These initiatives identified between LEED Lab students and the facilities management were approved by the Director of Ground Management yet still needed to be addressed in many locations on campus. The biggest focus includes (1) maintaining soil compactions, (2) minimizing water runoff, and (3) managing vegetation. The Site improvement Plan that was submitted and achieved as a credit followed these three main focuses by providing (1) documentation of general soil structure, preservation of healthy soils, remediation of compacted soils, and identification of previously developed areas; (2) protection and improvement of water bodies on-site, rainwater management and reuse opportunities, and potable water-use reduction; and (3) documentation of existing vegetation on-site, turf area reduction, management of native and invasive plants, and protection of threatened, endangered or unique species.

For the first focus (1), students and staff determined that constant soil turning and loosening would need to occur. These soil loosening treatments would be implemented in areas not covered by vegetation like grass or exotic plants. In order to keep the soil loose, grounds keepers would need to turn the soil monthly in order to prevent any soil clumping.

Soil is a significant factor when dealing with water runoff. To promote water run-off reabsorption, The Catholic University has taken measures to aerate the soil every few months. There is no specific timetable of when and what areas need aerating, but when there is ponding in a certain area after a rainwater event, the university takes immediate action in uncompacting the soil.

In terms of documenting the types of soil on campus, we used an online source to find areas that contained a certain type of soil. To tackle this part of the plan, we resorted to the soil records of websoilsurvey.nrcs.usda.gov to find the necessary data. To document the soil, we made a map of where each soil type was located on campus. The 17 soils found on campus were identified on a campus map (Figure 6.8). Areas where there was a type of sandy loam soil would need little maintenance due to the richness and its resistance towards compaction.

Since stormwater runoff is closely linked to soil type, we assembled a contour map of the campus grounds (Figure 6.9) and then identified where water is most likely diverted across the contours (Figure 6.10). To prevent rainwater runoff (2), students and staff determined that several actions needed to be taken with this information at hand, with the ultimate goal of conserving the water that ran off on the impervious surfaces. A few methods were implemented; for instance, a method was established to create vegetated swales. Vegetated swales are small dips in the earth filled with vegetation which allow penetration of the water to the roots, keeping water on site. A small retrofit with the appropriate gravel and filtration medium to an existing swale converted it to a water retention and percolation vehicle. By preventing soil compaction, the soil was prepared to absorb the water and not let it runoff when there is significant rainfall. When the water runs off from the impervious surface into these vegetated dips in the land, there is theoretically no waste of water. However, these vegetated swales are not necessarily enough to hold all of the water runoff so other methods were used.

Students paid such close attention to this credit that they created a sub-group within LEED Lab called CUARain – dedicated to increasing rainwater harvesting by designing and constructing custom cisterns throughout the campus. In order to effectively reach CUARain's goal of successfully irrigating plants solely with water from runoff, a plan was executed to manufacture these cisterns by the students and eventually propagate their cistern design for all of the buildings on campus. In addition to these cisterns, the university began installing green roofs on existing and new buildings.

The third focus of vegetation management (3) included the removal of invasive species as a new road was constructed

SITE

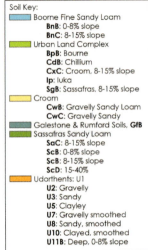

Fig 6.8 *The Catholic University of America Campus Master Plan, April 2012*

Note: This plan illustrates the various soil types that exist on campus

Source: Derived from The Catholic University of America Strategic Master Plan Document. Diagrammed by Elizabeth Meyers, 2020

to the campus. Another smaller project was creating a set of community gardens for the campus – for food, restoration of green space, and tree revival. In the past five years, the average number of trees planted annually has been an average of 44, according to the vendor Casey Trees, Inc. The parking lot in the center of campus was scheduled to be demolished and replaced with trees and vegetation, for example.

Throughout the past seven years, the university has kept records of the trees and other vegetation on campus. This includes grass, types of trees, and any plant that may be growing that needs to be irrigated. This credit requires a log of these plants and their quantity on campus. A list was compiled to document various types of native or invasive species on campus (Figure 6.11). Here we recorded the area of a certain vegetation in a particular section of campus to visualize locations which needed more assistance with regulating invasive species. Apart from listing the vegetation on-site, a few methods for managing

SITE

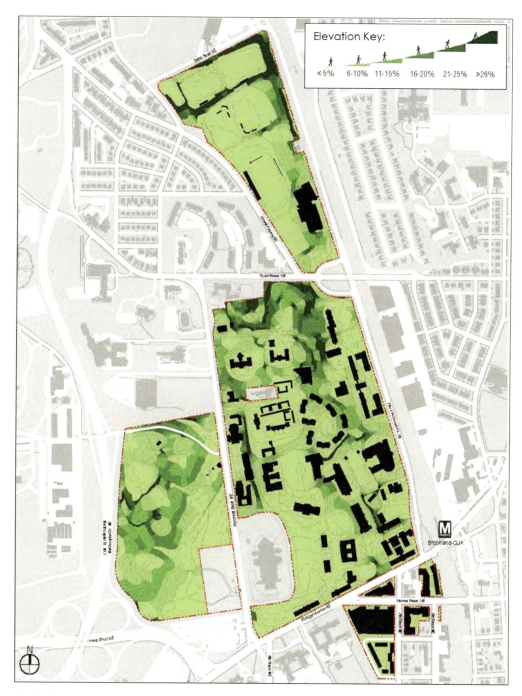

Fig 6.9 Terrain elevation map of The Catholic University of America, Campus Master Plan, April 2012
Note: This plan illustrates the different elevations of the terrain around the campus
Source: Derived from The Catholic University of America Strategic Master Plan Document. Diagrammed by Elizabeth Meyers, 2020

SITE

Fig 6.10 *The Catholic University of America Campus Master Plan, April 2012*
Note: This plan illustrates the water flow direction on the impervious surfaces on campus
Source: Derived from The Catholic University of America Strategic Master Plan Document. Diagrammed by Elizabeth Meyers, 2020

SITE

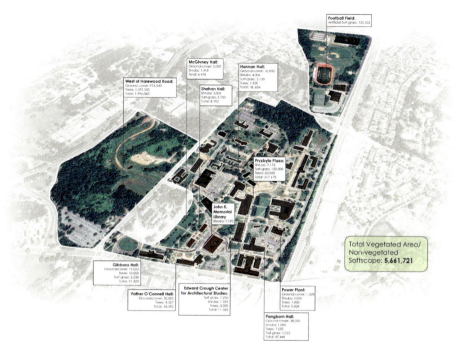

Fig 6.11 The Catholic University of America, area of vegetation on campus
Source: Created by Dallas Chavez. Diagrammed by Elizabeth Meyers, 2020

irrigation were promoted. One of those sustainable methods was letting the turfgrass go dry throughout the winter. The cool season turfgrass (grass that grows best at temperatures from 65 F to 80 F) would need about 4 ml of water per day in order to maintain health. Since the majority of campus had turfgrass on the lawns, by not watering the turfgrass in the winter, there would be a significant reduction in water loss – reducing runoff from sprinklers, although not contributing to any credit which warrants indigenous or native species.

There were many other options that could have improved The Catholic University of America's ecological sustainability, but the expenses involved with making them a reality were budget-prohibitive. The three main sustainable initiatives focusing on rainwater management, onsite vegetation and prevention of soil compaction were successful and executed into awarding several synergistic credits in addition to the Site Improvement Plan.

6.5 Exercises

The questions on the next page are derived from the aforementioned case study. Questions testing knowledge of the breadth of tools, tasks and techniques are important for LEED Lab; the investigation

| 103

SITE

required in answering these exercises helps students to approach their credit assignments from a synergistic perspective.

Exercise Scenario 1

In addition to the initiatives proposed for the campus' Sustainability Improvement Plan, what additional credit or credits may be earned considering the LEED Lab student's initiatives of starting the CUARain student organization?

Exercise Scenario 2

Which synergistic credits could have been awarded to this project if all three of the focuses (1), (2) and (3) were fully successful?

Exercise Scenario 3

If the cost of replacing turfgrass with adaptive foliage is relatively low, and the university pursued this strategy, which additional credits may be awarded?

Exercise Scenario 4

Your university is located in Singapore and your LEED Lab class is interested in using the local rating system to fulfill green assessment requirements for the site. Which assessment system would best fit this option?

Exercise Scenario 5

Your LEED Lab team is confused about where to turn to seek strategies that would mitigate stormwater and rainwater run off from the site. Where could your team turn for resources to help navigate options?

Notes

1. US Green Building Council, "Sustainable Sites: Overview," *Reference Guide for Building Operations and Maintenance* (Washington, DC: US Green Building Council, 2013): 57.
2. Ibid.
3. Green Building Initiative, *Green Globes® for Existing Buildings 2007 Technical Reference Manual, Version 1.21 December 2019* (Green Building Initiative, Inc., 2019): 173, 178, 181, 185. www.thegbi.org/files/training_resources/Green_Globes_EB_2007_Technical_Reference_Manual.pdf
4. S. Summerson, J. Atkins and A. Harries, *BREEAM In-Use: Driving Sustainability through Existing Buildings* (Watford: Building Research Establishment Ltd.): 2. www.breeam.com/filelibrary/BREEAM%20In%20Use/KN5686---BREEAM-In-Use-White-Paper_dft2.pdf
5. BREEAM, *BREEAM In-Use Technical Manual SD221 2.0:2015* (Watford: BRE Global Ltd, 2016): 164, 285, 385.
6. Green Building Council of Australia, "Ecological Value," "Groundskeeping Practices," and "Stormwater," *Green Star – Performance v1.2 – Initial Certification Submission Template r1*. www.gbca.org.au/greenstar-manager/resources/?filter-rating-tool=101&_ga=2.107716033.213355384.1592333897-29415128.1591753717

7. Green Building Institute of Australia, *Green Star – Performance Portfolio Certification – Release v1.0* (Green Building Council of Australia, 2015): 30. www.gbca.org.au/uploads/160/36000/Green%20Star%20Portfolio%20Certification%20Guide_160715%20Release%20v1.0.pdf
8. US Green Building Council, "Site Management Policy: Behind the Intent," *Reference Guide for Building Operations and Maintenance* (Washington, DC: US Green Building Council, 2013): 67, 75, 83, 115.
9. *Green Mark for Non-Residential Existing Buildings, Version NRB/4.1* (Singapore: Building and Construction Authority (BCA), Ministry of National Development, 2013): 8.
10. *BEAM Plus Existing Buildings Version 2.0 (2016.03): Comprehensive Scheme* (Hong Kong: Hong Kong Green Building Council, 2016): 2.
11. Manuel Duarte Pinheiro, *LiderA: Voluntary System for the Sustainability of Built Environments: Working Version V2.00c1* (Lisbon: Manuel Duarte Pinheiro, 2011). www.lidera.info/resources/_LiderA_V2.00c1%20sumario_ingles.pdf
12. Ibid.
13. *The Pearl Rating System for ESTIDAMA Emirate of Abu Dhabi, Pearl Building Rating System: Design & Construction, Version 1.0* (Abu Dhabi: Abu Dhabi Urban Planning Council, April 2010): 115. www.upc.gov.ae/-/media/files/estidama/docs/pbrs-version-10.ashx?la=ar-ae&hash=58A67F549081968086D016E8D3757366BF29B10F
14. Ibid., 135.
15. The Egyptian Green Building Council, *The Green Pyramid Rating System First Edition – April 2011* (Egyptian Green Building Council, 2011).
16. Ibid., 12.
17. *BeHQE: Join the Movement for Performance and Quality of Life* (Paris: Cerway, 2018). www.behqe.com/documents/download/19
18. US Green Building Council, "Site Management Policy: Step-by-Step Guidance," *Reference Guide for Building Operations and Maintenance* (Washington, DC: US Green Building Council, 2013): 61.
19. Ibid.
20. See website: www.usgbc.org/resources/ssp-site-management-policy-template
21. See website: www.epa.gov/sites/production/files/2016-01/documents/gi_tech_asst_summary_508final010515_3.pdf
22. Jenny Carney, "EBOM-v4 SSp1: Site Management Policy," BuildingGreen, 2018. https://leeduser.buildinggreen.com/credit/EBOM-v4/SSp1
23. Samantha Longshore, "EBOM-v4 SSc5: Site Management," BuildingGreen, 2018. https://leeduser.buildinggreen.com/credit/EBOM-v4/SSc5
24. Trista Little, "EBOM-v4 SSc1: Site Development – Protect or Restore Habitat," BuildingGreen, 2018. https://leeduser.buildinggreen.com/credit/EBOM-v4/SSc1.
25. Jenny Carney, "EBOM-v4 SSc6: Site Improvement Plan," BuildingGreen, 2018. https://leeduser.buildinggreen.com/credit/EBOM-v4/SSc6
26. Samantha Longshore, "EBOM-v4 SSc3: Heat Island Reduction," BuildingGreen, 2018. https://leeduser.buildinggreen.com/credit/EBOM-v4/SSc3
27. "Urban Runoff: Low Impact Development," United States Environmental Protection Agency, 2020. https://tinyurl.com/48ahesyp; Shikha Ranjha, "Green Infrastructure: Planning for Sustainable and Resilient Urban Environment." Brief for GSDR – 2016 Update. https://tinyurl.com/54uybb93; description of LID Technologies: www.wbdg.org/resources/low-impact-development-technologies; case studies analyzing the economic benefits of low impact development and green infrastructure programs: www.epa.gov/sites/production/files/2015-10/documents/lid-gi-programs_report_8-6-13_combined.pdf
28. See www.climate.gov/maps-data/dataset/past-weather-zip-code-data-table
29. See www.epa.gov/water-research/storm-water-management-model-swmm
30. Gail Vittori, "EBOM-v4 SSc2: Rainwater Management: Runoff Calculations and Rainwater Harvesting," BuildingGreen, 2018. https://leeduser.buildinggreen.com/forum/runoff-calculations-rainwater-harvesting
31. "Light Pollution Wastes Energy and Money," International Dark Sky Association, 2020. www.darksky.org/light-pollution/energy-waste/
32. "Light Pollution Effects on Wildlife and Ecosystems," International Dark Sky Association, 2020. www.darksky.org/light-pollution/wildlife/
33. "Human Health," International Dark Sky Association, 2020. www.darksky.org/light-pollution/human-health/
34. US Green Building Council, "Light Pollution Reduction: Step-by-Step Guidance," *Reference Guide for Building Operations*

and Maintenance (Washington, DC: US Green Building Council, 2013): 98.
35 Ibid.
36 See website: www.instrumart.com/categories/5639/light-meters
37 Bill Swanson, "EBOM-v4 SSc4: Light Pollution Reduction," BuildingGreen, 2018. https://leeduser.buildinggreen.com/credit/EBOM-v4/SSc4
38 This report was originally prepared by Dallas Chavez, a high school student, for the purpose of summarizing his experience on the SITE team while auditing CUA's 2014 LEED Lab course.

CHAPTER SEVEN

WATER

7.1 Theory

LEED Lab approaches water use in the Water Efficiency (WE) set of credits holistically, combining all uses of water on a building site: indoor, outdoor, specialized uses (e.g., HVAC, showers in a dormitory or hospital, water fountains), and metering. The reason is to calculate present water efficiency, to propose methods to reduce usage of potable water, and then to address through credits the use of non-potable water and alternate water sources.

Concern over water usage and disposal in a building is very important due to the increasing scarcity of fresh water and the environmentally unfriendly manner in which waste water is treated in most commercial buildings. Developed nations rely upon extensive piping systems to deliver potable water from far away sources, and then upon another system of conduits to take waste water to a processing plant, where the waste water – though treated – still contains contaminants but is nevertheless reintroduced into the environment by emptying into bodies of water.[1] Further, the energy expended in treating waste water or in purifying it for drinking, and in the transportation to and from the required locales, consumes great amounts of energy.

This category of building assessment also introduces alternative sewage conveyance techniques as another method to minimize water consumption. The USGBC has estimated that in the United States, buildings account for 13.6 percent of potable water use.[2] Through the avenues presented in this category, water in building consumption can be reduced or even eliminated by removing the need for irrigation, the installation of water-efficient fixtures and reusing water. LEED projects have already significantly reduced water usage in the United States, and through the use of the WE category's three major components (indoor water, irrigation water, water metering), and projects can add to this achievement. There are similar goals of water reduction across other global green rating systems.

DOI: 10.4324/9780429449703-7

WATER

7.2 Comparison

The introductory overview for the WE section of LEED O+M addresses the complexity and importance of water use management in existing buildings. As with the majority of other rating systems, the goal is to encourage reduction of total water use.[3] It is important to notice that all rating systems address water use in certain phases of a building's life (Figure 7.1). The two major challenges addressed by all rating systems for existing buildings are a reduction of water use, and a reduction of energy needed for wastewater treatment and reuse or preservation.

The scarcity of available potable water and the hydrological cycle in various climates creates a nuance in the way different rating systems prioritize credit allocation in this category (Figure 7.2). Typically, most building water cycles through the structure and then flows off-site as wastewater. In industrially developed countries, potable water usually comes from a public water supply system a great distance away from the building site, and wastewater exiting the site must be piped to a processing plant, and then emptied into a distant water body. This pass-through system reduces streamflow in rivers and depletes freshwater aquifers, causing water tables to drop and wells to go dry. In

Fig 7.1 Global sustainable existing building sustainability assessment tools

Source: Created by Patricia Andrasik and Milan Glisić, 2017

| 108 |

WATER

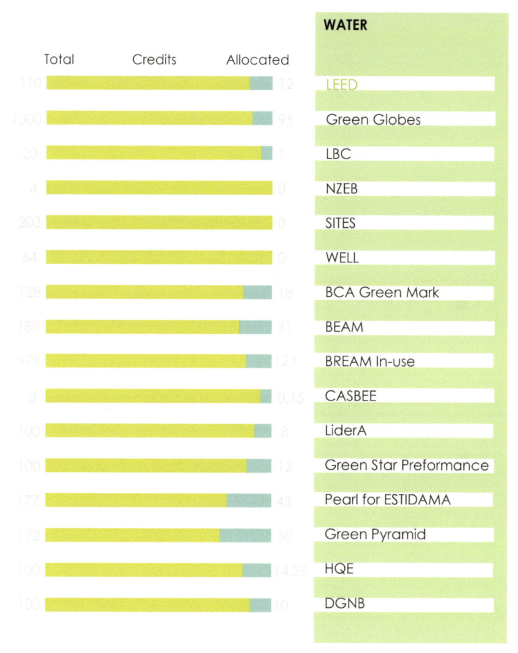

Fig 7.2 *Global sustainable existing building sustainability assessment tools*
Source: Created by Patricia Andrasik and Milan Glisić, 2017

60 percent of European cities with populations greater than 100,000, groundwater is not being replenished at a positive rate.[4]

7.2.1 Green Globes for Existing Buildings (EB)

The focus which the Green Globes EB program places on the water category is articulated in three distinct areas: consumption, conservation, and management.[5] As with other rating

WATER

systems, Green Globes primarily assesses the environmental impact of building operations and use. The principle steps in the assessment process are filing an on-line survey, and performing an independently done on-site assessment and a post-assessment after the completion of the Performance Period. The water-related points in this rating system are 11 percent of all available points (114 out of 1,000).[6] Unlike LEED this rating system does not have prerequisites, but buildings must achieve at least a 35 percent score from all available categories to be certified.

HOW?

This rating system has three areas – Energy, Water, and Emissions and Other Impacts – under which six topics are focused on water. In order to obtain points, water consumption is obtained on an annual basis as part of a self-assessment and is a part of an on-line survey. The on-site assessment provides multiple conserving choices and on-site treatment references as optional tool tips for improvement and Performance Period assessment. Similar to other rating systems, policy and management strategies, as well as regular water audits, are parts of a successful assessment.

7.2.2 BREEAM In-Use

A water category appears in each of the three major categories of BREEAM: Asset Performance, Building Management, Occupier Management. The goal is to evaluate the environmental impact of water asset performance and then provide opportunities for improvement through two management phases. Water category credits account for 123 credits (11.1 percent).[7] The rating system utilizes a Key Performance Indicator (KPI) (Side Lesson A: Key Performance Indicators, KPIs).

Side Lesson A – 7.2.2: Key Performance Indicators (KPIs): A KPI is used by companies or organizations to evaluate performance through specific quantifiable measurements. BREEAM In-Use uses ten KPIs to assess environmental performance for these categories; energy, water, materials, pollution, land use & ecology, health & wellbeing, waste, transport, & management (see https://tools.breeam.com/filelibrary/BREEAM%20In%20Use/KN5686-BREEAM-In-Use-White-Paper_dft2.pdf).

HOW?

The Asset Performance Category creates a number of questions addressing metering and equipment efficiency, leak issues and preventions, and the reduction of main building consumption. Each issue awards a certain number of credits with respect to the level of water asset environmental impact.

The Building Management Category pushes the potential for further by addressing water metering and the consumption, refurbishment, recycling, and overall treatment of water in building operations. The rating system considers the building's features along with water management. The same issues related to management and targets with consumption rates are addressed through Occupier Management separately.[8]

7.2.3 Green Star Performance

The Green Star Performance Rating System recognizes the reality that potable water in the thousands of gallons is used daily for ongoing building operations, particularly for cooling, irrigation and as part of occupant amenity. As a responsible reaction to this reality, the water category considers and rewards the reduction in potable water use together with applicable reuse and substitution with collected rainwater or greywater (also called graywater) (Side Lesson B: Greywater). These account for a total of 12 points. Water is also addressed in the stormwater sub-category of Emissions, which offers two possible points. Thus, 14 points are available related to water usage, which constitutes 12.8 percent of Green Star's total.[9]

Side Lesson B – 7.2.3: Greywater is the gently used water that comes from baths, washing machines, sinks, and kitchen appliances. This water contains at most traces of food, dirt, grease, household cleaning products, and hair (see https://greywateraction.org/greywater-reuse/).

HOW?

The Performance Period is an essential element of this rating system, similar to LEED. The Potable Water category and credits evaluate building performance over the established baseline period of one year. Besides providing a method, the credit category has a flexibility which gives to the building owners/management the ability to set a goal and improve water use over time.

The registered project prepares and collects documentation for submittal to the Green Building Council of Australia. Upon the submittal, documentation and performance scores are evaluated by an independent panel of experts before eventual certification by a third party.[10]

Additional points are awarded under the Fire Protection Systems Testing credit where the building owner has adopted the less frequent monthly testing regime. Further points are awarded where no potable water is used for fire systems testing and maintenance.[11]

7.2.4 LEED Operations and Maintenance (O+M)

As emphasized in the starting paragraph of this chapter, the LEED O+M Water Efficiency category actually tackles three modes of water use: indoor, irrigation and water metering. The core synergy is in the linear dependence between installed water meters and tracked/documented actual or identified reduction in use, therefore indicating savings in building operations. LEED assigns 13 of all available credits to the water category. The WE section, as the name suggests, is focused on efficiency in water conservation and the reduction of potable water use, and as a consequence additionally promotes the use of non-potable and reused water.[12]

HOW?

Indoor and outdoor water use reduction is mandatory as is building level metering. As prerequisites are established, the stated periods of metering and required reductions relative to the baseline are fundamental for further credit achievements. Several options are usually at the disposal of the project teams. In order to comprehensively assess water efficiency, LEED O+M requires the presentation of site plans, plumbing fixture datasheets, alternative water sources (reuse, harvesting) and occupancy usage calculations. The credits are significantly interrelated: LEED recognizes synergies between installed water meters and actual documentation requirements, requesting and promoting building level metering and sub metering during and beyond Performance Period.[13]

7.2.5 Other Rating Systems

As an essential area of sustainability, water efficiency and use/reuse is assessed not only by most global assessment systems (also identified in Chapter 3.3), local assessment systems may be considered as an alternative for LEED O+M within LEED Lab due to their focus on water usage related to geographic relevance and/or regional reputation.

- ***BCA Green Mark.*** The Singaporean BCA Green Mark focuses on alternative and suitable sources for non-potable uses: water efficient fittings (7), a landscape irrigation system (1), reduction in water consumption of cooling towers (2.5), water monitoring and leak detection (1), water usage portal and dashboard (1), and use of alternative water sources (2). It allocates 14.5 (8.7 percent) of the total 165 points. The numerous options identified as viable sources are rainwater, greywater, AHU condensate and water recycled from approved sources.[14]

  Points are awarded based on the percentage of the reduction in potable water usage of applicable uses. Further points are awarded in case of the implementation of water metering, efficient fittings and also certain specific residential issues, such as common area washing and washing of water tanks.[15]

- ***BEAM Plus for Existing Buildings.*** Although Hong Kong has long enjoyed a reliable economic supply for most of its fresh water needs from Mainland China, the Hong Kong Green Building Council's Building Assessment Method (BEAM) nevertheless addresses the water category.

  With the increased industrialization of Guangdong Province in Mainland China there is likely to be greater competition for water, meaning that water conservation may become a significant issue for Hong Kong. BEAM Plus looks into ways to improve the utilization and conservation of water resources and allocates 23 credits plus eight bonus credits (15.5 percent) of BEAM's overall 200.[16]

  Water Conservation and Water Management are addressed through several separately identified requirements and assessment criteria. The water uses and conservation measures are evaluated together with established audit criteria. Eighty percent of Hong Kong residents are supplied with seawater for flushing toilets, creating a direct impact on the environment. The load on the environment unless proper measures are applied on the municipal level. The load on municipal treatment plants can be reduced drastically through reduced water usage and efficient fixtures.[17]

- **CASBEE.** The approach of Japan's Comprehensive Assessment System for Build Efficiency (CASBEE) is quite specific: it evaluates the environmental load of the house itself as imposed on the external environment and then the environmental quality of the building itself. The major approach to the water category is reduction of use and wastewater production.

  In the category LR2 (Resources and Materials) water is addressed in the subcategory Water Resources, which contains the criteria 1.1 Water Saving (40 percent of Water Resources) and 1.2 Rainwater and greywater (60 percent of Water Resources).[18] Water Conservation accounts for 15 percent of LR2, and 4.5 percent of the overall CASBEE-EB criteria.[19]

- **LiderA.** As mentioned before, the LiderA Rating System, in use in Portugal since 2005, is heavy in new developments. Nevertheless, the water category is recognized as an important area in ongoing building functioning and management.

  The two criteria addressed under the Resource category are Potable Water Consumption and Local Water Management.

  > The challenge for water demand in sustainability ... is based on seeking the reduction of potable water consumption (C10) by joining its good quality to more noble and demanding uses and in seeking to manage waters (C11) in the intervened areas.[20]

  LiderA allocates 8 percent (two of 43) of all credits to the water category.

- **Pearl for ESTIDAMA (PORS).** The Water Resources Master Plan for Abu Dhabi (EAD 2009) says that

  > one of the most important challenges for the Emirate is to balance water supply and demand as efficiently as possible given that the per capita consumption of fresh water is among the highest in the world and new water supplies are expensive.[21]

  Having in mind the above-mentioned urgent situation, Pearl predominantly addressed the water requirements of new construction. However, each of the credit titles under the "Precious Water" category also outline the ongoing requirements for building operations, focusing on indoor/outdoor water use reduction and monitoring, leak detection and storm water management. Pearl allocates 43 (24.2 percent) of its total 177 credits to the water area.[22]

- **Green Pyramid.** In line with some of previous rating systems, Green Pyramid of Egypt outlines requirements for new developments as well. In the same manner, the

Water Efficiency Category fosters the development of operation and maintenance strategies and plans. The goal is to reduce the use of potable water for non-critical actions like irrigation and at the same time to reduce the generation of wastewater.

Water use monitoring is mandatory for the application of this rating evaluation to any building, and 50 of a total 172 credits is available under water related areas.

Several credits are available for a certain percentage of documented improvements in indoor water efficiency, landscaping water use, cooling systems, leakage detection, and wastewater management.[23]

- **HQE Exploitation.** France's *Haute Qualité Environnementale* (HQE), or High-Quality Environmental Standard, Certification for Buildings in Operation promotes continuous progress in environmental performance. Process oriented, it is concerned with water management and building impact on local, regional and global environment.

  The certification process is divided into three areas: 1) assessing owner engagement, 2) water management and 3) user activities considered separately and jointly. In order for a building to be certified, it must satisfy a number of fundamental prerequisites and justify performances beyond current practice.[24] Within the Sustainable Use categories, Target 4 – Water (27 points) and Target 14 – Water Quality (ten points) address this area. Water Management concerns the reduction and monitoring of water consumption and Water Quality the temperature and protection of the indoor system and the management of legionella risk. Together, these total 37 points, 11.5 percent of the total.[25]

- **DGNB In Use.** Of the six main criteria groups, only three are considered in the Deutsche Gesellschaft für Nachhaltiges Bauen (DGNB) In Use scheme (developed by the German Sustainable Building Council in 2011) for the accreditation of an existing building: Ecological Quality, Economic Quality, Sociocultural and Functional Quality.

  Relating to water, the goal of DGNB In Use is to reduce drinking water requirements and wastewater volume in order to disturb the natural water cycle as little as possible. This is handled by a single criterion, domestic water consumption and volume of wastewater, which can award 20 points towards accreditation.[26]

  The presumption is that the water consumption value is strongly influenced by user behavior. Thus, qualitative measures must be considered in order to reduce the drinking water requirement.[27]

LEED O+M recognizes that the increased scarcity of potable water is a serious issue as many countries around the world face severe shortages and deteriorated water quality. Its precisely tailored prerequisites direct occupied buildings to take control

WATER

of reduction in water use. The global impacts of climate change, highly unsustainable water use patterns combined with cyclical nature of water movement, and the continued diminishing of major aquifers pose significant problems for the future. As such, students in LEED Lab must understand the specifics of water calculations since they are the prime determinant of how much their facility is ultimately consuming – both indoors and outdoors.

7.3 Credits

7.3.1 Indoor Water Use Reduction

(*Refer also to page 135 in the LEED O+M v4 Reference Guide*)

Using drinkable or potable water in buildings for purposes other than drinking creates an unnecessary depletion of a valuable resource. Reducing this overall quantity by selecting efficient fixtures, proposing alternative methods of sewage conveyance, and using recycled or reclaimed water for purposes other than human consumption can be a significant marker of efficiency in a building. Fixtures such as those with the WaterSense Label (Side Lesson C: The WaterSense Label) which use 20 to 50 percent less water than code-required levels are becoming popular and frequently specified in new buildings. Such fixtures may also be specified in existing buildings to meet credit compliance for LEED Lab projects.

Some campus facilities may have heavy process water (Side Lesson D: Process Water) usage. In these cases, the credit allows for some exemptions. However, there are cases where reclaimed water may be used in certain systems such as evaporative condensers. In general, the category optimizes efficiency in existing fixtures and builds upon this model in subsequent credits.

Tasks

The basic requirement prior to enacting further credits is to calculate the total water consumption of the facility as a 'baseline' and then determine how much potable water can be saved in subsequent credits. The LEED Lab student should start by identifying all of the sources of water consumption in the facility and then calculate the baseline water use using the online calculator, or if fixtures are already metered, document a baseline from the record of metering for one year.

☐ If the first option – Calculated Water Use – is pursued, use USGBC's online calculator (see Tools on the next page) to determine the *calculations for the water-use baseline*.

In identifying this information, consistency is important. For example, if one LEED Lab student is assigned to this prerequisite and another is assigned to calculate indoor lighting requirements, the same occupancy must be used for both. All credits must possess the same base information.

Side Lesson C – 7.3.2: The WaterSense Label was developed by the EPA to identify independently certified products that meet criteria for efficiency and performance. Some of these criteria include: providing water savings, water efficiency achieved through several different technologies, performing better than their product counterparts, and realizing water savings (see www.epa.gov/watersense/watersense-label).

Side Lesson D – 7.3.2: Process Water is nonpotable water that has been run through machinery or electrical equipment for a variety of manufacturing purposes. For example, process water can be make-up water for cooling towers or boilers. Process water undergoes extensive treatments such as desalination, distillation and microfiltration (see www.waterprofessionals.com/process-water/).

| 115

WATER

Box 7.1 Option 1: calculated water use tasks

1. Identify the following information:
   - Number of occupants _____
   - Gender distribution of occupants _____
   - Days of operation _____
   - Fixture types _____, _____, _____ etc.

There are caveats to this baseline calculation: namely, if facilities were modified after 1995 – a significant year for updating plumbing codes to more efficient standards. These can be found in the LEED O+M v4 Reference Guide on page 138. Otherwise, the next step is fairly simple.

2. Complete the **calculations for the installed fixtures**. In this case, identify the following information:
   - Fixture types _____, _____, _____ etc.
   - Flow rates _____, _____, _____ etc.
   - Manufacturer _____, _____, _____ etc.
   - Occupant use _____, _____, _____ etc.

3. Use this information in the LEED v4 Indoor Water Use Calculator (see Tools).

If the calculation is for a simply occupied building, the following equation can be used to determine both baseline and installed fixtures in lieu of the calculator (Figures 7.3 and 7.4).

☐ If the second option – Metered Water Use – is pursued because there are already meters for the water flow, follow these steps which are simplified from those in the Reference Guide.

☐ If there are no meters, pursue Option 1, install meters, and use this option for the recertification in five years. Often the Performance Period may not be an adequate-enough time frame to accommodate the installation of water meters (for at least 80% of the fixtures), their calibration, and recording them for one full year unless other meters are also being installed to pursue other credits.

If meters are already installed and tracking water consumption data, follow these steps:

Box 7.2 Option 2: metered water use tasks

☐ Determine the *water-use baseline for one year*.
☐ Retrofit existing fixtures to decrease potable water use during Performance Period.
☐ Track water use of *retrofitted fixtures for one year*.
☐ Compare the baseline data with the Performance Period data to determine the percentage reduction.

 Tools

The tools indicated here represent those which are useful for delivering Option 1 – the online calculator and the equation for deriving water-use reduction, whichever one the student chooses to apply.

WATER

STEP 1: Only if building is built before 1995, and renovated later. Determine the Baseline Multiplier (A value between 120-150%)

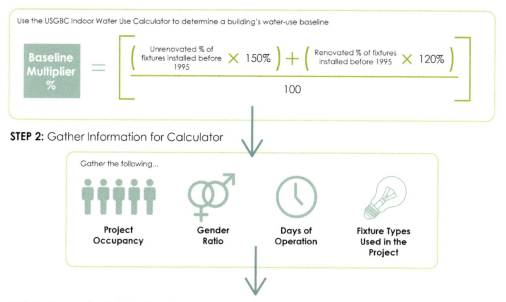

STEP 2: Gather Information for Calculator

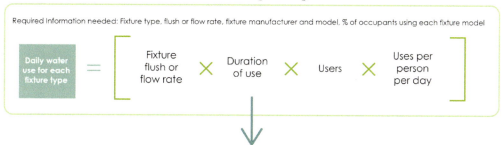

STEP 3: Complete Calculation for Baseline Existing Building

STEP 4: Complete the Same Calculation from Step 3, but for the Performance Design

STEP 5: Calculate for the Improvement from the Baseline, but taking the difference

Fig 7.3 Water Efficiency Prerequisite, Indoor Water Use Reduction: Option 1
Source: Derived from LEED O+M v4 Reference Guide. Diagrammed by Elizabeth Meyers, 2020

| 117

WATER

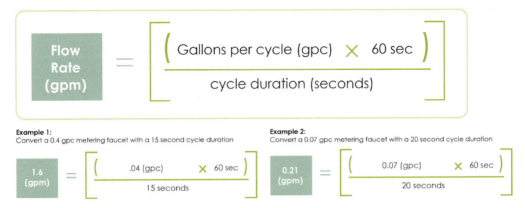

Fig 7.4 *Water Efficiency Prerequisite, Indoor Water Use Reduction: faucet flow rate conversion*
Source: Derived from LEED O+M v4 Reference Guide. Diagrammed by Elizabeth Meyers, 2020

Remember, the final calculation is a *reduction* of overall water usage, so the delta will have to be communicated in terms of how much water was *saved from the overall consumption*. This means that the total water consumption (performance) of the facility divided by its baseline case should be subtracted from 100 in order to achieve a water use reduction percentage (Figure 7.5).

- **LEED V4 Indoor Water Use Calculator**[28]

 Techniques

There are a few strategies which can improve the chances of achievement for the LEED Lab student using the following techniques:

- ☐ Take advantage of high-intensity water usage areas such as a university gymnasium or a dormitory for retrofits such as water reclamation for toilet use and low-flow fixtures.
- ☐ Utilize low-cost upgrades such as investing in automatic controls or aerators.
- ☐ Identify any state or university-wide rebates or incentives reducing the cost of upgrades.
- ☐ If metering occurs conjointly, obtain instructions from the manufacturer or facility personnel about how to document each use for a full year.[29]
- ☐ If there are systems which are non-functional, repair or stop water flow permanently.
- ☐ Identify personnel who can and will track continuous upgrades and measures after certification.
- ☐ Any new retrofit should be accompanied with manufacturer's cut sheets upon final submission to USGBC.

Table 7.1 Reduction of water use in flow fixtures

Fixture Groups							Flow Rate (GPM/GPC)			Annual Water Consumption (kGal)	
Select	Display	Fixture ID[1]	Fixture Family	Fixture Type	Default	Total Daily Uses[2]	Duration (Secs)[3]	Baseline	Installed[4]	IPC/UPC Baseline	Performance Case
FTE_Main Level	FTE Main Level	FTE_ML	Public Lavatory Facility	IPC/UPC (Conversion)	☒	51	30	0.5	0.5	2.55	2.55
T_Main Level	T_Main Level	T_ML	Public Lavatory Facility	IPC/UPC (Conversion)	☒	41	30	0.5	0.5	0	0
FTE_Basement Level	FTE_Basement Level	FTE_BL	Public Lavatory Facility	IPC/UPC (Conversion)	☒	51	30	0.5	0.5	2.55	2.55
T_Basement Level	T_Basement Level	T_BL	Public Lavatory Facility	IPC/UPC (Conversion)	☒	41	30	0.5	0.5	0	0
Total calculated flow fixture water use annual volume, baseline case (kGal)									5.1		
Total calculated flow fixture water use annual volume, performance case (kGal)									5.1		Calculate
Percent reduction of water use in flow fixtures (%)									0		

(FTE = Full Time Equivalent)
(T = Transient)

Source: USGBC

Notes:
1 Define a reference name or descriptor that can be used to identify each fixture family/type.
2 May be modified for special circumstances. Deselect the "Default" checkbox in order to insert the modified Total Daily Uses value.
3 May be modified for special circumstances. Provide a narrative in the Special Circumstances section below to justify modifications.
4 For public metering/autocontrol lavatory faucets, convert all flow rates in gallons per minute (GPM) to gallons per cycle (GPC) using a default 12-second duration of flow.

WATER

Select one of the following:

- ☐ Manufacturer or supplier data was available to verify flow rates for each flush fixture type that differs from UPC/IPC efficiency requirements.
- ☐ Manufacturer or supplier data was not available for each flush fixture type that differs from UPC/IPC efficiency requirements, so measured flush rates for at least 20% (by number of fixtures) of each type were used.
- ☐ All flow fixtures are listed as UPC/IPC (Conventional) fixture type in Table 7.1.

Table 7.2 Flush and flow summary statistics

IPC/UPC baseline annual water use (kGal)	33.66
Number of fixtures substantially completed before 1994	9
Number of fixtures substantially completed in 1994 or later	17
LEED O+M baseline multiplier (%)	134
LEED O+M annual water use, baseline case (kGal)	45.1
Calculated annual water use, performance case (kGal)	33.66
Percent water use reduction in all fixtures (%)	25.37

Note: The total calculated performance case must less than or equal to the LEED O+M baseline case to document compliance with WE Prerequisite 1

Partnering Credits

Indoor Water Use Reduction is a logical segue to this prerequisite. If the following questions may be answered affirmatively, this credit should be pursued:[30]

- ☐ Has your institution has taken measures to decrease potable water consumption in your facility during the Performance Period that exceed the baseline?

Or

- ☐ Does your facility already exceed the baseline without any modifications or additional measures?

7.3.2 Building Level Water Metering

(*Refer also to page 149 in the LEED O+M v4 Reference Guide*)

Is water use optimized in the facility which your LEED Lab course is evaluating? This prerequisite ensures that there is a record of documenting what a standard baseline of water consumption should be, and how your facility exceeds or falls short of achieving that threshold. Even if conservation is not optimal, there is room for improvement via LEED Lab! As student/personnel teams begin to understand the usage throughout the year, opportunities exist for improvement, change or modifications to fixtures or systems which can be implemented during the Performance Period.

Tasks

- ☐ Identify all water fixtures in the project. Since this credit is ineligible for an aggregated campus approach, only building-specific outlets of potable water supply should be listed:

Amenity	Quantity	Location	Meter
Lavatories			
Toilets			
Showers			
Dishwashing			
Irrigation			
HVAC			
Other processes			

☐ Track each fixture during the Performance Period. LEED Lab students can track for the full Performance Period if this time overlaps with another LEED Lab course.

Tools

There are various methods of measuring water supply. These are a few tools that can aid the LEED Lab student:

- **Water meter** (Figure 7.5). Procuring a water meter may be a good option for your institution for not only certification but for future tracking.
- **Water use calculator**[31]

Pulse water meters typically use a simple switch and magnet system to detect water flow. This type of meter can be used to detect water leakages in buildings.

The Pulse Counting Unit: contains a switch connection to exterior wires

Magnetized Dial: after completely a revolution sends a signal to close the switch

Pipe Connection

Wire Connection to Pulse Input Meter: connect these wires to a pulse input meter in order to get a pulse count

Fig 7.5 Building-level water metering: stainless steel pulse output water meter
Source: Derived from EKM Metering. Diagrammed by Elizabeth Meyers, 2020

WATER

*Side Lesson E – 7.3.1:
Downstream vs. Upstream.
Downstream refers to water
that flows away from the
source to an outlet, with a
current. Upstream is when
the water flows against
a current from an outlet
towards the source.*

 Techniques

This category is reliant on meters to calculate the overall consumption of water in the building. However, there are specific recommendations for LEED Lab that can facilitate compliance:

☐ Working with the individual facility personnel who measure or track water supply data is a great first step to this credit.
☐ Can automatic loggers be installed for future readings or is there a procedure established for reading water data manually?[32]
☐ If the project is served by a public water supply then the standard building meter can suffice for tracking.
☐ Usually, buildings use one source of potable water. However, if more than one source is used multiple meters are required for accurate tracking – additional meters should be procured prior to the Performance Period.
☐ A single meter installed downstream of multiple potable water supply systems may be used if it is upstream (Side Lesson E: Downstream vs. Upstream) of all project water uses.[33]

*Side Lesson F – 7.3.3:
The Landscape Water
Requirement (LWR):*

*Evapotranspiration
(ET) is the amount of
water lost to the atmosphere
from a plant area due to
evaporation. The word
"evapotranspiration" is the
combination of "evaporation"
and "transpiration." ETo is a
value that represents location-
based weather data and its
effect on plant water. ETo
standardizes and simplifies
the ET rate of plants and
crops at specific locations.*

*The Adjustment Factor (AF)
is a pre-set number given
by different jurisdictions,
it establishes the site's
maximum water allowance
or water budget. 0.623 is a
conversion factor that changes
water depth in inches to
water volume in gallons (see
https://bseacd.org/uploads/
BSEACD_Irr_Demand_
Meth_Rprt_2014_
Final_140424.pdf).*

Partnering Credit

Water Metering builds upon this prerequisite. If the following questions can be answered affirmatively, this credit should be attempted:

☐ There is permanently installed submetering in place for at least two water subsystems, or such additional metering will be installed during the Performance Period.
☐ There is a standard protocol for weekly data recording of water metering; or, can either automatic loggers or manual readings be installed during the Performance Period?[34]

7.3.3 Outdoor Water Use Reduction

(*Refer also to page 153 in the LEED O+M v4 Reference Guide*)

According to the Environmental Protection Agency (EPA), the average American family uses a significant amount of water simply to water its lawn. Nearly 50 percent of water used for this purpose is wasted due to evaporation, wind, or runoff, often caused by faulty methods and systems.[35] In this country, water is treated to potable standards – so the question about why it is used to be placed back into our natural environment is always at the forefront of any sustainably minded student.

When creating an efficient landscape, many factors must be considered, often indicated directly in the type of foliage and irrigation chosen for the site: e.g., the evapotranspiration rate, the density of foliage, site location, and of course the type of irrigation – if any – that is chosen. All factors combine to measure a Landscape Water Requirement or Allowance (LWR, LWA) (Side Lesson F: The Landscape Water

Requirement (LWR)). This is an estimation derived through a water budget that allows the LEED Lab team to arrive at an estimate of how much water the landscape requires, and how the team can fulfil that requirement, preferably without using potable water.

Equation: Water Requirement (gal.) = ETo (in.) × Adjustment Factor × Landscape Area (sq. ft) × 0.623

There is a considerable amount of research required to achieve this credit if there is existing landscaping on the site of your facility. This credit is particularly more successful if there is an active member of the facility personnel familiar with the species planted collaborating with your LEED Lab class.

Tasks[36]

A large part of the research mentioned includes understanding the factors of your site which contribute and don't contribute towards water use reduction. It is typical to presume that turf grass would contribute towards this credit and many LEED Lab students approach it by admitting these areas in their calculations. Although it easily can help attain reduction of a heat island or contribute towards pervious areas for stormwater runoff, it will not help achieve water reduction Turf grass requires regular mainenance and consistent watering, thus it is often often overlooked as a reason this credit may not be achieved.

Located in the Tools section below, there are resources which aid in finding this information. Critical site factors identify the following:

- Areas of foliage
- Types of foliage
- Irrigation type
- Precipitation*
- Climate*
- Peak month of water consumption*

*These are automatically included in the Water Budget calculator.

Tools

This credit is dependent on the prerequisite for water use reduction to earn points, much like the Indoor Water Use Reduction credit. Thus, it entails a few resources which can help the LEED Lab student calculate the total outdoor water consumed and also understand the site factors indicated above. The LEED O+M v4 Reference Guide provides standard equations for calculating the end result. Note the following tools which can facilitate attempting this credit:

- **Water Budget Tool calculator:**[37] The Water Budget Tool is available as an Excel platform released June 2020 by the EPA. Although EPA does not support the web application version of this tool, it still remains a relevant calculator for the purposes of this credit.[38]

WATER

- **Plant guides:**[39] Identifying the best options for foliage in your region and locale.
- **Irrigation systems:**[40] A gupersonnelide to identifying which irrigation systems are good options for your site. Remember that no irrigation may be the best option.

Techniques[41]

Side Lesson G – 7.3.3: Xeriscaping is a type of landscape design that can reduce or eliminates the need for water and irrigation. A xeriscaped landscape needs no other water than what the natural climate provides. In the western and dry regions of the United States, the practice of xeriscaping is very common (see www.nationalgeographic.org/encyclopedia/xeriscaping/).

Techniques for achieving this credit include a good analysis of existing landscaping conditions. The LEED Lab student should be working with the grounds keeping facility personnel to understand where irrigation currently occurs and if there are mitigation alternatives. Some helpful principles:

☐ A 'low-hanging fruit' option for this credit on campuses always includes evaluating current irrigation practices. Is water being introduced regularly without consideration for the current weather? Altering watering schedules is the low-budget alternative which may lead to achievement.

☐ Indigenous species can be introduced in place of annuals or non-native plants. The native plantings require no additional watering, thus can decrease your water budget. This is another low-cost alternative for LEED Lab. Xeriscaping (Side Lesson G: Xeriscaping) can be implemented where current foliage requires heavy irrigation.

☐ More intensive efforts for achievement include replacing hardscape with foliage, introducing greywater or reclaiming water systems for irrigation. These are often pursued in connection with an overall campus strategic plan.

Side Lesson H – 7.3.4: Cooling Towers: A Cooling Tower is a mechanical system that helps remove the heat from a building. Cooling towers can also be used in industrial processes to cool down water. Cooling towers use a heat exchange system to cool the system. It brings air and water in contact with each other in order to cool down the temperature of hot water. Hot water that is used from industrial processes is usually pumped directly into the cooling tower. When air and water are in contact, small portions of the water evaporate and start the cooling process. This new colder water will then get pumped back into the equipment that absorbs the heat. This loop is repeated to constantly cool down the heated equipment (see https://tinyurl.com/ywzfa38f).

7.3.4 Cooling Tower Water Use

(*Refer also to page 173 in LEED O+M v4 Reference Guide*)

What is a cooling tower (Side Lesson H: Cooling Towers)? A simple answer is a mechanism associated with removing heat from a building. On a campus, a cooling tower usually sits on top of a building or beside it depending on the facility size (Figure 7.6). It is identified by the generation of the airflow system used, the heat transfer mechanism or design.

Water is a typical medium for removing heat in a cooling tower. As it evaporates, small particles called scale (Side Lesson I: Scale) deposit in the cooling tower's mechanical system – almost like residue collecting on the inside of a dryer. If it is not removed after every wash, the dryer decreases in efficiency. Similarly, in a cooling tower, the scale gathers on the interior mechanical equipment and renders it less efficient. Regular maintenance is the key to reducing scale and creating a smoothly operating system. One way of accomplishing this is through a process called blowdown or bleed off (Side Lesson J: Blowdown). In non-chemical cooling water treatment systems (Side Lesson K: Non-chemical Cooling Water Treatment Systems), this blowdown can be directly introduced into the landscaping – sometimes in the form of irrigation (Figure 7.7). To accommodate the loss of this

WATER

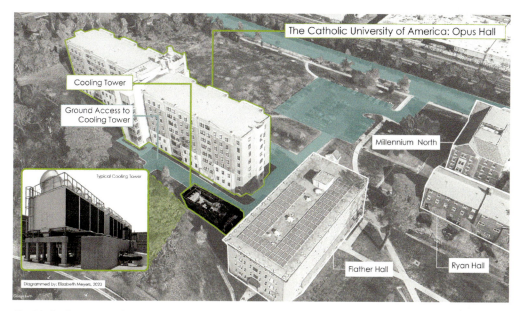

Fig 7.6 Cooling tower at Opus Hall, The Catholic University of America
Source: Diagrammed by Elizabeth Meyers, 2020

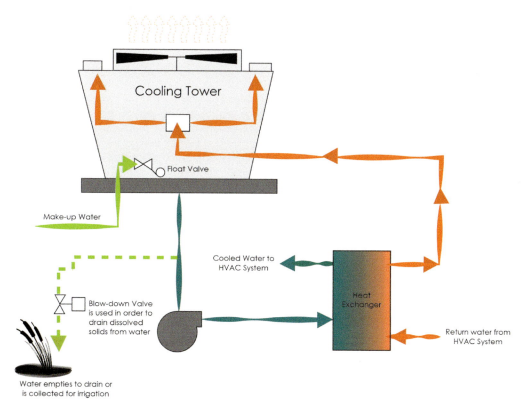

Fig 7.7 Typical low chemical water treatment system
Source: Derived from BWI Solutions, Inc, Dolphin Water Treatment System (https://tinyurl.com/4jry9vu8). Diagrammed by Elizabeth Meyers and Patricia Andrasik, 2020

| 125

WATER

Side Lesson I – 7.3.4: Scale is material buildup, commonly found inside of water pipes. Scale in water occurs when there is a high level of minerals present; calcium carbonate and magnesium are the most common scale forming minerals found in water (see https://tinyurl.com/37cysbsr).

Side Lesson J – 7.3.4: Blowdown is the water removed from the boiler. The purpose of blowdown is to reduce corrosion, scale, carryover, and other potential issues during the continuous evaporation of steam. Steam pressure in the boiler blows out the water (see www.suezwatertechnologies.com/handbook/chapter-13-boiler-blowdown-control).

Side Lesson K – 7.3.4: Non-chemical Cooling Water Treatment Systems are systems designed to treat water that runs through cooling towers and chiller condensers without the use of conventional chemicals. Examples of some of these systems include: electro-magnetic field, ultra-violet (UV), electric field, and ozone generation devices (see https://tinyurl.com/5vakr2th).

blowdown, makeup water (Side Lesson L: Makeup Water) is then added to replace evaporative losses and the volume which the blowdown originally occupied. This is why cooling towers were included in the category of Water in LEED O+M and other rating systems – they often account for large quantities of water consumption and since they are considered a process system, can be substituted for clean yet non-potable water sources or more efficient systems.

Tasks[42]

Cooling towers use water in cycles. Analyzing the cycles in terms of their maximum levels of chemical composition of calcium, alkalinity, silicone dioxide, chemical ionization and conductivity can identify waste or efficiency for optimization. The analysis of water cycles in a cooling tower is the single most critical aspect of credit achievement. Unfortunately, unless the LEED Lab student or the facility personnel is a trained analyst, a third-party evaluation is necessary. The following tasks help to accomplish this analysis in order to identify more efficient operating methods:

- ☐ Engage an expert to analyze the cooling tower cycles.
- ☐ Identify how many times water cycles efficiently without exceeding the chemical parameters.
- ☐ Adjust the cooling tower settings for these parameters.
- ☐ Optional: Add non-potable water to the system.

Tools

Cooling towers are water-conservation tools which require continuous performance evaluation. Any downtime caused by lack of maintenance is costly and careless.[43] It is therefore recommended that the LEED Lab class actively work with the facility personnel regarding this credit since expertise in analyzing the cooling tower is required. The credit is achieved by submitting the analysis online and verifying the cycle concentration maximums based on the analysis report.

Techniques

This is a credit based solely on the work of an external evaluator or internal staff person, but final submission and compliance is dependent on the LEED Lab student. The online submission will guide you to the correct documentation yet there are a few strategies which can facilitate ease of compliance:

- ☐ Research rebates available through local or campus water utility organizations for cooling tower improvements or retrofits.[44] These may abate costs or incentivize campus officials to upgrade maintenance or sustainability initiatives.
- ☐ Identify any options for non-potable water usage, or any areas of reusing blow down for irrigation depending on the purity of the water treatment system.

- ☐ The facility you are analyzing may not use a cooling tower, thus the class may determine that this credit may not be pursued.
- ☐ However, the team may opt to review the No Cooling Tower pilot credit requirement to gauge relevance to the specific project.[45]

7.4 Case Study

In 2015, The Catholic University of America (CUA)'s LEED Lab class attempted several campus Master Site credits. The same year, the United Nations deemed 2015 the International Year of Soils.[46] Soil health has a profound influence on human life, yet soils are largely overlooked when considering the ecological needs of regions, and often campus maintenance. Erosion, salinization, compaction, acidification and chemical pollutants are common threats to the condition of soils. When healthy soil is sustained, the benefits include reduced irrigation needs and improved plant development.

A combination of these facts led CUA to increase sustainability efforts by improving student and faculty awareness and understanding of sustainable land management through university-led innovative soil improvement techniques. One such endeavor was the 'Biochar Curricular & Campus Integration Plan'[47] born from LEED Lab's Innovation in Operations (IO) initiative. While this plan was captured in LEED O+M's IO category, it incorporated CUA's mission of education into the environmental improvement efforts and also synergized several credits such as Water Use Reduction, Rainwater Management, Site Improvement Plan and Site Management.

Biochar (Side Lesson M: Biochar), or Biocarbon, is a highly porous material which is made from composting food (Figure 7.8). It looks like charcoal and is produced by burning this biomass. It is perfectly suited to host beneficial microbes, retain nutrients, hold water, and act as a delivery system for a range of beneficial compounds suited to specific applications. The Biochar Curricular & Campus Integration Plan was designed to provide a direct communication and collaboration between multiple parties on campus in order to implement an ongoing composting process. With cooperation between the landscape management division, the food service division, and the CUA Student Green Club, biochar was to be made through scientific experimentation then integrated into CUA's Community Garden to serve the charitable and sustainable efforts of the CUA Green Club. The technique had an applied research and educational element that showcased student efforts through a highly valuable sustainable end-product.

There are many benefits to biochar. Because it is carbon negative, every pound of carbon added to the community garden sequesters 50 percent of the carbon that plants absorb. Additionally, studies on the soil additive have shown a high decrease in watering needs. Other benefits include water filtration and microbial improvement, which was planned to

Side Lesson L – 7.3.4: Makeup Water is water added to an industrial or mechanical system to replace the water lost from processes like blowdown and evaporation. Makeup water must be pre-treated externally before being added to the system. External treatment includes removing impurities such as hardness, alkalinity, dissolved solids, dissolved iron, and dissolved gases (see https://tinyurl.com/2xhf2jdj).

Side Lesson M – 7.3.4: Biochar is a porous charcoal that is created through the process of pyrolysis or the anaerobic thermal decomposition of organic materials in order to produce special fuels for electricity and heat. Pyrolysis is the controlled process of burning biomass which is organic material from forestry or agricultural wastes. Biochar removes carbon dioxide from our atmosphere by safely storing it. It is also a great product for landscape architecture because it helps to retain water (https://extension.usu.edu/dirtdiggersdigest/2018/what-is-biochar).

WATER

Fig 7.8 *Examples of biochar*
Source: Diagrammed by Elizabeth Meyers, 2020

be observed through improvements in plant health and plant yield.

The process of creating this product on the campus included selecting landscape maintenance materials (grass, plant clippings, etc.) from campus that will be added to on-site compost bins periodically. Once the biochar was made, LEED Lab students were set to experiment and measure quantifiable differences of water usage and plant health with plants in regular soil, soil with charcoal, soil with compost, and soil with biochar in order to measure and compare which soil additive showed the most success. Further measurements to be made were the amount of carbon sequestered, water usage, and approximate improvement in plant yields. This process was set to continue each year and had the capacity to expand composting amounts to larger volumes. Table 7.3 describes the areas of savings. All of the produce grown in the CUA Community Garden was to be given away to an interfaith, community-based organization that exists to help the poor and homeless in Washington, DC (Figure 7.9).

7.5 Exercises

The questions on the next page are derived from the aforementioned case study. Questions testing knowledge of the breadth of tools, tasks and techniques are important for LEED Lab; the investigation required in answering these exercises helps students to approach their credit assignments from a synergistic perspective.

WATER

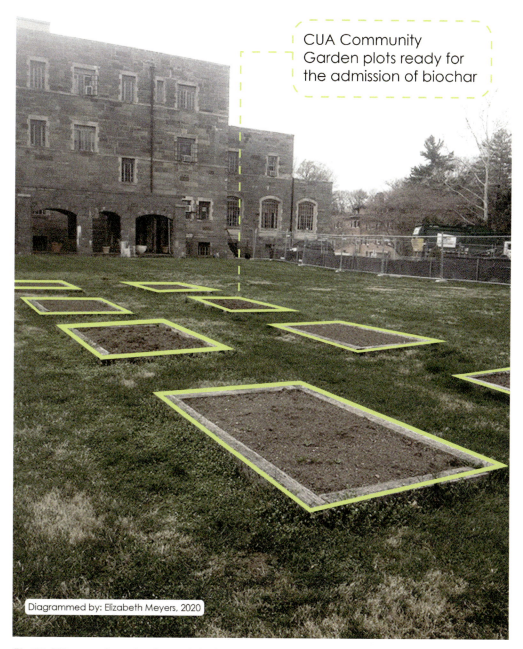

Fig 7.9 CUA community garden plots ready for the admission of biochar
Source: Photo by Patricia Andrasik. Diagrammed by Elizabeth Meyers, 2020

WATER

Table 7.3 Innovation savings chart: the building operating plan for the Crough School of Architecture and Planning

Innovation in operations	Intent/goal	Performance measurement unit
Integration of biochar in the CUA Community Garden	Generate environmental, educational, and charitable benefits through improvements in soil health by collaboration between CUA students, faculty, and staff	Amount of CO_2 sequestered Water usage by gallons

Source: Patricia Andrasik and Elizabeth Myers, 2020

Side Lesson N – 7.3.4: Micro-spray Irrigation is one of three types of Micro-irrigation (in addition to trickle and subsurface drip). These sprinklers provided water to the plants in a low-pressure system with very fine water droplets. This type of irrigation is most ideal for low volume irrigation such as greenhouses, flowers, fruits, horticultural crops, and gardens (see https://tinyurl.com/cme2v3fy).

Exercise Scenario 1

The Case Study is about the use of a product to help soil quality. What is the main element of the biochar which is associated with the outdoor water use reduction?

Exercise Scenario 2

When considering that the Case Study was originally submitted as an Innovation in Operations credit yet synergizes with other categories, which credits in the Sustainable Sites would the reduction of outdoor water use impact positively?

Exercise Scenario 3

Describe how water use reduction indoors could help to be achieved by reducing water outdoors.

Exercise Scenario 4

Using the EPA's WaterSense Budget Tool, the LWA for the city of Philadelphia with zip code 19019 based on the site's peak watering requirement is 27,342 gallons per month. If 2,000 sf of groundcover with a high-water usage and micro spray irrigation (Side Lesson N: Micro-spray Irrigation) is used in addition to biochar on a 5,000-sf site, what percent below the baseline would the credit yield?

Notes

1. US Green Building Council, "Water Efficiency (WE): Overview," *Reference Guide for Building Operations and Maintenance* (Washington, DC: US Green Building Council, 2013): 133.
2. "WE Overview," US Green Building Council, 2020. www.usgbc.org/resources/we-overview
3. Ibid.
4. US Green Building Council 2013, 135, op. cit.

5 Green Building Initiative, *Green Globes® for Existing Buildings 2007 Technical Reference Manual, Version 1.21 December 2019* (Green Building Initiative, Inc., 2019): 77–87. www.thegbi.org/files/training_resources/Green_Globes_EB_2007_Technical_Reference_Manual.pdf

6 Ibid., 15–17. Broken down, the water categories are: Hot Water (12 points), Water Consumption (30 points), Water Conserving Features (32 points), Water Management (18 points), Waste-Water Effluents (20 points), Drinking Water (lead and bacteria) (two points).

7 BREEAM, *BREEAM In-Use Technical Manual SD221 2.0:2015* (Watford: BRE Global Ltd, 2016): 16–17.

8 Ibid., 131, 263, 349.

9 Green Building Council of Australia, "Potable Water," "Fire Protection Testing Water" and "Stormwater," *Green Star – Performance v1.2 – Initial Certification Submission Template r1.* www.gbca.org.au/greenstar-manager/resources/?filter-rating-tool=101&_ga=2.107716033.213355384.1592333897-29415128.1591753717

10 Green Building Institute of Australia, *Green Star – Performance Portfolio Certification – Release v2.0* (Green Building Council of Australia, 2016): 28. https://gbca-web.s3.amazonaws.com/media/documents/green-star-portfolio-certification-guide-24062016-release-v2.0.pdf

11 Ibid., 30.

12 US Green Building Council 2013, 133–135, op. cit.

13 Ibid.

14 Singapore Building and Construction Authority, *BCA Green Mark GM ENRB: 2017: Technical Guide and Requirements* (Singapore: Building and Construction Authority, 2017): 50.

15 Ibid.

16 *BEAM Plus Existing Buildings Version 2.0 (2016.03): Comprehensive Scheme* (Hong Kong: Hong Kong Green Building Council, 2016): 33. www.beamsociety.org.hk/files/download/BEAM%20Plus%20Existing%20Buildings%20v2_0_Comprehensive%20Scheme.pdf

17 Ibid., 126.

18 Japan Sustainable Building Consortium (JSBC), *CASBEE for Market Promotion* (Tokyo: Japan Sustainable Building Consortium, 2011): 16.

19 Thilo Ebert et al., *Green Building Certification Systems: Assessing Sustainability – International System Comparison – Economic Impact of Certifications* (Detail, 2013): 60. http://ebookcentral.proquest.com/lib/cua/detail.action?docID=1075570

20 Manuel Duarte Pinheiro, *LiderA: Voluntary System for the Sustainability of Built Environments: Working Version V2.00c1* (Lisbon: Manuel Duarte Pinheiro, 2011): 42. www.lidera.info/resources/_LiderA_V2.00c1%20sumario_ingles.pdf

21 *The Pearl Rating System for ESTIDAMA Emirate of Abu Dhabi, Pearl Building Rating System: Design & Construction, Version 1.0* (Abu Dhabi: Abu Dhabi Urban Planning Council, April 2010): 116. www.upc.gov.ae/-/media/files/estidama/docs/pbrs-version-10.ashx?la=ar-ae&hash=58A67F549081968086D016E8D3757366BF29B10F

22 Ibid., 117–137.

23 The Egyptian Green Building Council, *The Green Pyramid Rating System First Edition – April 2011* (Egyptian Green Building Council, 2011): 17–19. www.eg.saint-gobain-glass.com/download/file/fid/1246

24 "What is HQE?" BeHQE, 2018. www.behqe.com/presentation-hqe/what-is-hqe

25 *Assessment Tool for the Environmental Performance of Buildings in Operation (EPB) Non Residential Buildings* (Paris: Cerway, 2017). www.behqe.com/documents/download/215

26 Thilo Ebert et al. 2013, 53–54, op. cit.

27 Ibid., 52.

28 See website: www.usgbc.org/resources/indoor-water-use-calculator (note the tab for 'Summary for D+C Rating Systems' may be deleted when submitting for LEED Lab projects).

29 Dan Ackerstein, "EBOM-v4 WEp1: Indoor Water Use Reduction," BuildingGreen, 2018. https://leeduser.buildinggreen.com/credit/EBOM-v4/WEp1

30 Ibid.

31 See note 28.

32 Ben Stanley, "EBOM-v4 WEp2: Building-Level Water Metering," BuildingGreen, 2018. https://leeduser.buildinggreen.com/credit/EBOM-v4/WEp2

33 Ibid., 150–151.

34 Ben Stanley, "EBOM-v4 WEc4: Water Metering," BuildingGreen, 2018. https://leeduser.buildinggreen.com/credit/EBOM-v4/WEc4

35 "Outdoor Water Use in the United States," United States Environmental Protection Agency, 2020. https://tinyurl.com/yufm6dss

36. Dan Ackerstein 2018, op. cit.
37. "Water Budget Tool," United States Environmental Protection Agency, 2020. www.epa.gov/watersense/water-budget-tool
38. Ibid.
39. See website: https://plants.sc.egov.usda.gov/java/
40. See website: www.cdc.gov/healthywater/other/agricultural/types.html
41. Dan Ackerstein, "EBOM-v4 WEc1: Outdoor Water Use Reduction," BuildingGreen, 2018. https://leeduser.buildinggreen.com/credit/EBOM-v4/WEc1
42. US Green Building Council, "Cooling Water Tower Use: Step-by-Step Guidance," *Reference Guide for Building Operations and Maintenance* (Washington, DC: US Green Building Council, 2013): 175–176.
43. John Neller and Dennis A. Snow, "Cooling Towers," *Plant Engineer's Reference Book*, 2nd Edition (Amsterdam: Elsevier, 2002).
44. Ashwini Arun, "EBOM-v4 WEc3: Cooling Tower Water Use," BuildingGreen, 2018. https://leeduser.buildinggreen.com/credit/EBOM-v4/WEc3
45. See website: www.usgbc.org/credits/WEpc94OM
46. "International Year of Soils," USDA Natural Resources Conservation Service Soils, 2020. www.nrcs.usda.gov/wps/portal/nrcs/main/soils/yos/
47. This credit and narrative were originally devised by Erin Sandlin, a politics major and LEED Lab student in 2015.

CHAPTER EIGHT

ENERGY

8.1 Theory

There is no doubt or surprise that energy has taken a leading role in the discussion of buildings. The US Energy Information Administration's staggering data[1] indicates that the amount of greenhouse gas emissions (GHG) (Side Lesson A: Greenhouse Gases (GHG)) from building operations is 72% (Figure 8.1). Most of this comes from electricity generation.[2]

The current worldwide mix of energy resources is weighted heavily toward oil, coal and natural gas. In addition to emitting GHG, these resources are non-renewable, their quantities are limited or cannot be replaced as fast as they are consumed. Though estimates regarding the remaining quantity of these resources vary, it is clear that the current reliance on non-renewable energy sources is not sustainable and involves increasingly destructive extraction processes, uncertain supplies, escalating market prices and national security vulnerability.[3]

With building assessment and stronger building green code enforcement applied at the onset of a building design project, designing inefficient energy-consuming structures is slowly becoming a practice of the past. Yet if the high numbers attributed to energy consumption derive from *existing* buildings, how can we ensure how much they consume – and is that efficient enough? Energy 'benchmarking' is a familiar concept that means tracking a building's energy and water use and using a standard metric to compare the building's performance against past performance and to those of its peers nationwide.[4] Such comparisons become catalysts to increase energy efficiency upgrades, increase property values, create a more desirable facility, and most importantly reduce the global carbon footprint. It is ironic therefore that mandatory energy benchmarking has only recently begun to proliferate in the US (see Chapter 1, Figure 1.2).

A large percentage of annual commercial building utility bills can be saved through low-cost Operations and Maintenance

Side Lesson A – 8.1: Greenhouse Gases (GHG) are gases in the atmosphere that trap solar heat through the absorption and emission of radiant energy. This process is known as the greenhouse effect. The main greenhouse gases located in the atmosphere are ozone, methane, carbon dioxide, water vapor, and nitrous oxide. A certain number of greenhouse gases are healthy. The average temperature of Earth's surface is 59°F, without greenhouse gases it would be 0°F. However, too much is leading to penetrations in the atmosphere and global warming. Since the Industrial Revolution, 1750, there has been a 40 percent increase in carbon dioxide CO_2 in the atmosphere. Since then, combustion of fossil fuels, oil, natural gas, and coal have been the leading cause of carbon dioxide emissions (see www.ipcc.ch/pdf/assessment-report/ar4/syr/ar4_syr_appendix.pdf).

ENERGY

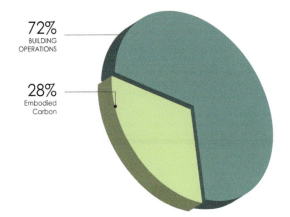

Fig 8.1 Annual global building CO_2 emissions by sector
Source: Derived from Architecture 2030. Diagrammed by Elizabeth Meyers, 2019

Side Lesson B – 8.1: Building-Level Energy Metering requires the use of energy meters or submeters to provide data on the building's total energy consumption. Energy meters track data like electricity, water, oil, steam, and natural gas. They are important tools to pinpoint and correct environmental and consumption issues in buildings (see www.usgbc.org/credits/core-and-shell/v4-draft/eap3).

(O+M) improvements, only if they are planned then implemented. Efficient building operation lowers operating costs and maintains comfort, which may lead to increased capital value, and *that* is a goal worth pursuing. This means that certain goals for operational energy efficiency for buildings must be established in a strategic plan and optimally in a campus' business plan simultaneously. To accomplish this, we must first understand the mission of the university and then involve senior management in further savings possibilities.

Building managers at campuses can apply such measures to their campuses in a few steps. First, by establishing policies, equipment and procedures; second, by measuring success within a Performance Period; third, by tracking the performance of their equipment; and fourth, by taking measures to increase renewables and decrease global impacts of future operations. The LEED Operations and Maintenance (O+M) rating system outlines these steps through a series of prerequisites and credits in the category of Energy and Atmosphere which makes implementation into the campus strategic plan simpler. The prerequisites are best started from Building-Level Energy Metering, since this is the foundation of accomplishing the majority of the remaining prerequisites in LEED's Energy category (Side Lesson B: Building-Level Energy Metering) (Figure 8.2). However, there is an array of other building assessment systems which present very similar variables for achieving energy efficiency on campus.

8.2 Comparison

The LEED O+M Energy and Atmosphere (EA) category approaches energy from a holistic perspective, addressing energy use reduction, energy-efficient design strategies, and renewable energy sources. Such sub-categories are also an integral part of many sustainability rating systems worldwide – not only with the aim of reducing ongoing energy costs but also encouraging the use of more efficient building systems and rewarding the use of renewable energy generation. In fact, rating systems for building operations and maintenance with respect to energy are primarily based on benchmarking the building's relative energy performance and redirecting the current dependence on fossil fuels as

ENERGY

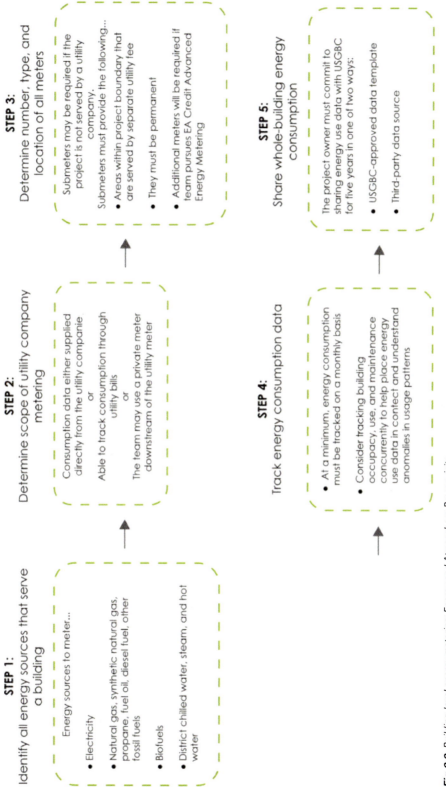

Fig 8.2 *Building-level energy metering: Energy and Atmosphere Prerequisite*
Source: Derived from USGBC LEED O+M v4 Reference Guide. Diagrammed by Elizabeth Meyers, 2020

| 135

ENERGY

Fig 8.3 Global sustainable existing building sustainability assessment tools for energy

Source: Created by Milan Glisić and Patricia Andrasik, 2017

the primary energy source[5] (Figure 8.3). Energy sub-categories may be termed 'credits' and within the credits, 'points' are awarded in LEED. The *approach* to evaluating their weight is, however, unique to the rating system being used (Figure 8.4). Let's take a closer look within the energy categories of the global top O+M rating systems mentioned in Chapter 3.3 which may be used within the LEED Lab course, particularly if LEED is not a common rating system within the specific locale.

8.2.1 Green Globes for Existing Buildings (EB)

Utilizing an online survey, on-site assessment, and post-assessment to achieve certification and recognition, the Energy category in Green Globes EB comprises 350 credits, exactly 35 percent of the credits of this rating system. Unlike LEED, it includes transportation and carbon dioxide (CO_2) and addresses ozone (O_3) depletion under the area of Emissions, Effluents and Pollution Control.[6]

Energy is the most important area affecting the sustainability of a building according to Green Globes; therefore, it carries the highest point value of all the assessment areas within the Existing Building (EB), New Construction (NC) and Sustainable Interiors (SI) programs.[7]

ENERGY

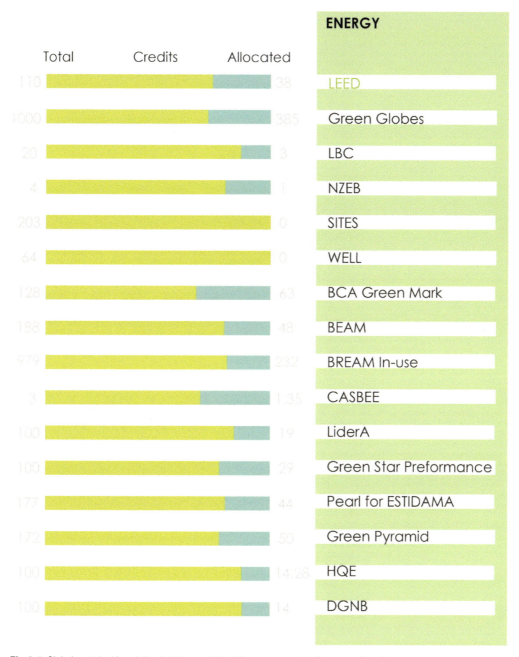

Fig 8.4 Global sustainable existing building sustainability assessment tools: comparison for energy
Source: Created by Milan Glisić and Patricia Andrasik, 2017

HOW?

With almost 20 different area topics under the Energy category alone, a Building Assessor should be supplied with answers, required data and benchmarking according to the Energy Star® energy target by the staff, similar to what is required of LEED: energy consumption figures and/or bills for the 12-month period, Energy Star® documentation, an energy audit conducted during the last three years, and a written plan that address energy management issues, budget,

| 137

training and maintenance schedules. There should be evidence of maintenance schedules and preventive maintenance as well as built drawings/specifications and/or O+M manuals for lighting systems, boilers, chillers, controls, hot water heaters and other energy efficiency features. A copy of a contract to verify credit for Renewable Energy Certificates (RECs) or other documentation to verify credit for Green Energy are required, along with a building envelope assessment and/or specification for envelope components.

8.2.2 BREEAM In-Use

Out of the three-part evidence-based process used to certify a building, BREEAM In-Use (BIU) attributes the greatest emphasis on its Energy category. Part 1 (Asset Rating with 26.5 percent), Part 2 (Building Management Rating with 31.5 percent) and Part 3 (Organizational or Occupier Management Rating with 19.5 percent) are all dedicated to assessing Energy,[8] which comprises almost 26 percent of the entire credits of this rating system. Similar to LEED, BREEAM's concept for energy reduction is "to manage and monitor energy consumption and to encourage the use of equipment that supports the sustainable use and management of energy in the asset."[9] Unlike LEED, there are 30 specific credits out of which 28 are given points based on calculations from an 'energy model' via an asset energy calculator.

HOW?

In-Use Buildings Assessors in Part 1 first assess an asset energy score via the performance of end-use components like heating, cooling and ventilation informed by their subcomponents (solar gains, efficiency of heat generation, building fabric, etc.). A final score – the Asset Rating – is calculated by adding together the weighted end use component scores. The assessment is then submitted to the BREEAM In-Use (BIU) team for either an unverified score, or towards certification.

Part 2 is attained by providing the building users appropriate guidance which enables them to understand and use the building via a Building User Guide. This is a Technical Overview of the building and its environmental strategy with respect to energy, water and waste efficiency policy-strategy and how users should engage with and deliver the policy-strategy. Part 3 is attained by documenting the organizational policies, reports and objectives as they pertain to energy, water and waste, and if targets have been met.

8.2.3 Green Star Performance

As with the preceding rating systems, the energy category in Green Star comprises the majority of the 'points' this rating system affords (14.6 percent) but does not span the breadth of subcategories. In fact, there are only two categories – Greenhouse Gas Emissions and Peak Electricity Demand. The former establishes a baseline from historical GHG emissions data of comparable buildings within the market and compares it against a building's current operations during a specific Performance Period. It accounts for 23 of the 24 points in this category, and therefore requires refined calculations of the implementation of strategies and actions to measure and reduce a building's operational energy. In Peak Electricity Demand, points are awarded where the building's peak demand performance meets the network's peak demand ratio benchmark. Both reward the users on decreasing reliance on energy supply and GHG emissions of the grid.[10]

HOW?

Similar to LEED, this rating system – used in Australia – is based on the assessment of a building's operations during a one-year 'Performance Period.' The Green Star rating is determined by comparing the number of available points achieved. After the project is registered, documentation of all the energy strategies for the two credits is accumulated along with the desired credits in other categories and is submitted to the Green Building Council of Australia (GBCA). An independent panel of energy experts assign a score to the categories, and third-party certification (valid for up to three years) may ensue.[11]

8.2.4 LEED Operations and Maintenance (O+M)

The Energy and Atmosphere (EA) category is almost 35 percent of the total categories of the LEED O+M rating system. This category recognizes that the reduction of fossil fuel use extends far beyond the walls of the building. It provides opportunities for renewable energy application, demand response engagement and also global warming potential (GWP) reduction. Projects are encouraged to evaluate the existing building benchmarking and 'commissioning' – a set of discrete tasks that include monitoring system performance, executing functional tests and verifying equipment operation.[12]

HOW?

The majority of energy credits are achieved through the auditing and commissioning process in LEED as self-assessments which are verified via reviewers at GBCI. Inefficiencies and opportunities for improvement are identified and prioritized, generally according to cost and benefit. The many no- and low-cost items often uncovered during the initial auditing process can generate savings and efficiencies without significant capital investment.

In an operationally effective and efficient building, the staff understands what systems are installed and how they function. Metering and ongoing commissioning do not add to what the staff does on an ongoing basis and they allow staff to track energy use and identify issues consistently. Staff must have initial and continuous training so that they can learn new methods for optimizing system performance.[13] Credits like those which measure GWP, renewables and renewable energy credits (RECs), may not be a part of ongoing operations and are achieved through specific calculations indicted in the LEED O+M v4 Reference Guide.

8.2.5 Other Rating Systems

Beyond the most propagated global assessment systems used to evaluate energy (also identified in Chapter 3.3), other

ENERGY

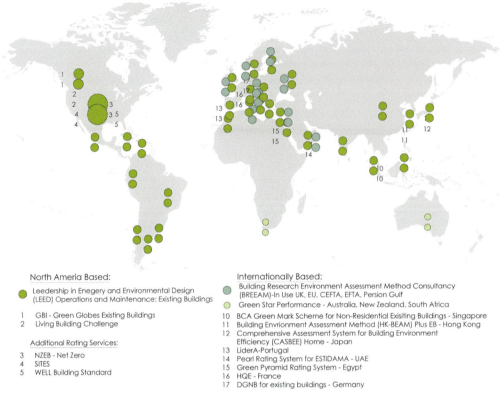

Fig 8.5 Global assessment systems: North America based and internationally based
Source: Unknown. Redrawn by Elizabeth Meyers, 2019

contenders may be considered as a substitute rating system for LEED O+M's Energy category due to their geographic relevance and/or regional reputation (Figure 8.5).

- **Building and Construction Authority (BCA) Green Mark.** Launched in 2005 to guide Singapore's construction industry in the creation of environment-friendly buildings, the BCA Green Mark rating system allocates 40 of the total 128 available points of the Non-Residential Existing Building Criteria to energy, comprising 31 percent of the total point weight.[14]

- **BEAM Plus for Existing Buildings.** From its inception in 2010, Hong Kong Green Building Council's (HKGBC) existing building rating system – called Building Environmental Assessment Method (BEAM) – has targeted the owners of Hong Kong's existing buildings to adopt green building management. The category Energy Use comprises 24 percent of the overall credit weighting of this rating system, but also is evident in the Management category as 'energy management', 'staff training' and 'building users involvement' which contributes towards the energy score.[15]

  This rating system offers either a Comprehensive or Selective scheme in which energy is measured towards certification: the former is designed for previously certified BEAM New Construction-Certified buildings, or buildings that will be upgraded, while the latter provides a certification for each aspect on an individual aspect and enables applicants to implement assessments that match their building's needs.[16]

- **CASBEE Existing Buildings (EB).** Japan's Comprehensive Assessment System for Built Environment Efficiency (CASBEE) has various scales of evaluation from detached residences to cities where it incorporates energy metrics into various scales of evaluation from detached residences to cities. The Building Design/Existing Building (BD/EB) path is the best comparison to LEED O+M, targeting existing buildings with an energy operations record for at least one year after completion while serving as an asset value tool. The LR1 is the energy category and is divided between thermal load (30 percent), natural energy utilization (20 percent), efficiency of building service system (30 percent), and efficient operation (20 percent). LR1 comprises 20 percent of the overall weight of CASBEE-EB categories.[17]

- **LiderA.** The prime rating system of Portugal since 2005 encompasses different building types at various stages, including plan and design, construction and management simultaneously. This means the assessment of energy occurs in terms of reducing any unnecessary consumption evidenced by an Energy Certification (C7), evaluating Passive Design Performance (C8) such as bioclimatic design, and harnessing renewable sources, which will translate into low-carbon emissions through measuring the Carbon Intensity of Existing Equipment (C9). Together, these comprise 17 percent of the overall credit weight.[18]

- **Pearl for ESTIDAMA (PORS).** Specifically designed for the arid climate of the Middle East, the Pearl Operational Rating System (PORS) released in 2013 is the alternative to LEED O+M in the United Arab Emirates. It assesses the built-in features and operational performance of an existing building,[19] and verifies operational performance to ensure the design's intent has achieved its stated objectives.[20] Energy is integrated into four main sections: Integrated Operation Management, Systems and Procedures, Building Performance and Operations + Maintenance. Different building uses have a different number of credit points for each particular component. This is intended to reinforce the critical issues that should be addressed for particular building use.[21]

- **Green Pyramid.** The Egypt Green Building Council's Green Pyramid Rating System (GPRS) which originated in 2010 currently only focuses on guidelines for new construction in Egypt, although much of the energy criteria closely aligns with existing building evaluation. Objectives include an evaluation of the mechanical, electrical and plumbing (MEP) systems inventory, reduction of energy demand, minimizing appliance loads and addressing peak loads. The Energy Efficiency category comprises 50 points, 29 percent of all available credits within this rating system.[22]

- **HQE Exploitation.** France's Green Building Council developed *Haute Qualité Environnementale* (High Quality Environmental) Standard (HQE) Certification for Buildings in Operation (HQE Exploitation) in 2005 as their counterpart

ENERGY

to BREEAM In-Use and LEED O+M.[23] This scheme is divided into three certification areas for valuing, respectively, the engagement of the owner, the manager and the use, independently or jointly.[24] Being process-oriented, HQE is focused on ongoing management and efficiency of ecological energy use and uses an auditor who inspects the building and analyzes the documentation. The Sustainable Use set of targets handles existing building, and Target 4 addresses energy with two subcategories of monitoring energy consumption and responsible purchasing and usage, comprising a total of 19 points, 6 percent of the total points available.[25]

- **DGNB In Use.** Developed by the German Sustainable Building Council in 2011, existing or renovated buildings are considered in the Deutsche Gesellschaft für Nachhaltiges Bauen (DGNB) In Use scheme in only three categories: Ecological Quality, Economic Quality, Sociocultural and Functional Quality. In this rating system, energy use is addressed by two credits in the Ecological Quality category under the Utilization of Resources and Arising Waste subsection: Non-renewable primary energy demand (30 pts) and Total primary energy demand and proportion of renewable primary energy (20 pts). Together, there are 50 possible points dedicated to energy, roughly 9 percent of the In-Use total.[26]

As we can see, there are many similarities and differences between these rating systems and LEED O+M. Many – particularly those native to a certain international locale – may be creatively utilized and perhaps even provide a stronger platform for an academic application. Yet the strength of LEED O+M as the basis for LEED Lab exists due to USGBC's established protocol of offering a certification pathway for such a collegiate application. At this time LEED O+M is the rating system we can break down with certainty and experience to describe credit achievement responsibilities required for this course. Navigating first the Prerequisites of the Energy category, then the credits and the points – often in that order – it becomes clear how LEED O+M becomes a logical conduit for the education of not only students, but also facilities staff and administrators.[27] Understanding the theory of this category and its comparison to other rating systems, let's explore how to accomplish specific prerequisites and credits.

 ## 8.3 Credits

8.3.1 Best Management Practices

(*Refer also to page 189 in the LEED O+M v4 Reference Guide*)

Creating Best Management Practices (BMPs) is one of the most important prerequisites to meet when establishing a building's energy sustainability. It begins with identifying best practices to ensure that the proper procedures are in place. It is a 'top-heavy' endeavor relying chiefly on those personnel in charge of facilities, documented by LEED Lab students. In many cases, students help to confirm that BMPs are in fact in place and are being implemented on campuses.

Identifying best practices to ensure that the proper procedures are in place is one of the most important prerequisites to meet when establishing a building's energy sustainability. However, many building personnel do not actively engage in a building's energy diagnostics as a part of their daily maintenance or operations, which is why LEED Lab can become a conduit for the education of not only students, but also of facilities staff and administrators via this prerequisite.

The LEED O+M v4 Reference Guide identifies eight steps towards credit completion which can be condensed into two main steps for LEED Lab: (1) Creating a comprehensive document (O+M Assessment) that outlines or documents existing best practices, and/or can help to identify new best practices for operations and maintenance procedures; (2) Establishing an energy baseline for efficiency and consumption via a report. The reason for the truncation of steps is simple: some campuses have established documents which do not need these specific steps, and some do not have any documents – or have disorganized documents which require many more intermediate steps than what is listed. Regardless of the state of documents, students require a deeper explanation of what these are. This two-step combination provides a good basis to identify opportunities for reduction with all parties responsible for participating in the course.

8.3.1.1. The O+M Assessment

This is the initial document that outlines best practices for operations and maintenance procedures. It may already exist or may be facilitated by LEED Lab students in conjunction with facility personnel. It is best completed simultaneously with the establishment of the energy baseline since identifying how much energy a building consumes impacts the measures used to optimize it, and vice versa.

The Assessment does not have a specific template derived from a reference standard like we will see with the Energy Baseline in item 2 below. Rather, it is a combination of diverse data documentation requirements of the campus' operational procedures. This comprises:

- **Current Facility Requirements (CFR).** According to the Building Commissioning Association (BCA), the CFR defines the Owner's current operational needs and requirements for a building. It should note any integrated requirements such as controls, fire and life safety, warranty review, service contract review and security systems.[28] In the case of LEED Lab and LEED O+M assessment, the sustainable systems are key components.
- **Space requirements.** A List of rooms and spaces.
  1. *Functional* – A schedule of how the rooms and spaces are occupied and cleaned.
  2. *Operational* – A schedule of temperature, humidity and lighting level setpoints (targets) for the rooms and spaces.
- **Existing building drawings.** Also termed 'as-builds', these are technical 2D or 3D architectural working drawings which graphically describe the building systems. They

ENERGY

are typically located in the set of drawings used for construction with the labels of "E" or "M" preceding a page number such as E101, etc. (Figure 8.6).

- **Operations and Maintenance Plans (O+M Plans).** An O+M Plan familiarizes the employees, users and managers of a facility with the systems and activities which are required to operate it. There are many various templates, forms and methods of accomplishing this (Table 8.1), and industry standards vary based on the type of organization and building being evaluated. Common elements to these plans, and the requirements of LEED are similar and constitute the following:
- **Systems Narrative.** A few paragraphs describing an overview of plumbing, electrical and mechanical systems.
- **Building Systems Description.** More extensive written details of how the plumbing, electrical and mechanical systems work, along with their current status.
- **Building Operating Plan (BOP).** A roadmap that can describe to anyone in detail how to operate the building during standard and after-hours using the data from the items above.
- **Sequence of Operations (SOP).** The engineer's instructions outlining the process how items A and B react to external conditions.
- **Preventative Maintenance Plan (PMP).** Description of regularly executed work on functioning systems equipment in order to reduce the possibility of failure.

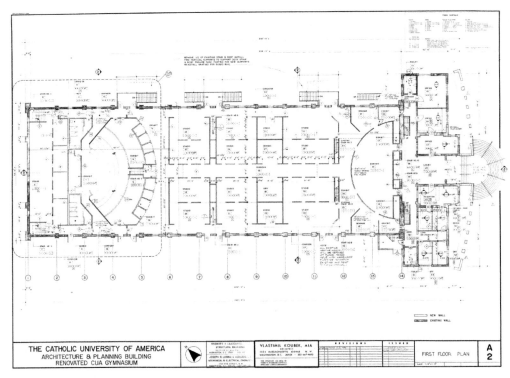

Fig 8.6 Existing building plan

Source: Plans drawn by Vlastmil Koubek, AIA

Table 8.1 Sample of an O+M plan

Required	Typical for building	Grad Studio Set A AHU-1	Koubek (Lecture Hall) Set B AHU-2	Main Studio AHU-3 and 4	Computer Lab AHU-3	1st Floor Offices AHU-5 and 8	2nd Floor offices/ Locraft AHU-6 and 7	Elevator Room AHU-9	Basement AHU-10 and 11	Paintbooth AHU-12
Air temp. for cooling and heating seasons and set points	Occupied: 70F; Unoccupied summer: 74F To Unoccupied winter: 70F	Same	Same	Same	Same	Same	Same	Same	Same	Same
Humidity	AHU coils provide dehumidification while running. No control system except for temperature	None	None	None	None	None	None	None	None	None
Dehumidification	See above	None	None	None	None	None	None	None	None	None
Pressure relationship	(+) 0.03 pressure differential between building interior and outside environment	Same	Same	Same	Same	Same	Same	Same	Same	Same
Filtration	MERV 13	MERV 13	MERV 13	MERV 13	MERV 13	MERV 13	MERV 13	MERV 13	MERV 13	MERV 13
Ventilation	Fixed outside air damper position	Same	Same	Same	Same	Same	Same	Same	Same	Same
Outside air	a	a	Meets ASHRAE 62.1–2007	a	a	a	a	a	a	100 percent OA Unit
Sound and noise level	c	c	c	c	b	b	b	b	b	b

(Continued)

ENERGY

Table 8.1 (Continued)

Required	Typical for building	Grad Studio Set A AHU-1	Koubek (Lecture Hall) Set B AHU-2	Main Studio AHU-3 and 4	Computer Lab AHU-3	1st Floor Offices AHU-5 and 8	2nd Floor offices/ Locraft AHU-6 and 7	Elevator Room AHU-9	Basement AHU-10 and 11	Paintbooth AHU-12
Normal operating schedule for occupancy[d]	24/7	Same	Same	Same	Same	Same	Same	Same	Same	Same
Weekend schedule[d]	24/7	Same	Same	Same	Same	N/A	N/A	Same	Same	Same
Holiday schedule[d]	24/7	Same	Same	Same	Same	Same	Same	Same	Same	Same
Process and office equipment status after-hours	e	None	None	None	None	e	e	None	None	None
Process and office equipment status during holiday hours	e	None	None	None	None	e	e	None	None	None
Process and office equipment status during scheduled maintenance shutdowns	e	None	None	None	None	e	e	None	None	None
Cleaning schedules	M-F=7am to 3pm	Same	Same	Same	Same	Same	Same	Same	Same	Same

ENERGY

Lighting levels[f]	Artificial lighting available for all spaces. Levels between 10fc and 300fc	Daylight levels between 10fc and 300fc	No daylight. Artificial lighting levels between 30fc and 150fc	Daylight levels between 10fc and 200fc	No daylight. Artificial lighting levels between 30fc and 150fc	Daylight levels between 10fc and 180fc	Daylight levels between 10fc and 200fc	No daylight. Artificial lighting levels between 30fc and 150fc	Daylight levels between 5fc and 150fc	No daylight. Artificial lighting levels between 10fc and 300fc

Source: Data from the Crough Center documentation for the LEED O+M certification, 2014

Notes:
[a] It meets 10 CFM per person.
[b] This is an independent isolated room with sound attenuation measures added to the wall construction.
[c] This building comprises mainly open studio spaces due to the nature of the architectural studio profession. Sound and noise levels are expected to be high and are modulated with moveable panels for pin up space flexibility.
[d] Classroom buildings on campus are powered up at 7am and powered down at 7pm unless the school requests otherwise. However, this particular building, the Crough Center for Architecture Studies, operates 24/7 based on the nature of the school's architectural mission, thus is in a different operational case all together.
[e] All equipment is equipped with a power saver mode, or is turned off by staff in the respective space.
[f] During the Performance Period, automatic shut off switches were installed for the main overhead pendant lighting due to a sufficient amount of daylight being available.

| 147

ENERGY

The documents required of the O+M Assessment frequently overlap. It is perfectly acceptable to combine them as long as they are each clearly identifiable to the LEED reviewers, applicable to the facilities staff, and understandable to students. Students should be able to garner clear answers to questions such as: "Is the energy-consuming equipment efficient?"; "Is there a need to replace old equipment with greener alternatives?"; "Is energy procurement sustainable and reliable?"; "Are there plans to replace equipment?" Such questions draw the staff personnel into their learning experience.

8.3.1.2. The Energy Baseline

The Energy Baseline is an overall account of existing systems. It is the tool used for 'benchmarking,' (described at the start of this chapter) – a common practice of comparing buildings within weather fluctuations, use types, occupancy and other metrics in order to gauge the energy efficiency of a building.[29] The energy baseline – called the Level 1 Energy Audit – is most easily accomplished through a protocol which has already been established by the American Society of Heating and Refrigeration Engineers (ASHRAE), a global society advancing technical measures in buildings.[30] Its mission is "to advance the arts and sciences of heating, ventilating, air conditioning and refrigerating to serve humanity and promote a sustainable world"[31] and is the global source of both technical and educational information, making the organization *the* primary provider of heating, ventilating, air conditioning and refrigerating guidance in the United States.[32]

ASHRAE's Level 1 Energy audit format, formally referred to as *Procedures for Commercial Building Energy Audits*, 2nd Edition, results in the data necessary to establish the current usage of a building. This includes a physical audit, analysis and report of hours of operation, quantity of people who regularly occupy spaces, types of equipment, fuel end-use breakdown, space types, whole building energy and water usage data, and an Energy Star Statement of Energy Performance. Any audit documentation done within five years prior to the Performance Period may be supplemented to reflect current conditions (Table 8.2 and Figure 8.7).

Both the O+M Assessment and the Energy Baseline provide solid documentation that can maintain continuity to facilitate future energy adjustments and will guide decisions about energy goals and performance improvement. They may be localized to one building and/or in conjunction with an overall site assessment of the campus as LEED Lab facilities.

There exists an interesting irony on some campuses – many times, personnel who are responsible for operating and maintaining the building receive the least information about its energy use. This is because the system which *tracks* energy may be independent from the system which *manages* it. The entire process of usage, tracking and adjustment can be termed the Energy Accounting Feedback Loop (EAFL) (Figure 8.8). When Tasks and Tools are applied to accomplish the critical feedback loop (EAFL) enacted with the baseline and assessment, a solid protocol for energy efficiency management is very achievable.

ENERGY

Table 8.2 Combined fuel end-use breakdown for the Crough School of Architecture and Planning. Data from the Crough Center ASHRAE Level 1 Walkthrough documentation for the LEED O+M certification, 2014, developed by Westlake Reed Leskosky

		Conversion factor to kBtu
Electricity – Input Unit 1	kWh	3.412142
Steam – Input Unit 2	kBtu	1
Input unit 3		0
Combined Output Units	kBtu	1
Building Gross Floor Area	44,700	
Floor Area Units	ft^2	

	Input energy units			Combined energy use	
End Use	kWh	kBtu	%	kBtu	%
Space heating	35,161	162,723	–	282,697	9%
Cooling	175,805		–	599,872	19%
Ventilation	193,386		–	659,860	21%
Water heating	26,371	12,248	–	102,230	3%
Lighting	272,498		–	929,802	29%
Refrigeration	43,951		–	149,967	5%
Office equipment	8,790		–	29,993	1%
Computers	70,322		–	239,949	8%
Miscellaneous	52,742		–	179,963	6%
Total estimated	879,026	174,971	–	3,174,333	100%
Historical billing	889,780	765,395	–	3,801,451	
Percent of actual	98.8%	22.9%	0%	83.5%	
Total per ft^2	19.7	3.9	–	71	

Source: WRL Engineering, 2011

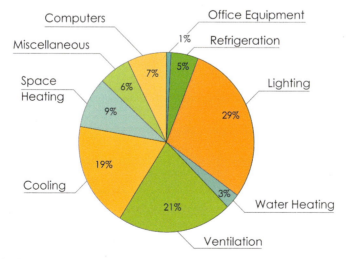

Fig 8.7 *Combined fuel end-use breakdown for the Crough School of Architecture and Planning*
Source: Data from the Crough Center ASHRAE Level 1 Walkthrough documentation for the LEED O+M certification, 2014, developed by Westlake Reed Leskosky, and WRL Engineering, 2011

ENERGY

Fig 8.8 Energy Accounting Feedback Loop (EAFL)

Source: Diagrammed by Elizabeth Meyers, 2020

Tasks

It is critical to know prior to these analyses who is responsible for the EAFL and if such a procedure exists. If there is not already an EAFL, addressing it with the building staff, management and/or any external consultants involved with the building will inherently occur when conducting the Assessment and Baseline. If such an individual or team does not exist, discuss the potential for such an appointment within the in-house staff. A skilled staff member who can implement a full EAFL, and even long-range goals of an energy plan, is a necessity if these analyses are to be seriously considered in any long-term sustainable impacts on the building or campus.[33] With this guidance, the two analyses can be accomplished easily and quickly. Certain Tasks are required for not only the creation but also upkeep of these documents:

I. The O+M Assessment

　A. **Current Facility Requirements (CFR)**

　　☐ *Establish* a meeting with a skilled staff member who can implement a full EAFL – it may be the same person responsible for managing the building to identify current documentation and assistance to complete the items below. This can be a representative from the facilities department or a designated individual.

　　☐ *Obtain* the existing building drawings as explained in "(1) The O+M Assessment."

　　☐ *Refer* to the floor plan of the building in the existing building drawings.

　　☐ *Fill in* the matrix provided here in this template. List all of the rooms and spaces first, then include the Functional and Operational schedules as described under "(1) The O+M Assessment."

　B. **Systems Narrative + Building Systems Description** – A written description of the building's various systems:

　　• Writing a combination of the Systems Narrative and Building Systems Description is an efficient way to save time when describing equipment. It includes capacities, flow rates and set-points for cooling, heating, ventilation, lighting, building control systems and any renewable or non-renewable energy systems. The Narrative must be documented during the Performance Period of the project.

C. **BOP** – Building Operating Plan (or The Owner's Operating Requirements) – A roadmap to the building's various systems:

- Write the Building Operating Plan as a bird's eye overview of the Systems Narrative and Building Description. The document should describe the occupancy and cleaning schedules, noise levels, air filtration, ventilation, pressure and reiteration of the setpoints for the occupied spaces of the building. The Plan must be enacted and be engaged for the duration of the Performance Period of the project.

D. **SOP** – The current Sequence of Operations for the building's various systems:

- Write the SOP for all building systems protocols from start-up to shut-down – typically provided by the original systems engineer. Facilities staff should possess this document in some form already since it is necessary to operate existing equipment.
- The document provides a solid understanding of how systems operate and how they are controlled. In a new building project, it is typically included in the specifications of the project, but in an existing building it should be written – if not already created – to identify the Description of Control (garage fans, handling units, etc.) and the Mode (occupied, unoccupied). Cooling, heating, ventilation, lighting, building control systems and any renewable or non-renewable energy system are examples of systems to be included. The SOP must be documented during the Performance Period of the project.

E. **PMP** – A Preventative Maintenance Plan of how to minimize decline of the building's various equipment:

- The PMP is a written schedule which most buildings already possess. The focus of the Plan in this assessment is to assure that equipment is properly operated to avoid premature equipment failure which would lead to increased maintenance – and to prevent energy waste due to improper scheduling, controls or ill-functioning equipment. Specifics of the PMP include:
    - Forms for data gathering/tracking procedures for actual v. expected performance.
    - Description of work
    - Frequency of equipment check
    - Method of addressing non-conformance/ Method of resolving performance deficiencies (When equipment does not meet the expected performance criteria, it may indicate a need for

ENERGY

- improved or more frequent maintenance procedures (cleaning, lubricating, etc.) or different operating parameters (setpoints, lockout strategies, capacity control strategies, etc.)).
- How to monitor operating sequences and schedules
- Activities critical to the energy efficiency of the building (such as monthly cleaning of rooftop PVs).
- The plan must be enacted and engaged for the duration of the Performance Period of the project.

2. *The Energy Baseline: ASHRAE Level I Energy Audit – The ASHRAE preliminary energy use baseline walkthrough audit*

This Baseline document can be conducted for a cost using external consultants or as additional time spent for existing facilities building personnel. Alternatively, energy utility companies may provide a no-cost audit that can be supplemented with information from the building personnel to achieve ASHRAE requirements. Regardless of the vehicle for completion, it should be accomplished in collaboration with LEED Lab peers.

The ASHRAE Level 1 Walkthrough Energy Audit, as defined in the ASHRAE Procedures for Commercial Building Energy Audits, should be scheduled in advance with building personnel and engineers. An energy audit is an investigation into the depth of energy savings. ASHRAE offers three various audit levels but only two of them are addressed in the LEED certification. The levels are consecutive: as audit complexity increases, so does thoroughness of the site assessment, the amount of data collected, and the detail provided in the final audit report, yielding higher energy savings.

The LEED O+M certification *requires* a Level I: Site Assessment or Preliminary Audit. It identifies no-cost and low-cost energy saving opportunities and offers a general view of potential capital improvements. It may be cost effective while conducting this Level I audit to consider administering Level II: Energy Survey and Engineering Analysis Audit as an option for the Existing Building Commissioning Analysis credit, which identifies no- or low-cost opportunities and provides energy efficient recommendations aligned with capital-intensive energy savings opportunities. This audit includes an in-depth analysis of energy costs, energy usage and building characteristics and a more refined survey of how energy is used in your building and is thoroughly explained later in Chapter 8.3.5.

The third level of evaluation is Level III: Detailed Analysis of Capital-Intensive Modification Audits (sometimes referred to as an "investment grade" audit) and although not formally required for any LEED credit, provides solid recommendations and financial analysis for major capital investments. In addition to Level I and Level II activities, Level III audits include monitoring, data collection and engineering analysis.[34]

The Audit comprises an on-site survey of the existing building to identify any problems or needs that may affect the building energy use and/or the operation cost and a review of the current building operation and maintenance plan with at least one year of utility bills collected for building energy use analysis.

ENERGY

In consultation with the building personnel/engineer, and using the ASHRAE template:

A. Produce a preliminary review of energy use:
   - ☐ Collect metered data
   - ☐ Calculate EUI and compare to similar facilities (use Portfolio Manager®, see Tools further on) (Figure 8.9):
     - ☐ Establish online account at www.energystar.gov/buildings/facility-owners-and-managers/existing-buildings/use-portfolio-manager
     - ☐ Add a Property (your site)
     - ☐ Enter metered data (Energy and Water Data from meters)
     - ☐ View Results and Progress
     - ☐ Assess energy efficiency improvement potential.
B. Conduct a site assessment (Figure 8.10):
   - ☐ Interview building staff
   - ☐ Visually inspect building systems and equipment
   - ☐ Compile energy use breakdown with building staff and/or maintenance crew knowledgeable about the systems.

ENERGY STAR® Statement of Energy Performance

70
ENERGY STAR® Score[1]

CUA Sustainability Initiative
Primary Property Function: K-12 School
Gross Floor Area (ft²): 44,700
Built: 1919

For Year Ending: October 31, 2012
Date Generated: April 15, 2014

[1] The ENERGY STAR score is a 1-100 assessment of a building's energy efficiency as compared with similar buildings nationwide, adjusting to climate and business activity.

Property & Contact Information

Property Address	Property Owner	Primary Contact
CUA Sustainability Initiative 620 Michigan Avenue, NE Washington, District of Columbia (D.C.) 20064	( ) -	( ) -

Property ID: 3604885
Unique Building Identifier:
Project ID 1000015979 Access ID 3976829842201245 Block Title:
CUA Sustainability Initiative Block ID 1000015977 LEED for Existing Buildings

Energy Consumption and Energy Use Intensity (EUI)

Site EUI	Annual Energy by Fuel		National Median Comparison	
71 kBtu/ft²	Electric - Grid (kBtu)	2,999,364 (94%)	National Median Site EUI (kBtu/ft²)	86.1
	District Steam (kBtu)	174,971 (6%)	National Median Source EUI (kBtu/ft²)	261.1
			% Diff from National Median Source EUI	-18%
Source EUI			Annual Emissions	
215.4 kBtu/ft²			Greenhouse Gas Emissions (MtCO2e/year)	395

Fig 8.9 *Statement of Energy Performance for the Crough School of Architecture and Planning*
Source: Data from the US Environmental Protection Agency (EPA), ENERGY STAR Portfolio Manager Tool, April 2014, page 1, and the Crough Center documentation for the LEED O+M certification, 2014

| 153

ENERGY

Fig 8.10 *LEED Lab students are introduced to the central plant by a staff operator indicating the operation of the boilers to produce steam*

Source: Photo by Patricia Andrasik, 2015

C. Create an energy and cost analysis consisting of the following:
- ☐ Indices for energy cost, energy demand, energy use and an energy reduction target
- ☐ A final report on no-cost or low-cost energy conservation measures and/or building operation improvements
- ☐ An abbreviated financial assessment related to implementing these measures or improvements.

3. *The EAFL*

After conducting the Baseline and Assessment during the Performance Period, prioritizing which improvements are most cost-effective is easy. The process becomes a catalyst for insight into low-cost and inexpensive changes which we like to call the 'low hanging fruit'; procedures or changes which improve building operation rather than expensive, technology-intensive improvements which impact capital. For example, adjusting controls such as lighting and thermostats regularly prove to save a significant amount of overall energy. Behavioral modifications of occupants are also valued as cost- and energy-saving measures. Ensuring this process exists and identifying a person to oversee the EAFL is not required in any formal LEED O+M deliverable; in LEED Lab however it is a necessary accompaniment to the Baseline/Assessment pair to ensure that a process is in place for subsequent LEED Labs and recertification. Logically this also becomes a long-term benefit to the campus' operational goals.

A. Identify a staff team or individual to permanently oversee and administer the EAFL and serve as a liaison to LEED Lab students.
B. Develop an EAFL spreadsheet to include:
    ☐ Energy Usage – A competent record of how much energy the building uses, derived from Energy Baseline results.
    ☐ Energy Tracking – The instruments and process responsible for documenting energy metering data.
    ☐ Energy Adjustment – The process of how energy metering data is applied to systems.
C. Generate one document (EAFL) from the three items above using the Baseline and/or Assessment. This must be understandable to both LEED Lab students and administration. Include:
    ☐ The person(s) responsible for Tracking and Adjustment of systems
    ☐ A finance mechanism for identifying 'low hanging fruit'
    ☐ Long-term measures.

Tools

There are certain tools that are critical to learn as a part of accomplishing the Tasks further on (or at least in understanding them) which are not fully explained in general certification protocol. It is common for the operation of these tools to be delegated to building staff engineers, personnel, or outside consultants. However, learning how to diagnose building performance is the main focus of LEED Lab as a research course and the education gained by knowing what each tool accomplishes is advantageous to any participant.

A. **BAS.** The Building Automation System (BAS) or Building Management System (BMS) is a central control platform for a building's major systems that has been in existence for many years. It controls the facility's equipment such as lighting systems, air-handling units, and fan coils, and alerts building personnel in the event of an irregularity or in an emergency. Although the BAS automates control of these systems (Figure 8.11), it cannot provide building energy efficiency optimization feedback and adjustment simultaneously without some intervention of personnel and more analytics. A modern BAS can integrate energy meters to track and control data simultaneously (via the Energy Management System or EMS).

ENERGY

B. **EMS.** The modern Energy Management System (EMS) is a cloud-based platform for visualizing and tracking usage of various forms of energy (gas, electric, etc.) and similar facility analytics that are fed through meters installed in the central plant or mechanical equipment base. Data is used by personnel to streamline repairs and O+M by allowing a probing view into usage patterns and is frequently used to calibrate the BAS for the ultimate goal of facility performance optimization. The EMS comprises two parts: the actual software and the point meters (Figures 8.12, 8.13 and 8.15). The points for data collection fed through energy meters are often permanent in the EMS, making it difficult to take measurements in areas other than where they are installed. For these scenarios, another device is appropriate – the Data Logger.

C. **Data Loggers.** Data Loggers are portable battery-powered devices which track lighting, relative humidity, electrical current, temperature, occupancy and other variables, and which are capable of storing a multitude of data at any programmable frequency of easily understood data. Loggers may be USB, Web-based, wireless or Bluetooth compatible. They are ideal for buildings which do not possess an EMS system, or as supplements for buildings with limited points of metering to optimize equipment operation. The data logger and operating software can be procured with a relatively inexpensive budget and may require integration into the BAS depending on the EAFL goals.

Fig 8.11 A Building Automation System (BAS) or Building Management System (BMS)

Note: This diagram illustrates the connections in this type of system

Source: Diagrammed by Elizabeth Meyers, 2020

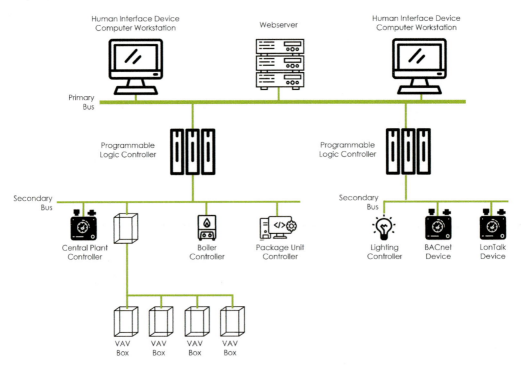

ENERGY

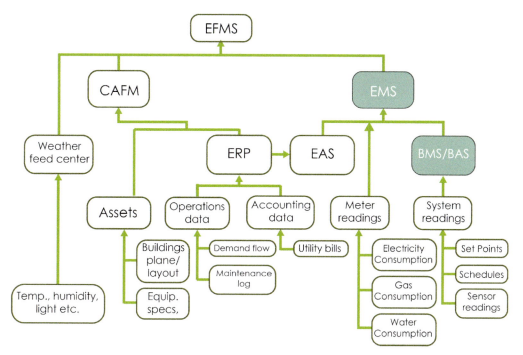

Fig 8.12 Energy and Facility Management Software (EFMS) for buildings
Source: Diagrammed by Elizabeth Meyers, 2020

Fig 8.13 Energy and Facility Management Software (EFMS) for Buildings Feedback Loop
Source: Diagrammed by Elizabeth Meyers, 2020

Techniques

Sometimes the energy *tracking* system is independent from the energy *management* system on campuses, although they are symbiotic in function. The tracking detects usage, and usage impacts tracking; in other words, the ability to increase efficiency

| 157

or conservancy in usage is identified via tracking, and tracking indicates success or failure in doing so.

The techniques of accomplishing the tasks of this credit include:

- ☐ detecting and troubleshooting both maintenance and operational problems
- ☐ record keeping to track operating changes, improvements and deficiencies
- ☐ informing building personnel with critical information for comparing past and current conditions of equipment and system performance.

How and by whom are these tasks completed? Best Management Practices include procedures that need to be conducted by knowledgeable in-house personnel or an external third person or organization. The following are recommendations for LEED Lab students to help accomplish such goals with their partnering facility personnel:

- ☐ Outsourced analyses often require a mechanical engineering or energy management firm with a service contract that clearly states which measurements and tasks are related to efficient operation. The benefits include the experience the firm may possess and the consistency by which the analyses are provided to the building staff. However, this technique also means a financial obligation to conduct the initial and ongoing analysis and having to check the firm's work.
- ☐ If outsourcing is not an option, in-house staff may be used to complete the Tasks. The main benefits of this technique include saving money (which would otherwise be given to an external party) and providing the in-house staff with a direct – not 'second hand' – knowledge. Additionally, in-house building staff conducting these Tasks may find this to be a good training exercise for the entire crew. The cons of using in-house staff are that their job descriptions may not warrant such analyses, they may possess limited experience to conduct the tasks, and the quantity of personnel may not be sufficient.
- ☐ A third option includes hiring an external party for a limited time to train in-house staff. This option proves to be a win-win scenario with minimum upfront expenditures. Staff can repeat the assessment themselves in the future for subsequent building analyses, are less likely to disable systems that they don't understand if they are trained and are more able to manage the systems in the event that an external contract expires. For example, when personnel are trained to understand the metering software and how it impacts preventative maintenance or sequence of operations (SOP) of the building systems collectively, they are better able to control occupant satisfaction and save energy simultaneously; they can customize software control 'logic' for their building BAS or EMS, and also their equipment control for a variety of conditions,

- such as occupancy, heat load of the interior and external temperature fluctuations.
- ☐ Since it is essential to continually track all energy and water usage data for the building as it is required during certification and recertification, creating an account in the US Environmental Protection Agency, Energy Star® Portfolio Manager (Portfolio Manager) is a critical technique for documentation. An Energy Star® *rating* necessary for certification may be established once all data is uploaded. This rating is established by comparing the analyzed building performance against performances of similar-type buildings available within the Portfolio Manager. The Portfolio Manager tool may also aid project teams in establishing energy use and cost reduction targets.
- ☐ When metered data is available *prior* to commencing the Performance Period, the ASHRAE Level 1 Walkthrough Energy Audit is recommended to evaluate whether and how the energy improvements for this prerequisite may be achieved during the Performance Period. Energy conservation measures (ECMs) recommended by the walkthrough report can greatly improve the building's energy use prior to starting the Performance Period to achieve the best results for this prerequisite.
- ☐ Although students of LEED Lab can easily establish accounts or follow existing accounts of their buildings' performance on Portfolio Manager, the ASHRAE Level 1 Walkthrough Energy Audit should be performed by members of the building operations staff or by an independent member.
- ☐ The audit team may include the owner, property manager, building engineering staff, energy auditor, a controls contractor and other maintenance staff or necessary contractors to perform testing and balancing procedures.
- ☐ A list of capital improvements may also be identified within the ASHRAE Level 1 Walkthrough Energy Audit; however, it is not required for this prerequisite. When O+M changes are made during this process – as they always will be in order to maximize energy efficiency – regular performance tracking provides timely feedback on the effect and success of those changes on equipment efficiency.
- ☐ There are also techniques which can assist in the implementation of this prerequisite. At the onset, identify which professionals or stakeholders within the organization should be contacted for gathering information prior to developing the initial required documentation.
- ☐ Explain to the building's management how this strategy fits into their mission by developing specific goals from these documents.
- ☐ The LEEDuser forum identified in Chapter 3.3.1.6.3 Resources is a particularly great repository for tips and information about this prerequisite.

ENERGY

 Partnering Credit

The Commissioning Credit Trio explained in Chapter 8.3.4 serve indirectly as the Partnering Credits to Best Management Practices Prerequisite. If the following questions may be answered affirmatively, these Partnering Credits may be attempted:

1. ***Existing Building Commissioning – Analysis***
   a. Does an existing building commissioning plan exist, or will one be executed within the Performance Period?
   b. Does an ASHRAE Level 2 Energy Survey exist or will one be conducted within the Performance Period?

2. ***Existing Building Commissioning – Implementation***
   a. Has the existing building commissioning plan been executed to include
      ☐ Low cost improvements phased within a five-year plan or less?
      ☐ Training personnel?
      ☐ Tracking / Verification for systems?

3. ***Ongoing Commissioning***
   a. Is your team able to verify with building personnel that your institution have an established commissioning plan?

8.3.2 Minimum Energy Performance

(*Refer also to page 201 in the LEED O+M v4 Reference Guide*)

This prerequisite synergizes with most of the energy credits and impacts many other LEED categories. There is no need to simulate data for this prerequisite because it entails the actual metered data from tracking the energy consumed by the systems and occupants of the existing campus building. Most energy meters on campuses are owned by the university or institution, and as evidenced by the Best Management Practices, require regular tracking in order to obtain data and to adjust needs to fulfill both energy conservation and occupant satisfaction goals. *Calibrating meters, tracking energy, and obtaining an energy score are the main goals of this prerequisite;* if Best Management Practices have been fulfilled in their entirety in the previous prerequisite, obtaining a Minimum Energy Performance is very easily accomplished.

Minimum Energy Performance is focused on the function of one primary instrument: the energy meter. This is different from a utility meter. Your building may have a utility meter which tracks consumption of water, gas or electricity by the utility company to which a bill is paid. For example: In Washington DC, a major electric utility company is Potomac Electric Power Company (PEPCO). Buildings on the CUA campus typically have electricity meters owned by PEPCO located on the outside of the facility where service personnel may access them. However, these types of meters do not inform the occupant where that energy is being consumed, who is using the energy or how it is being consumed; these are not the sub-meters necessary for acquiring this prerequisite. Energy sub-meters make use of individual water, gas or electricity meters and break them down further from the

ENERGY

Fig 8.14 A utility submeter system in a building
Source: Mraybin/iStockphoto.com

utility meter, so specific usage may be monitored (Figure 8.14) (more is discussed in the Tools section of this chapter).

The LEED O+M v4 Reference Guide presents seven steps for success to fulfill Minimum Energy Performance. However, a shortened version is necessary for LEED Lab, particularly since most of these 'activities' tend to occur simultaneously with the Best Management Practices or have already been considered earlier in this book – such as establishing the Performance Period in Chapter 4.3.

1. Calibrating

Is your institution connected to a District Energy System (DES), meaning that there is a central plant either on campus or in the vicinity providing energy to your building? Or is your building associated with an independent energy system or off-grid sustainable alternative energy system? Either scenario requires energy meters for electricity, steam, gas or any form of energy production which runs your building. If these energy meters are already installed by a third-party such as a utility company, they are presumed to be running efficiently and do not require calibration. However, if energy meters are owned and operated by your campus facilities staff, they need to be 'calibrated.'

Calibrating energy meters simply means that the instrument should be functional to a set engineering tolerance of operability. More often than not, the manufacturer of the instrument calibrates it prior to installation and may be called back prior to the Performance Period to ensure it is calibrated. Calibration is different from 'qualification,' which ensures the quality of an instrument model range, because of its design and manufacturing process: although a specific meter may be qualified because it is part of a model range and never lose this qualification, it may drift out of calibration.[35]

ENERGY

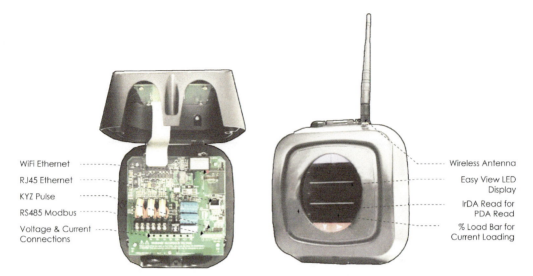

Fig 8.15 Shark Meter diagram

Note: This is an example of a device that can track energy consumption. The Shark Meter can track pulses from multiple meters

Source: Derived from ElectroIndustries Gauge Tech. Redrawn by Elizabeth Meyers, 2020

Side Lesson C – 8.3.2: HVAC&R Systems (heating, ventilation, air conditioning, and refrigeration) are used to regulate the indoor air quality and temperature. Refrigeration systems are typically designed by mechanical engineers for commercial and industrial buildings. These systems serve cold storage warehouses, ice rinks, supermarkets, convenience stores, and food processing facilities (see www.ccsgroup. net.au/what-is-hvacr/).

2. Tracking

The ongoing collection of metered data retrieved from the energy meter comprises tracking. Tracking begins after establishing from Chapter 4.3 (1) a Performance Period in order to know when to begin and end tracking, and from the previous Best Management Practices Prerequisite (2) an Energy Star® Portfolio Manager Profile. Tracking is accomplished as either a standard internal or external operational protocol – gathered by facilities staff or a third party – on a regular basis.

The basic concept of tracking is to introduce a digital platform which reads the meters. Often this platform is cloud-based and records pulses of energy sources (e.g., electricity, water or gas) in increments of 60, 30 or 15 minutes. Once the pulses are recorded on the digital platform, they may be read through that platform or in some cases a more user-friendly graphic platform. The LEED Lab student, facility staff person or building authority reads the tracked data and optimally makes decisions based on the trends of that data. For example, if there is a constant surge in electricity consumption when the building is not typically occupied, there may be an issue with the setpoints of the heating, ventilating, air-conditioning and refrigeration (HVAC&R) system (Side Lesson C: HVAC&R Systems), or simply negligence! LEED Lab students should become familiar with this concept of tracking by becoming actively involved with actual data collection (Figure 8.15), or at least observation, since it will be their responsibility for uploading this data to the Portfolio Manager platform and obtaining the Energy Star® Performance Rating.

ENERGY

3. Obtaining

Obtaining a performance benchmark is the last – and often the most exciting – goal to accomplish. LEED Lab students engaged in tracking energy are eager to know where their building stands in energy efficiency, and an actual metric can relate that information. There are several ways of attaining a benchmark. All entail comparing your building to other similar buildings once energy data is logged into Portfolio Manager for 12 months during the project's Performance Period (see Best Management Practices or Tools). To aid in your decisions, let's review some basics of the Environmental Protection Agency (EPA)'s and USGBC's tasks for accomplishment.

Tasks

USGBC relies on the Portfolio Manager Tool to accomplish this prerequisite. Basically, Energy meter data is manually input from the meter into the online Portfolio Manager® platform, and a score is assessed which will be used in this prerequisite.

1. ***Calibrate.*** The procedure to set up tracking equipment should not be attempted by the uneducated LEED Lab student, but rather by a qualified professional or the manufacturers' representative due to its technical complexity.
2. ***Track.*** Record the building energy use for a full year of continuous operation in Portfolio Manager so that there is data collected for the various seasons of the year. This task is derived from Best Management Practices, where the establishment of metered data is introduced.
   Produce a preliminary review of energy use:
   ☐ Collect metered data
   ☐ Calculate EUI and compare to similar facilities (use Portfolio Manager®, see Tools further on) (Figure 8.16)
   ☐ Establish online account at www.energystar.gov/buildings/facility-owners-and-managers/existing-buildings/use-portfolio-manager
   ☐ Add a Property (your site)
   ☐ Enter metered data (Energy and Water Data from meters)
   ☐ View Results and Progress
   ☐ Assess energy efficiency improvement potential
3. ***Obtain.*** There are several conditions your buildings must meet to attain an energy benchmark, and USGBC has prepared various paths for accomplishment. How do you know which path your building should follow? The diagram on page 205 of the LEED O+M v4 Reference Guide, also referred to in Figure 8.17, is a good resource for navigating this choice in conjunction with reading this section.

The two 'cases' introduced in this credit may be difficult to interpret to the novice. An abbreviated summary will help the LEED Lab student navigate which option may be the best to follow.

Case 1 in a nutshell

EPA's Energy Star® label is the trusted, government-backed symbol for energy efficiency helping us all to save money and

| 163

ENERGY

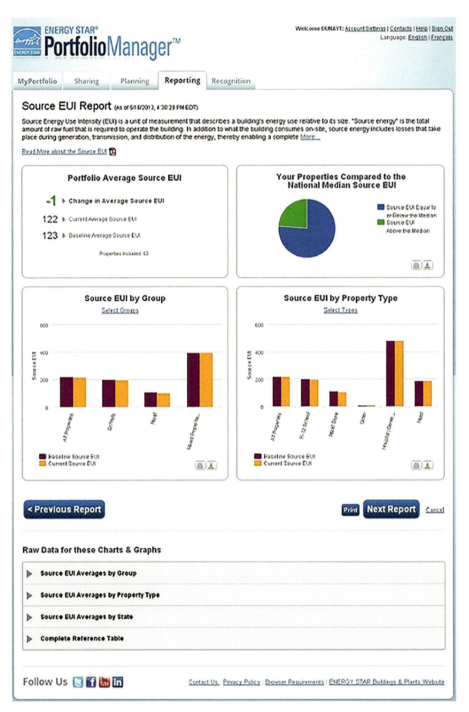

Fig 8.16 Energy Star Portfolio Manager

Source: Data from the Crough Center documentation for the LEED O+M certification, 2014

ENERGY

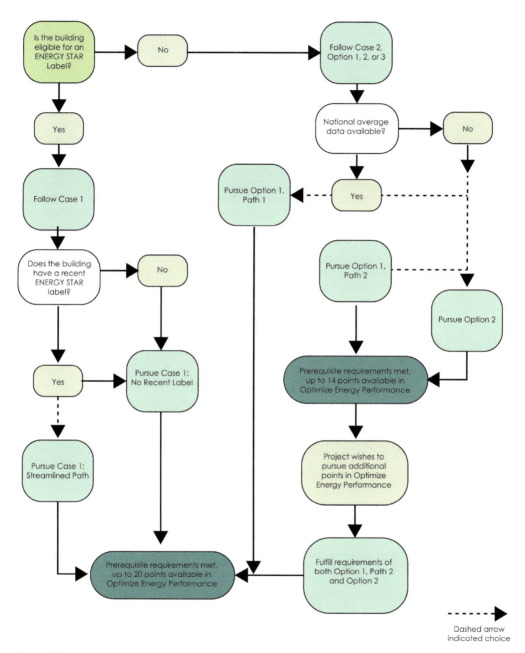

Fig 8.17 *Energy and Atmosphere Prerequisite: minimum energy performance diagram*
Source: Derived from LEED O+M v4 Reference Guide. Redrawn by Elizabeth Meyers, 2020

ENERGY

to protect the environment through energy-efficient products and practices.[36] It is a certification which, based on the national average, indicates that a building uses 35 percent less energy and causes 35 percent fewer greenhouse gas emissions than comparable buildings across the country.[37]

The Label allows teams to lock in its energy rating for 12 months, even if the building's performance fluctuates or if changes to the Energy Star® algorithm affect the benchmark.[38] Although there is no cost to apply for certification, the application must be verified and stamped by a licensed Professional Engineer (PE) or Registered Architect (RA). This means this person will sign off on your reported property use characteristics (including square footage of the building), your energy data, and whether each of the indoor environment criteria has been met.[39] Achieving a score of at least 75 (from a range of 1–100) when energy performance data is input into the Performance Manager tool will earn this label. If an Energy Star label is earned within 12 months before your Performance Period ends, the project may pursue "Case 1" for fulfilling this prerequisite.

The project may have an Energy Star® label older than one year, or cannot obtain a label because it is outside[40] of the US. In this scenario, Portfolio Manager® should similarly be engaged for a minimum of 12 months for tracking within the Performance Period. If the project earns a rating of 75 before the end of the Performance Period, it still may pursue "Case 1" for fulfilling this prerequisite.

Case 2 in a nutshell

Most buildings are eligible to receive an EPA Energy Star® rating because they contain typical functional spaces such as banks, hotels, offices and retail establishments. If space types in your building are not typical – for example if more than 10 percent of your spaces are in a classification of use which is not found in the Portfolio Manager® tool.[41] The project is considered to be ineligible for an Energy Star® rating. The project may still obtain the prerequisite via Portfolio Manager® by demonstrating that its building energy is 25 percent more efficient than similar buildings either compared with national energy data (Option 1, Path 1), at least three similar buildings (Option 1, Path 2), or compared with three years of its own performance (Option 2).

Despite these options, a uniquely functioning building not possessing previous energy data may be challenging to benchmark. Creativity in this case is required. For example, if your campus building is not listed in EPA's Property Types eligible to receive a 1–100 Energy Star® score, comparative buildings and performance metrics may be accessed on the Commercial Buildings Energy Consumption Survey (CBECS)[42] (see Tools below) and Case 2, Option 1, Path 1 may be the vehicle for achievement. There are many similar examples of challenging benchmarking found on LEEDuser.[43]

Tools

Energy meters tied into the EMS require an external mechanism to disseminate data to a broader audience for evaluation, transparency and energy efficiency awareness; namely, so buildings may be benchmarked and compared to similar buildings in similar environments. This comparison is expressed in common units of energy per square foot per year or Energy Use Intensity (EUI).

1. **ARC Performance Platform.** Referring to Chapter 3.3, the Performance Platform called ARC is able to track energy by logging in data directly from the campus' energy meters. There are two approaches to tracking performance. (1) Enter utility bills directly to the online platform. (2) Report your data and utility bills through ENERGY STAR Portfolio Manager. Portfolio Manager syncs directly with ARC.

2. **EPA Energy Star® Portfolio Manager®.** In 2007, the Environmental Protection Agency (EPA) launched the Energy Star® Portfolio Manager®, a free online tool used to log data from energy meters and bills in order to benchmark the performance of one building or a whole portfolio of buildings. The Portfolio Manager® is linked to a regularly updated repository of similar building types through CBECS in order to establish a benchmark. CBECS is a national sample survey that collects information on the stock of US commercial buildings, including their energy-related building characteristics and energy usage data (consumption and expenditures)[44] and is administered through the US Energy Information Association, an agency within the Department of Energy. For most types of commercial buildings, including buildings on campuses, the 1–100 Energy Star® score is based on CBECS. This includes schools, hospitals, correctional institutions and buildings used for religious worship, in addition to traditional commercial buildings such as stores, restaurants, warehouses, and office buildings.[45]

3. **Labs 21.** In 1999, the US Environmental Protection Agency (EPA) and the US Department of Energy (DOE) collaborated to create "Laboratories for the 21st Century" (Labs21) initiative. It is a free, voluntary web-based benchmarking system designed to improve the environmental performance of US laboratories. Labs 21 is similar to Portfolio Manager® but compares the energy use of specifically *laboratory* buildings with that of similar facilities in the USA. It contains owner-submitted energy use information from more than 200 laboratory facilities and allows users to benchmark energy performance in terms of whole-building metrics (e.g., BTU/sf-yr).[46] The tool is hosted by Lawrence Berkeley National Lab (LBNL) and is maintained by LBNL and the Benchmarking Working Group of the International Institute for Sustainable Labs (I²SL).[47] Like Portfolio Manager®, it requires an initial set up with facility data such as climate zones, occupancy and function.[48]

Techniques

Since there is very little besides metering and documenting that metering which needs to be accomplished for this prerequisite,

ENERGY

Side Lesson D – 8.3.2: District Energy System (DES): Most buildings operate energy using boilers and chillers. Boilers heat the water so it can be used as energy by the natural state of the heated water, or via steam. Chillers do the opposite – they cool the water so it can be used for air conditioning, or to cool water before it is introduced to other systems in the building or the public utility. DESs are arrangements of hot and cold-water pipes that are located underground so that individual buildings can be heated and cooled more efficiently than having a multitude of chillers and boilers. DES may be used to supplement various systems such as chilled water used for electricity or fuel, hot water/steam used for electricity or fuel or combined heat and power (CHP). If your building is dependent on DES, LEED requires projects to "prorate" the energy consumption. Prorating simply implies proportionally assessing the systems' energy. The prorated energy that is required to be entered into Portfolio Manager® is a ratio of the DES energy inputs to the DES energy generated. This ratio is then multiplied by the thermal energy measured by the meters and accounts for any losses such as when the energy is lost into soil that surrounds the pipes. It is recommended that an internal staff member who operates these systems or an external consultant guide your documentation if your building uses DES.

techniques simply revolve around specifics of that metering and benchmarking. Here are some helpful suggestions:

- ☐ It is critical prior to beginning this prerequisite to verify that metering equipment is installed per manufacturers' recommendations if the facility personnel is installing them, and to confirm that each building has an individual whole-building energy meter regardless if it produces its own energy, is tied to a central plant, or uses a district energy system (DES) (Side Lesson D: District Energy System (DES)) (Figure 8.18).

The type of energy should be indicated. For example, does the facility have CHP?

- ☐ It is required to calibrate meters prior to the Performance Period.
- ☐ CHP is an energy efficient technology that generates electricity and captures the heat that would otherwise be wasted to provide useful thermal energy – such as steam or hot water – that can be used for space heating, cooling, domestic hot water and industrial processes. CHP can be located at an individual facility or building or be a district energy or utility resource. CHP is typically located at facilities where there is a need for both electricity and thermal energy.[49]
- ☐ During benchmarking, profile accounts of all projects, regardless of the tool used for benchmarking, must agree to be shared with USGBC. Although not specified in the LEED O+M v4 Reference Guide, in Case 1, buildings lacking a signed statement from a professional architect or engineer will require additional documentation submission for data and performance verification.
- ☐ In Case 2, projects that have at least 10 percent of their gross area used for the function of being a laboratory should use the Labs21 tool.[50] An Energy Star® rating is not offered for such functions, thus Case 1 does not apply.
- ☐ In Case 2 projects, data may be 'normalized' within the Portfolio Manager tool (Side Lesson E: Normalization). Both actual and required 'normalized' data as well as the normalization methodology must be provided. At the project team's discretion, projects may be further normalized to account for inconsistencies in operating hours, occupancy, number of computers and other characteristics in order to clarify the conditions for both the LEED Lab student and also the GBCI Reviewer.
- ☐ It is essential but frequently overlooked to continually update all energy consumption data, number of occupants and vacant spaces and space type changes within the project Portfolio Manager® Account by the LEED Lab student not only *during* the Performance Period but also for recertification. This will occur while recording the building energy use for a full year of continuous operation so that various seasons of the year may be sampled. After the project receives LEED certification, data-recording period must start for recertification.

ENERGY

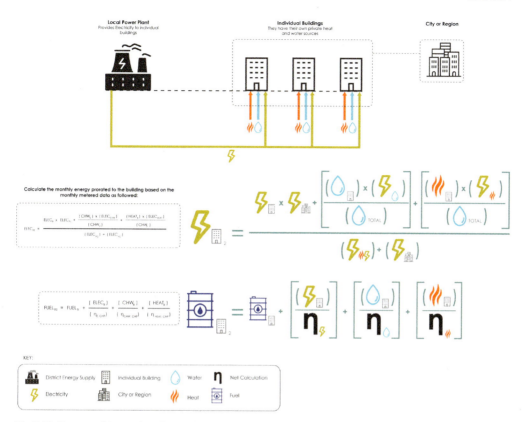

Fig 8.18 Energy and Atmosphere Prerequisite: minimum energy performance calculations for district energy supply
Source: Derived from LEED O+M v4 Reference Guide. Redrawn by Elizabeth Meyers, 2020

 *Partnering Credit*

Optimize Energy Performance is the Partnering Credit to the Minimum Energy Performance Prerequisite. It builds upon it by requiring an Energy Star score *beyond* 75 or being *over* 25 percent more efficient than similar buildings. If the infrastructure for using a benchmark (conducted in the Minimum Energy Performance Prerequisite) to facilitate enhancements does not yet exist, and the ASHRAE Level I Audit (conducted in the Best Management Practices Prerequisite) revealed opportunities for further energy-savings which will be implemented prior to the end of the Performance Period.

☐ Enhancing energy efficiency during the Performance Period may be categorized into a correlational hierarchy of cost/effort: Behavioral, Procedural and Mechanical, respectively. The least expensive modification requires the greatest effort. For example, turning off lights, vacating spaces after-hours and unplugging unused devices do not necessarily incur cost but require occupants to alter their behavior in order to decrease energy consumption (Behavioral). Adding formal guidelines to making equipment more economical may incur additional labor

Side Lesson E – 8.3.2: Normalization is the process of rearranging data to avoid redundancy and logically related items together and is necessary for the accuracy of comparing performance in the database.

| 169

and material cost to facilitate operation (Procedural) and upgrading equipment to sustainable standards requires the cost of upgrading it up front for additional maintenance (Mechanical). This concept may be helpful when communicating with facility personnel about exceeding the due diligence of the prerequisite. Your facility already has protocol for such progressive energy efficiency modifications.

If the following questions may be answered affirmatively, this Partnering Credit should be attempted:

- ☐ Are *all* energy sources which serve the facility able to be metered for 12 months?
- ☐ Is metered data available for various intervals?
- ☐ Will Behavioral, Procedural and/or Mechanical enhancements be implemented during the Performance Period to improve energy efficiency through standard facility protocol or as identified by the ASHRAE Level I Audit?

8.3.3 Energy Metering

(*Refer also to page 217 in the LEED O+M v4 Reference Guide*)

Perhaps the most complex part of understanding this simple credit is determining the types of energy sources and working with the facilities staff to confirm if those are metered. In many LEED Lab courses, energy meters are in fact installed in the facility and may be calibrated and tracked easily per the requirements of the preceding prerequisites; however, they are not installed for the full spectrum of energy sources. To solve the latter case, additional meters must be installed, delaying the anticipated certification or completion of certain credits for the aim of the course. Following a few specific tasks can ensure a successful outcome.

Tasks

The primary goal of this prerequisite is to have established and functioning energy meters in the building. Since there is no way for students to know their number, location and reason for placement, the direct assistance of a facility staff member is required for all of these steps. Therefore, the list of steps to ensure satisfaction of this prerequisite are condensed from those in the LEED O+M v4 Reference Guide, specifically for LEED Lab.

1. **Source.** Most large campuses have a central plant, which is common for the generation of energy. However not all buildings on campus are necessarily dependent on this energy source and may have their own energy generation or rely on direct utilities to power the facility. Figure 8.19 describes a variety of energy sources on a campus.

ENERGY

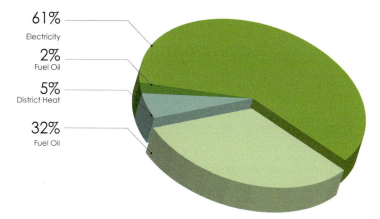

Fig 8.19 Shares of major energy sources used in commercial buildings, 2012

Note: Education uses about 10 percent of total energy consumed by commercial buildings

Source: Derived from the US Energy Information Administration (EIA) (www.archtoolbox.com/materials-systems/sustainability/refrigerants-used-in-buildings-and-hvac-equipment.html). Redrawn by Elizabeth Meyers, 2020

Box 8.1 Energy sources on campus

What are the sources of energy that are being delivered to power your facility?

Gas _____

Water _____

Steam _____

Electricity _____

Heat _____

Cooling _____

---

2. **Locate.** Energy meters for any energy source identified in Task 1 in this chapter should be permanently installed, functional and ready for operation – if not already in use. If one or more of these energy sources does not have a meter associated with it, your facility staff member should procure it prior to the Performance Period.
   ☐ Where do the energy meters exist in your facility to track the consumption of your various power sources?
3. **Procure.** There is no specific direction in LEED regarding the brand of meters which should be obtained to track energy, but incorrect meter selection and installation negatively impacts the quality of metered data. There are

| 171

ENERGY

certain basic questions to help make the decision if new or supplemental meters are required.

    a. **What is your communication protocol?** This is an arrangement of instructions in telecommunication which enable information to be transmitted between several objects of a system. For example, when the meters record energy data, the data may be transmitted to a central location and then to an internet platform where it can be read by several parties. Each entity needs to relay information to the other within the system. The 'language' used is called the protocol. In procuring additional or initial meters, knowing the communication protocol of your existing telecommunication system will help to select the correct device. Pursuing the Partnering Credit for Advanced Metering becomes more desirable because it requires that all energy sources should link to a communications infrastructure where data can easily be accessed remotely.

    b. **How many phases are needed for your communication system?** Most meter manufacturers sell "single-phase" and "three-phase" power meters. Three-phase electric power is continuous, and often used in large facilities where more equipment that demands consistency and efficiency of power exists. Single-phase power is used in small retail or commercial properties where less power is desired. If your facility operates on a single-phase alternating current system from which data is logged, a single-phase meter is preferred.

    c. **How many amps are used by the system?** An amp measures electrical current or the flow *rate* of electricity, a volt measures the *pressure* of electricity, and an ohm measures electrical *resistance*. These basic units of electricity play a role in the type of meter to be procured.

4. **Calibrate.** Any new or additional energy meters require calibration. Please take the next step after procurement to learn about calibration in Minimum Energy Performance Chapter 8.3.2 Tasks.

 Tools

While Minimum Energy Performance involves Portfolio Manager® as the tool for tracking facility energy to obtain a baseline rating, Building Level Energy Metering involves a different category of 'tool' to establish the facility's metering infrastructure. The LEED Lab student will most likely not be permitted to *install* any meters towards this credit but should be *knowledgeable* about their compliance standards.[51]

    1. **ANSI C12.20 – Electricity Meters.** The American National Standards Institute (ANSI) standard for electricity meters establishes performance standards for electricity meters through testing protocols, maintenance intervals and accuracy

requirements. Class .02 refers to an accuracy of +/- .2 percent of true value at a full load.[52]
2. **EN 1434 (CEN/TC 176) – Thermal Energy Meters.** Thermal energy systems comprise DES, hydronic systems, geothermal and CHP (see Chapter 8.3.2). This European Standard specifies the general requirements of such heat meters, covers only closed systems, and indicates the quantity of heat.

Techniques

- ☐ This prerequisite should be accomplished prior to attempting Minimum Energy Performance since it may require the installation of new meters or employ existing building-level energy meters.
- ☐ This prerequisite may be earned rather easily if your facility has existing meters that are able to track whole-building energy use on a monthly interval and software to compile energy-use summaries which can be shared for minimally five (5) years with USGBC through Portfolio Manager.
- ☐ In order to complete Task 1 (Source) it is easiest to identify all fuel energy sources utilized by the building, including electricity, fossil fuels, biofuels and district chilled water, steam and hot water which should be metered. Locally generated and consumed renewable energy such as photovoltaics, wind-generation, and geothermal or solar thermal cells do not require metering unless the Partnering Credit Advanced Energy Metering is being pursued (see Partnering Credit on the next page).
- ☐ When completing Task 2 (Locate) it is helpful to know that if the building shares utility meters with other buildings, or has functions with varying occupancies, sub-meters are required – which will assist in pursuing Advanced Energy Metering (see Partnering Credit on the next page). If such new meters are introduced, they should be in locations of easy access for maintenance. They should also be installed prior to the Performance Period since that is the timeframe to capture metering data towards a baseline.
- ☐ If utility-owned meters do not provide immediate data, or provide undisclosed data to the facility personnel, the LEED Lab students may request that they install a private meter adjacent to the utility meter. If this is not possible, energy bills which reflect the utility-owned metered data may be submitted.
- ☐ When selecting private meters for Task 3 (Procure), it is essential to identify equipment that conforms to the strict accuracy standards of the local regulations governing revenue-grade metering or otherwise is highly accurate.
- ☐ Private meters must be calibrated per the manufacturer's recommendations and must be permanent. Monthly energy data from owner-provided or private energy meters may be compiled in two ways: via the BAS, EMS or other energy-reporting software, or via the facility personnel through manual meter readings which are, however, not permitted when pursuing Advanced Energy Metering (see Partnering Credit on the next page).

ENERGY

Side Lesson F – 8.3.3: Energy End Use is building equipment or processes requiring power in order to successfully function for its occupants. Energy categories for buildings are space cooling, space heating, receptacles, service hot water, with lighting contributing towards the single largest use of electricity in commercial buildings. Energy modeling software pulls data from these categories to view the building's overall energy use. Tenant level-metering does not qualify for as an end-use and therefore cannot be used for this credit. This is because tenant-level meters monitor energy use for plug loads, lighting, and supplemental cooling (see https://tinyurl.com/7kyk6xut).

 Partnering Credit

Advanced Energy Metering is the Partnering Credit to the Building-Level Metering Prerequisite. It builds upon it by requiring advanced metering capabilities and sub-metering. This credit requires a holistic approach to the way the entire facility's energy is managed and will likely be a time-consuming endeavor if the facility is not already compliant. Many buildings with utility-owned meters will not meet the requirements of this credit, even if all of the energy sources are individually metered. Using solely energy monitoring software will not meet this credit either, since a physical meter for monitoring end uses is necessary (Side Lesson F: Energy End Use). An early decision on whether to pursue this credit will help inform accordance with the prerequisite. It should be assigned to the same LEED Lab student/group as the prerequisite.

This credit requires permanently metering end uses which comprise a portion of the total annual consumption (excluding plug loads) via utility meters or the BAS or EMS (Side Lesson G: Plug Loads). Referring to the ASHRAE Level 1 walk-through analysis required for Energy Efficiency Best Management Practices alternatively will help to determine which end uses to meter. Students will need to develop an energy baseline for both demand and consumption using this metered data. The BAS or EMS should be programmed to generate an alarm which sounds if the actual consumption and demand exceeds that baseline by 5 percent.

If the following questions may be answered affirmatively, this Partnering Credit should be attempted:

Side Lesson G – 8.3.3: Plug Loads are the energy consumption caused by equipment and appliances plugged into wall outlets. Sixty-six percent of plug loads come from computers and monitors. Plug loads are not associated with general building HVAC, lighting, and watering heating. They are a large energy consumer and can take up to as much as 50 percent of the total building energy consumption (see https://tinyurl.com/2vbmxmv2).

- ☐ Are meters able to capture any renewable energy sources if applicable?
- ☐ Are energy sources and major energy end uses already sub-metered?
- ☐ Are inputs and outputs of fuel, electricity and recovered heat from non-renewable energy sources being metered?
- ☐ Are end uses which comprise over 20 percent of the overall energy consumption being metered?
- ☐ Is the metering system able to store data for at least three years?
- ☐ Are meters capable of logging data at hourly (or less), daily, monthly and annual intervals?
- ☐ Do electricity meters record both consumption and demand, or power factor?
- ☐ Is the metered data accessible remotely?
- ☐ Does a BAS or EMS exist to support any new sub-metering?
- ☐ Does the BAS or EMS have alarm capabilities?

 ### 8.3.4 Refrigerant Management

(*Refer also to page 223 in the LEED O+M v4 Reference Guide*)

The main purpose of this prerequisite is a global endeavor: to minimize depletion of the Earth's ozone layer (Side Lesson H: Ozone Layer).[53] Without the filtering action of the ozone layer, solar radiation penetrates the atmosphere and over-heats the earth's surface[54] (Figure 8.20).

ENERGY

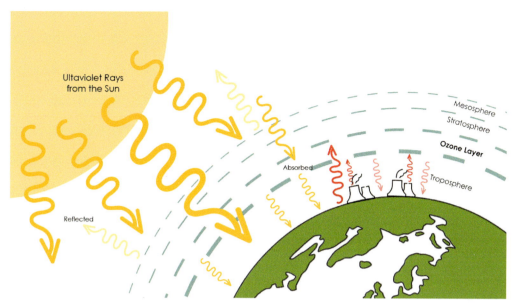

Fig 8.20 *The ozone layer*

Note: Radiation from the sun enters the atmosphere and penetrate the ozone layer when it has holes in it, thus increasing the trespass of harmful UV rays to the earth's surface. These penetrations are caused by substances such as CFCs, while HFCs trap and increase the heating of the earth

Source: Diagrammed by Elizabeth Meyers, 2020

Table 8.3 Comparison of refrigerants: global warming potential and ozone depletion potential

Refrigerant type	Ozone depletion potential	Global warming potential
CFC	High	Very high
HCFC	Very low	Very high
HFC	Zero	High
HC	Zero	Negligible
CO_2	Zero	Negligible

Source: Derived from ArchToolBox (www.archtoolbox.com/materials-systems/sustainability/refrigerants-used-in-buildings-and-hvac-equipment.html). Condensed from https://tinyurl.com/ey9y4mae by Elizabeth Meyers, 2020

Refrigerants (Side Lesson I: Refrigerants) used in mechanical building equipment contain chemicals that contribute towards this depletion (Table 8.3). Minimizing its depletion was actively realized through the Montreal Protocol in 1987, which phased out chemicals that erode this protective layer of the earth when they are exposed to the atmosphere. The United States has been a leader implementing the Protocol throughout its existence and has taken strong domestic action to phase out the production and consumption of ozone-depleting substances such as chlorofluorocarbons (CFCs) and halons.[55]

Side Lesson H – 8.3.4: Ozone Layer: The earth's atmosphere is made up of five major layers; troposphere, stratosphere, mesosphere, thermosphere, and exosphere. A layer of the molecule, ozone, exists in the stratosphere, which is referred to as "the ozone layer." Ozone acts as a shield keeping out harmful ultraviolet radiation from the sun. It is incredibly important to life, without this layer humans would be more susceptible to impaired immune systems, skin cancer, and cataracts (see www.nasa.gov/audience/foreducators/postsecondary/features/F_Ozone.html).

| 175

ENERGY

Side Lesson I – 8.3.4: Refrigerants: A refrigerant is a type of substance, typically in the form of a fluid, that is used in a refrigeration cycle and heat pump in order to cool a space. They cool spaces by capturing and releasing heat using a thermodynamic phenomenon of phase changes; where fluid turns to gas and vice versa (see www.archtoolbox.com/materials-systems/sustainability/refrigerants-used-in-buildings-and-hvac-equipment.html).

In 1990 the US Congress assigned the EPA the responsibility of reducing ozone depletion through managing air quality and atmospheric protection by giving it regulatory powers.[56] CFCs can no longer be manufactured or imported into the USA effective January 1, 1996; however, refrigerant manufactured before this date or refrigerant recovered and recycled can be used.[57]

To maintain conformance to this regulation in existing buildings, a small activity has a significant aggregate effect: limiting the leakage and use of harmful refrigerants in HVAC&R systems. The application of this concept to a standard new commercial building is relatively easy to accomplish since all new mechanical equipment must conform to these strict regulations. However, the application of this concept to an existing campus building evaluated by LEED Lab students – typically an older structure – involves the facility personnel in helping them access mechanical equipment. This way they may see for themselves the labels on the equipment which indicate the refrigerant contents and learn more about the equipment's refrigerants to help them choose a path for compliance.

Tasks

The primary task in accomplishing this prerequisite is to document the type of refrigerant that existing mechanical equipment contains. LEED O+M recognizes the significant expense of mechanical equipment and that it may be fiscally impossible to replace it on a campus in order to utilize an eco-friendlier chemical. Other options therefore exist: either confirming that existing HVAC&R equipment does not possess a CFC-based refrigerant or reducing its leakage rate if it is economically unfeasible to replace it until it is phased it out.

1. **Identify:**
   - ☐ Identify the responsible campus party and/or facility personnel who record all refrigerants used for the equipment in your facility.
   - ☐ Identify the equipment type, refrigerant type and installation date.

   Refrigerant functions in equipment through the process of phase conversion (Side Lesson J: phase Conversion) (Figure 8.21). The chemicals used in refrigerants enable them to change at relatively low temperatures, facilitating this process. A label identifying the type of refrigerant is required to be located somewhere visible on the equipment. With the assistance of the facility personnel, *identify the chemical refrigerant which is present in your mechanical equipment.* Building equipment that uses refrigerant includes:

   a. **Air Conditioning (AC).** This is a method of cooling a space by pushing refrigerant through coils located inside of a space to absorb heat from the interior environment, thus cooling the air – then circulates to coils outside of the space to release the heat (Figure 8.22).
   b. **Water Cooling.** This is a method of removing heat from computers or heavy commercial or industrial

ENERGY

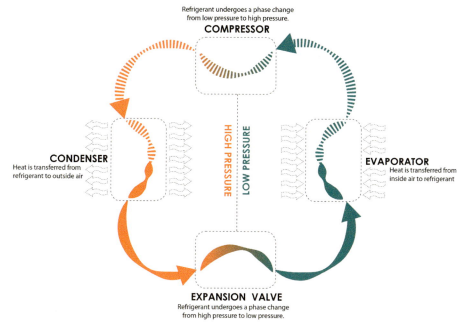

Fig 8.21 *The physics of the refrigerant cycle*
Source: Diagrammed by Patricia Andrasik, 2020

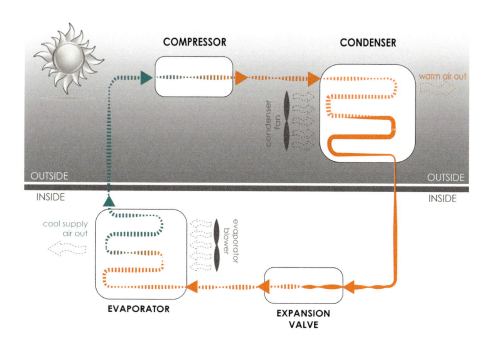

NOTE: This diagram indicates a 'split system' where part of the equipment is outside and part inside. A 'packaged unit' locates all of the equipment outside.

Fig 8.22 *Diagram of how a refrigerant is processed in an air conditioner*
Source: Diagrammed by Patricia Andrasik, 2020

ENERGY

Side Lesson J – 8.3.4: Phase Conversion: There are a few basic components to the refrigeration cycle; the condenser, fluid refrigerant, an expansion device, a compressor, and the evaporator. The process:

1. *The compressor raises the pressure of the refrigerant vapor through constriction and pushes it to the condenser.*
2. *The condenser turns the refrigerant into a high pressure liquid refrigerant.*
3. *The high-pressure liquid refrigerant cools down the air while absorbing the heat.*
4. *The cycle starts over again once the refrigerant is expelled as a gas back into its primary destination.*

(See https://tinyurl.com/wk5wf69v).

equipment and power plants using water as a heat conductor. New water cooler models condense, evaporate and compress water to accomplish this. Older water coolers – many which are found on campuses in aging buildings – often use CFC-based refrigerant to remove heat. This term is also used to describe the process for water fountains which typically hold around seven ounces of refrigerant and would not be included in this prerequisite because of the insignificant quantity.

c. **Heat Pumps.** This term refers to equipment which functions using the same process as the air conditioner – absorbing heat from the interior environment, thus cooling the air – then circulating it to coils outside of the space to release the heat. Both systems compress refrigerant in order to facilitate a phase change, but heat pumps are able to reverse the process in order to provide heating to the interior in colder months. Because heat pumps can cool and heat, they offer year-round functionality (see Figure 8.23).

d. **Refrigerators.** This equipment is available for large or small commercial and institutional and industrial uses, and uses the same process of refrigeration as AC, water cooling and heat pumps.

2. **Analyze.** If the equipment you have identified does not contain CFCs, it is sufficient to simply indicate this in the submission in order to complete the prerequisite. Otherwise, the system requires *an analysis to determine prerequisite compliance*. Answering a few short questions will help this endeavor:

   a. **Is it feasible financially to upgrade existing equipment?** The LEED O+M v4 Reference Guide provides a clear equation for determining payback (Figure 8.24) (see LEED O+M v4 Reference Guide p. 225). If that payback is longer than ten years, an upgrade is not necessary. However, the information for this equation should be researched with your facility personnel partner. The three variables of the equation include:

      1. **"Cost of replacement or conversion."** The general rule-of-thumb in the HVAC industry is when the cost of repair meets or exceeds 50 percent of the value of your air conditioning system, it is logical to replace your system.
      2. **"Resulting annual energy cost difference."** [Energy cost of upgraded equipment – energy cost of existing equipment] This indicates the energy cost your new, upgraded system expends subtracted from the original energy cost prior to upgrade. The cost is easily be detected via energy bills if this equipment is the only change to your systems. If there are other system upgrades occurring simultaneously, a careful evaluation using energy sub-metered data before and after upgrades will aid in providing this figure if it is available.

ENERGY

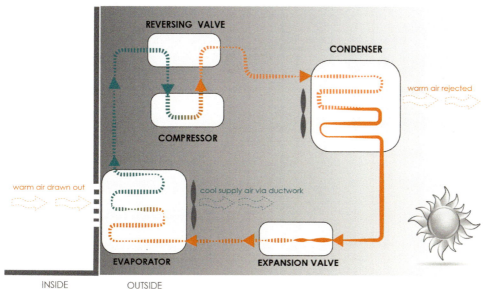

COOLING MODE of heat pump

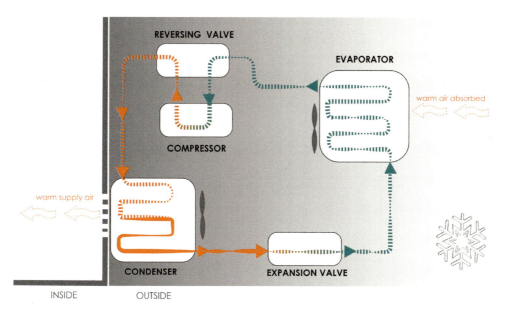

HEATING MODE of heat pump

Fig 8.23 Diagram of how refrigerant is processed in a heat pump

Note: This diagram indicates a 'package unit' which means all components are located outside. A 'split system' locates part of the equipment outside and part inside.

Source: Derived from https://energyeducation.ca/encyclopedia/Heat_pump. Diagrammed by Patricia Andrasik, 2020

3. **"Resulting annual maintenance and refrigerant cost difference"** (Figure 8.25). Refrigerant cost is fairly easy to attain from your campus procurement or facility personnel, or even from a standard pricing chart you may find on a refrigerant manufacturer's website. Simply find out how much the upgraded

ENERGY

Fig 8.24 *Equation from LEED O+M v4 Reference Guide for simple payback for equipment replacement or conversion*
Source: Derived from LEED O+M v4 Reference Guide. Redrawn by Elizabeth Meyers, 2020

Fig 8.25 *Resulting annual maintenance and refrigerant cost difference equation*
Source: Diagrammed by Elizabeth Meyers, 2020

| 180 |

equipment's refrigerant costs against the original equipment's refrigerant. Often maintaining the existing harmful refrigerant is much costlier because it is being phased out of existence, and less supply of a discontinued item results in its higher cost. Equipment upgrades in this case ultimately become a welcome reduction to operating costs. Annual maintenance cost requires you to know how *frequently* the refrigerant needs to be serviced – including being recharged – by the facility personnel. This frequency is multiplied by the *cost* of the labor to perform it (Side Lesson K: Refrigerant Charge).

b. **Is there a Phase-Out Plan for the refrigerant?** If the payback for financial feasibility to upgrade the equipment amounts to fewer than ten years, proof that the existing equipment will eventually be upgraded within this timeframe is required. This should be accomplished by a descriptive Phase-Out Plan which also addresses how any leakage of the existing refrigerant will be minimized prior to the upgrade. The Plan may be written by the LEED Lab student as long as it is informed by the facility personnel, if it does not already exist.

Side Lesson K – 8.3.4: Refrigerant Charge can be defined as the amount of refrigerant gas required for the effective operation of the HVAC system. Refrigerant charging is the act of replenishing these refrigerant gases with levels depleted due to system repairs or leaks (see https://tinyurl.com/hpzmz7xr).

Tools

Besides investing in a flashlight for identifying refrigerant on HVAC equipment and a calculator to assess the financial feasibility of existing equipment, the only 'tools' involved in attempting this prerequisite are two important reference documents. The following will aid LEED Lab students' understanding of the theory behind assessing refrigerants:

1. **US EPA Clean Air Act, Title VI, Section 608, Stationary Refrigeration and Air Conditioning.** This is a portion of a United States federal law which was designed to control air pollution on a national level.[58] The Clean Air Act is the country's first and most influential of the modern environmental laws and is also among the most inclusive air quality laws in the world.[59] In 1970, Congress established much of its basic structure as a result of dense, visible smog in many of the nation's cities and industrial centers. Major revisions in 1977 and 1990 were designed to improve its effectiveness and to target newly recognized air pollution problems such as acid rain and damage to the stratospheric ozone layer.[60] This specific section identifies the importance of protecting the ozone layer, defines the National Recycling and Emission Reduction Program, controls venting of ozone-depleting substances (ODS) and regulates certifications of technicians and service, among other maintenance factors.

2. **The Montreal Protocol on Substances That Deplete our Ozone Layer.** This is a global agreement to protect the stratospheric ozone layer by phasing out the production and consumption of ODS. The Montreal Protocol on Substances that Deplete our Ozone Layer is a system of

ENERGY

rules enacted in 1989 as a part of the Vienna Convention for the Protection of the Ozone Layer; an international treaty created to phase out the production of numerous harmful substances responsible for ozone depletion. As a result of this protocol, hydrogen, chlorine, fluorine and carbon (HCFC's) which have a *lower* potential to destroy ozone than CFCs, are being used temporarily to replace them but are still harmful since they are greenhouse gases that trap heat in our atmosphere.

Techniques

1. This prerequisite suggests the use of best practices *in addition to* the requirements of the Clean Air Act, Title VI, Rule 608 for minimizing refrigerant leakage. However, when reading it, note that many of the best management practices suggested in the LEED O+M v4 Reference Guide (see page 226) are already included in this document.
2. The ten-year CFC Phase-Out Plan may be developed jointly by the facility personnel and LEED Lab student but must be signed by the owner. If such a plan exists and is scheduled to commence within five years, the feasibility study is not necessary. If the feasibility study is required however, a third-party company is *recommended* to perform or to be involved in its creation. It is better to create this plan for CFC-based refrigerants in older equipment which are nearing the end of their functional lives, and to perform the economic feasibility analysis in newer CFC-containing equipment.
3. A plan for minimizing refrigerant leakage is required regardless of whether the equipment will be phased out, converted, or remain in place due to financial feasibility.
4. If equipment which has a refrigerant rate below .05 lb. is procured during the Performance Period or beyond, it is required to be CFC-free even if similar existing equipment is exempt.
5. Any equipment owned and maintained by individual schools or departments on campus (e.g., an experimental but functioning AC unit used for continuous applied research in the facility by faculty) must be accounted for under this prerequisite if it contains more than .05 lb. of refrigerant.

Partnering Credit

Enhanced Refrigerant Management is the Partnering Credit to the Fundamental Refrigerant Management Prerequisite. If your facility does not have a CFC-free equipment infrastructure, or if your facility is in the midst of an upgrade, this credit will be difficult to achieve and will rely on aggregate equipment calculations which may or may not prove compliance. In the latter case, one equation is used on each piece of refrigerant-using equipment in your facility, and then calculated with a weighted average of all base building equipment. This Calculation of

Refrigerant Impact uses the following important variables which require understanding:

1. **Lifecycle Ozone Depletion Potential.** LCODP is the measure of ozone degradation this piece of equipment will cause over its lifetime.
2. **Lifecycle Direct Global Warming Potential.** LCGWP is the measure of how much emission energy the gases from this equipment will trap in the atmosphere throughout its lifetime.
3. **Global Warming Potential.** GWP of the refrigerant is the measure of how much emission energy the gasses from this refrigerant will trap in the atmosphere throughout its lifetime.
4. **Ozone Depletion Potential.** ODP is the measure of ozone degradation this refrigerant will cause over its lifetime.
5. **Refrigerant Leakage Rate.** LR is the measure of speed which this equipment expels refrigerant into the atmosphere due to a leak. A default rate of 2 percent and not the actual measured quantity is used for this calculation.
6. **End-of-life Refrigerant Loss.** MR refers to the measure of leakage or extraction of refrigerants from equipment when it is removed from service. A default of 10 percent is used for this calculation unless otherwise documented.
7. **Refrigerant Charge.** RC is the amount of refrigerant necessary for the equipment to work correctly (see side lesson in Tasks).
8. **Equipment Life.** Life is the measure of time in which a specific piece of equipment operates, from installation until it is removed from service. A default of 10 years should be used for existing equipment not indicated in the LEED O+M v4 Reference Guide, Table 2, page 297. Manufacturers' specifications also may be admitted as documentation for equipment life for this credit.

If the following questions may be answered affirmatively, this Partnering Credit should be attempted:

- ☐ Does this facility operate on a chilled-water or otherwise non-CFC central cooling plant?
- ☐ and/or
- ☐ Is the facility's equipment CFC-free without a need to create a Phase-Out Plan, or is there not one in progress?
- ☐ Do the facility personnel currently have a refrigerant management plan to reduce leakage?
- ☐ Does this facility have a record-keeping protocol for refrigerants?

8.3.5 Commissioning

The Energy Efficiency Best Management Practices Prerequisite, discussed in Chapter 8.3.1, involved certain measures to be in place regarding the operations and maintenance of systems.

ENERGY

Building upon this requirement, Commissioning (Cx) includes a trio of credits which addresses a deeper understanding of how your facility uses energy and can both improve its performance and ensure that the operational and comfort needs of building occupants are met.[61] It is unlike the commissioning we may expect of new buildings. New building commissioning is typically accomplished by a "qualified employee of the owner, an independent consultant, or an employee of the design or construction firm who is not part of the project's design or construction team, or a disinterested subcontractor of the design or construction team."[62] Commissioning existing buildings, sometimes referred to as 'retro-commissioning' (if it is being done for the first time), on the other hand may be accomplished by in-house individuals or third parties who are qualified to conduct certain analyses and tasks. ASHRAE has recently begun validating commissioning competency through the Building Commissioning Professional (BCxP) certification.[63] However, no such formal professional commissioning qualifications are required to achieve any credits under this category.

While new building commissioning is a prerequisite for new LEED–certified buildings and involves verifying mechanical, plumbing, electrical, fire and life safety, building envelope, lighting, wastewater, controls, security and other systems responsible for creating an operational occupant facility in order to cater to the client or property owner's requirements, existing building commissioning involves *enhancing* existing facility performance. The Building Commissioning Association (BCA) defines Existing Building Commissioning (EBCx) as

> a systematic process for investigating, analyzing, and optimizing the performance of building systems through the identification and implementation of low/no cost and capital-intensive Facility Improvement Measures and ensuring their continued performance. The goal of EBCx is to make building systems perform interactively to meet the Current Facility Requirements and provide the tools to support the continuous improvement of system performance over time. The term EBCx is intended to be a comprehensive term defining a process that encompasses the more narrowly focused process variations such as retro-commissioning, re-commissioning and ongoing commissioning that are commonly used in the industry.[64]

Lighting, process loads, domestic water heating, HVAC&R, renewable energy, energy-producing or consuming equipment in a system is required to be verified. The process involves many facets of ensuring that systems are operating efficiently. Otherwise in this publication, related credits are associated by the Partnering Credit subchapter. In this case however, LEED O+M's Commissioning credits in particular will be presented in unison due to their specific relationship to each other. LEED O+M certification respectively offers the following Commissioning Credits:

1. Commissioning Analysis
2. Commissioning Implementation
3. Ongoing Commissioning

ENERGY

Tasks

1. Commissioning Analysis
(*Refer also to page 229 in the LEED O+M v4 Reference Guide*)

There are two basic tasks to successfully demonstrate enhanced facility operational efficiency through this credit: commissioning and auditing. Both require detailed site visits and lengthy processes of evaluating energy operations. The former uses a routine evaluation in which the LEED Lab student may directly participate, while the latter utilizes a prescribed ASHRAE procedure typically conducted by an external engineering firm. Both include a thorough O+M assessment and identify ways of improving energy efficiency by addressing equipment failure, primary low-cost measures and the return on investment of higher costing improvements such as upgrading the BAS or control systems. If energy consumption is higher than anticipated, or if there is a significant occupant change or a change in the intended function of spaces, either analysis will identify successes and challenges to a facility's energy management. There are however differences to these two methods.

A. **Commissioning** (Credit Option 1) is more often conducted on facilities that are under five years old and/or when there are occupant complaints. It is also conducive to LEED Lab students that the internal facility staff conduct the process because they may more easily be included in the analysis. This process engages Functional Performance Testing (FPT) so that equipment may flow through its entire sequence of operations to check response to the BAS or EMS, identifying which equipment may have digressed from its intended operation (Side Lesson L: Functional Performance Testing (FPT)[65] Consequently, small adjustments in lieu of significant equipment replacement may be made to improve energy efficiency.

B. **Auditing** (Credit Option 2) usually is preferred when equipment is older and an upgrade to major mechanical, electrical or plumbing systems is expected. It also is ideal when there is neither a sufficient documentation of a sequence of operations nor a set of drawings detailing the systems. In Auditing, operational issues can be identified via the BAS or EMS by consultants through evaluating setpoints and schedules of the equipment, but normally do not require any testing. This process requires more up-front cost for external personnel unless the LEED Lab class can obtain these services pro bono.

- ☐ Identify with the facility personnel who will comprise the Cx Team.
- ☐ Assemble the data for all metered equipment which you have previously identified for end uses in Chapter 8.3.3 so that there is a history of performance for each piece of equipment.
- ☐ Create a hierarchy of which pieces of equipment should be targeted for energy reduction.
- ☐ Using performance specifications generated under

Side Lesson L – 8.3.4: Functional Performance Testing (FPT) is an essential component of the building commissioning process. FPT is the process of putting the Direct Digital Control (DDC) system through a series of tests with HVAC equipment and control conditions. The goal is to manipulate the DDC and test out every possible condition; switches from cooling to heating, occupied to unoccupied mode, normal power to emergency power, or unsatisfied to satisfied temperature. This DDC testing ensures that the system will function properly. Only once the DDC passes this series of testing can the contractors hand over the building to the owner. The design engineer is the one that creates the control's sequence language, which is what also gets worked through with the testing. Through testing, one can understand the engineer's reasoning for different performances and reactions. For example, testing could verify that the economizer mode is triggered with the outside air dampers open to 100 percent during certain outside conditions (see https://buildingenergy.cx-associates.com/2013/04/functional-performance-testing-of-your-hvac-system-brains/).

ENERGY

          EA Prerequisite Energy Efficiency Best Management Practices (see Chapter 8.3.1), create a Commissioning (Option 1) or Auditing (Option 2) Plan with a timeline.
- ☐ Commence the Plan, logging ECMs – issues and opportunities – with financial repercussions.
- ☐ Identify in-house facility staff who will be responsible for maintaining this Plan. An ASHRAE Level 2 audit encompasses these tasks in its prescribed assessment.
- ☐ Update the O+M Plan developed for Energy Efficiency Best Management Practices per this analysis process.

2. **Commissioning Implementation**
(*Refer also to page 243 in the LEED O+M v4 Reference Guide*)

This credit is relatively easy to accomplish when the previous credit is attempted. If either Commissioning or an Audit occurred up to two years prior to the end of the Performance Period or project submission, it may qualify for Implementation. If it occurred after two years, the results will have to be updated. It is based on the application of the primary low-cost ECMs identified in the Commissioning Analysis, a five-year Plan for more significant upgrades, and staff training. The LEED Lab student may effectively participate in the preparation of a Plan and help to train staff but this will depend on the facilities staff to accomplish the 'low-hanging fruit' of equipment modifications within the Performance Period. The following tasks are necessary for a successful outcome:

- ☐ Identify with the facility personnel who will comprise the Cx Team.
- ☐ Implement primary low-cost ECMs identified in the previous Analysis.
- ☐ Create a five-year plan for implementing major equipment upgrades.
- ☐ Create a mechanism for tracking implementation.
- ☐ Train staff so that upgraded equipment may be effectively maintained.
- ☐ Identify in-house facility staff who will be responsible for maintaining this Plan.
- ☐ Update the O+M Plan developed for Energy Efficiency Best Management Practices per this implementation process.

3. **Ongoing Commissioning**
(*Refer also to page 251 in the LEED O+M v4 Reference Guide*)

At this point, the variety of plans and analyses from the Energy Prerequisites to the commissioning trio may become a gray zone, one running into the other. This Energy credit collection can be perceived as independent endeavors which synergize, one overlapping the other, yet remaining autonomous in their composition. For example, if your LEED Lab class' goals include obtaining the preceding commissioning analysis and Implementation credits, it is very cost-effective, simple and logical to pursue this subsequent credit for mutual scholastic and institutional benefits.

Although it requires yet another plan, ongoing commissioning is about the due diligence of continuous improvement opportunities for energy efficiency for at least two years. Take note however, that your staff counterpart may contend that there is

ENERGY

already a running commissioning plan or may insist that the documentation gathered for the energy efficiency best management practices will suffice for ongoing equipment maintenance. For this credit to be met however, the plan must "go beyond preventive maintenance and system trending"[66] and activities conducted towards ongoing commissioning should be achieved and documented quarterly. For example, FPT, something which the ASHRAE Audit does not require, must be implemented in this 'ongoing' maintenance, as will regularly scheduled testing of fire alarms, safety alarms and meters.

Critical to credit compliance but not emphasized in the LEED O+M v4 Reference Guide is updating the Systems Manual (Side Lesson M: The Systems Manual), a document that describes the schedule, details and components of the mechanical equipment and is typically assembled by the Commissioning Team. Equally important for this credit is using data patterns from metering (trend data) to regularly evaluate performance. This task in itself becomes "like a gold mine which could be exploited for the purpose of ongoing commissioning."[67] Paul Torcellini, Principal Engineer for the Commercial Buildings Research Group at the National Renewable Energy Laboratory (NREL), even recommends the use of a dedicated system for monitoring required HVAC variables,[68] but such a measure would be beyond the extent of the minimum credit requirements – though a cost-saving investment to your campus facility. Data collection and monitoring for the successful completion of this credit may be facilitated if the facility's BAS or EMS is equipped with DDC. However, manual ongoing tracking is perfectly acceptable as well. Specific tasks for success include:

- ☐ Identify with the facility personnel who will comprise the Cx Team.
- ☐ Create an ongoing Cx Plan with Quarterly Reports.*
- ☐ Use the Implementation Tracking Mechanism created in the Cx Implementation credit to document corrective action which occurs in the Cx Plan.
- ☐ Identify facility staff who will be responsible for maintaining this Plan.
- ☐ Update existing Systems Manual if significant equipment changes occur as a result of Ongoing Cx.
- ☐ Update the O+M Plan developed for Energy Efficiency Best Management Practices (Chapter 8.3.1) per this ongoing process.
- ☐ Request that the facilities personnel include an explanation of the documents generated in the Commissioning trio credits in your institution's facility staff training guides.

Side Lesson M – 8.3.4: The Systems Manual includes a description of the system/s, Updated Sequence of Operation, Flow Diagrams, O+M Data, images of equipment and functioning, setpoints and explanations on DDC graphics. The Manual is much easier accomplished by an experienced external Cx firm than by an internally staffed team who may not understand the breadth of this document. It is also different from the O+M manual, which is more detailed (see www.eeperformance.org/uploads/8/6/5/0/8650231/systemsmanualsgdl1_4-201x__chair_approved.pdf).

Tools

There are many resources to aid in understanding Commissioning for the LEED Lab student which serve this chapter as useful tools. Many of these fall into standards which are published by various third-party trade organizations. These are not necessarily required for accomplishing the credits listed, per the USGBC,

ENERGY

but are recommended to be investigated so that facility personnel and students alike can understand the thoroughness needed to accomplish the various phases required for analysis, implementation and ongoing commissioning. The following publications function as tools to this aim:

1. ***New Construction Building Commissioning Best Practices, 3rd Edition.***[69] Written and peer-reviewed by industry professionals, this is the first industry publication to include details for hands-on manual and monitoring-based Ongoing Commissioning (OCx) and Building Existing Commissioning (BECx) project management.[70]

2. ***Best Practices in Commissioning Existing Buildings.***[71] This document defines the qualities and characteristics of best commissioning practices in order to promote those practices in the built environment.[72]

3. ***Return on Investment Calculator.*** The Cash Flow Opportunity Calculator helps inform strategic decisions about financing energy efficiency projects. Using the tool, you will be able to estimate how much new equipment you can finance using anticipated savings, as well whether you should finance now or wait for a lower interest rate. Questions such as "How much new energy efficiency equipment can be purchased from the anticipated savings?" "Should this equipment purchase be financed now, or is it better to wait and use cash from a future budget?" or "Is money being lost by waiting for a lower interest rate?"[73] can be easily answered to help the strategic energy efficiency planning of your facility.

 Techniques

A strong initial Cx team that will endeavor these credits is the key to successful accomplishment of one or all of them. The LEED Lab student should keep in close contact with the individuals who comprise this team, namely their facilities staff counterpart, throughout the semester. Commissioning is an excellent method of making staff responsibilities more efficient especially if there is miscommunication or no communication between the facilities staff operating the meters, the BAS or EMS, and the field personnel. Some recommendations for success include the following:

☐ Current training of these individuals should be simultaneous and include the basics of analyzing energy use and operating schedules along with identifying/rectifying deficiencies and must also include their commitment to *maintain* energy savings if a successful Commissioning trio of credits is to be attained.

☐ If this facility was previously audited and major systems have been upgraded since then, a collection of those documents should be requested from facilities staff. This will greatly facilitate the analysis.

☐ Synergies may be reaped between credits if your LEED Lab class is pursuing Demand Response (Chapter 8.3.5)

where the Cx Plan must include the control sequences for the Demand Response event, and the Occupant Comfort Survey in Chapter 10.3.8.
☐ Complaints from building occupants often indicate thermal discomfort, poor ventilation and lighting or other system malfunctions which should be addressed through commissioning.

8.3.6 Demand Response

(*Refer also to page 273 in the LEED O+M v4 Reference Guide*)

Demand response (DR) is an electricity tariff or program established to motivate changes in electric use by end-use customers, designed to induce lower electricity use typically at times of high market prices or when grid reliability is jeopardized.[74] This program allows utility companies to call on institutions to decrease their building's electricity use during peak times in exchange for monetary compensation to the facility. Depending on the region of your campus, either the utility provider or the An Independent System Operator (ISO) will implement the program in your locale (Side Lesson N: Independent System Operators (ISO)). Facilities accomplish the DR by setting control sequences during a time of high energy consumption during seasons and times of the day (peak energy events) on their BAS or EMS. This reduces the excess grid energy and the need to strain the load on power plants, decreasing their proliferation. Logically sequeing from the Commissioning trio of credits, the activities which DR requires need to be formally documented in the Cx Plan.

DR as a credit to pursue LEED Certification seeks *specifically* a peak energy reduction in the facility. The process is linear and begins when the BAS or EMS accepts a signal from the utility during peak hours of operation to reduce the building's load. In order to do this, it should be fully or semi-automated. The BAS or EMS reduces the electricity load via the energy-saving measures outlined by the facility personnel. For example, if lighting loads are reduced, plug loads are minimized or electrical activities are limited to off-peak hours, the peak load is lowered (Figure 8.26). When demand is reduced continuously with such measures instead of only during peak events, it is called Permanent Load Shifting (PLS) and is also an acceptable option of compliance.

LEED Lab students who: (1) create a plan at their facility and coordinate with the facility personnel and a utility company to implement it, or (2) work with these individuals to install controls necessary for the DR program during the Performance Period (to be in operation once their local utility provides it) can successfully achieve this credit.

Side Lesson N – 8.3.5: Independent System Operators (ISO): An ISO is an organization that monitors and controls electrical power system operations, either statewide or sometimes regional. An ISO can only be formed at the recommendation of the Federal Energy Regulatory Commission (FERC). There are Regional Transmission Organizations (RTOs) that do the same thing, however they cover a larger geographic area than ISOs (see https://tinyurl.com/ynhb2tvv).

Tasks

Being the catalyst to develop a DR Plan for your institution as a LEED Lab student may be a very rewarding experience. An institution's reluctance to such an endeavor resides in either a lack among personnel to develop and execute the Plan, a lack of

ENERGY

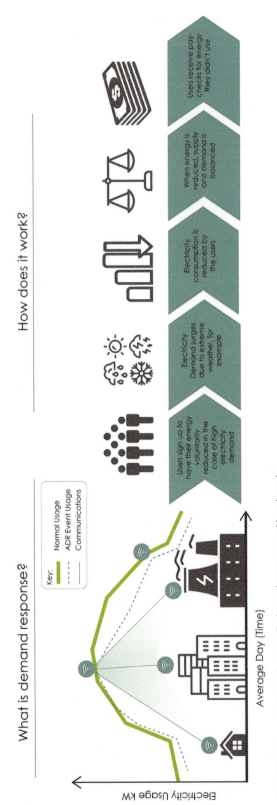

Fig 8.26 Energy and Atmosphere credit: demand response and how it works
Source: Derived from Energy Central and Schneider Electric. Diagrammed by Elizabeth Meyers, 2020

ENERGY

funding to obtain the infrastructure to engage the Plan, or a lack of time for a thorough testing of the Plan. In any case, the long-term benefits outweigh this initial investment. Note that utilities typically provide monetary incentives to even initially launch a DR Program at your institution in addition to the ongoing pay-back of saving energy.

Demand Response is such a locale-dependent endeavor, that the simple Independent System Operator (ISO) investigation into whether your local energy company provides it is the first task! The methods of accomplishing this credit are sufficiently out-lined in the LEED O+M v4 Reference Guide but are repeated here with a slightly different organization in order to facilitate applica-tion in the LEED Lab class:

- ☐ Verify with local utility if DR is available.
- ☐ Verify with facility personnel if a BAS or EMS controls the facility.
- ☐ Decide with your facility personnel which option is ideal for your institution.
- ☐ Follow the steps on pages 275–277 in your LEED O+M v4 Reference Guide.
- ☐ Create a DR Plan with facility personnel.
- ☐ Update the O+M Plan developed for Energy Efficiency Best Management Practices (Chapter 8.3.1) per this DR process.
- ☐ Include the Control sequence in the Cx Plan (Chapter 8.3.4) if your LEED Lab class is pursuing it.

Tools

The DR process begins with a simple question: "Does our utility company provide a DR Program?" Whether or not they do, the implementation of the program may be straight-forward, but the actual evaluation of *which* strategies will yield the most savings may be time-consuming whether conducted manually, through examining energy bills, by assessing submetering data, or through a simulation. Marcus Sheffer, Enviroenergist at 7group explains that

> the utility infrastructure peak load typically occurs on a hot, summer, weekday afternoon when there is a high cooling demand. That means that daylighting controls at perimeter spaces with windows are usually an effective DR strategy because they can be applied to reduce both lighting power and cooling load. Summer peak loads also sometimes coincide with a high percentage of staff being gone for vacation, making the building sparsely occupied. This might present an opportunity to temporarily relocate staff within the building, allowing HVAC and lighting to be shut down in entire sections or floors of buildings. Specialty HVAC systems – like data center cooling, kitchen cooking and dishwasher exhaust and make-up air – and process HVAC should also be included.[75]

Since many of these strategies may rely on adjusting set-points, BAS and EMS controls, creating an energy model of your facility is one option to determine aggregate impacts of peak-reducing strategies which is not elaborated in the LEED O+M

ENERGY

v4 Reference Guide. It consists of a digital model simulating all mechanical and architectural aspects of your facility and then allows the person doing the modeling to adjust variables and test their impact on energy efficiency. This proves a valuable exercise especially if your facility is complicated mechanically. The LEED Lab student may be involved with the facility personnel in creating a Plan but will need to yield to a professional if an energy model is the method chosen to evaluate strategies. The following tools are helpful in answering the initial DR question of availability, and the intermediate question of which strategies should be applied in peak reduction:

List of utility companies in the United States (Table 8.4):

☐ **Demand Response Quick Assessment Tool (DRQAT).**[76] This is a software-based assessment tool which uses prototypical simulation models to calculate the energy and demand reduction potential under certain demand responsive strategies. It is based on the most popular feature and capabilities of EnergyPlus® software to conduct a simulation using an energy model[77] and will require the assistance of an engineer skilled at running energy simulation models.

 Techniques

- Facilities with large mechanical systems which can be shut down during peak consumption times or ones which already have load-shifting as a part of their operation, and/or ones which operate on a BAS or EMS, will find this credit relatively easy to achieve.
- The effort of this credit typically occurs when analyzing which strategies prove most effective to reduce demand by 10 percent.
- If your facility is already enrolled in a DR Program, obtain from your facility personnel the written plan which was executed so that the terms may be evaluated to see if they are acceptable for meeting this credit.
- The greatest hurdle to achieve this credit for those facilities which do not have a DR program already, or those facilities located in locales which do not yet provide DR programs, is ensuring that the infrastructure of your systems will accommodate it.
- A new facility or recently upgraded equipment in an existing campus facility will most likely possess a connection to a BAS or EMS. This ensures controlling the equipment and the ability to program modifications to such appliances as lighting or ventilation. In this case, a DR Program would simply incur a fee for additional programming of the BAS or EMS.
- Renewable resources applied as means of alleviating the peak grid load such as photovoltaics or wind turbines do not reduce the amount of energy which the facility's base electricity load produces, and therefore will not successfully achieve this credit.

ENERGY

■ Alabama
- Alabama Municipal Electric Authority
- Alabama Power, a part of the Southern Company
- PowerSouth
- Tennessee Valley Authority
- Wiregrass Electric Cooperative

◆ Alaska
- Alaska Electric Light & Power
- Chugach Electric Association
- Copper Valley Electric Association
- Golden Valley Electric Association
- Kodiak Electric Association
- Municipal Light & Power

■ Arizona
- Arizona Public Service
- Salt River Project
- Tucson Electric Power
- UniSource Energy Services

■ Arkansas
- Southwestern Electric Power Company
- Entergy Arkansas, Inc.

◆ California
- Alameda Municipal Power
- Anaheim Public Utilities
- Azusa Light & Water
- Burbank Water & Power
- Direct Energy
- East Bay Municipal Utility District
- Glendale Public Service Department
- Gridley Municipal Utilities
- Healdsburg Municipal Electric Department
- Imperial Irrigation District
- Los Angeles Department of Water and Power
- Nevada Irrigation District
- Pacific Gas and Electric
- Pasadena Water & Power
- Pacific Power
- Riverside Public Utilities
- Sacramento Municipal Utility District
- San Diego Gas & Electric
- Santa Clara Electric Department
- Sierra-Pacific Power
- Southern California Edison
- Southern California Public Power Authority
- TID Water & Power - Turlock Irrigation District

■ Colorado
- Public Service Company of Colorado
- Colorado Springs Utilities
- Platte River Power Authority
- United Power, Inc.

▬ Connecticut
- AVANGRID (The United Illuminating Company)
- Direct Energy
- Eversource Energy (Connecticut Light and Power)
- Northeast Utilities

◀ Delaware
- Ambit Energy
- City of Dover Electric Department
- City of Milford Electric Department
- City of Newark Electric Department
- City of Seaford Electric Department
- Delaware Electric Cooperative
- Delaware Municipal Electric Corporation
- Delmarva Power, a subsidiary of Exelon
- Lewes Board of Public Works
- Municipal Services Commission of the City of New Castle
- Town of Clayton Electric Department
- Town of Middletown Electric Department
- Town of Smyrna Electric Department
- Direct Energy

◆ District of Columbia
- PEPCO, a subsidiary of Exelon
- Direct Energy

▽ Florida
- Beaches Energy Services
- Central Florida Electric Cooperative
- Choctawhatchee Electric Cooperative
- City of Alachua Public Services Department
- City of Bartow Electric Department
- City of Blountstown Electric Department
- City of Bushnell Utilities Department
- City of Chattahoochee Electric Department
- City of Fort Meade Utilities Department
- City of Green Cove Springs Utilities Department
- City of Lake Worth Utilities Department
- City of Moore Haven Utilities Department
- City of Mount Dora Electric Utility
- City of New Smyrna Beach Utilities Commission
- City of Newberry Electric Utility
- City of Quincy Utilities Department
- City of Starke Utilities Department
- City of Tallahassee Utilities
- City of Vero Beach Electric Utilities
- City of Wauchula Utilities
- City of Williston Utilities Department
- City of Winter Park Electric Utility Department
- Clay Electric Cooperative
- Clewiston Utilities
- Duke Energy Florida, a part of Duke Energy
- Escambia River Electric Cooperative
- Florida Keys Electric Cooperative
- Florida Municipal Power Agency
- Florida Power & Light, a part of NextEra Energy
- Florida Public Utilities, a part of Chesapeake Utilities
- Fort Pierce Utilities Authority
- Gainesville Regional Utilities
- Glades Electric Cooperative
- Gulf Coast Electric Cooperative
- Gulf Power Company, a part of NextEra Energy
- Homestead Public Services
- JEA
- Keys Energy Services
- Kissimmee Utility Authority
- Lakeland Electric
- Lake Worth Utilities
- Lee County Electric Cooperative
- Leesburg Electric Department
- Ocala Electric Utility
- Okefenoke Rural Electric Membership Corporation
- Orlando Utilities Commission
- Palm Peach
- Peace River Electric Cooperative
- Progress Energy Florida

(Continued)

| 193

Table 8.4 (Continued)

- PowerSouth Energy Cooperative
- Reedy Creek Energy Services
- St. Cloud Utilities
- Seminole Electric Cooperative
- Sumter Electric Cooperative
- Suwannee Valley Electric Cooperative
- Talquin Electric Cooperative
- TECO Energy, a part of Emera
- Town of Havana Utilities
- Tri-County Electric Cooperative
- West Florida Electric Cooperative
- Withlacoochee River Electric Cooperative

▶ **Georgia**

- Georgia Power, a part of the Southern Company
- Municipal Electric Authority of Georgia (MEAG Power)
- Oglethorpe Power
- Tennessee Valley Authority
- Altamaha EMC
- Amicalola EMC
- Blue Ridge Mountain EMC
- Canoochee EMC
- Carroll EMC
- Central Georgia EMC
- Coastal Electric Cooperative
- Cobb EMC
- Colquitt EMC
- Coweta-Fayette EMC
- Diverse Power Inc. - Pataula District
- Excelsior EMC
- Flint Energies
- Grady EMC
- GreyStone Power Corp.
- Habersham EMC
- Hart EMC
- Irwin EMC
- Jackson EMC
- Jefferson Energy Cooperative
- Little Ocmulgee EMC
- Marietta Power
- Middle Georgia EMC
- Mitchell EMC
- North Georgia EMC
- Ocmulgee EMC
- Oconee EMC
- Okefenoke REMC
- Planters EMC
- Rayle EMC
- Satilla REMC
- Sawnee EMC
- Slash Pine EMC
- Snapping Shoals EMC
- Southern Rivers Energy
- Sumter EMC
- Three Notch EMC
- Tri-County EMC
- Tri-State EMC
- Upson EMC
- Walton EMC
- Washington EMC
- Direct Energy

▶ **Hawaii**

- Hawaiian Electric Company (HECO), Oahu subsidiary of Hawaiian Electric Industries
- Hawaiian Electric Light Company (HELCO), Island of Hawaii subsidiary of Hawaiian Electric Industries
- Kauai Island Utility Cooperative (KIUC)
- Maui Electric Company (MECO), Maui County subsidiary of Hawaiian Electric Industries

▶ **Idaho**

- Avista
- Clearwater Power
- IDACORP (Idaho Power)
- PacifiCorp (Rocky Mountain Power)

▶ **Illinois**

- Ambit Energy
- Ameren
- Champion Energy
- City Water, Light & Power (Springfield, Illinois)
- ComEd, a subsidiary of Exelon
- Direct Energy

▶ **Indiana**

- American Electric Power (Indiana Michigan Power)
- Cinergy Corporation
- Duke Energy
- Indiana Municipal Power Agency
- Indianapolis Power & Light
- NiSource
- Northern Indiana Public Service Company
- Vectren (Southern Indiana Gas & Electric Company)

▶ **Iowa**

- Interstate Power and Light Company, a part of Alliant Energy
- MidAmerican Energy

▶ **Kansas**

- Kansas City Board of Public Utilities
- Kansas City Power and Light Company
- Westar Energy

▶ **Kentucky**

- American Electric Power
- Cinergy Corporation
- Direct Energy
- Duke Energy
- Kentucky Utilities
- Louisville Gas & Electric
- Owensboro Municipal Utilities
- Tennessee Valley Authority

▶ **Louisiana**

- CLECO
- Entergy
- SWEPCO, a subsidiary of American Electric Power

▶ **Maine**

- AVANGRID (Central Maine Power)
- Direct Energy
- Emera (Bangor Hydro Electric)

▶ **Maryland**

- A&N Electric Cooperative
- Agway Energy Services
- Allegheny Electric Cooperative
- Ambit Energy
- Baltimore Gas and Electric, a subsidiary of Exelon
- Berlin Electric Utility Department
- Champion Energy
- Choptank Electric Cooperative
- Conectiv, a subsidiary of PEPCO which is a subsidiary of Exelon
- Delmarva Power, a subsidiary of Exelon
- Direct Energy
- Easton Utilities
- FirstEnergy (Potomac Edison)
- Hagerstown Light Department
- Just Energy
- Southern Maryland Electric Cooperative (SMECO)
- Town of Thurmont Municipal Light Company
- Town of Williamsport Utilities

▶ **Massachusetts**

- Ashburnham Municipal Light
- Berkshire Company (WMECO)
- Braintree Electric Light Department
- Boylston Electric Light Department
- Chester Municipal Electric Light
- Chicopee Electric Light Department
- Concord Municipal Light Plant

ENERGY

- Danvers Electric Department
- Eversource Energy (NSTAR, Western Massachusetts Electric)
- Georgetown Electric Department
- Gosnold Municipal Electric Plant
- Groton Electric Department
- Groveland Light Department
- Hingham Municipal Light Department
- Holden Municipal Light Department
- Holyoke Gas and Electric
- Hudson Light and Water Department
- Hull Electric Light Department
- Ipswich Electric Light Department
- Littleton Electric Light and Water Department
- Marblehead Municipal Light Department
- Mansfield Municipal Light Department
- Merrimac Light and Water Department
- Middleboro Municipal Gas and Electric Department

- Middleton Municipal Light Department
- National Grid (Massachusetts Electric, Nantucket Electric)
- North Attleboro Electric Department
- Northeast Utilities
- Norwood Electric Light Department
- NSTAR
- Paxton Municipal Light Department
- Peabody Municipal Light Plant
- Princeton Electric Light Department
- Reading Municipal Light Department
- Rowley Electric Light Department
- Russell Municipal Light Department
- Shrewsbury Electric Light Department
- South Hadley Electric Light Department
- Sterling Electric Light Department
- Taunton Municipal Light Plant
- Templeton Municipal Light Company
- Unitil Corporation
- Wakefield Municipal Gas and Light Department

- Wellesley Municipal Light Plant
- West Boylston Municipal Lighting
- Westfield Gas and Electric Department
- PTI Electric Department
- Direct Energy

Michigan
- Alger Delta Electric Cooperative
- Alpena Power Company
- American Electric Power (Indiana Michigan Power)
- Cherryland Electric Cooperative
- Cloveriand Electric Cooperative (Cloverland acquired Edison Sault Electric Company in 2009)
- Consumers Energy
- DTE Energy (DTE Energy Electric Company)
- Great Lakes Energy Cooperative
- Holland Board of Public Works
- Homeworks Tri-County Electric Cooperative
- Lansing Board of Water & Light
- Lowell Light and Power

- Midwest Energy & Communications (Cooperative)
- Ontonagon County REA (Cooperative)
- Presque Isle Electric & Gas Cooperative
- Thumb Electric Cooperative
- Upper Peninsula Power Company
- We Energies
- Wyandotte Municipal Services

Minnesota
- Basin Electric Power Cooperative
- Dairyland Power Coop
- East River Electric Power Co-op
- Freeborn-Mower Co-op Services
- Great River Energy
- Hutchinson Utilities Commission
- Interstate Power and Light Company
- L&O Power Co-op
- Marshall Municipal Utilities
- Minnkota Power Cooperative,
- Minnesota Power
- Missouri River Energy

- Northern States Power Company, a subsidiary of Xcel Energy
- People's Co-op Tri-County Electric
- Otter Tail Power Company
- Rochester Public Utilities Commission
- Southern Minnesota Municipal Power Agency
- Willmar Municipal Utilities
- Xcel Energy

Mississippi
- Cooperative Energy, formerly South Mississippi Electric Power Association
- Entergy Mississippi
- Magnolia Electric Power
- Mississippi Power, a part of the Southern Company
- Pearl River Valley EPA
- Tennessee Valley Authority
- Yazoo Valley Electric Power Association

Missouri
- Ameren
- Aquila

- City Utilities of Springfield
- Empire District Electric Company
- Independence Power and Light
- Kansas City Power and Light Company

Montana
- Central Montana Electric Power Cooperative
- Montana-Dakota Utilities (MDU)
- Montana Electric Cooperatives' Association
- Northwestern Energy

Nebraska
- Nebraska Public Power District
- Omaha Public Power District
- Lincoln Electric System

Nevada
- NV Energy (Nevada Power)
- Sierra Pacific Power

New Hampshire
- Eversource Energy (Public Service Company of New Hampshire)

(Continued)

| 195

Table 8.4 (Continued)

- Liberty Utilities (including Granite State Electric)
- New Hampshire Electric Cooperative
- Northeast Utilities
- National Grid
- Unitil Corporation

◆ **New Jersey**

- GANDU Electric, heavy electric
- Atlantic City Electric, a subsidiary of Exelon
- Borough of Madison Electric Utility
- Borough of Milltown Electric Department
- Borough of Park Ridge Electric Department
- Borough of Seaside Heights Electric Utility
- Borough of South River Electric Department
- Butler Power and Light
- Direct Energy
- FirstEnergy (Jersey Central Power and Light Company)
- Lavallette Electric Department
- Northeast Utilities

- Pemberton Borough Electric Department
- Public Service Electric and Gas Company
- Rockland Electric
- South Jersey Industries
- Sussex Rural Electric Cooperative
- Vineland Municipal Electric Utility

■ **New Mexico**

- El Paso Electric
- Public Service Company of New Mexico
- Southwestern Public Service Company

◄ **New York**

- Central Hudson Gas 8, Electric
- CH Energy Group
- Consolidated Edison Company of New York
- Direct Energy
- East Coast Power & Gas
- Long Island Power Authority (LIPA)
- National Grid (Niagara Mohawk)

- New York Power Authority (NYPA)
- New York State Electric & Gas, subsidiary of AVANGRID
- Orange and Rockland
- Northeast Utilities
- Rochester Gas & Electric

◄ **North Carolina**

- Albemarie Electric Membership Corporation
- Blue Ridge Energy
- Brunswick Electric Membership Corporation
- Cape Hatteras Electric Cooperative
- Carteret-Craven Electric Cooperative
- Central Electric Membership Corporation
- City of Concord Electric Department
- Dominion North Carolina Power
- Duke Energy
- Edgecombe-Martin County Electric Membership Corporation

- EnergyUnited
- Four County Electric Membership Corporation
- French Broad Electric Membership Corporation
- Halifax Electric Membership Corporation
- Haywood Electric Membership Corporation
- Jones-Onslow Electric Membership Corporation
- Lumbee River Electric Membership Corporation
- North Carolina Electric Membership Corporation
- Pee Dee Electric Membership Corporation
- Piedmont Electric Membership Corporation
- Pitt 8, Greene Electric Membership Corporation
- Randolph Electric Membership Corporation
- Roanoke Electric Cooperative

- Rutherford Electric Membership Corporation
- South River Electric Membership Corporation
- Surry-Yadkin Electric Membership Corporation
- Tennessee Valley Authority
- Tideland Electric Membership Corporation
- Tri-County Electric Membership Corporation
- Union Power Cooperative
- Wake Electric Membership Corporation

■ **North Dakota**

- Basin Electric Power Cooperative
- Central Power Electric Cooperative
- Montana Dakota Utilities (MDU)
- Minnkota Power Cooperative
- Northern States Power Company

- Otter Tail Power Company
- Upper Missouri Power Cooperative
- Xcel Energy

▶ **Ohio**

- American Electric Power
- Cinergy Corporation
- Cleveland Electric liluminating Company
- Consolidated Electric Cooperative
- Dayton Power & Light
- Direct Energy
- Duke Energy
- FirstEnergy
- Ohio Edison
- South Central Power Company
- Toledo Edison

▶ **Oklahoma**

- East Central Electric Cooperative
- Oklahoma Gas & Electric
- Public Service Company of Oklahoma
- Western Farmers Electric Cooperative

ENERGY

Oregon
- Claverack Rural Electric Cooperative
- Columbia River Public Utility District
- Direct Energy
- Eugene Water & Electric Board (EWEB)
- Duquesne Light
- FirstEnergy
- IDACORP (Idaho Power)
- Lansdale Electric
- PacifiCorp (Pacific Power)
- New Enterprise Rural Electric Cooperative
- Portland General Electric
- Northeast Utilities
- West Oregon Electric Cooperative
- Northwestern Rural Electric Cooperative
- PECO, a subsidiary of Exelon
- Perkasie Borough Electric Department

Pennsylvania
- Pike County Light & Power
- Adams Electric Cooperative
- PPL Electric Utilities
- Allegheny Electric Cooperative
- REA Energy Cooperative
- Bedford Rural Electric Co.
- Rural Valley Electric Cooperative
- Borough of Ephrata Electric Division
- Somerset Rural Electric Cooperative
- Borough of Hatfield Electric Utility
- Sullivan County Rural Electric Cooperative
- Borough of Kutztown Electric Department
- Tri-County Rural Electric Cooperative
- Borough of Quakertown Electric Department
- UGI Utilities
- Borough of Schuylkill Haven Utilities Department
- United Electric Cooperative
- Valley Rural Electric Cooperative
- Central Electric Cooperative
- Warren Electric Cooperative
- Citizen's Electric Company
- Wellsboro Electric Company

Puerto Rico
- Autoridad de Energía Eléctrica
- EcoElectrica

Rhode Island
- Direct Energy
- National Grid
- Northeast Utilities
- Pascoag Utility District

South Carolina
- Aiken Electric Co-Op
- Central Electric Power Cooperative, Inc.
- Duke Energy
- Progress Energy Carolinas
- Santee Cooper
- South Carolina Electric & Gas Company
- Tri-County Electric Co-Op

South Dakota
- Black Hills Power
- East River Electric Cooperative
- MidAmerican Energy Company
- Montana-Dakota Utilities (MDU)
- Northern States Power Company

- Northwestern Energy
- Otter Tail Power Company
- Rushmore Eletric Cooperative
- Xcel Energy

Tennessee
- Appalachian Power, a unit of American Electric Power
- Citizens Utilities Board[where?]
- EPB (Electric Power Board), Chattanooga, Hamilton County
- Knoxville Utilities Board
- Lenoir City Utilities Board
- Memphis Light, Gas and Water
- Nashville Electric Service, metro Nashville, Davidson County
- Tennessee Valley Authority

Texas
- American Electric Power
- Amigo Energy
- Austin Energy
- Bartlett Electric Cooperative
- Brazos Electric Power Cooperative
- CenterPoint Energy
- City of Bryan
- City of Greenville
- Comanche Electric Cooperative
- CoServ Electric
- Cosery Electric
- CPS Energy
- Denton Municipal Electric
- Direct Energy
- dPi Energy
- El Paso Electric
- Electric Database Publishing
- Entergy
- Entrust Energy
- Fort Belknap Electric Cooperative
- Garland Power & Light
- GDF SUEZ Energy Resources
- Golden Spread Electric Cooperative
- Hamilton County Electric Cooperative
- Heart of Texas Electric Cooperative
- HILCO Electric Cooperative
- J-A-C Electric Cooperative
- Lower Colorado River Authority
- Luminant
- MidSouth Synergy
- Navarro County Electric Cooperative
- Navasota Valley Electric Cooperative
- Oncor Electric Delivery (Formerly TXU)
- Pedernales Electric Cooperative
- PenTex Energy
- Reliant Energy
- South Plains Electric Cooperative
- Southwestern Public Service Company
- Texas Electric Service Company
- Texas New Mexico Power
- Tara Energy
- Tri-County Electric Cooperative
- TXU Energy
- United Cooperative Services
- Wise Electric Cooperative

Utah
- Intermountain Power Agency (IPA)
- PacifiCorp (Rocky Mountain Power)

Vermont
- Burlington Electric Department
- Central Vermont Public Service
- Gaz Metro (Green Mountain Power)

(Continued)

| 197

Table 8.4 (Continued)

• Vermont Electric Cooperative • Washington Electric Cooperative ◂ **Virginia** • A&N Electric Cooperative • Appalachian Power • BARC Electric Cooperative • Community Electric Cooperative • Craig-Botetourt Electric Cooperative • Danville Utilities	• Dominion Virginia Power • Mecklenberg Electric Cooperative • Northern Neck Electric Cooperative • Northern Virginia Electric Cooperative • Old Dominion Electric Cooperative • Prince George Electric Cooperative • Rapahannock Electric Cooperative • Shenandoah Valley Electric Cooperative • Southside Electric Cooperative	▰ **Washington** • Avista Utilities • Benton County Public Utility District • Chelan County Public Utility District • Clark Public Utilities • Douglas County Public Utility District • Franklin County Public Utility District • Grant County Public Utility District • Klickitat Public Utility District • Mason County Public Utility District 3
• Orcas Power and Light Coop (OPALCO) • PacifiCorp (Pacific Power) • Peninsula Light Co • Pend Oreille County Public Utility District • Puget Sound Energy • Seattle City Light • Snohomish County Public Utility District • Tacoma Power • Tanner Electric Coop ◂ **West Virginia** • Allegheny Electric Cooperative (Allegheny Power)	• Appalachian Power • FirstEnergy • Wheeling Electric Power (AEP Ohio) ▰ **Wisconsin** • Dairyland Power Cooperative • Madison Gas and Electric • Northern States Power Company-Wisconsin • We Energies • Wisconsin Power and Light Company	• Wisconsin Public Service Corporation • Xcel Energy ▰ **Wyoming** • Cheyenne Light, Fuel & Power • Lower Valley Energy • PacifiCorp (Rocky Mountain Power)

Source: https://en.wikipedia.org/wiki/List_of_United_States_electric_companies

8.3.7 Renewable Energy and Carbon Offsets

(Refer also to page 283 in the LEED O+M v4 Reference Guide)

This credit provides options to achieve the most predictable source of power for any sustainable building – renewable resources. It is more difficult to achieve however in existing buildings. It is clear that renewable energy systems, such as geothermal, biomass, and those discussed in Chapter 8.3.3, are able to replace in entirety or partially a reliance on the energy grid, thus limiting the amount of fossil fuel used to power the facility's systems (see also restrictions to what type of renewables are acceptable in the LEED O+M v4 Reference Guide, page 287). However, there are many limiting factors to installing renewable systems on campus such as budget, location, lack of infrastructure, or timing (a new renewable energy system must be in place during the Performance Period). In these cases, a Renewable Energy Certificate (REC) and Carbon Offsets become attractive options to achieve independence from the energy grid. What may not be clear are the concepts behind these strategies, and how these factor into accomplishing the same goal as other measures of energy efficiency.

Both of these documents represent how applying environmental measures can minimize GHG emissions. Carbon Offsets and RECs are guided by regulations on how they are used and retired. Each has a unique identification number which is placed in a database to prevent double usage. "Offsets and RECs, however, are fundamentally different instruments with different impacts, representing different criteria for qualification and crediting in the context of inventory or emissions footprint."[78] Offsets represent emissions avoided or reduced, while RECs represent renewable electricity generation.

The energy sources of RECs may include a wind turbine farm or a PV array in a field, among others. However, despite the source, its location or its proximity to the buildings benefitting from it, RECs *do not directly transfer energy to a building*. Also known as Tradable Renewable Certificates (TRCs), Solar Renewable Energy Certificates (SRECs) or Green Tags, RECs are

> market-based instruments that represents the property rights to the environmental, social and other non-power attributes of renewable electricity generation. RECs are issued when one megawatt-hour (MWh) of electricity is generated and delivered to the electricity grid from a renewable energy resource.[79]

They represent environmental attributes of renewable energy generation, can be used almost like environmental currency that can be bought or sold separately from the electricity,[80] and can only be used to mitigate the effects from Scope 2 emissions (Figure 8.27).

Carbon Offsets, similar to RECs, are certificates used in measuring environmental attributes: both are a form of trade. They differ in the units of what they measure and how these are

ENERGY

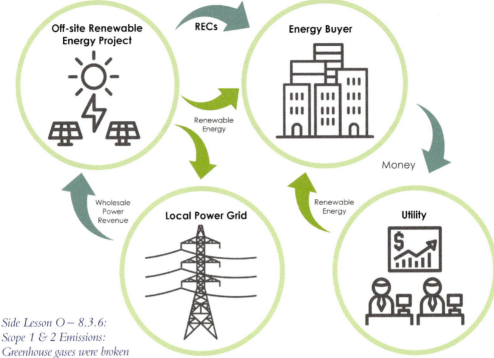

Fig 8.27 Renewable Energy Certificate

Source: Derived from Urban Grid (www.urbangridsolar.com/guide-to-virtual-power-purchase-agreements/). Diagrammed by Elizabeth Meyers, 2020

Side Lesson O – 8.3.6: Scope 1 & 2 Emissions: Greenhouse gases were broken down into three categories or "scopes" by the Greenhouse Gas Protocol. Each scope is defined by the source of the greenhouse gas emissions. Scope 1 is all direct emissions. Examples of this include on site fuel combustion from company vehicles, gas boilers, and air-conditioning leaks. Scope 2 is all indirect emissions. Examples of this include emissions created during the production of energy. Scope 3 is all other indirect emissions from a company or organization that are out of their control, such as travel, water, and water. Scope 3 typically has the highest level of emissions (see https://compareyourfootprint.com/difference-scope-1-2-3-emissions/).

calculated. Where RECs represent energy offsets by a renewable source, Carbon Offsets represent CO_2 emissions offset by the reduction of emissions made elsewhere. They allow your institution to 'pay' for the reduction of GHGs universally instead of proposing extreme and often unrealistic reductions on campus. Carbon offsets may be used to mitigate the effects from both Scope 1 emissions or Scope 2 emissions.

Logically, enabling all of the options the credit offers simultaneously will lead to an aggregate reduction of global GHGs. But regardless of how it is achieved – installing renewable systems, purchasing RECs or Carbon Offsets – simply achieving this credit may be an excellent testimony to your institution's commitment to global climate change mitigation. It may be capitalized through the campus' public relations and media outreach.

Tasks

The conditions to achieve credit for using renewable energy or carbon offsets again require the close participation of your

ENERGY

facility personnel. Decisions about which method to accomplish for offsetting grid energy are a significant measure for any large institution. However, the calculations required for documentation, as well as informing facility staff of advances in the field of green power, are the ways in which LEED Lab students may be instrumental as catalysts for advancing renewables on campus. The following steps illustrate a path derived from the LEED O+M v4 Reference Guide specifically for LEED Lab:

Box 8.2 Main tasks for renewable energy and carbon offsets

1. **Investigate:** Provide green power options to the facility personnel.
    Students are encouraged to provide a summary of research regarding the green power options which their local utility and private companies provide to their facility personnel. If the sustainability coordinators of the campus already are aware of such options, or if such research is already being accomplished administratively, LEED Lab students should communicate with these individuals to inform them of their credit pursuit (see Tools on the next page for guidance).

2. **Calculate:** Determine the amount of energy being offset from the grid.
    Many sources of offsetting from the grid may be considered if the power is being directly offset from the institution's energy or the institution directly receives power from the renewable energy sources (Figure 8.28).

    ☐ Check off the following that apply, then calculate the amount of energy from that source.

    A. **Renewable Energy Sources**

    _____ ON-site, owned by the institution
    _____ ON-site owned by third party
    _____ OFF-site owned by the institution
    _____ OFF-site owned by third party

    ☐ Identify the annual total building energy use from the Minimum Energy Performance Prerequisite (*Chapter 8.3.2*). _____.
    ☐ Identify the annual renewable energy generated through actual metered data _____.
    ☐ Calculate.
    ☐ Total Renewable Energy Source Points = _____
    ☐ Establish contract to install renewable energy during the Performance Period.

    B. **RECs**

    _____ REC from Green-E Certified Equivalent source
    _____ REC from Equivalent

    ☐ Identify the annual total building energy use from the Minimum Energy Performance Prerequisite (*Chapter 8.3.2*). _____.
    ☐ Subtract this figure item (1) from any existing or proposed Renewable Energy Source you have in your facility (item 2 above). _____.
    ☐ Calculate.
    ☐ Total REC Points= _____
    ☐ Establish contract with the REC provider during the Performance Period.

ENERGY

> C. **Carbon Offsets**
> ☐ Identify the annual total building energy use from the Minimum Energy Performance Prerequisite (*Chapter 8.3.2*). _____.
> ☐ Calculate the amount of CO2 your institution generates_____.
> ☐ Subtract this figure from any existing or proposed Renewable Energy Source or REC you have in your facility (item 2). _____.
> ☐ Calculate.
> ☐ Total REC Points= _____
>
> (*Please see Tables 1 and 2 on pages 288 and 289 of LEED O+M v4 Reference Guide*)
>
> ☐ default emissions factors established by Energy Star® Portfolio Manager®.
>
> Add all of the points from Renewable Energy Sources, RECs and Carbon Offsets.
>
> 3. **Establish:** Install all systems considered for on-site or off-site green power Performance Period. Generate digital copies of all contracts for each renewable resource product.

EQUATION 1: Renewable Energy Systems Contribution

$$\left[\left(\frac{\text{Renewable energy generated}}{\text{(Total) building energy use}}\right) \% \div 1.5\% = \text{Total Renewable Energy Source Points}\right]$$

EQUATION 2: Percentage of Energy Purchased or Offset by RECS, Green Power, and Carbon Offsets

$$\left[\left(\frac{\text{Quantity of RECs in kWh}}{\text{Annual building energy use in kWhs}}\right) + \left(\frac{\text{Purchased green power in kWh}}{\text{Annual building energy use in kWh}}\right) + \left(\frac{\text{Purchased carbon offset}}{\text{Annual building energy use in kWh}}\right)\right] = \% \text{ Energy Purchased or Offset}$$

EQUATION 3: Contribution from RECS, Green Power, and Carbon Offsets

$$\left[\text{Energy purchased or offset \%} \div 25\%\right] = \text{Points}$$

Fig 8.28 *Energy and Atmosphere credit: renewable energy and carbon offsets equations*
Source: Derived from LEED O+M v4 Reference Guide. Redrawn by Elizabeth Meyers, 2020

 Tools

If Renewable Energy Systems, RECS or any of the methods above are already a part of your campus' strategic plan, or if your campus will be installing them in the near future, this credit is achievable. If there is a question about the process for acquiring them for your campus, there are tools which may accompany the LEED Lab student to meetings with facility personnel to facilitate discussions that can determine which measure or combination of measures would be the most prudent for your specific institution. The following publications function as tools to wards this aim:

Green Power Procurement Process. The EPA created a Green Power Partnership in 2001 to protect human health and the environment by increasing organizations' voluntary green power. It was intended to advance the American market for green power and the development of those renewable electricity sources.[81] "As of January 2018, the Partnership has more than 1,700 Partner organizations voluntarily using billions of kilowatt-hours (kWh) of green power annually."[82] The following resources serve as tools for assisting the assessment of your institution's priorities and potential with selecting which renewable resources are most appropriate for your institution:

- www.epa.gov/greenpower/green-power-procurement-process
- www.epa.gov/sites/production/files/2016-01/documents/purchasing_guide_for_web.pdf

Green-e Energy Certified Resources. Once the decision to procure renewable resources is made, this website will help your institution decide which green trade product specifically to pursue. Some examples include Agera Energy's "Pure Wind" product (100 percent wind power), Alliant Energy's "Second Nature" product (comprising 85 percent wind, 13 percent biogas and 2 percent solar), or Bonneville Environmental Foundation's "BEF Carbon Mix" product (various constitution of landfill Gas Capture, Renewable Energy, Organic Waste Composting and SF6 Reduction). Green-e certified renewable energy and carbon offset products meet the most stringent environmental and consumer protection standards in North America. You can search for certified green power and renewable energy certificate programs for your home or business and carbon offset products to offset your emissions from certain activities.[83] The LEED O+M v4 Reference Guide also provides instructions for Green-e Certified equivalents, which are also permitted. www.green-e.org/certified-resources.

Techniques

- ☐ If your institution already purchases RECs and Carbon Offsets for certain facilities on campus, it may be easier to meet this credit if the amount could be increased to accommodate your specific facility. If not, researching providers and products may be facilitated through the Tools in this chapter.
- ☐ Note that RECs may be procured on the open market *or* through a utility provider.
- ☐ Carbon Offsets for projects in the US must be derived from GHG reduction projects within the US and may be applied only toward nonelectric energy uses.
- ☐ Green power and RECs must be applied only to electric uses. Green power, Carbon Offsets and RECs all must be Green-e Energy Certified or the equivalent.

ENERGY

- If your LEED Lab class and facility personnel choose *not* to install or purchase Green-e Energy and Green-e Climate products and opt for demonstrating equivalency, it will take much more time to document.
- Renewable resource systems, also called "Green Power," may be installed on- or off-site if they still provide direct energy to the facility. In the latter case, they must be accompanied with a purchase agreement of power with the third party showing at least the next 10 years of partnership, where that party provides renewable energy to your facility.
- The amount of energy produced and consumed – regardless of whether it is on or off site – must be capable of being sub metered.
- If renewable energy is sold *back* to the grid the project must procure the same number of RECs for a minimum of 10 years.

8.4 Case Study

The Edward M. Crough School of Architecture and Planning was certified under LEED O+M 2009 with a commitment to share whole-building energy and water usage data through the Energy Star® Portfolio Manager® Tool and USGBC Release Form (Figure 8.29).

The Crough building is served by electricity, steam (from the university's central plant), and potable water. The whole-building energy consumption metering is collected by one electricity meter and one steam meter. The whole-building water metering is collected by one potable water meter for indoor uses – save for process water – and one irrigation meter. Process water is not used at the Crough building as it does not house any cooling towers, chillers or boilers. All meters are permanently installed at the site specifically for the Crough Center. A central meter located at the University's central plant collects the data from all meters. This data is not directly connected to the existing BAS system, and any HVAC adjustments required for optimizing building energy performance must be coordinated manually by the university's operation and maintenance staff (Figure 8.30). This limitation in building automated operations or direct digital controls as well as the absence of sub-meters for the Crough Center's major energy end uses did not allow the LEED Lab team to pursue the energy credit for Advanced Energy Metering.

The Crough Center energy and water meters are owned by The Catholic University of America. As part of this prerequisite's requirement, the school is in charge of meter maintenance and calibration. The meters' performance is regularly and continuously overseen by the facilities maintenance and operations staff through the BAS and central meter as well as through the data management system. Any discrepancies or deviations in data can be readily recognized via daily or monthly readings and checks. Per the manufacturer's recommendations, the Crough

ENERGY

6. Must Commit to Sharing Whole-Building Energy and Water Usage Data

☒ I commit to sharing with USGBC and/or GBCI all available actual whole-project energy and water usage data. This commitment will start upon certification acceptance or on the date that the LEED project begins typical physical occupancy and will continue for at least 5 years. I understand that sharing this data includes supplying information on a regular basis in a free, accessible, and secure online tool, OR allowing USGBC to access the whole-project metering facility where such meters are in place, OR taking any action necessary to authorize USGBC, GBCI or their designee to collect project information directly from service or utility providers. I will use reasonable efforts to ensure that this commitment carries forward in the event that the building or space changes ownership or lessee.

Furthermore, I understand that the purpose of data collection is for research and to aid in improving the LEED program. I understand that any whole-project energy and water usage data that is made publicly available shall be presented in an aggregate form with no identifying project-specific characteristics.

Furthermore, I understand that if my project does not have meters in place that measure energy and/or water usage for the entire LEED certified gross floor area, I will not be required to supply energy or water usage data unless and until such meters are installed. I understand that if the LEED project is altered, sold, assigned or otherwise transferred in such a way that the data for the original LEED project becomes impractical to collect, I will no longer be required to provide the data or provide access to the data.

Select one of the following:
- ⦿ **Option 1.** Share Data through ENERGY STAR's Portfolio Manager Tool and the USGBC Release Form
- ○ **Option 2.** Project Owner Commitment to Apply for LEED for EB: O&M Recertification
- ○ **Option 3.** Share Data Through Approved Format

ENERGY STAR's Portfolio Manager and the USGBC Release Form

Required Signatory PIf1-1. Owner/Agent

The project is registered in ENERGY STAR's Portfolio Manager tool.
USGBC - LEED Performance Reporting has master account access to the project in Portfolio Manager.
Subsequent to LEED Certification (at certification acceptance or upon typical physical occupancy), the project will report energy and water data into the Portfolio Manager project on a monthly basis for a duration of five years.

Note: Master account "USGBC - LEEDPerformanceReporting" is not the same master account as offered in EA Prerequisite 2/Credit 1. For instructions on registering in ENERGY STAR Portfolio Manager or sharing access with a master account, refer to PI Form 1 Credit Resources section in LEED Online.

LEED 2009 for Existing Buildings: Operations & Maintenance
PI Form 1: Minimum Program Requirements
Page 2 of 4

Save Form

Version 4.0
Copyright © 2009 U.S. Green Building Council. All Rights Reserved.

Fig 8.29 *Minimum project requirement for the Crough School of Architecture and Planning, Item 6*
Source: Data from the Crough Center documentation for the LEED O+M certification, 2014 and from USGBC LEED O+M 2009, PI Form1: Minimum Program Requirements, page 2

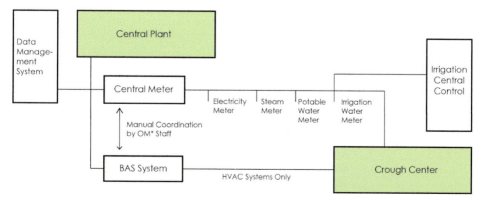

Fig 8.30 *Metering Management System at the Crough Center*
Source: Data from the Crough Center documentation for the LEED O+M certification, 2014. Diagrammed by Ana R. Paraon and Elizabeth Meyers, 2020

Center's meters require calibration after a period of at least two years. As was required, these meters were initially calibrated at installation by the manufacturer, and calibration data was found on the Certificate of Calibration issued by the manufacturer.

Data recording and management for electricity, potable water and steam for this project was initially documented by a third-party engineering firm. Over time, LEED Lab team members received training on specific management software programs to track and document this data on their own. Consequently, the costs associated with contracting a third-party engineering firm to perform this task were eliminated. However, maintaining consistency and continuity of meter data management became an apparent concern. The University's maintenance and operation team became the most appropriate group for supervising this data, and as such they required and received the same training as the original LEED Lab students. The University's new maintenance and operation staff now handle the data management system.

Irrigation water metering is only taken when the system is activated by the climate-sensitive central control, to which the water meter is connected. The occurrence of irrigation is determined according to current weather conditions and parameters specified at the central control. Typically, irrigation at the Crough Center site occurs annually from April to October.

Based on the whole-building energy metering and analysis done during the Crough LEED O+M Performance Period, lighting and equipment carried the highest demand for energy at the Crough Center. One of the most effective strategies implemented for reducing this demand was to install an automatic shut off switch for the existing general lighting at the ground floor. Through this strategy, general lighting is turned off at 8:00 am throughout the year. Lights are turned on at 6:00 pm during the summer and at 4:00 pm during the winter months. The application of this strategy resulted in an overall 30 percent reduction in energy consumption. Implementing this strategy was made possible by coordinating the energy prerequisites with the credit EQ c2.4 Daylight and Views (LEED O+M 2009) which analyzed daylighting availability at the Crough Center.

The process for achieving the Energy and Atmosphere prerequisites was especially challenging in this case study because two major complications existed: (1) the steam meter failure during the original Performance Period and (2) the lack of pre-existing baseline data or precise classification for 'schools of architecture.' Continuous preventive maintenance of installed meters was extremely important to guarantee not only accuracy but also continuity of data recording, especially during the Performance Period.

During the Performance Period, one of the meters for the Crough Center failed to provide such continuous reading and extra time was required to adjust all energy data to an acceptable 12-month timeframe of data reporting. Since a specific energy baseline for schools of architecture did not exist within the Energy Star® Portfolio Manager®, the main challenge was to establish an acceptable energy baseline that would most accurately reflect the energy consumption at the Crough Center.

Initial attempts to utilize the existing 'Laboratory' definition per CBECS and Energy Star's® Portfolio Manager® did not meet the School of Architecture program and operations requirements, which extended beyond laboratories alone. Finally, as agreed and approved by USGBC, a baseline was established utilizing the 'K-12 school' definition which required supplemental data and additional energy requirements. As a result, this project was eligible to be developed under the Case 1 – Energy Star® rating.

The Crough Center as an architecture school is not a typical campus educational building: it is open 24 hours a day, seven days per week and many students work in the building late into the night. All laboratories and studios remain open and the building runs at full capacity almost every day of the year minus the Thanksgiving, Christmas, Spring and Easter breaks. Because the Crough Center has operating hours and power-operated equipment unique to the School of Architecture, it still differs from a K-12 building type. Thus, in an effort to more accurately analyze the school EUI, a chart with all power-operated equipment and their consumption was developed. The results of this chart's calculations represented the number of computers used in the Portfolio Manager® tool under the K-12 type option (Table 8.5). Additionally, the building was divided into three parts: education, laboratory (lab), other (Figure 8.31).

"Education" as a category comprises one-third of the building square footage and consists of classrooms, an auditorium, faculty spaces, offices and conference rooms. Faculty and office spaces are only open from 9:00 am to 5:00 pm but the auditorium, classrooms and conference rooms are available for meetings at night, on weekdays and over the weekends. Mechanical equipment, storage and hallways are classified as "Other" and make up a second third of the building's total area (refer to Figure 8.31). Spaces designated as "Laboratory" comprise the last third of the building square footage and consist of studio spaces, computer labs, digital media labs, the woodshop, the prefabrication lab, the spray room and the 3D-printing lab. All of these spaces use an extensive amount of electricity. These labs and studio spaces are considered "dry labs," and the variety and abundance of electrically powered instruments in these dry labs predominantly require high-capacity plugs. Moreover, each student is required to have a computer and uses one or two computer monitors in their studio space.

Given the long and irregular periods of work, a few students keep mini-fridges in their studio spaces, which have become a common component in the school. In Table 8.5, students' computers are represented as the number of transient occupants, since transient occupants often bring their own computers.

The program for the laboratories at the Crough Center is the part that most differs from K-12 schools. Students in these areas use drills and other hand tools when constructing models and various projects. The woodshop, metal shop, Computer Numeric Control (CNC) machine for prefabrication, spray room, 3D-printing machines and laser cutters are available to students 24 hours a day, seven days per week. These lab spaces and the server room are the major contributors to the building energy use.

ENERGY

Table 8.5 Daily energy use at the Crough School of Architecture and Planning

Location	Item	Qty	Watts/hour active mode	Hours Active/day	Watts/day
Server room	Dell r310 server	1	400	24	9,600
Server room	Boxx nodes type a (render nodes)	10	520	8	41,600
Server room	Boxx nodes type b (render nodes)	10	520	8	41,600
Server room	Drobo b800i (storage area network array)	1	164	24	3,936
Server room	Cisco 3560g (multi-purpose switch)	1	160	24	3,840
Server room	Cisco 3750g (storage area network switch)	1	540	24	12,960
Server room	Apc acf400 (air removal unit for rack)	1	1,200	8	9,600
General	Large copy machines	5	1,200	8	48,000
Faculty	Laserjet printers	5	110	8	4,400
Printing lab	Small scanners	3	33.6	8	806.4
Printing lab	Medium scanners	3	144	8	3,456
Printing lab	Plotters	5	720	8	28,800
Digital lab	Wacom_interactive pen display monitor_23in	10	71	4	2,840
General	Task lighting 22w fluorescent bulb	24	22	6	3,168
General	Microwave	3	750	1	2,250
General	Mini fridge	20	75	24	36,000
Classroom	Projectors (ceiling mounted)	3	600	9	16,200
Classroom	Digital portable projectors	2	306	3	1,836
Classroom	Flat screen 52in to 65in	4	120	6	2,880
Digital lab	Audio system	2	500	6	6,000
Woodshop	Laser cutter	2	2,000	8	32,000
Woodshop	Cnc machine	1	5,700	5	28,500
Woodshop	Cnc machine dust collector	1	3,200	5	16,000
Lab	3D printer	2	4,500	8	72,000
Woodshop	Table saw	2	3,200	4	25,600
Woodshop	Chop saw	1	2,800	4	11,200
Woodshop	Planner	1	3,000	4	12,000
Woodshop	Joiner	1	3,000	4	12,000
Woodshop	Bandsaw	1	2,100	6	12,600
Woodshop	Sander, oscillating	1	746	6	4,476
Woodshop	Lathe	1	746	3	2,238
Woodshop	Dust extraction system - laser cutter	2	3,200	8	51,200
Woodshop	Welding machine	1	5,589	4	22,356
Woodshop	Compresser	2	4,450	8	71,200
Paint booth	Exhaust fan at paint booth	1	1,456	4	5,824
Paint booth	Paint spray gun and turbine	1	1,260	4	5,040
			Total watts per day[a]		664,006
Number of computers per equivalence of equipment above					426
Number of existing computers at Crough Center/owned by the School					107
Number of computers per transient occupant (students)					161
Total number of computers					694

Source: Data from the Crough Center documentation for the LEED O+M certification, 2014. Table by Ana R. Paraon

Note: Most equipment will have negligible idle mode consumption with some exceptions, as per ASHRAE Fundamentals 2013

[a] Based on the typical consumption of 65W/hour per computer as per ASHRAE Fundamentals 2013, Chapter 18, Table 8, Note a.

ENERGY

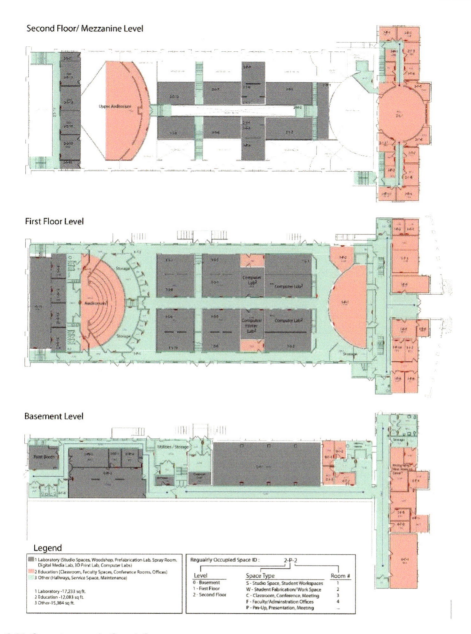

Fig 8.31 *Space types at the Crough Center*
Source: Data from the Crough Center documentation for the LEED O+M certification, 2014, developed by LEED Lab, 2013

All projects must use the Energy Star® Portfolio Manager® tool to track energy consumption data, even when not eligible for an Energy Star® rating. In addition to consumption data from all energy sources, other project information is or may be required by the Portfolio Manager® tool: total and space-type areas, building type, operating hours, building occupancy, number of computers and servers, and finally, area exclusions as permitted by LEED. The main documentation developed under the Portfolio Manger tool is the Statement of Energy Performance. The building in this case study was eligible for an Energy Star rating of 70 under LEED O+M version 2009. The statement reports valuable project information for achieving or documenting this prerequisite as well as other energy credits, such as the site and source EUI, annual energy use by fuel type, the national median comparison data, the annual greenhouse gas emissions and the Energy Star® rating (refer to Figure 8.9).

LEED Lab students worked closely with CUA Facilities Maintenance and Operations staff to compile and document all required information for this prerequisite. A mechanical engineer volunteered his office's services to develop the essential ASHRAE Level 1 Walkthrough Assessment and Report (Westlake Reed Leskosky). Some information required for the Current Sequence of Operations, the Building Operating Plan, the Systems Narrative and the Preventive Maintenance Plan were readily available for the Crough Building. Missing information, such as an additional HVAC unit and the lighting around the building structure, were surveyed and updated into the existing plans and documentation as required. In addition, an integrated coordination, especially among the energy prerequisites, was required to assure that all information was consistent across the prerequisites and credits, as well as to assure that the minimum project requirements of the LEED O+M rating system and code regulation was achieved and implemented during the project Performance Period (e.g., ASHRAE 62.1 Ventilation for Acceptable Indoor Air Quality and Minimum Outdoor Air Supply).

Tables 8.1 and 8.6 indicate some of the final documentation submitted. Under the ASHRAE Level 1 Walkthrough Energy Audit and Report, the summary of findings which refer to the building EUI must indicate a target index and the potential cost savings associated with it. This target index is determined in the Energy Star® Portfolio Manager® tool. The audit report should also include an analysis of energy consumption by major system types or end-uses and should include all fuel sources (refer to Table 8.2 and Figure 8.7). The report on no- to low-cost energy conservation measures (ECMs) should also include the correspondent annual energy demand savings, energy cost savings and maintenance cost savings achievable through these measures. In this case study, the engineers identified several energy conservation measures that ranged from no-cost to capital-cost, within which five were low- to no-cost solutions with an "estimated implementation cost of $12,000 or less ... [for] combined energy savings of $11,000"[84] (Table 8.7 and Figure 8.32).

The Crough Center also helped to generate the "The Catholic University of America – Operating and Maintaining HVAC Systems Policy" as part of the documentation for this prerequisite. This policy describes the protocol for outdoor air measurement as well as the operating and maintenance program for the campus HVAC systems. This program includes recommended practices, assignment of responsibilities, HVAC documentation requirements, standards for inspection and maintenance of HVAC systems and components, standards for temperature and humidity control, standards for inspections and maintenance recording and requirements for training personnel on personal protective equipment and safety standards.

Table 8.6 Preventive maintenance schedule for the Crough School of Architecture and Planning

Equipment (system)	Pm activity	Frequency									
		Every week	By vendor	Every month	By vendor	Every quarter	By vendor	Semi-annual	By vendor	Every year	By vendor
Supply fans (ventilation)	1. Lube pillow block 2. Thoroughly clean unit 3. Inspect complete unit 4. Record name plate data 5. Inspect belts and sheaves 6. Inspect filters and replace as needed 7. Check amps and record							X			
Return fans (ventilation)	1. Lube pillow block 2. Inspect belts 3. Inspect all mountain points 4. Clean fan and blades 5. Log nameplate data 6. Record amp reading							X			
Air compressors only[a] (cooling)	1. Lube motor 2. Record amperage readings							X			
Heating zone pumps[b] (heating)	1. Lube motor 2. Record amperage readings							X			
Hot water circulation pumps (heating)	1. Clean and inspect unit							X			
BAS controls (heating)	1. Software upgrade and inspection			X	X						
Interior general lighting (lighting)	1. Check proper function			X							

(Continued)

Table 8.6 (Continued)

Equipment (system)	Pm activity	Frequency								
		Every week	By vendor	Every month	By vendor	Every quarter	By vendor	Semi-annual	By vendor	Every year	By vendor
Exhaust fan 1[c]; exhaust fan 3[d]; exhaust fan 4[e] (ventilation)	1. Lube blower 2. Lube motor		X								
	3. Check operation	X									
Exhaust fan 2 (restrooms at lower level south) (ventilation)	1. Lube blower 2. Lube motor			X							
	3. Check operation	X									
Exhaust fan 5 (paint booth) (ventilation)	1. Lube blower 2. Lube motor			X							
	3. Check operation			X							

Source: Data from the Crough Center documentation for the LEED O+M certification, 2014

Notes:

The steam to hot water convertors should be cleaned on an annual basis by facilities management, in order to prevent chemical build up, which impedes heat transfer; a schedule that allows for task lighting to replace significant use of overhead lighting will be implemented and enforced. This tactic can help minimize lighting loads and in turn, energy consumption; air filters will be inspected once a month and replaced because the standard for this facility has changed from MERV 8 to MERV 13 during the Performance Period; refrigerant levels should be monitored monthly, to determine levels and identify potential leakage.

[a] Maintenance should be done at the beginning and end of the cooling season. The Crough Center has DX units for AC, no chiller or pumps.
[b] Maintenance should be done at the beginning and end of the heating season.
[c] Located at restrooms at basement level, north.
[d] Located at men's bathroom at main level, north.
[e] Located at ladies' bathroom at main level, north.

Table 8.7 Energy conservation measures for the Crough School of Architecture and Planning

Eccm		Category	Energy use for category	Estimated first cost	Annual energy consumption savings		Annual energy demand savings[1]	Annual maintenance savings	Total annual energy (consumption and demand) cost savings		Simple payback
ID	Description			$	%	kBtu	kW	$	kBtu	$	years
L-1	Switch halogen in studio space and lights throughout to LED.	Lighting	Lighting	$37,454	5	46490	2.5	$500	46490	$1,533	24.4
L-2	Provide more controllability of lighting - occupancy sensors throughout, task lighting at studio, daylight sensors for studio general lighting, break studio halogen lights into smaller circuits for more zones.	Lighting	Lighting	$74,928	25	232450	12.4	$	232450	$7,664	9.8
H-1	Repair insulation of refrigerant piping and provide insulation on fittings and branch piping of HHW to studios.	HVAC	Space heating, Cooling, Ventilation, Refrigeration	$11,086	2.5	42310	2.3	$ -	42310	$1,297	8.5
H-2	Auditoriums and enclosed classrooms should have setback cooling/heating setpoint based on occupancy season/schedule.	HVAC	Space Heating, Cooling, Ventilation, Refrigeration	$11,036	10	169240	9	$ -	169210	$5,190	2.1
H-3	More means of preventing stratification in high ceiling studio space should be used (ceiling fans on/air pear fans at top).	HVAC	Space Heating, Cooling, Ventilation, Refrigeration	$22,171	10	169240	9	$ -	169540	$5,190	4.3
H-4	One or two central entrances/exits at studio should be used instead of 12 (other only for emergency) Means to prevent infiltration should be used - air door, vestibule, alarm if door popped open for certain time period, etc.	HVAC	Space Heating, Cooling, Ventilation, Refrigeration	$6,543	5	84620	4.5	$ -	84620	$2,595	2.5

(Continued)

ENERGY

Table 8.7 (Continued)

Eccm		Category	Energy use for category	Estimated first cost	Annual energy consumption savings	Annual energy demand savings[1]	Annual maintenance savings	Total annual energy (consumption and demand) cost savings	Simple payback
H-5	Addition of insulation on exterior wall/roof should be investigated.	HVACC	Space Heating, Cooling, Ventilation, Refrigerator	$ 216,097	15	253859	13.5	$ -	253859	$ 7,785	27.8
H-6	Mechanical system should be tied to operable windows of some alarm of visual signal to show one or the other is being used to prevent both fighting each other.	HVAC	Space Heating, Cooling, Ventilation, Refrigerator	$ 27,712	5	84620	4.5	$ -	84620	$ 2,595	10.7
P-1	Limited use of elevator should be encouraged, alternative route to basement.	Process	Miscellaneous	$ 1,000	5	8998	0.5	$ -	8998	$ 297	3.4
P-2	Projectors and other equipment should be turned off and not be in stand-by when un-used.	Process	Miscellaneous	$ 1,000	2.5	4499	0.2	$ -	4499	$ 148	6.7

Source: Data from the Crough Center ASHRAE Level 1 Walkthrough documentation for the LEED O+M certification, 2014, developed by Westlake Reed Leskosky

Note:
1 Utility rate structure provided by university is average rate, which takes into account all consumptions and demand charges. Broken out demand structure not provided by university for analysts. Low-to-No-Cost Energy Conservation Measures identified by Westlake Reed Leskosky.

ENERGY

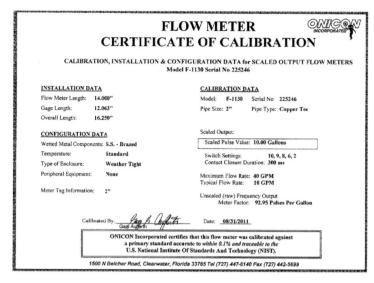

Fig 8.32 Sample Meter Certificate of Calibration
Source: Data from the Crough Center documentation for the LEED O+M certification, 2014

The requirements for the Fundamental Refrigerant Management Prerequisite were achieved through the Crough's phase-out plan to replace CFC-based air-handling units within five years of the LEED O+M certification date. The existing units serving the Crough Center use the HCFC–22 refrigerant. According to the plan, the units are to be replaced with equipment fitted with the compliant refrigerant R-134A or R410. Collectively, these energy strategies, analyses and accomplishments helped the school to achieve LEED O+M certification; the first of its kind for any architecture school.

8.5 Exercises

The questions below are derived from the aforementioned case study. Questions testing knowledge of the breadth of tools, tasks and techniques are important for LEED Lab; the investigation required in answering these exercises helps students to approach their credit assignments from a synergistic perspective.

Exercise Scenario 1

Circulating pumps push the water to each air handling unit through a coil and fans which blow air over the coil to heat the air to a pre-determined set point. Research what constitutes a set point modification, and understand that even a small change in temperature has a significant impact on energy efficiency.

| 215

ENERGY

a. What is a 'setpoint'?
b. How can the setpoint for Crough Center be modified?
c. What would the benefit of this modification be?

Exercise Scenario 2

Sections in the ENERGY chapter of the Reference Guide provided documentation that directly synergized with determining Best Management Practices for Energy Efficiency. After reading various sections in this chapter (Minimum Energy Performance, the ASHRAE Level 1 Walkthough Energy Audit and Report, etc.) which are the two most symbiotic credits?

a. Which are the two most symbiotic credits with respect to this section?

Exercise Scenario 3

A 'low hanging fruit' modification to the lighting successfully accomplished a reduction in energy. Students are challenged to study the document in this Case Study and realize that integrating information from the baseline into the assessment is necessary to BOTH identify AND implement modification to operations that can yield measurable differences.

a. How was this accomplished?
b. Referring to the Combined Fuel End-Use Breakdown diagram, why was this specific item in the Sequence of Operations chosen?

Exercise Scenario 4

Significant measures to actual improvement or replacement of the standard equipment have not been accomplished in the Case Study. They will explore the various sections of this chapter to find that there are credits that ensure the advancement of the foundations proposed in this section. Existing Building Commissioning Analysis or Implementation and Ongoing Commissioning: this prerequisite documentation describes the required operation and maintenance of the systems that may be commissioned, as well as recommendations for energy conservation measures that will be implemented under the Existing Building Commissioning credit).

a. Is there an established EAFL? Where would you recommend this information to be located in your LEED Lab facility's assessment?
b. What chapter section can ensure that the proper preventative maintenance, systems narrative and overall sequence of operations and maintenance are being advanced regardless of replacing equipment?

Exercise Scenario 5

The Facilities Manager at CUA speculated the application of using Renewable Energy for a facility which is scheduled to be used as the LEED Lab case study certification building in 2020. The building has an annual energy use of 8,000,000 kWh in electricity only without other energy use. A PV array installed in 2005 has already generated approximately 300,000 kWh in the same time period.

a. Using Equation 1, calculate the contribution of solar energy to its total energy use.

Notes

1. "How Much Energy is Consumed in U.S. Residential and Commercial Buildings?" US Energy Information Administration: Independent Statistics and Analysis, May 3, 2018. www.eia.gov/tools/faqs/faq.php?id=86&t=1
2. "Why the Building Sector?" Architecture 2030, 2017. http://architecture2030.org/buildings_problem_why/
3. US Green Building Council, "Energy Efficient Best Management Practices," *Reference Guide for Building Operations and Maintenance* (Washington, DC: US Green Building Council, 2013): 198.
4. "Use Portfolio Manager," Energy Star, 2018. www.energystar.gov/buildings/facility-owners-and-managers/existing-buildings/use-portfolio-manage
5. *International Sustainability Systems Comparison: Key International Sustainability Systems: Energy and Water Conservation Requirements* (CoreNet Global/ARUP, 2014): 31.
6. Green Building Initiative, *Green Globes® for Existing Buildings 2007 Technical Reference Manual, Version 1.21 December 2019* (Green Building Initiative, Inc., 2019): 15–16. www.thegbi.org/files/training_resources/Green_Globes_EB_2007_Technical_Reference_Manual.pdf
7. Ibid.
8. *BREEAM In-Use International Technical Manual SD221 2.0:2015 – February 2016* (BRE Global Ltd, 2015): 218–330. https://tools.breeam.com/filelibrary/Technical%20Manuals/SD221_BIU_International_2015_Re-issue_V2.0.pdf
9. Ibid.
10. Green Building Council of Australia, "Greenhouse Gas Emissions" and "Peak Electricity Demand," *Green Star – Performance v1.2 – Initial Certification Submission Template r1*. www.gbca.org.au/greenstar-manager/resources/?filter-rating-tool=101&_ga=2.107716033.213355384.1592333897-29415128.1591753717
11. "Living Green Star: Green Star is an Internationally Recognised Sustainability Rating System," Green Building Council Australia, 2015. https://new.gbca.org.au/green-star/rating-system/
12. US Green Building Council 2013, 187, op. cit.
13. Ibid., 186.
14. Singapore Building and Construction Authority, *BCA Green Mark GM ENRB: 2017: Technical Guide and Requirements* (Singapore: Building and Construction Authority, 2017): 7–8.
15. *BEAM Plus Existing Buildings Version 2.0 (2016.03): Comprehensive Scheme* (Hong Kong: Hong Kong Green Building Council, 2016): 15. www.beamsociety.org.hk/files/download/BEAM%20Plus%20Existing%20Buildings%20v2_0_Comprehensive%20Scheme.pdf
16. "New Options Under EB V2.0," Hong Kong Green Building Council, 2018. www.hkgbc.org.hk/eng/EB_2-0Scheme.aspx
17. Japan Sustainable Building Consortium and Japan Green Building Council, *Comprehensive Assessment System for Built Environmental Efficiency: CASBEE* (Tokyo: Institute for Building Environment and Energy Conservation, 2016). www.ibec.or.jp/CASBEE/english/document/CASBEE_brochure_2016.pdf
18. Manuel Duarte Pinheiro, *LiderA: Voluntary System for the Sustainability of Built Environments: Working Version V2.00c1* (Lisbon: Manuel Duarte Pinheiro, 2011): 16. www.lidera.info/resources/_LiderA_V2.00c1%20sumario_ingles.pdf
19. Abu Dhabi Urban Planning Council, *Pearl Building Rating System: Design & Construction, Version 1.0, April 2010* (Abu Dhabi, UAE: Abu Dhabi Urban Planning

Council, 2010): 13. www.upc.gov.ae/-/media/files/estidama/docs/pbrs-version-10.ashx?la=ar-ae&hash=58A67F549081968086D016E8D3757366BF29B10F
20 Ibid.
21 Ibid., 12.
22 The Egyptian Green Building Council, *The Green Pyramid Rating System First Edition – April 2011* (Egyptian Green Building Council, 2011): 17–19. www.eg.saint-gobain-glass.com/download/file/fid/1246
23 France GBC, *International Environmental Certifications for the Design and Construction of Non-Residential Buildings: The Positioning of HQE Certification Relative to BREEAM and LEED* (Paris: France GBC, 2015). www.behqe.com/documents/download/254
24 *BeHQE: Join the Movement for Performance and Quality of Life* (Paris: Cerway, 2018). www.behqe.com/documents/download/19
25 *Assessment Tool for the Environmental Performance of Buildings in Operation (EPB) Non Residential Buildings* (Paris: Cerway, 2017). www.behqe.com/documents/download/215
26 Thilo Ebert et al., *Green Building Certification Systems: Assessing Sustainability – International System Comparison – Economic Impact of Certifications* (Detail, 2013): 53–54. http://ebookcentral.proquest.com/lib/cua/detail.action?docID=1075570
27 Important to note is that Best Management Practices for Energy Efficiency in Buildings is a prerequisite in the LEED certification protocol. This means it is required in order to obtain certification. If your intent is not to obtain certification, this chapter will still guide you to fulfill the necessary steps for achieving a solid set of best management practices for energy efficiency.
28 "Best Practices in Commissioning Existing Buildings," The Building Commissioning Association. www.bcxa.org/wp-content/pdf/BCA-Best-Practices-Commissioning-Existing-Construction.pdf
29 "Jurisdictions," BuildingRating: Sharing Transparency for a More Efficient Future, 2014. www.buildingrating.org/jurisdictions
30 "ASHRAE: Shaping Tomorrow's Built Environment Today," ASHRAE, 2018. www.ashrae.org/
31 "ASHRAE's Mission and Vision," ASHRAE, 2018. www.ashrae.org/about/mission-and-vision
32 Ibid.
33 The cost savings generated by the savings after implementing an EAFL could possibly cover the salary of an experienced energy manager who may be hired for such a role.
34 US Department of Energy, "A Guide to Energy Audits – Pacific National Laboratory Technical Report" (US Department of Energy, 2011). www.pnnl.gov/main/publications/external/technical_reports/pnnl-20956.pdf
35 Herman Carstens et al., "Low-Cost Energy Meter Calibration Method for Measurement and Verification," *Applied Energy* 188 (2017): 563–575.
36 "How a Product Earns the ENERGY STAR Label," Energy Star, 2018. www.energystar.gov/products/how-product-earns-energy-star-label
37 "ENERGY STAR Certification," Energy Star, 2018. www.energystar.gov/buildings/about-us/find-energy-star-certified-buildings-and-plants
38 LEED O+M v4 Reference Guide, p. 208.
39 "How to Apply for ENERGY STAR Certification," Energy Star, 2018. www.energystar.gov/buildings/facility-owners-and-managers/existing-buildings/earn-recognition/energy-star-certification/how-app-1
40 LEED O+M v4 Reference Guide, p. 208.
41 See website: www.energystar.gov/buildings/facility-owners-and-managers/existing-buildings/use-portfoliomanager/identify-your-property-type
42 "Commercial Buildings Energy Consumption Survey (CBECS)," US Energy Information Administration Independent Statistics and Analysis, 2018. www.eia.gov/consumption/commercial/
43 See website: https://leeduser.buildinggreen.com/
44 Ibid.
45 See website: https://portfoliomanager.energystar.gov/pm/signup
46 "Energy Benchmarking: Part of the Labs21 Toolkit," I2SL: International Institute for Sustainable Laboratories, 2018. https://lbt.i2sl.org/
47 "Benchmarking," Labs21 Benchmarking, 2018. https://labs21benchmarking.lbl.gov
48 LEED Lab students can begin to benchmark here: https://labs21benchmarking.lbl.gov/
49 "What is CHP?" United States Environmental Protection Agency, 2018. www.epa.gov/chp/what-chp
50 Labs21 Benchmarking, 2018, op. cit.
51 ANSI B109: The ANSI standard for Natural Gas for Vehicles Installation Code is listed in the LEED Reference Guide as a Reference Standard as well; however, it does not pertain to achieving this credit (cf. https://webstore.ansi.org/RecordDetail.aspx?sku=CSA+B109-2017).

52. Brad Kelechava, "ANSI C12.20–2015 – Electricity Meters – 0.1, 0.2, and 0.5 Accuracy Classes," ANSI: American National Standards Institute, 2017. https://blog.ansi.org/?p=6964
53. "Science: Ozone Basics," Stratospheric zone: Monitoring and Research in the NOAA, 2018. www.ozonelayer.noaa.gov/science/basics.htm
54. Ibid.
55. "The Montreal Protocol on Substances That Deplete the Ozone Layer," US Department of State, 2018. www.state.gov/e/oes/eqt/chemicalpollution/83007.htm
56. "EPA 608 Certification Study Guide," HVAC Training Solutions, 2015. www.hvactrainingsolutions.net/EPA.pdf
57. Ibid.
58. "The Plain English Guide to the Clean Air Act," United States Environmental Protection Agency, 2007. www.epa.gov/clean-air-act-overview/plain-english-guide-clean-air-act
59. "Clean Air Act Text," United States Environmental Protection Agency, 2017. www.epa.gov/clean-air-act-overview/clean-air-act-text#toc
60. "Clean Air Act Requirements and History," United States Environmental Protection Agency, 2017. www.epa.gov/clean-air-act-overview/clean-air-act-requirements-and-history
61. LEED O+M v4 Reference Guide, p. 231.
62. CxA Requirements – v4," US Green Building Council, 2018. www.usgbc.org/credits/reqea21r6
63. "A Guide to Commissioning and Auditing Credentials," BuildingGreen, 2018. https://leeduser.buildinggreen.com/tipsheet/guide-commissioning-and-auditing-credentials
64. The Building Commissioning Association, op. cit.
65. Katie Mason, "Functional Performance Testing of your HVAC System Brains," Building Energy Resilience, Cx Associates, 2013. https://buildingenergy.cx-associates.com/2013/04/functional-performance-testing-of-your-hvac-system-brains/
66. "EBOM-v4 EAc3: Ongoing Commissioning," BuildingGreen, 2018. https://leeduser.buildinggreen.com/credit/EBOM-v4/EAc3
67. Hadrien Vandenbroucke and Radu Zmeureanu, "Use of Trend Data from BEMS for an Ongoing Commissioning of HVAC Systems," *Energy Procedia* 78 (2015): 2415–2420.
68. Ibid.
69. See website: www.bcxa.org/wp-content/uploads/2018/06/BCA-New-Const-Best-Practices-2018-05-14.pdf
70. "Resources: Building Commissioning Handbook," Building Commissioning Association, 2018. www.bcxa.org/knowledge-center/building-commissioning-handbook/
71. See note 28.
72. "Best Practices and Tools," Building Commissioning Association, 2018. www.bcxa.org/knowledge-center/best-practices/
73. "Cash Flow Opportunity Calculator," Energy Star, 2018. www.energystar.gov/CFOcalculator
74. "Demand Response – Policy," US Department of Energy, 2018. www.energy.gov/oe/services/electricity-policy-coordination-and-implementation/state-and-regional-policy-assistanc-4
75. Marcus Sheffer, "EBOM-v4 EAc6: Demand Response," BuildingGreen, 2018. https://leeduser.buildinggreen.com/credit/EBOM-v4/EAc6#tab-cost.
76. See website: https://drrc.lbl.gov/tools/demand-response-quick-assessment-tool-drqat
77. "Demand Response Quick Assessment Tool (DRQAT)," Demand Response Research Center, 2018. https://drrc.lbl.gov/tools/demand-response-quick-assessment-tool-drqat
78. "Renewable Energy Certificates (RECs)," United States Environmental Protection Agency, 2018. www.epa.gov/greenpower/renewable-energy-certificates-recs
79. Ibid.
80. "Quick Guide: Renewable Energy Certificates (RECs)," Federal Energy Management Program, US Department of Energy, 2011. www.energy.gov/sites/prod/files/2013/10/f3/rec_guide.pdf
81. "Green Power Partnership Program Overview," United States Environmental Protection Agency, 2018. www.epa.gov/greenpower/green-power-partnership-program-overview
82. Ibid.
83. "Find Green-e Certified," Green-e. www.green-e.org/certified-resources
84. Westlake Reed Leskosky, Crough Center for Architectural Studies: ASHRAE Level 1 Energy Audit, 2014: 13, Table 8.5: Daily Energy use at the Crough School of Architecture and Planning.

CHAPTER NINE

MATERIALS AND RESOURCES

 ## 9.1 Theory

The use of building materials does not cease with the completion of construction but continues throughout the life of a building. Regular operations, maintenance, and additional construction mean the introduction of more materials whose excavation and formation can adversely affect the environment in a greater or lesser way: water and air pollution, depleted natural resources, and the introduction of volatile organic compounds (VOCs) are all possibilities. This is cause for concern and should be a prompt to those who formulate operations and maintenance plans to carefully select materials which are both suitable for requisite tasks and crafted in a way that is least impactful on the environment. The Materials and Resources (MR) category looks at such procedures.

There are two different streams of focus for this category. One is associated with the exterior environment and the other with human health. Environmental impacts of any material are caused by its origin, manufacturing, distribution, and disposal – basically, its very existence. The way to calculate the aggregate of these factors is called Life Cycle Assessment (LCA) (Side Lesson A: Life Cycle Assessment (LCA)). The goal of LCA studies according to the Environmental Protection Agency (EPA) is to identify key processes within a building product that are likely to pose the greatest impact, including occupational and public toxicity impacts (Figure 9.1).[1] As an independent certification of a material's environmental sustainability, the Environmental Product Declaration (EPD) (Side Lesson B: Environmental Product Declaration (EPD)) was created and helps to navigate its life cycle success.

Human health is evaluated through the amount of chemical input and output of the material. Input may mean that the product contains formaldehyde (Side Lesson C: Formaldehyde), a typical by-product of many interior building products, or

Side Lesson A – 9.1: Life Cycle Assessment (LCA) is a way to analyze and assess a product's environmental impact from its development all the way to its disposal or reuse. It tracks energy consumption from each point of the product's "life": from raw material extraction, to procession, manufacture, distribution, use, and disposal. Two ways of analyzing a product's LCA is cradle-to-grave and cradle-to-cradle. Cradle-to-grave is when a product is eventually disposed of. Cradle-to-cradle is when a material or product can be used and reused indefinitely or is able to decompose naturally (see www.sciencedirect.com/topics/earth-and-planetary-sciences/life-cycle-assessment).

MATERIALS AND RESOURCES

Results per life cycle stage, itemized by division

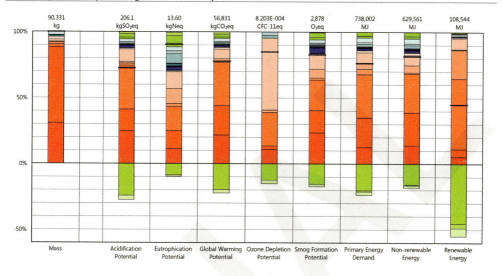

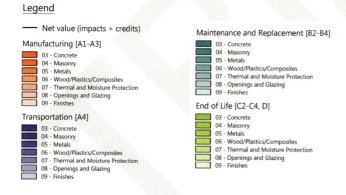

Fig 9.1 A sample of an LCA Report from the Revit plug-in TALLY
Note: This report was created on the trial version of TALLY
Source: Patricia Andrasik, 2017

another toxin. Output indicates the amount of off-gassing (Side Lesson D: Off-gassing) the product emits. Similar to the EPD, as an independent certification of a material's health impacts on occupants, the Health Product Declaration (HPD) (Side Lesson E: Health Product Declarations (HPD)) was created to navigate its success of improving air quality and lessening harmful effects to occupants. Interestingly, this science has only recently evolved to be a key point in evaluating a building, and thus is a smaller portion of LEED O+M's assessment system. The environmental evaluation is, however, pivotal in achieving several credits in this category. Additionally, meeting the prerequisites (policies for

Side Lesson B – 9.1: Environmental Product Declaration (EPD) is a report that communicates products life cycle assessment as well as the materials used in the product. It is meant to be as transparent and informative as possible. LEED v4 rewards credits for products with a verified EPD (see www.environdec.com/).

| 221

MATERIALS AND RESOURCES

purchasing, use and waste), can fulfill many of the other credits in this category (see Partnering Credits in this chapter).

9.2 Comparison

In order to promote a healthy life cycle for products and materials, this credit category focuses on the constant flow of products being purchased and discarded to support building operations.[2] The optimal goal of this category in the LEED Lab course is to train or confirm training of facility personnel so they are capable of addressing all environmental issues related to materials and resource procurement, use and disposal/reuse. There are some institutions who have mastered this, and others who will find LEED Lab student intervention helpful to provide sustainable purchasing ideas to improve their operations.

Similar to LEED O+M, other rating systems identify well-established policies supported through continual adaptive purchase monitoring as essential in achieving resource-efficient and environmentally preferable practices. Though, as always, the approaches and methodology applied by different rating systems around the world depend on numerous local particularities (Figure 9.2).

Side Lesson C – 9.1: Formaldehyde is a strong smelling and colorless gas that is used in the production of household products and building materials. A lot of wood products use formaldehyde in the manufacturing process: fiberwood, particle wood, and plywood. Formaldehyde can be fatal when ingested. Long-term exposure to low levels in the air can cause asthma, skin irritation, and cancer (see https://tinyurl.com/vdmfsjr5).

9.2.1 Green Globes for Existing Buildings (EB)

Through standardized steps, as in LEED, the categories of Resources (55 pts) and Environmental Management System (55 pts) focus on materials and comprise 11 percent of the available credits (1,000 pts) in this rating system. Unlike the LEED O+M category Materials and Resources, here subcategories related to materials are not combined into one category.

Green Globes EB addresses waste reduction and recycling separately by means of the Resource category. The focus is on facilities for storing and handling of recyclable materials, and a work plan. The parts of the Environmental Management System category dedicated to the environmental assessment are purchasing (25) and documentation (30) (Figure 9.3).[3]

Side Lesson D – 9.1: Off-gassing is the process to release volatile organic compounds (VOCs), trapped, frozen, absorbed, and trapped in a product. This process is a common practice for new construction, major renovations, and furniture manufacturing. The duration of off-gassing depends on the type of chemicals used in the manufacturing process. Summer is the most ideal time to off-gas because high temperatures provoke more VOC emission (see https://foobot.io/resources/off-gassing/).

HOW?

Resources and Environmental Management System create questionnaires for an assessor and provide tooltip/reference information for each topic separately.

Required are:

- Written policy (waste reduction work plan) intended to minimize construction waste.
- Waste Management contract, waste audit, and/or other records of waste either by volume or weight, including the diversion rate.
- Records of waste either by volume or weight including diversion rate;
- Documentation that addresses a recycling program incorporating all fiber and consumable products.
- Phase 1 Environmental Assessment or other documentation to verify the site is free from pollution.

MATERIALS AND RESOURCES

Fig 9.2 Global sustainable existing building sustainability assessment tools for materials
Source: Created by Patricia Andrasik and Milan Glisić, 2017

The Environmental Management set of requirements specifically addresses issues related to purchasing:

- Written environmental-purchasing policy and documentation of products purchased.[4]

9.2.2 BREEAM In-Use

Materials and Resources are addressed in the two categories of Materials and Waste in all three major subdivisions: Asset Performance (30), Building Management (20), and Occupier Management (165). The overall weight of the Material and Resources category, 215 points, in this rating system comprises 19% of all

*Side Lesson E – 9.1:
Health Product Declarations (HPD) provide full disclosure of potentially harmful chemicals that are found in products and materials. Similar to EPDs, however, HPDs are more concerned with the user's health. HPDs can be used in green building qualification systems such as LEED v4, Google Portico, Living Product Challenge, and WELL (see www.hpd-collaborative.org/).*

| 223

MATERIALS AND RESOURCES

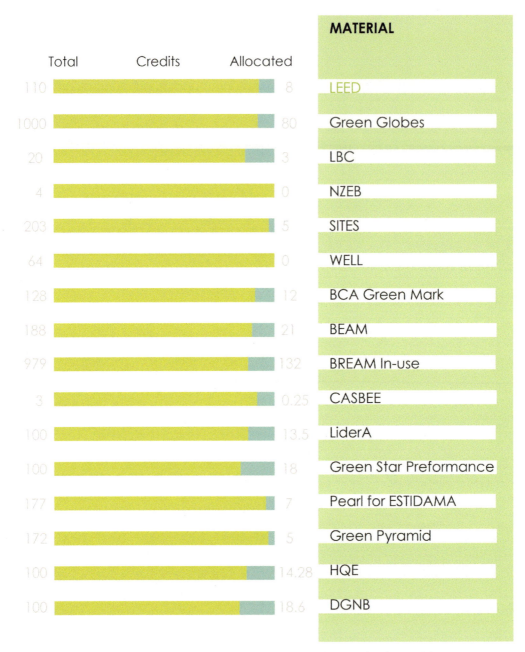

Fig 9.3 Global sustainable existing building sustainability assessment tools comparison for materials
Source: Created by Patricia Andrasik and Milan Glisić, 2017

available points (1109). Though each area can be assessed separately, it is advisable to perform all of them simultaneously to define the overall environmental impact of targeted categories.

Similar to previous categories, Material and Waste are assessed under each area. Significant differences and detailing are assigned depending on areas, while policies and practices related to procurement, cleaning and waste handling are also assessed under several issues within the Building Management area.[5]

MATERIALS AND RESOURCES

HOW?

BREEAM In-Use defines Materials and Waste as separate environmental categories. In Part 1, Materials and Waste are assessed under eight separate asset evaluations. The asset is to a great extent the equivalent of the Project Boundary in LEED and could be just the floor of the building, for example, in BREEAM.

In Part 2, assets are evaluated through seven subcategories for robustness of management practices relating to the implementation of emergency plans, consideration of the environmental impact when procuring materials, and other management activities which may have an impact on procured materials. Defined assets are also assessed for the success of management practices related to providing adequate space for recycling activities.

The greatest weight in this rating system is given to the Occupier Management area and subcategories related to the Materials and Waste, with a total of 16 defined areas. These areas are concerned with the improvement of occupant awareness, managing occupant activities, monitoring waste production, segregation and other occupant management procedures and activities which improve the impacts related to waste generation.[6]

9.2.3 Green Star Performance

There are several areas within this rating system focused on materials, accounting for a total of 12 points, up to 9% of all available points: Hazardous Materials (2) under Indoor Environmental Quality and the three subcategories of Materials: Procurement and Purchasing (3), Waste from Operations (4) and Waste from Refurbishments (3).[7] The materials category focuses on materials that go into or come out of a building during the operational phase of its lifecycle.[8] The policies and practices related to green cleaning are required in order to reduce waste and suppress the use of harmful substances, capable of impacting environmental quality, occupant health, and natural systems. Under Indoor Environmental Quality, the Hazardous Materials credit is intended to promote practices and policies established to reduce the health risk to building occupants from the materials commonly found in older buildings.

HOW?

Similar to LEED, this rating system has standard steps which need to be performed upon registration of the project with the Green Building Council of Australia. The credits are awarded based upon the submission of documentation and the adoption of required policies and principles, followed by furthering the targeted goals through benchmarking during the Performance Period. Materials related to procurement and purchasing, waste from operations and waste from building refurbishments are all identified separately. The assessment is performed by an independent panel of sustainable experts.[9]

9.2.4 LEED Operations and Maintenance (O+M)

Materials and Resources are addressed through the entirety of the building life cycle and its ongoing operations and maintenance.

MATERIALS AND RESOURCES

In LEED O+M, this category recognizes a separate issue related to purchasing for building maintenance and renovation as well as purchasing and waste related to ongoing operations. As the longest part of a building's life cycle, operations phase complexity and cross-cutting issues are targeted.[10] The Material and Resources category comprises seven to eight points, 7 percent of all categories and available points in LEED O+M.[11] This rating system imposes prerequisites in this category related to adopted policies.

HOW?

Each prerequisite and credit outline the exact scope of the requirements. The prerequisite and credit requirements are divided into two categories: products purchased on an ongoing basis (e.g., lamps, paper goods, office equipment) and materials purchased for periodic maintenance or renovation work. The calculations for purchasing credits are based on product and material cost, excluding the labor required for installation or replacement.

Many sustainable criteria in the MR category apply to the entire product, as is the case for product certifications and programs.[12] Some of the available credits in the Material and Resources category depend on how effectively the procured materials and product tracking systems are adopted and how well they function during the Performance Period.

9.2.5 Other Rating Systems

Many globally and locally recognizable certification systems in addition to those aforementioned are tackling materials and resources and can be considered as a substitute rating system for LEED O+M. The developmental particularities of certain regions are sometimes beyond the scope of narrowly designed systems, whereas matured systems – e.g., BREEAM, LEED, etc. – are flexible enough to successfully address even regional requirements.

- **BCA Green Mark.** From 2005 the Singaporean BCA Green Mark rating system allocates to material issues 15.5 of a total 165 available points of the Non-Residential Existing Building Criteria.[13]

    Within this system, it is highly relevant to establish a building management plan or strategy around the sustainability goals. This plan should address all sustainability criteria, and be activated and regularly monitored during building operations. The other important issue addressed here is required waste management by all active participants, occupants, tenants, and visitors.

    Points are awarded for each of the areas addressed in the Resource Stewardship section: Green Products and Materials (7), Recycling Facilities (3.5), Storage Area for Recyclable Waste (1), Promotion of Waste Reduction (2), Waste Monitoring (2).[14]

- **BEAM Plus for Existing Buildings.** This rating system, called Building Environmental Assessment Method for

MATERIALS AND RESOURCES

Existing Buildings (BEAM-EB), tackles the specific situation in Hong Kong. The majority of its 42,000 existing buildings are over 30 years old and it is essential to reward building owners who adopt sustainable and green building management techniques and are willing to upgrade their service systems. BEAM-EB offers either a comprehensive or a selective scheme in which materials and resources are measured towards certification. Within the selective scheme, the option for building management of aged existing buildings is rewarded for every effort made towards reducing the building environmental load.[15]

Materials and Resources are treated by the Building and Site Operations and Maintenance section of Management, which gives two credits total, one credit for "demonstrating the operation of a planned program of regular inspection, cleaning and maintenance of the building's fabric and structure under the control of the Applicant" and one "for demonstrating the operation of a planned program of regular inspection, cleaning and maintenance of external areas and facilities."[16]

In the Materials and Waste Aspects section, there are various combinations which permit the awarding of a total of 17 credits and 7 bonus credits, provided that certain ones are awarded. Issues addressed are defined under purchasing policies and practices, the application of green products, as well as various aspects and levels of waste management procedures, collection arrangements and equipment, and food waste management.[17]

There is a total of 19 credits and seven bonus credits possible.

- **CASBEE Existing Buildings.** Japan's Comprehensive Assessment System for Build Environment Efficiency (CASBEE) for Existing Buildings aims to "ensure a long service life" through basic maintenance, functionality, and "life performance."[18] The two major areas are building environmental quality and building environmental loadings, and unlike its counterparts, CASBEE EB evaluates those separately through Built Environment Quality (Q) of the interior enclosed space and Built Environment Load (L) of exterior factors, and then graphs these on a Built Environment Efficiency (BEE) Chart.[19] The Building Design/Existing Building (BD/EB) path is the best comparison to LEED O+M, targeting existing buildings operations records for at least one year after completion while serving as an asset value tool.[20]

For implemented policies and procedures, the Functionality subdivision of Q2 Service Performance has three minor criteria: functionality and ease of use (40 percent), amenity (30 percent), and maintenance (30 percent). The Functionality category constitutes 40 percent of Q2, or 6 percent of the total CASBEE-EB weight.[21]

Waste issues are addressed by the Reducing Usage of Non-Renewable Resources subdivision of LR2 Resources and Materials, which comprises six criteria: 1) reducing usage of materials (7 percent); 2) continuing usage of existing building skeleton (24 percent); 3) use of recycled materials as structural frame materials (20 percent); 4) use of recycled materials as non-structural materials (20 percent); 5) timber from sustainable forestry (5 percent); 6) reusability of components and materials (24 percent). Reducing Usage of Non-Renewable resources comprises 63 percent of LR2, or 9.5 percent of all CASBEE-EB criteria.[22] (Material Point Allocation chart-Milan).

- **LiderA.** Created primarily for Portugal in 2005, LiderA compasses different building types at various stages: plan and design, construction and management.[23] Of the six principles recognized as focal points for sustainability, the promotion of the efficient use of resources and the sustainable use of the built environment are the two oriented toward the materials category.

    The LiderA Materials category awards up to 5 percent of its overall weight to durable (C12), local (C13), and low impact (C14) materials used in existing building operations. Further, the Waste category accounts for up to 3 percent of credits devoted to effective control (C19), management (C20), and valorization (C21). The issue of management is addressed under the Sustainable Use Category with 6 percent for environmental information (C41) and environmental management system (C42) criteria. Thus, a total of 14 percent of LiderA credits relate to Materials and Resources.[24]

- **Pearl for ESTIDAMA (PORS).** As an alternative to LEED O+M in Abu Dhabi and the entire United Arab Emirates, the Pearl Operational Rating System (PORS) launched in 2013. Adjusted for the desert climate, it assesses the built-in features and operational performance of an existing building,[25] and verifies operational performance to ensure design intent has achieved its stated objectives.[26] The Stewardship Materials section is focused on materials and the handling of resources.

    This section of the Pearl Rating System encourages teams to consider a building's 'whole-of-life' cycle when selecting and specifying materials, with an overall objective to improve the social and environmental outcomes associated with their manufacture, transport, installation, and disposal.[27]

There are two requirements, similar to LEED prerequisites: 1) targeting whole building in-use cycle, related to elimination of hazardous materials and 2) basic operational waste management. Upon achieving these fundamentals, certain credits are awarded for use of non-polluting materials, improved operational waste management, and organic waste management. Up to seven (3.9 percent) of a total of 177 credits available can be achieved under this category.

MATERIALS AND RESOURCES

- ***Green Pyramid.*** The Egypt Green Building Council's Green Pyramid Rating System (GPRS), which originated in 2010, currently only focuses on guidelines for the construction of new buildings in Egypt.[28]

    The overall aim of this rating system applicable to existing buildings is to raise awareness of resource scarcity, ways to mitigate demand for these resources, and to minimize the environmental impact of buildings while maintaining their function and comfort as well as the health and well-being of their occupants and of the community.

    The goal is also to encourage innovative solutions that minimize environmental impact and raise awareness of the benefits of buildings with reduced impact on the environment.[29]

    Green Pyramid, similar to LEED, has requirements which must be fulfilled before optional credits are awarded in a particular area. Since the majority of requirements are related to the construction phase, only the subcategory Credits for Building User Guide, under the Management category, is targeting ongoing functions during the in-use phase. Total awarded credits can be five (3 percent) of a total of 172.

- ***HQE Exploitation.*** *Haute Qualité Environnementale* or High-Quality Environmental Standard (HQE) Certification for Buildings in Operation (HQE Exploitation) is "process-oriented, focused on ongoing management, efficiency, and use/disposal of materials.[30] The Sustainable Use list of credits handles existing buildings. An independent auditor inspects the building and ongoing operations and analyzes the documentation.

    The primary goals of the materials category are to minimize waste in operations, building maintenance and repairs, while advancing the hygiene and cleanliness of indoor spaces. HQE does this through Target 6: Waste and Target 7: Maintenance.

    Target 6: Waste has two subcategories with several prerequisites and 43 possible points to be awarded for the reduction of user waste. Target 7: Maintenance comprises a total of 21 possible points. Together these constitute 64 points (20 percent) of the 321 possible points in HQE.[31]

- ***DGNB In Use.*** The Deutsche Gesellschaft für Nachhaltiges Bauen (DGNB) In Use scheme, developed by the German Sustainable Building Council in 2011, only considers three out of the six main criteria groups for existing or renovated building assessment. These include Ecological Quality, Economic Quality, Sociocultural and Functional Quality.

    Within the Ecological Quality group, there are six criteria which relate to materials and resources: Global warming potential, Ozone depletion potential, Photochemical ozone

MATERIALS AND RESOURCES

creation potential, Acidification potential, Eutrophication potential, Sustainable uses of timber and resources. Together these comprise 80 points. Within the Economic Quality group, one criterion applies: Building-related life cycle costs, for 30 points. Together these comprise 110 points, 20 percent of DGNB In Use.[32] Evaluation assessment for each criterion is developed as multiphase questionnaires, supplemented with required documentation and benchmarked performances.

The materials category is addressed slightly differently in the various rating systems (Figure 9.3) yet the terminology is consistent. This means sub-categories can be defined as credits and points, as in LEED, Green Globes, BREEAM and CASBEE-EB. LEED O+M addresses broad aspects of materials and resource related issues during the building in-use life and renovation phase, and as such, is a good basis for LEED Lab and the phased steps of assessment application.

9.3 Credits

9.3.1 Ongoing Purchasing and Waste Policy

(*Refer also to page 311 in the LEED O+M v4 Reference Guide*)

Side Lesson F – 9.3.1: Ongoing Goods and Durable Goods: Ongoing goods are products that are constantly being purchased and replaced. Examples of ongoing goods include office supplies like paper, envelopes, notepads, cartridges, batteries, binders, and notebooks. These types of products are constantly being bought, thrown out, and replaced.

Durable goods are the more constant products that last longer before being thrown out or replaced. Examples of durable goods include appliances and electronically powered equipment (see www.usgbc.org/credits/ existing-buildings-schools-existing-buildings-data-centers-existing-buildings-hospitality--1).

There are a few important policies which a LEED Lab team should have in place prior to engaging any of its subsequent environmentally impacting material credits: a Purchasing/Waste Policy and a Maintenance/Renovation Policy. The former ensures that any product procured for occupant use meets sustainability criteria while the latter addresses the sustainability of any product procured for the building's use. These prerequisites can only be achieved with knowledge of the university's procuring patterns, thus requiring the LEED Lab student to work closely with the facility personnel.

Although many campuses already possess some form of a material life cycle program, these policies may be written by the LEED Lab student and verified by campus authorities. The Ongoing Purchasing and Waste Policy identifies the process of selecting products used frequently (ongoing goods), and more substantial equipment infrequently procured (durable goods) (Side Lesson F: Ongoing Goods and Durable Goods) by the building staff, students, and faculty that comprise sustainable materials and low LCA impacts. It also identifies the process of removing and disposing all waste: e.g., paper, aluminum, organics, equipment (ongoing and durable goods) and hazardous materials, with the latter including the mercury (Side Lesson G: Mercury) found in lighting fixtures. Crafting an environmentally favorable purchasing plan and a guide for waste or debris disposal is advantageous not only to the environment but also to the building occupants.[33] The credit name leads the LEED Lab student to believe that there is only one policy, but actually there are a few which are submitted together to fulfill this prerequisite.

MATERIALS AND RESOURCES

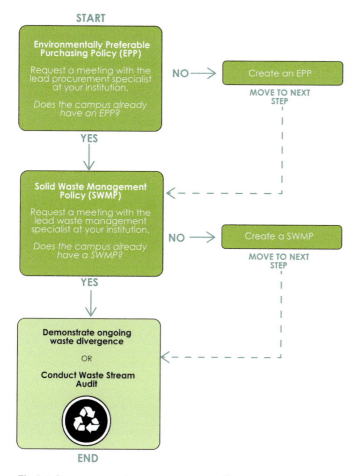

Fig 9.4 Procurement and waste management policy map
Source: Diagrammed by Elizabeth Meyers and Patricia Andrasik, 2020

Tasks

Tasks to complete a procurement and waste management policy require a significant amount of time in coordination with the respective facility personnel. The way these materials are used by occupants and how they are disposed is also considered a part of a product's life cycle and needs to be documented. The LEED O+M v4 Reference Guide provides details to fulfill these requirements and they should be thoroughly understood. The following steps are advised for LEED Lab students as a *prelude* to understand the details in the LEED O+M v4 Reference Guide. This will greatly help students decide which course of action to pursue (Figure 9.4).

1. **Environmentally Preferable Purchasing Policy (EPP).** Request a discussion with the lead procurement specialist at your institution. At this meeting answer the following questions:

Side Lesson G – 9.3.1: Mercury is a naturally occurring chemical element and can be found in rock along the earth's crust. It takes a liquid form when stored at room temperature. Mercury was used in old thermometers, electrical switches, high intensity discharge (HID) lamps, neon signs, and fluorescent light bulbs. Light bulbs using mercury are more energy efficient and last longer than the counterparts. Using a bulb containing mercury does not pose a health risk. However, the workers assembling the bulbs at the facility are the ones at risk of exposure (see www.cdc.gov/niosh/topics/ mercury/default.html).

| 231

MATERIALS AND RESOURCES

      a. **Existing EPP:** Does the campus already have an EPP which includes the specifics of this prerequisite? If yes, skip to Solid Waste Management Policy. If not, proceed below.
      b. **Create EPP:** Review annual purchasing records to identify the items required for documentation. Paper, toner, cartridges, binders, batteries, and desk accessories are items that are required for the policy and are most likely used by university officials. Note that the 'five most purchased categories' may already include these items.
      c. Use examples in Tools below to compose an EPP.

2. **Solid Waste Management Policy (SWMP).**[34] Request a discussion with the lead waste management specialist at your institution. At this meeting answer the following questions:
      a. **Existing SWMP:** Does the campus already have a SWMP which includes the specifics of this prerequisite? If yes, skip to Waste Stream Audit. If not, proceed as below.
      b. **Create SWMP:** Does the campus outsource waste management? If so, request that the campus' lead waste management specialist and the vendor collaborate with the LEED Lab student to create the policy along with the provisions in the Reference Guide.
      c. Does the campus manage waste within its organization? If so, request that the campus' lead waste management specialist and LEED Lab student collaborate to create the policy.
      d. Use examples in Tools below to compose a SWMP.

3a. Demonstrate ongoing waste divergence (see Partnering Credits on the next page).
or
    b. Conduct Waste Stream Audit.[35]

Tools

The tasks and techniques associated with this prerequisite lead to the same goal – the establishment of policies which foster a greater awareness and action towards material sensibility in campus facilities. These are particularly aimed at ongoing and durable goods. The following are templates or examples of various EPPs:

- USGBC Policy Template[36]
- Lehigh University EPP[37]
- University of Utah Environmentally Preferable Purchasing Guidelines (EPP)[38]
- Harvard University Sustainable Purchasing Guidelines (EPP)[39]
- University of California Davis (SWMP)[40]
- Northwestern University (SWMP)[41]

Techniques[42]

The following advice may assist the LEED Lab student in achieving this credit.

MATERIALS AND RESOURCES

1. Do not include the following items in the top five purchases:
   - Notebooks or pads
   - Envelopes
   - Writing tools
2. Many EPPs include construction waste as well. LEED requires these two documents to be submitted separately. If requirements for the EPP and the SWM Policy are integrated into one document, submit this single document to both prerequisites.
3. Use, in all contracts with general contractors and all external vendors, the language used in the policy.

Partnering Credits

All of the credits for the Materials category are very tightly related to the two aforementioned prerequisites. It is particularly important for the LEED Lab student to review the possibilities of achieving subsequent credits. If the following questions may be answered affirmatively, **Purchasing – Ongoing** should be attempted:[43]

- ☐ Does the facility have an existing process for tracking ongoing and durable goods purchases?
- ☐ Can a process for tracking purchases for the facility be created during the early stages of the Performance Period if one does not exist – or – can existing tracking processes be revised to include the requirements of this credit?
- ☐ Do the majority of all ongoing consumables (60 percent by cost) contain either post consumer recycled content or bio-based materials, use sustainable agriculture, have extended use, source ingredients locally, or are they certified by the Forest Stewardship Council (FSC) or USGBC-approved equivalent?
- ☐ Does the majority of all equipment (40 percent by cost) meet either a silver Electronic Product Environmental Assessment tool (EPEAT) or an ENERGY STAR rating?

If the following questions may be answered affirmatively, **Purchasing – Lamps** should be attempted:

- ☐ Are specifications available to confirm mercury contents, output and lifespan for the bulbs in all light fixtures of the facility?
- ☐ Can high-mercury-containing existing light fixtures/bulbs be replaced with low-mercury alternatives during the Performance Period and thereafter be maintained?

If the following questions may be answered affirmatively, **Solid Waste Management – Ongoing** should be attempted:[44]

- ☐ Does the facility have an existing process for disposal and diversion of ongoing and durable goods waste tracking?
- ☐ Does the facility have an existing process for safely disposing batteries and mercury-containing lamps?
- ☐ Can students, faculty and staff be better educated about the waste disposal stream so they become engaged participants?

MATERIALS AND RESOURCES

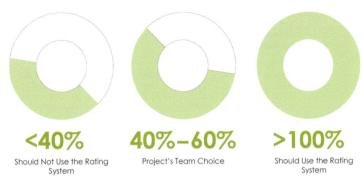

Fig 9.5 Percentage of floor area appropriate for a particular rating system
Source: Derived from USGBC LEED O+M v4 Reference Guide. Diagrammed by Elizabeth Meyers, 2020

 ### 9.3.2 Facility Maintenance and Renovation

(*Refer also to page 325 in the LEED O+M v4 Reference Guide*)

The spectrum of impacts of new building construction may not seem important to consider in LEED Lab since the course focuses on existing buildings. Yet what happens when renovations occur in an existing building? The steps in ensuring that the LCA bears an insignificant impact on the earth is the same as that of a new construction project; materials should be sustainably sourced, procured, and disposed of. In fact, any renovation of existing facilities should be first evaluated to understand if the project warrants certification as a LEED New Construction (LEED NC) or a LEED O+M project, since projects with a larger scope may mandate substantial upgrades (Figure 9.5). As such, the LEED NC rating system's requirements are at their core applied to fulfill this prerequisite and subsequent credits, particularly in the disposal of construction material, which includes all waste produced on a construction site (even cans consumed by construction personnel) if a building is renovated.

Campus renovations of an existing facility are far more successful when there is preparation for accomplishing the goals of this prerequisite. Landfill tax or tipping fees (Side Lesson H: Landfill tax or tipping fees) are saved when waste is recycled, reused, resold, or otherwise disposed of in a sustainable manner. Indoor air quality is increased when proper measures are taken to subside any debris. Earthly impact is decreased and LCA becomes more successful when sustainable building products are procured and maintained. This prerequisite ensures attention to all of these factors and, like the Purchasing and Waste prerequisite, comprises three different policies which may be integrated or separated based on the organization of your campus' administration.

Side Lesson H – 9.3.2: Landfill tax or tipping fees are charges that based on the quantity of waste a user drops off or gives to a waste processing facility. Landfill taxes are used to offset the cost of maintaining, closing, and opening the site (see www.infrastructurereportcard.org/glossary/tipping-fee/).

Tasks[45]

The tasks to complete the Facility Maintenance and Renovation Policy prerequisite are fairly straightforward for a LEED Lab

MATERIALS AND RESOURCES

student, yet they demand a significant amount of time in coordination with the respective facility personnel. The LEED O+M v4 Reference Guide provides details to fulfill these requirements, and they should be followed intently. The following steps are advised for LEED Lab students as a *prelude* to understand the details in the LEED O+M v4 Reference Guide. This will greatly help students decide which course of action to pursue (Figure 9.6).

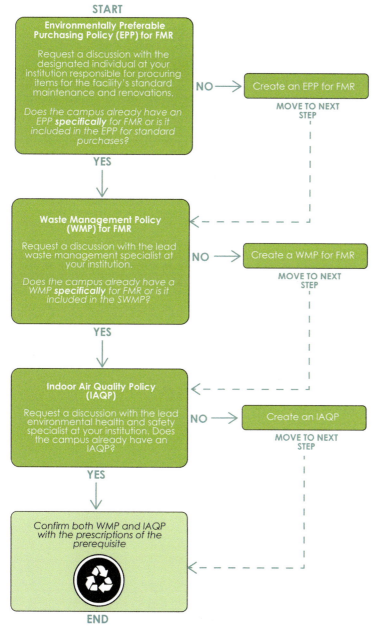

Fig 9.6 *Facility Maintenance and Renovation (FMR) Policy Prerequisite map*
Source: Diagrammed by Elizabeth Meyers and Patricia Andrasik, 2020

| 235

MATERIALS AND RESOURCES

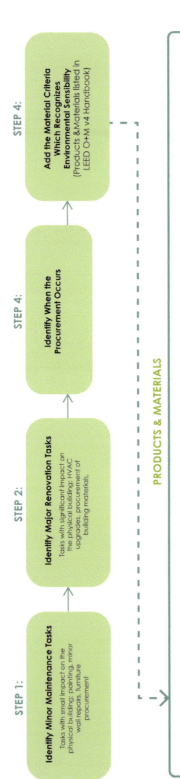

Fig 9.7 Environmental Purchasing Policy (EPP) for Facility Maintenance and Renovation (FMR) steps

Source: Derived from USGBC LEED O+M v4 Reference Guide. Diagrammed by Elizabeth Meyers, 2020

MATERIALS AND RESOURCES

1. ***Environmental Purchasing Policy (EPP) for FMR (Facility Maintenance and Renovation).*** Request a discussion with the designated individual at your institution responsible for procuring items for the facility's standard maintenance and renovations. At this meeting answer the following questions:
   - ***Existing EPP for FMR:*** Does the campus already have an EPP which includes the specifics of this prerequisite? If yes, skip to Solid Waste Management Policy. If not, proceed below.
   - ***Create EPP for FMR:*** An easy way to begin this policy is to organize the items to be procured into two different categories: Minor and Major FMR items (Figure 9.7).
   - Identify minor maintenance tasks. These include any task which occurs with frequency and has a small impact on the physical building.
   - Identify major renovation tasks. These include any task which occurs less frequently and has a significant impact on the physical building.
   - Identify when the procurement occurs.
   - Add the material criteria which recognizes environmental sensibility.
   - Use examples in Tools on the next page to compose an EPP.

2. ***Waste Management Policy (WMP) for FMR.*** Request a discussion with the lead waste management specialist at your institution – this may be the same person as the aforementioned WMP. At this meeting answer the following questions:
   - ***Existing WMP:*** Does the campus already have a WMP which includes both facility maintenance and renovation waste? If yes, skip to Indoor Air Quality Policy. If not, proceed as below.
   - ***Create WMP:*** Does the campus outsource waste management for maintenance projects? If so, request that the campus' lead waste management specialist and the vendor collaborate with the LEED Lab student to create the policy according to the provisions in the LEED O+M v4 Reference Guide.
   - Does the campus manage waste for maintenance projects within its organization? If so, request that the lead waste management specialist and LEED Lab student collaborate to create the policy.
   - Does the campus outsource waste management for renovation projects via an external contractor? If so, request that the campus' main point of contact for renovation work collaborate with the LEED Lab student to create the policy along with the provisions in the Reference Guide.
   - Use examples in Tools on the next page to compose a WMP for FMR.

3. ***Indoor Air Quality Policy (IAQP).*** Request a discussion with the lead environmental health and safety specialist

MATERIALS AND RESOURCES

Side Lesson I – 9.3.2: Flush-out Process: Flush-out introduces air to a newly built space in order to eliminate pollutants that are off-gassed from the new materials, paints, finishes, furniture, and other products. This process has to be completed before occupation. In most cases, the construction may not be complete in time for the flush out to occur. In that case, it may be phased throughout occupation. IAQ testing is much more costly, yet is a good alternative if a phased or standard flush out process is unable to be achieved (see https://tinyurl.com/rtskz6eb).

at your institution. At this meeting answer the following questions:

☐ **Existing IAQP:** Does the campus already have an existing IAQP which includes both facility maintenance and renovation air quality? If yes, skip this section and confirm both the WMP and the IAQP with the prescriptions of the prerequisite. If not, proceed below.

☐ **Create IAQP:** Does the campus have a third party managing the IAQ of maintenance and/or renovation work? If so, request that a representative from that vendor, the campus lead environmental health and safety specialist and the LEED Lab student collaborate to create the policy along with the provisions in the LEED O+M v4 Reference Guide.

☐ Use examples in Tools below to compose an IAQP for FMR.

☐ Include (either in the policy or as a standard protocol for the facilities department) a process for flushing out or testing the air quality (Side Lesson I: Flush-out Process).

☐ Confirm (via a formal correspondence which will be submitted towards certification) that the environmental health and safety specialist shares the policy with those impacted by the chemicals contained in the materials they are handling. This ensures that the policy is being applied and may reduce the amount of questions from the USGBC after submission.

Tools

The tasks and techniques associated with this prerequisite lead to the same goal – to establish policies which foster a greater awareness and action towards material sensibility in campus facilities. The following examples include IAQP and WMP for FMR:

- USGBC Policy Template[46]
- University of North Carolina in Chapel Hill[47]
- University of Pennsylvania[48]
- New York University[49]

Techniques[50]

There are several techniques which can help the LEED Lab student achieve this prerequisite, but note that a strong alliance with campus facility personnel is very important. This is the case since personnel will be coordinating internally or externally with general contractors, builders, or otherwise construction personnel to renovate existing or future areas of the facility. Some helpful principles for the LEED Lab student to share with their campus counterparts include:

☐ Will an internal or external party be responsible for the actual tracking of material purchasing and waste management of materials during a renovation project?

MATERIALS AND RESOURCES

- ☐ Ensure that the policies can be implemented at some point during the Performance Period.
- ☐ For waste that is hazardous, identify confined areas of disposal within the facility and/or a specific campus location.
- ☐ Sorting or comingling of maintenance waste on campus, and its final destination, should be coordinated with ongoing and durable goods waste management.
- ☐ Collaborate during the completion of this policy with those LEED Lab students who are involved with the following synergistic credits: EQ Green Cleaning Policy, Indoor Air Quality Management Program and Enhanced Indoor Air Quality Strategies.[51]
- ☐ Include the language used in the policy in all contracts with general contractors and all external vendors.
- ☐ Identify in the policy how to minimize disturbances of air quality for currently occupied spaces.
- ☐ Whether this policy is new or if an existing policy is being revised for LEED Lab and certification, it is advised that a mechanism be developed to gauge how it has positively impacted air quality since implementation. This may include a simple questionnaire or an official research endeavor between LEED Lab students and other academic units on campus, to be used towards your five-year recertification.
- ☐ Note that the EPP-FMR may include other policies such as the WMP and the IEQP. Alternatively, these may be written as separate documents and submitted together.

Partnering Credits

The Purchasing and Solid Waste Management – Facility Maintenance and Renovation credits are tightly associated with this prerequisite. Since it is a requirement for the EPP-FMR policy to include criteria from this credit, it may be easily achieved by providing documentation that the materials identified in the policy were in fact obtained during actual maintenance or renovation within the Performance Period. Note that even if no alterations in the purchasing of materials occurs within the Performance Period, the credit point is nevertheless achieved.

If the following questions can be answered affirmatively, Purchasing – Facility Maintenance and Renovation should be attempted:[52]

- Do materials for building maintenance and/or renovation procured within the Performance Period adhere to the criteria of the EPP-FMR policy?
- Does the LEED Lab team have documentation that these procured materials meet the criteria (at least 50 percent by cost for products and materials and 75 percent by cost of total furniture) of the EPP-FMR policy?

If the following questions can be answered affirmatively, the former (Solid Waste Management – Facility Maintenance and Renovation credit) should be attempted:[53]

| 239

MATERIALS AND RESOURCES

- ☐ Do materials for building maintenance and/or renovation discarded within the Performance Period adhere to the criteria of the EPP-FMR policy?
- ☐ Does the LEED Lab team have documentation that these materials discarded from maintenance or renovations, and diverted from landfills, meet the criteria (at least 70 percent by weight or volume) of the EPP-FMR policy?
- ☐ Does the entity conducting the maintenance and renovation (internal or external party) have a tracking mechanism in place to consistently document waste from their activities?

Another Partnering Credit which is not in the Material category yet has a very logical association with the IAQP is the Indoor Air Quality Management Program, under the category Indoor Air Quality (see Chapter 10.3.1 and page 427 in the LEED O+M v4 Reference Guide).

9.4 Case Study

During the recertification of the Edward M. Crough School of Architecture and Planning at The Catholic University of America, two challenges emerged with the Materials and Resources Ongoing Purchasing and Waste Policy Prerequisite. First, there were changes in the requirements during the transition from LEED v2009 to LEED v4. Additionally, personnel changeover left a gap in institutional knowledge of purpose and procedures related to the policy. A LEED Lab student researched historic challenges, coordinated with stakeholders, and charted a course towards prerequisite achievement.

The previous semester's LEED Lab class attempted the Ongoing Purchasing and Waste Policy, yet it was denied because the students used material related to the initial certification under LEED O+M v2009 standards; however, the Crough Center recertification is based on LEED O+M v4. One of the reasons for the denial is that the new version combines the prerequisite of the Sustainable Purchasing Policy and the prerequisite Solid Waste Management Policy into one prerequisite. The submission by the former LEED Lab student separated them. To avoid this in the current submission, a template from USGBC.org was downloaded and used as a guide for developing the Environmental Preferable Purchasing (EPP) and Solid Waste Management (SWM) Policy by LEED v4 standards. The student used this document to engage the facility managers, procurement experts and custodians.

She then integrated aspects of the former policies into draft language to share with the stakeholders. Since she found that staff changeover after the initial LEED Certification left a records gap, her new draft of the updated policy became a way to move forward and fill them. She outlined information such as the list of ongoing and durable purchases and assembled a table of the many individuals and offices involved in the policy. Like many campus systems, there exists a mix of authority and responsibilities between the staff focusing on campus-wide facilities and the local day-to-day building management. Such was the case for this project. In some cases, there were hired vendors involved in purchasing items

MATERIALS AND RESOURCES

for Crough Center. The following list includes all of the parties involved in the development of the policy at this institution:

- Director of Facilities Administration and Services
- Assistant Director for Grounds & Fleet Maintenance
- Procurement Officer
- Administrative Staff of the Crough Center
- Crough Center Purchase Card Holder employees
- Parties purchasing materials on CUA Crough Center's behalf
- Waste Haulers
- Other venders

One way to harness this vast group of stakeholders was through the university's Sustainability Plan. This comprehensive plan focuses on encouraging, engaging, inspiring, and motivating CUA community members to take steps to reduce their carbon footprint and improve environmental quality. Initiative 3.3: Reduce Waste Streams, a section in the plan, is directly related to the Ongoing Purchasing and Waste Policy. The LEED Lab student drafted a policy and highlighted areas for stakeholder input and vetting.

Part of this policy requires establishing specific responsibilities for tracking sheets. This is a critical step to maintain documentation and to establish a procedure for updating metrics as purchasing and waste patterns change. The LEED Lab class recommended that this policy be developed at the campus level during charrettes (see Chapter 2.3) by using Crough Center as a proof of principle. This helped the CUA campus as a whole realize initiatives and actions within the CUA Sustainability Plan (Figure 9.8).

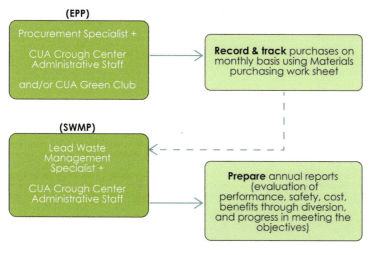

Fig 9.8 Procurement and Waste Management Policy for the CUA Sustainability Plan

Source: Diagrammed by Elizabeth Meyers and Patricia Andrasik, 2020

| 241

MATERIALS AND RESOURCES

 ## 9.5 Exercises

The questions below are derived from the aforementioned case study. Questions testing knowledge of the breadth of tools, tasks and techniques are important for LEED Lab; the investigation required in answering these exercises helps students to approach their credit assignments from a synergistic perspective.

Exercise Scenario 1

Review the Material and Resources Ongoing Purchasing and Waste Policy Prerequisite in the LEED O+M v4 Reference Guide. What is the relationship between the Ongoing Purchasing and Waste Policy Prerequisite and the Waste Stream Audit?

Exercise Scenario 2

Compare the various policy examples in Tools. Do all of the universities represented contain the necessary element to fulfill the prerequisite of the Ongoing Purchasing and Waste policy?

Exercise Scenario 3

Use the active link in the Tools menu to obtain the policy templates on USGBC's website. If the electrical appliances in Crough Center procured during the Performance Period were not EPEAT-rated, discuss a few ways the facility has still obtained certification.

Notes

1. "Design for the Environment Life-Cycle Assessments," United States Environmental Protection Agency, 2020. www.epa.gov/saferchoice/design-environment-life-cycle-assessments
2. US Green Building Council, "Materials and Resources (MR): Overview," *Reference Guide for Building Operations and Maintenance* (Washington, DC: US Green Building Council, 2013): 305.
3. Green Building Initiative. *Green Globes® for Existing Buildings 2007 Technical Reference Manual, Version 1.21 December 2019* (Green Building Initiative, Inc., 2019): 16, 17. www.thegbi.org/files/training_resources/Green_Globes_EB_2007_Technical_Reference_Manual.pdf
4. Green Building Initiative, *Eligibility Guidance for Certification of Sustainable Buildings under the Green Globes® NC, SI, and EB Programs: Green Globes for Existing Buildings, Pre-Assessment Check List* (GBI, 2015): 1.
5. BREEAM, *BREEAM In-Use Technical Manual SD221 2.0:2015* (Watford: BRE Global Ltd, 2016): 149–162; 189–195; 273–277, 284, 335–384. www.breeam.com/filelibrary/Technical%20Manuals/SD221_BIU_International_2015_Re-issue_V2.0.pdf
6. S. Summerson, J. Atkins and A. Harries, *BREEAM In-Use: Driving Sustainability through Existing Buildings* (Watford: Building Research Establishment Ltd.): 5. www.breeam.com/filelibrary/BREEAM%20In%20Use/KN5686---BREEAM-In-Use-White-Paper_dft2.pdf
7. Green Building Council of Australia, "Hazardous Materials," "Procurement from Purchasing," "Waste from Operations" and "Waste from Refurbishment," *Green Star – Performance v1.2 – Initial Certification Submission Template r1*. www.gbca.org.au/greenstar-manager/resources/?filter-rating-tool=101&_ga=2.107716033.213355384.1592333897-2941 5128.1591753717
8. Green Building Institute of Australia, *Green Star Performance: Summary of Categories and Credits* (Green Building Council of Australia, 2015): 32. www.gbca.

MATERIALS AND RESOURCES

9. Sustainability How-to Guide – Green Building Rating Systems. IFMA ESS SAG, 21.
10. US Green Building Council 2013, op. cit.
11. Ibid., 335, 345, 353, 373, 383.
12. Green Building Council of Australia 2015, 305–307, op. cit.
13. Singapore Building and Construction Authority, *BCA Green Mark GM ENRB: 2017: Technical Guide and Requirements* (Singapore: Building and Construction Authority, 2017): 8.
14. Ibid.
15. *BEAM Plus Existing Buildings Version 2.0 (2016.03): Comprehensive Scheme* (Hong Kong: Hong Kong Green Building Council, 2016): 6. www.beamsociety.org.hk/files/download/BEAM%20Plus%20Existing%20Buildings%20v2_0_Comprehensive%20Scheme.pdf
16. Ibid., 24.
17. Ibid., 26–28.
18. Japan Sustainable Building Consortium and Japan Green Building Council, *Comprehensive Assessment System for Building Environmental Efficiency (CASBEE), Technical Manual* (Tokyo: Institute for Building Environment and Energy Conservation IBEC, 2007): 8.
19. Dot Doan, Ali Ghaffarianhoseini, Nicola Naismith and Tongrui Zhang, "A Critical Comparison of Green Building Rating Systems," *Building and Environment* 123 (2017): 1–26.
20. *Comprehensive Assessment System for Built Environmental Efficiency: CASBEE* (Tokyo: Institute for Building Environment and Energy Conservation (IBEC), 2016). www.ibec.or.jp/CASBEE/english/document/CASBEE_brochure_2016.pdf
21. Thilo Ebert et al., *Green Building Certification Systems: Assessing Sustainability – International System Comparison – Economic Impact of Certifications* (Detail, 2013): 60. http://ebookcentral.proquest.com/lib/cua/detail.action?docID=1075570
22. Ibid.
23. Manuel Duarte Pinheiro, *LiderA: Voluntary System for the Sustainability of Built Environments: Working Version V2.00c1* (Lisbon: Manuel Duarte Pinheiro, 2011). http://lidera.info/resources/LiderA_English_Version_2_Presentation.pdf
24. Ibid., 20–27.
25. *The Pearl Rating System for ESTIDAMA Emirate of Abu Dhabi, Pearl Building Rating System: Design & Construction, Version 1.0* (Abu Dhabi: Abu Dhabi Urban Planning Council, April 2010): 13. www.upc.gov.ae/-/media/files/estidama/docs/pbrs-version-10.ashx?la=ar-ae&hash=58A67F549081968086D016E8D3757366BF29B10F
26. "Pearl Rating System Process," Department of Urban Planning and Municipalities, UAE, 2017. www.upc.gov.ae/en/estidama/estidama-program/pearl-rating-system
27. Abu Dhabi Urban Planning Council 2010, 170, op. cit.
28. "Green Pyramid Rating System Levels," Egyptian Green Building Council, 2009. www.egypt-gbc.gov.eg/ratings/index.html
29. The Egyptian Green Building Council, *The Green Pyramid Rating System First Edition – April 2011* (Egyptian Green Building Council, 2011): 7. www.eg.saint-gobain-glass.com/download/file/fid/1246
30. Harpa Birgisdottir, "Lessons Learned from Testing Four Different Certification Methods for Buildings – LEED, BREEAM, DGNB and HQE," SBI Danish Building Research Institute, 2009.
31. *Assessment Tool for the Environmental Performance of Buildings in Operation (EPB) Non Residential Buildings* (Paris: Cerway, 2017). www.behqe.com/documents/download/215.
32. Thilo Ebert et al. 2013, 53, op. cit.
33. US Green Building Council 2013, 306, op. cit.
34. US Green Building Council, "Ongoing Purchasing and Waste Policy: Step-by-Step Guidance," *Reference Guide for Building Operations and Maintenance* (Washington, DC: US Green Building Council, 2013): 315.
35. This should occur near the onset of the Performance Period.
36. See website: www.usgbc.org/credits/existing-buildings-schools-existing-buildings-data-centers-existing-buildings-hospitality--1?view=resources&return=/credits/Existing%20Buildings/v4/Material%20&%20resources
37. See website: https://financeadmin.lehigh.edu/sites/financeadmin.lehigh.edu/files/offices/ubs/purchasing/docs/Sustainable%20Purchasing%20Policy.pdf
38. See website: https://fbs.admin.utah.edu/purchasing/green/environmentally-preferable-purchasing-guidelines/#environmentally
39. This policy also includes some of the requirements for the subsequent Facility Maintenance and Renovation Policy. See website: https://internal.procurement.harvard.edu/files/procurement/files/

| 243

40. See website: https://sustainability.ucdavis.edu/local_resources/docs/zero_waste/solid_waste_management_policy.pdf
41. See website: https://policies.northwestern.edu/docs/sustainable-waste-management-FINAL.pdf
42. Dan Ackerstein, "EBOM-v4 MRp1: Ongoing Purchasing and Waste Policy," BuildingGreen, 2018. https://leeduser.buildinggreen.com/credit/EBOM-v4/MRp1
43. Dan Ackerstein, "EBOM-v4 MRc1: Purchasing – Ongoing," BuildingGreen, 2018. https://leeduser.buildinggreen.com/credit/EBOM-v4/MRc1
44. Dan Ackerstein, "EBOM-v4 MRc4: Solid Waste Management – Ongoing," BuildingGreen, 2018. https://leeduser.buildinggreen.com/credit/EBOM-v4/MRc4
45. US Green Building Council, "Facility Maintenance and Renovation Policy: Step-by-Step Guidance," *Reference Guide for Building Operations and Maintenance* (Washington, DC: US Green Building Council, 2013): 327–328.
46. See website: www.usgbc.org/resources/mrp-facility-maintenance-and-renovation-policy-template
47. See website: https://facilities.unc.edu/resources/design-guidelines/waste-reduction/construction-and-demolition-waste-management/
48. See website: www.facilities.upenn.edu/sites/default/files/Green%20Guidelines%20for%20Renovations%20October%202015.pdf
49. www.nyu.edu/life/safety-health-wellness/environmental-health-and-safety/waste-disposal/renovation-and-demolition-waste.html
50. Ashwini Arun, "EBOM-v4 MRp2: Facility Maintenance and Renovations Policy," BuildingGreen, 2018. https://leeduser.buildinggreen.com/credit/EBOM-v4/MRp2
51. US Green Building Council, "Facility Maintenance and Renovation Policy: Step-by-Step Guidance" 2013, 327, op. cit.
52. Ashwini Arun, "EBOM-v4 MRc3: Purchasing – Facility Maintenance and Renovation," BuildingGreen, 2018. https://leeduser.buildinggreen.com/credit/EBOM-v4/MRc3
53. Dan Ackerstein, "EBOM-v4 MRc5: Solid Waste Management – Facility Maintenance and Renovations," BuildingGreen, 2018. https://leeduser.buildinggreen.com/credit/EBOM-v4/MRc5

CHAPTER TEN

INDOOR ATMOSPHERE

10.1 Theory

Until a few decades ago, the quality of the interior environment had been undervalued as a feature of architectural design – it was not considered a part of base building architectural design. How important is the interior environment? Considering that Americans spend 87 percent of their time indoors,[1] 20 percent of all employees have a major illness related to indoor air pollution such as allergies, asthma, auto-immune diseases, etc., and 40 percent of all buildings pose a serious health hazard due to indoor air pollution, according to the World Health Organization. EPA estimates an 18 percent annual production loss to American business due to poor indoor air quality and cites that the average person in the US receives 72 percent of total chemical exposure in closed, indoor environments.[2]

The atmosphere of any new indoor occupied space, despite its function, requires a thorough set of criteria for an adequate design. Assessing an *existing* building's interior is no less complicated. The USGBC has provided myriad venues of credits to address interior issues. The credits within Indoor Air Quality (IEQ) (also called Indoor Environmental Quality – IEQ) span from the selection of filters for HVAC equipment to providing adequate outdoor ventilation. What is not clearly described in the LEED O+M v4 Reference Guide, however, is how all of the credits relate to each other and how they very specifically involve the Material (Chapter 9) and Energy (Chapter 8) categories.

Upon first glance, credits such as daylighting or assessing filters for HVAC appear to be two unrelated topics under one category. In fact, the variety of credits within the IEQ category is the most diverse among all of the credit categories. However, these seemingly disparate credits do in fact contribute to their functioning as a whole. An easy way of assimilating their disparity is to classify them into sub-topics of Health and Comfort of the indoor environment (Figure 10.1).

INDOOR ATMOSPHERE

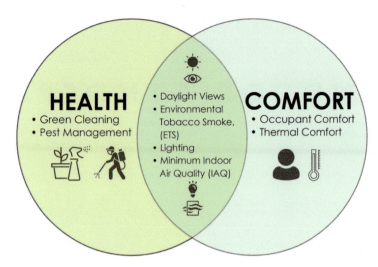

Fig 10.1 Health and comfort of the indoor environment
Source: Created by Patricia Andrasik, Milan Glisić and Elizabeth Meyers, 2020

Side Lesson A – 10.1: Sick Building Syndrome is when a building has a direct negative effect on the occupant's health. For example, poor indoor air quality can be a factor of the syndrome and can cause respiratory issues for the occupants. The amount of time spent in a building can be linked directly to the cause of illness (see www.epa.gov/indoor-air-quality-iaq/indoor-air-facts-no-4-sick-building-syndrome).

Side Lesson B – 10.1: Ergonomics is a scientific discipline that studies human interactions as a part of a larger system. This discipline uses data, theories, and principles to inform design for optimum well-being and performance (see https://rb.gy/ugmayk).

Health impacts of the interior environment. Indoor environments are highly complex and building occupants may be exposed to a variety of contaminants (in the form of gases and particles) from office machines, cleaning products, construction activities, carpets and furnishings, perfumes, cigarette smoke, water-damaged building materials, microbial growth (fungal, mold, and bacterial), insects, and outdoor pollutants. The indoor environmental benefits in green buildings translate to better self-reported health outcomes across several indicators, including fewer sick building syndrome (Side Lesson A: Sick Building Syndrome) symptoms, fewer respiratory symptom reports in children, and better physical and mental health. Occupants also report benefits that indicate improved work productivity in green buildings. In one study, the occupants reported fewer absenteeism and fewer work hours affected by asthma and allergies in green buildings. Also related to productivity, green buildings were associated with lower employee turnover and a decrease in the length of open staff positions. In a hospital setting, they noted improved quality of care in green buildings, fewer bloodstream infections, improved record keeping, and lower patient mortality.[3] Factors of indoor health are *directly* a result of how a building's interior is designed and maintained. These include noise pollution, which is sound that negatively or harmfully impacts activity of daily life for humans or animals, and ergonomics which dictates aspects such as the position of furniture as it relates to the human body (Side Lesson B: Ergonomics).[4] Circulation is also a part of ensuring a healthy environment because it dictates the walkability or how well people can navigate the interior environment.

Air pollution – either as toxic particulates which are invisible or visible to the eye – is one of the most critical factors to control in the interior environment. This includes smoking bans to reduce exposure to second-hand exposure. Mold (Side Lesson C: Mold), a type of fungus which releases spores into the air,[5] and dirt may possess invisible airborne particulates and bacteria thus may be considered a form of air pollution. Good ventilation often mitigates the impacts of the air pollution and is dependent on how air flows through a building. Filtration, which can be a simple perforated object which traps such airborne particles, is often a part of the same HVAC system that provides the ventilation.

Interior materials also play an important role in indoor health through their potential to contribute towards air pollution, although they constitute an entirely different chapter and credit category (see Material and Resources, Chapter 9). The composition of every item within an indoor environment – the wallcovering, the flooring, the paint, the mechanical systems, even the finish on furniture – has an aggregate effect on the indoor air. How? Some of the components of materials cause them to off-gas chemical substances, or volatile organic compounds (Side Lesson D: Volatile Organic Compounds (VOCs)), creating a potentially toxic indoor atmosphere. Current building standards are increasing their stringency of chemical composition for building products used in the interior environment, so not every material will off-gas.

Comfort within the interior environment. Closely linked to the health impacted *by* the interior environment is comfort *within* the interior environment. How effectively people function in a building has a direct correlation to their level of comfort in it. Temperature, air speed and humidity which indicates the amount of water vapor or moisture in the air, all impact this level of comfort. In fact, ASHRAE defines thermal comfort as a "condition of mind which expresses satisfaction with the thermal environment."[6] Regardless of which type of building you are assessing in your LEED Lab class, the *function* of the building is a key feature in determining where the building's thermal comfort zone (Side Lesson E: The Thermal Comfort Zone) will appear on a psychrometric chart (Figures 10.2, 10.3, 10.4, 10.5, and 10.6). Knowing the thermal comfort zone is helpful in understanding how the existing space/s in your facility may or may not be providing adequate thermal comfort for occupants. Comfort however is not limited to the thermal factors of the atmosphere. Many factors of comfort are *directly* a result of how a building is designed – one of the most important is lighting.

Used to aid working, exercising and all basic functions, lighting can evoke feelings of relaxation, energy or other emotions and impacts the quality of color perception. It can enhance or minimize patterns, textures on interior surfaces. The more light is able to be controlled by the occupants in a space, the more comfortable those occupants become.

Light can be either natural or artificial. Glare, either from either natural or artificial light, is intense brightness which may be debilitating if not controlled within the interior environment. Artificial Lighting includes incandescent, fluorescent, LED or any interior lighting source which requires power to provide illumination. Daylighting involves placing fenestration and reflective surfaces in positions

Side Lesson C – 10.1:
Mold is a type of fungus. There are some types of mold that produce toxins (mycotoxins) – these types are toxigenic. Toxigenic mold is rare to find in the household, but can create health issues for the occupants such as memory loss or pulmonary hemorrhage. Mold is everywhere, even if a very little amount. It can be present in air and on several surface types. Even non-toxigenic molds should be considered as a hazard (see www.cdc.gov/mold/stachy. htm).

Side Lesson D – 10.1:
Volatile Organic Compounds (VOCs) are small components of chemicals that become unattached from a material over a certain period of time through the process of off-gassing. These compounds are released in the form of a gas into the air. The most dangerous VOCs include Ethanol, Acetone, Formaldehyde chloroform, Phthalates, Ozone, Benzene, Perchloroethylene, Methylene chloride, and chemical flame retardants. VOCs can exist not only in solid materials but liquid as well. Even though it is an organic compound, organic does not always mean healthy or chemical-free. Many VOCs are cancerous, and can become harmful once mixing with other chemicals as gases (see www.epa.gov/indoor-air-quality-iaq/volatile-organic-compounds-impact-indoor-air-quality).

INDOOR ATMOSPHERE

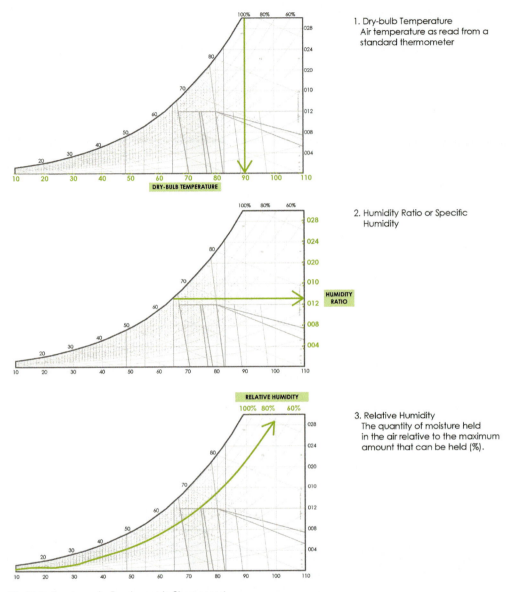

Fig 10.2 *How to read a Psychrometric Chart, page 1*
Source: Diagrammed by Elizabeth Meyers, 2020

accessible to direct or indirect sunlight to provide natural illumination. The use of daylighting in buildings has focused primarily on reducing energy consumption and providing pleasant interior environments, however it is also helpful to health through impacts on the body's circadian rhythms. Given that people spend a majority of their waking hours indoors, lighting has an impact on *both* health and comfort[7] in addition to being a primary contributor to the energy load.

Indoor air quality has a tenuous relationship with energy. For example, when a thermal comfort control in a dorm room is set to provide an optimum level of heating during the spring

INDOOR ATMOSPHERE

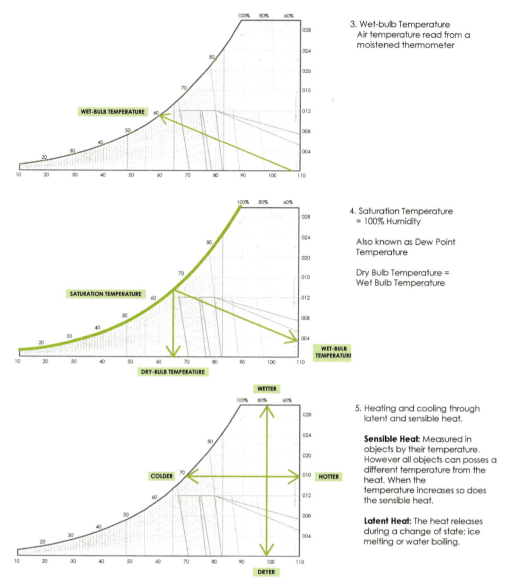

Fig 10.3 *How to read a Psychrometric Chart, page 2*
Source: Diagrammed by Elizabeth Meyers, 2020

break when the room is unoccupied; if individual thermostats in offices provide variable temperatures for different needs of its occupants; or when lighting is designed for the maximum occupancy in a classroom which is only filled one day per week; more energy than necessary is consumed, despite the comfortable environment provided. If your facility has a function which requires a significant power load such as a data center, creating a comfortable interior environment for occupants may draw more energy due to the increased HVAC demands. We can initially assess our indoor comfort priorities when we better understand the type of buildings we are evaluating.

Side Lesson E – 10.1: The Thermal Comfort Zone is the location within a psychrometric chart where 80 percent of occupants will find the environment thermally acceptable.

| 249

INDOOR ATMOSPHERE

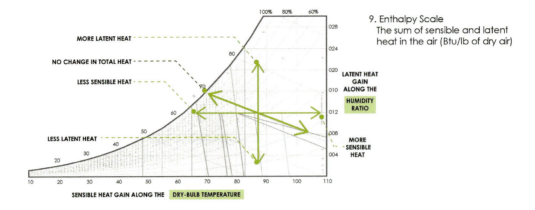

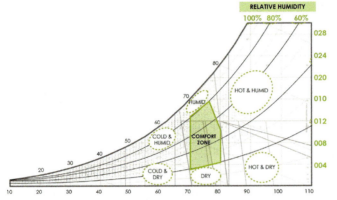

Fig 10.4 *How to read a Psychrometric Chart, page 3*
Source: Diagrammed by Elizabeth Meyers, 2020

Types of buildings. There are typically two types of facilities which exist on your campus – Internally Dominated and Externally Dominated Buildings. The latter are sparsely populated buildings with little activity or equipment and are generally dominated by "external loads" such as heat from the sun, or the wind from a winter gust. These usually constitute small residences, storage facilities, warehouses, or apartments, and any small commercial space. Internally Dominated buildings are more densely populated facilities with high activity or energy-intensive equipment. These are generally dominated by internal loads such as heat from computers, heat generated from the amount of people in a crowded auditorium or a library, and spaces which require hefty electrical requirements such as museums, and most offices. Depending on whether your campus facility is internally or externally dominated can provide a clue about where your focus may reside when considering indoor air quality. If your facility is a library for example, it is internally dominated. This means that it will be more difficult to reduce energy consumption since providing a well-ventilated and well-lit space is a priority for such a function where people occupy space for long periods of time. *The desire to provide an optimum environment may exceed a priority of energy reduction in this case.*

INDOOR ATMOSPHERE

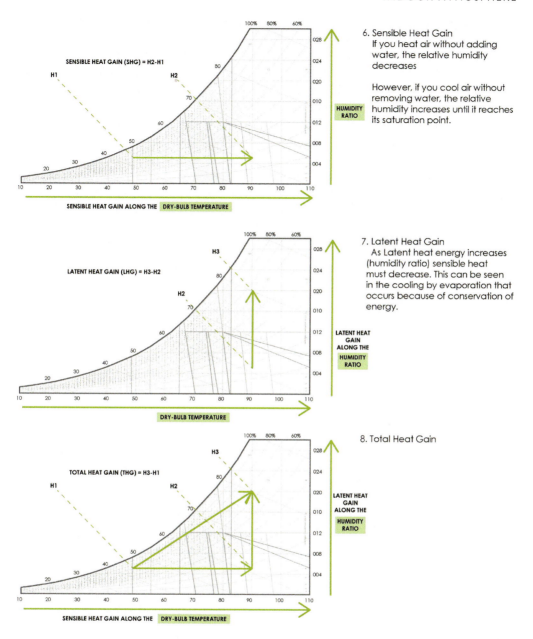

Fig 10.5 *How to read a Psychrometric Chart, page 4*
Source: Diagrammed by Elizabeth Meyers, 2020

An externally dominated building will be focused on the exterior climate to inform much of the energy requirements of the interior environment. For example, a small residence on your campus will be influenced by the climate more directly due to the proportion of the exterior wall space to the square footage of the building rather than the quantity of people occupying the

INDOOR ATMOSPHERE

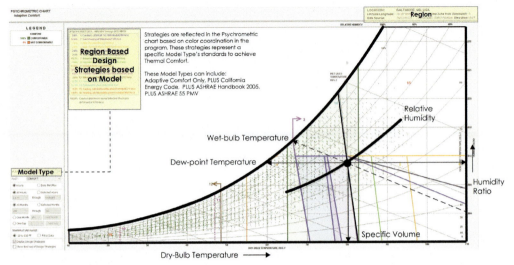

Fig 10.6 A Psychrometric Chart, a tool to help determine interior thermal comfort levels

Note: To create a similar chart, use ASHRAE 55

Source: Created by Patricia Andrasik using ASHRAE 55, 2017

interior. It is much easier to provide a good interior environment from the onset of design in this case, where the walls, floor and roof of the building (called the building envelope) can be modified to accept or reject environmental forces such as solar radiation or wind. *A superb indoor air quality for these types of facilities may be more difficult to achieve if the architecture was not well-informed by the climate, thus creating a necessity for increasing energy demand in this case.* Understanding the building's function and energy demands can help to prioritize energy and IEQ credits for your LEED Lab class' facility.

10.2 Comparison

Indoor Environmental Quality (IEQ) has a broad spectrum of importance and is a fundamental aspect of assessment in every major rating system. Indoor air pollution has many forms and is globally recognized as a critical feature of sustainable building maintenance. It may be in the form of smoke emitted from solid fuel combustion, such as in case of the households in developing countries, or a complex mixture of VOCs present in modern buildings.[8] The health effects from indoor pollution are diverse, could be immediately detected or, as often is the case, produce debilitating results on life after years of unnoticed exposure. According to the World Health Organization, indoor air pollution from solid fuel use was solely responsible for almost 2 million annual deaths and 2.7 percent of the global burden of disease in 2004.[9] The more mature existing building stock requires a proactive approach in building assessment simultaneously recognizing health and comfort related improvements applied by building owners. A variety of established global and local rating systems are currently addressing issues and credits similar to LEED O+M and in accordance to the specifics of the local environment (Figure 10.7).

Credit categories concerned with IEQ among various global systems are organized differently and have different weights per

INDOOR ATMOSPHERE

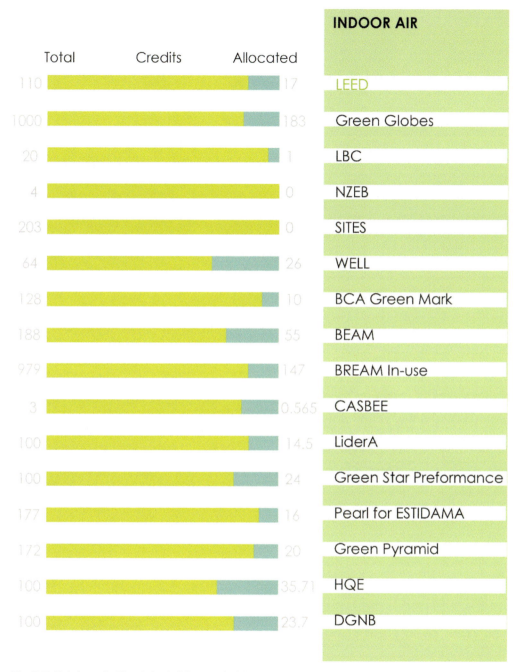

Fig 10.7 Global sustainable existing building sustainability assessment tools for indoor air quality
Source: Created by Milan Glisić, 2017

each rating system. For example, where LEED O+M uses the term IEQ, BREEAM in-Use uses the title "Health and Wellbeing." Green Star follows the LEED O+M approach and categorizes this as Indoor Environmental Quality while DGNB addresses assessment of IEQ through social-cultural and functional quality. Let's review the similarities and differences to LEED O+M in detail (Figure 10.8).

INDOOR ATMOSPHERE

Fig 10.8 Global sustainable existing building sustainability assessment tools: comparison for indoor air quality
Source: Created by Milan Glisić, 2017

10.2.1 Green Globes for Existing Buildings (EB)

Indoor Environmental Quality is second only to energy as a weighted area in the Green Globes rating system. Green Globes EB has ten categories under Indoor Environment: Ventilation System, Filtration System, Humidification System, Cooling Towers, Parking and Receiving, Control of Pollutants at Source, IAQ Management, Lighting Features, Lighting Management, Noise. Together, these credits comprise 185 credits, 18.5 percent of all credits. The goal is to create a report which would help building owners and LEED O+M facility personnel to evaluate current performance and offer suggestions for future improvements.[10]

HOW?

Along with six assessment areas within this rating system, the path of certification comprises three steps, starting with online survey-questionnaire and check-list, followed by on-site third-party assessment and post assessment related to Performance Period, similar to LEED O+M. Unlike LEED, this system doesn't have prerequisites for particular category assessment, but does apply a threshold for overall building performance across all categories. Each of the weighted criteria yields a certain number of points for appropriate answers on the preliminary on-line survey. The on-line submitted documentation and on-site assessment by accredited third party are next steps and require best management practices and benchmarked goals as continuing measures for compliance.[11]

10.2.2 BREEAM In-Use

Within its three-part process, BREEAM tends to IEQ through its Health and Wellness category. In Asset Performance, there are 11 categories totaling 33 credits; in Building Management, there are 12 categories totaling 37 credits; finally, in Occupier Management, there are five categories with 75 credits.[12] These categories include assessing indoor and outdoor space, glare control, lighting, illuminance, water provisions, microbial contamination, thermal and ventilation controls. The system recognizes that indoor air quality depends not only on physical features of the building but effectiveness and robustness of the building management systems and heavily relies on surveyed occupant answers.

HOW?

Undertaking all three assessment parts is required in order to determine the asset's overall IEQ performance. The Asset Performance area is Part 1 of the assessment process and requires asset's performance evaluation of air distributed cooling systems and/or mechanical and electrical ventilation equipment in order to award certain amounts of credits. The BREEAM In-Use team evaluates the level to which activities contribute to a healthy and comfortable environment for occupants. The main focus is under Management and Occupier Management Areas, Part 2 and Part 3 where a variety of issues are identified and addressed and achieved level through several credits.[13] The Part 2 is independent of Part 1 and allows users to identify and address management issues that impact well-being and comfort. Part 3 evaluates the quality of understanding and implementations of IEQ management systems, based comfort levels related to temperature, air quality, illuminance levels, and acoustics, the provisions of personal or zoned control systems, and other

INDOOR ATMOSPHERE

policies and technologies implemented to improve health and wellbeing within the asset.

10.2.3 Green Star Performance

Green Star allocates 18 percent of all available credits to the category of "Indoor Environmental Quality," following LEED O+M. Credits assess and reward strategies and actions taken to ensure buildings are healthy and comfortable places to live and work within. The Indoor Environment Quality category is subdivided in seven subcategories: Quality of Indoor Air (four points), Hazardous Materials (two points), Lighting Comfort (two points), Daylight and Views (two points), Thermal Comfort (three points), Acoustic Comfort (one point), and Occupant Comfort and Satisfaction (four points). These subcategories total a possible 18 points, 16.5 percent of the total 109.[14]

HOW?

Subcategories for this category are modeled to assess and reward processes in existing buildings which provide quality air supply and pollutant control with adequate overall capacities through a "Performance Period" similar to LEED O+M. After the project is registered, documentation of all indoor air quality strategies is accumulated along with the other desired credits in other categories and is submitted to the Green Building Council of Australia (GBCA). An independent panel of energy experts assign a score to the categories, and third-party certification (valid for up to three years) may ensue.[15] Points for monitoring intake air levels, CO concentrations, and hazardous materials on a regular basis are calculated, and an occupant comfort survey may be awarded with up to 4 points. The Green Star rating is determined by comparing the number of available points achieved.

10.2.4 LEED Operations and Maintenance (O+M)

The IEQ category comprises 22 credits, approximately 15.4 percent of the total categories of the LEED O+M rating system and is the second in line for weight after energy.[16] As with all of the rating systems, LEED O+M recognizes that IEQ is attributed to the ventilation and elimination of potential contaminants within building and rewards decisions made by project teams about thermal and visual comfort, and occupants' satisfaction. It also encourages building owners to determine priorities for improving the indoor environment by surveying occupants.

HOW?

While staff may understand which systems are installed and how they function, performance feedback and the opinions of the occupants are often beyond what traditional best management practices require, but what is necessary for accomplishing the goals of this category. Many credits are achieved through self-assessments – data collection of system performance and user response – which are verified via reviewers at GBCI. Three prerequisites related to minimum indoor air quality, tobacco smoke control, and Green Cleaning Policies must be met in order to further building performance and pursue available credits. Credits are focused on particularities of green policy implementation and related activities, employed equipment and resources are achieved through specific calculations indicated in the LEED O+M v4 Reference Guide.

10.2.5 Other Rating Systems

Regardless of being named to emphasize 'health', or 'comfort', rating systems around the globe recognize the importance of indoor air quality improvement. Many may be considered as a substitute rating system for LEED O+M within LEED Lab due their emphases of air quality relating to geography. Besides the most globally accepted assessment systems previously mentioned, there are others which are regionally oriented which may be substituted for LEED O+M within LEED Lab.

- **BCA Green Mark.** Launched in 2005 to drive Singapore's construction industry towards more environmentally friendly buildings, the BCA Green Mark rating system allocates 40 points within ten credit categories to the Smart and Healthy Building category, with an additional 15 points available for an advanced green effort; this equals 31 percent of the total 128 points. This involves providing confirmation that building air-conditioning systems and ventilation equipment functions within required operative levels. Reducing noise level, increasing lighting quality, minimizing airborne contaminants and improving air quality performance are subcategories which comprise this topic. The urban limitations of highly developed Singapore seem to warrant a greater focus on occupant comfort, but appear to focus on energy reduction as a higher priority.[17]

- **BEAM Plus for Existing Buildings.** Given that on average people in Hong Kong spend most of their time indoors, indoor environmental conditions in that city have a significant impact on the quality of life. Hong Kong Green Building Council (HKGBC) states that buildings should provide safe, healthy and comfortable indoor spaces and the design, management, operation and maintenance of buildings should seek to provide a good quality indoor environment, but with optimum use of energy and other resources.[18] This assessment system allocates a potential 28 points plus six bonus points of the overall 150 points (and 50 bonus points) to indoor environmental issues properly addressed, comprising a little over 18 percent of the rating system weight. This includes those aspects of building performance that impact on the health, comfort, or well-being of the occupants, as well as aspects of performance that improve quality and functionality.[19]

    As most rating systems, this category focuses on indoor air quality, ventilation, thermal comfort, lighting, and noise. It first requires the prerequisite under

Management (MAN) where policies ensure building operation of indoor strategies such as cleaning, renovation and user involvement. It also requires a Construction Indoor Quality Management Plan addressing potential problems caused by the renovation of the existing building. Within this category criteria awards credits and bonus credit for instalment and implementation of green cleaning. Finally, its own category of IEQ includes similar criteria as LEED O+M with the addition of hygiene and acoustics.

- **CASBEE EB.** Japan's Comprehensive Assessment System for Build Environment Efficiency rating system (CASBEE) dedicates 20 percent of its weight to Indoor Environmental Quality. The Q1 category is labeled Indoor Environment and consists of four subset categories – Noise and Acoustics, Thermal Comfort, Lighting and Illumination, and Air Quality. Examples of the granularity available within, for example, thermal comfort, are the following: room temperature control, humidity control, type of air conditioning system.[20]

- **LiderA.** LiderA – the prime rating system of Portugal since 2005 – encompasses different building types at various stages including plan and design, construction and management simultaneously. For this rating system, Indoor Environmental Quality is one of the factors with greatest impacts on occupants.

    LEED's IEQ has its parallel in the Environmental Comfort category, comprising Air Quality Levels (C24), Thermal Comfort (C25), Lighting Levels (C26) and Acoustic Insulation and Noise Levels (C27), together comprising 15 percent of the credits in LiderA. Under a separate category of Socioeconomic Experience, another 1 percent is attributed to the criteria Controllability (C36), bringing total of 16 percent of all points dedicated to IEQ. The system provides building occupants the ability to control comfort levels according to their needs, moderating temperature, humidity, pollutants, and noise levels control.[21]

- **Pearl for ESTIDAMA (PORS).** In the United Arab Emirates, most people spend most of their time indoors due to the extreme climate. The Pearl Operational Rating System (PORS) released in 2013 reflects this climate-driven lifestyle to health and wellbeing related issues. Similar to LEED O+M, PORS has a Livable Indoors (LBi) section with ten subsections: Ventilation Quality, Material Emissions, Construction Indoor Air Quality Management, Car Park Air Quality Management, Thermal Comfort and Controls, High Frequency Lighting, Daylight and Glare, Views, Indoor Noise Pollution, and Safe and Secure Environment. This totals 23 possible credits.[22]

    The system addresses thermal comfort by promoting beneficial outcomes that foster a well thought-through HVAC system and a greater degree of occupant control. Natural daylight, consistent and abundant in the region, together with appropriate artificial lighting is also a critical metric. Particular requirements such as mandatory ventilation, smoke control and legionella prevention are also directly addressed.

- **Green Pyramid.** The Egypt Green Building Council's Green Pyramid Rating System (GPRS) which originated in 2010 currently only focuses on guidelines for new construction of buildings in Egypt, although much of the indoor environmental criteria closely aligns with existing building evaluation. Category 5: Indoor Environmental Quality is focused on actual performance of the built environment with respect to the wellbeing and comfort of occupants. The subcategories are Optimized Ventilation, Controlling emissions from building materials, Thermal Comfort, Visual Comfort, Acoustic Comfort, for a total of 20 points.[23]

- **HQE Exploitation.** France's Green Building Council developed *Haute Qualité Environnementale* or High Quality Environmental Standard (HQE) Certification for Buildings in Operation (HQE Exploitation) in 2005 as their counterpart to BREEAM In-Use and LEED O+M.[24] The system is process-oriented, flexible and has three certification areas with 14 categories-targets, related to the complexity of building's external and internal environments. It is up to the client to distribute and define hierarchically all of them, including target performance levels, and to create a target profile for the building quality.[25]

    A scheme is set with a number of fundamental prerequisites and is divided into three certification areas for valuing the engagement of the owner, the manager and the user, independently or jointly. The Prerequisite level is obtained when all of the minimum requirements for a target are met, and the "Comfort and Health" target addresses particular aspects of indoor air quality. Performing and High Performing levels are obtained based on a percentage of points given per target, which allows for significant flexibility.

    HQE dedicates a significant number of its targets towards IEQ: Target 8 – Hygrothermal Comfort (11 points), Target 9 – Acoustic Comfort (9 points), Target 10 – Visual Comfort (16 points), Target 11 – Olfactory Comfort (15 points), Target 12 – Spaces Quality (20 points), Target 13 – Air Quality (24 points). Totaled, there are 95 points available towards IEQ in HQE, 29.5 percent of all credits available.[26]

- **DGNB In Use.** Existing or renovated buildings are considered in the Deutsche Gesellschaft für Nachhaltiges Bauen (DGNB) In Use scheme, developed by the German Sustainable Building Council in 2011. Of the six main criteria groups, only three can be used for the accreditation of an existing building: Ecological Quality, Economic Quality, Sociocultural and Functional Quality. The object of DGNB In Use is to develop and promote materials, means and solutions for the operation building processes to meet the criteria of sustainability. The consequences are important for the entire lifecycle of a building.

    Nearly the entire Sociocultural and Functional Quality group is dedicated to IEQ. Criteria numbers 18 through 25,

INDOOR ATMOSPHERE

comprising the Health, Comfort and User section, deals with thermal, acoustic and visual comfort and hygiene, safety and risk prevention; these total 160 points. Criteria numbers 26 through 28, from the Functionality section, handle accessibility for disabled persons, the efficient use of space, and a building's suitability for conversions, totaling 50 points. Together, these 210 possible IEQ points comprise almost 39 percent of the total points available for existing buildings.[27]

We can garner from the array of global rating systems that while indoor environment quality is an integral part of their structure, many requirements mimic LEED O+M. Additionally, some recognize noise pollution or emissions and hygiene, although emissions from products used in renovations, maintenance work, and furniture in LEED O+M are addressed in the Materials and Resources credit category.[28]

10.3 Credits

10.3.1 Air Quality Performance

(*Refer also to page 395 in the LEED O+M v4 Reference Guide*)

This is a prerequisite which should be analyzed early in the Feasibility Phase of your LEED Lab course. Basically, it ensures that occupants are receiving sufficient amounts of fresh air, promoting a healthy indoor environment and prevents spaces from being uncomfortable or 'stuffy' and formally establishes minimum thresholds of outdoor air ventilation and distribution in an existing building. If thresholds are not met, then modifications such as controlling pollutant sources, removing contaminants from the air, and supplying fresh air during the Performance Period are required. Monitoring this air rate regularly is also required.

The prerequisite applies to mechanical air-handling units (AHUs) and exhaust systems in order to verify that ventilation air is provided to all spaces which are occupied. Systems are either able to meet reference standards of ASHRAE or *Comité Européen de Normalisation* (CEN) International Standards, or not – and either may serve as a path for compliance. There is also an option for naturally ventilated spaces such as dormitories. The prerequisite is designed to measure the amount of fresh air proportional to the size of the space in square feet, the number of people occupying the space, and the activities being performed in the space. The precise rate of air output and delivery of air is dependent on the type and capabilities of the ventilation system being employed. The tasks of this prerequisite are most telling of the level of detail required to assess the outdoor air.

Tasks

Students must work intently with facility personnel who are in charge of the HVAC, outdoor air handling units supporting the HVAC system, or any equipment used to draw outdoor air into the facility, as these individuals will know *how* to – or *who* to engage when measuring outdoor air flow into the building. Often the designated individual is an external mechanical consultant who already works with the institution and should engage the LEED Lab student/staff.

INDOOR ATMOSPHERE

A. **Identification**

☐ Collect information from the facility
A few basic information-gathering steps must be performed before attempting to accomplish the credit by a specific path.
This should be completed by the LEED Lab student.
  ☐ Investigate if your project is located in a nonattainment area for particulate matter and ozone sufficiency (Side Lesson F: Nonattainment Areas). This is necessary to identify if the outdoor air quality interferes with the indoor air quality. If the outdoor air quality is poor, admitting 'fresh air' to aid in ventilation will pollute the indoor air, thus disqualifying the project from earning the prerequisite unless provisions for air-cleaning devices or a specific HVAC filter with a minimum efficiency reporting value (MERV 11) are met (Side Lesson G: The MERV Rating) (see Figure 10.9).

  Fortunately, the EPA has produced a handy online reference, the Green Book, easily provides data about the air quality of various counties in the USA (see Tools).

1. **Size + Space**
   ☐ Identify the size (square feet) and use of all the rooms in the project. Use a plan and identification system that is consistent with other documentation efforts of the project. The plan should recognize, at a minimum, the name of each space by its floor number, use, and room number. For example 2-S-7 is the 2nd Floor, Studio Space, Room #7. *It is vital that this style of room numbering is identical to the number and plans used for other credits. If the numbering system varies between credits, the documentation will not be considered acceptable, and the credit attempt will be considered "pending" upon clarification of documentation.*

2. **AHUs**
   ☐ Identify all air-handling units (AHUs) and exhaust systems in the facility. Identify these in a mechanical floor plan so they are clearly marked (Figure 10.10).

3. **Zones**
   ☐ Identify all system zones for the facility (Figures 10.11 and 10.12). To determine the amount of outdoor required by ASHRAE 62.1 the size, occupancy, and activity of each space must be noted on a diagrammatic plan. AHUs may serve a single space (Fig 2 – AHU 2), or they may serve multiple spaces.

   It is important to match the AHU to the spaces it serves. Generally, the easiest method to accomplish this is to map the lines of major ductwork. Finally, all the rooms served by one AHU unit should be grouped together and recognized as a Zone.

Side Lesson F – 10.3.1: Nonattainment Areas are locations in which violate air quality standards. The air quality must meet the National Ambient Air Quality Standards defined in the Clean Air Act Amendments of 1970 (PL, 91–604, Sec. 109), according to the United States environmental law. In order to meet the standard nonattainment areas must have a plan for implementation. Without an implementation plan, nonattainment areas may face the risk of losing federal financial assistance (see www.epa.gov/green-book).

Side Lesson G – 10.3.1: The MERV Rating is a metric used to rank air filters based on their effectiveness. In 1987, the American Society of Heating, Refrigerating, and Air-Conditioning Engineers (ASHRAE) designed the rating scale. The MERV rating ranges from 1 to 16, and bases effectiveness on ability to filter air particles. A high MERV rating means that a greater percentage of particles are captured through the filter. A filter rated MERV 16 can capture more than 95 percent of the particles from the air passing through it (see www.epa.gov/indoor-air-quality-iaq/what-merv-rating-1).

INDOOR ATMOSPHERE

Standard 52.5 Minimum Efficiency Reporting Values	Dust Spot Efficiency	Arrestance	Typical Controlled Containment	Typical Applications and Limitations	Typical Air Filter/Cleaner Type
20	n/a	n/a	<0.30 pm particle size	Cleanrooms	>99.999% ft. On. 10-20 pm
19	n/a	n/a	Virus (unattached)	Radioactive Material	Particles
18	n/a	n/a	Carbon Dust	Pharmaceutical Man.	Particles
17	n/a	n/a	All Combustion smoke	Carcinogenic Materials	Particles
16	n/a	n/a	0.30-1.0 pm particle size	General Surgery	
15	>95%	n/a	All Bacteria	Hospital Inpatient Care	• **Bag Filter:** Non-supported Micro-fine fiberglass or synthetic media, 12-36 in. deep, 6-12 pockets
14	90-95%	>98%	Most Tobacco Smoke	Smoking Lounges	• **Box Filter:** Rigid Style Cartridge Filters 6" to 12" deep may use lofted or paper media
13	89-90%	>98%	Proplet Nuclei (Sneeze)	Superior Commercial Buildings	
12	70-75%	>95%	1.0-3.0 pm Particle Size Legionella	Superior Residential	• **Bag Filter:** Non-supported Micro-fine fiberglass or synthetic media, 12-36 in. deep, 6-12 pockets
11	60-65%	>95%	Humidifier Dust or Lead Dust	Better Commercial Buildings	• **Box Filter:** Rigid Style Cartridge Filters 6" to 12" deep may use lofted or paper media
10	50-55%	>95%	Milled Flour or Auto Emissions	Hospital Laboratories	
9	40-45%	>90%	Welding Fume	Hospital Laboratories	
8	30-35%	>90%	3.0-10.0 pm Particle Size or Mold Spores	Commercial Buildings	• **Pleated Filters:** Disposable, extended surface area, thick with cotton-polyester blend media, cardboard frame
7	25-30%	>90%	Hair Spray or Fabric Protector	Better Residential	• **Cartridge Filters:** Graded density viscous coated cube or pocket filters, synthetic media
6	<20%	85-90%	Dusting Aids or Cement Dust	Industrial Workplace	• **Throwaway:** Disposable synthetic panel filter
5	<20%	80-85%	Pudding Mix	Paint Booth Inlet	
4	<20%	75-80%	>10.0 pm Particle Size Pollen	Minimal Filtration	• **Throwaway:** Disposable fiberglass or synthetic panel filter
3	<20%	70-75%	Dust Mites or Sanding Dust	Residential	• **Washable:** Aluminum Mesh
2	<20%	65-70%	Spray Paint Dust or Textile Fibers	Residential or Window A/C Units	• **Washable:** Aluminum Mesh
1	<20%	<65%	Carpet Fibers	Window A/C Units	• **Electrostatic:** Self-charging woven panel filter

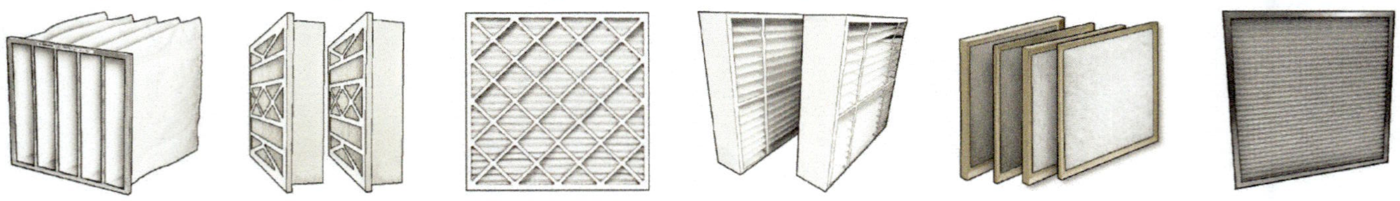

Typical Air Filter/Cleaner Type Image Key:

Bag Filter
MERV 11 8-Pocket
Synthetic Media
Aerostar® SoriQ Pocket Filter

Box Filter

Pleated Filters

Cartridge Filters
Bryant/Carrier FILXXFNC-0021
Cartridge Filter

Throwaway Filters
Koch Filter™ Disposable Polyester Filter

Washable/Electrostatic Filters

Fig 10.9 *MERV rating chart*

Source: Derived from Mechanical Reps Inc. (www.mechreps.com/PDF/PDF/Merv_Rating_Chart.pdf). Redrawn by Elizabeth Meyers, 2020

INDOOR ATMOSPHERE

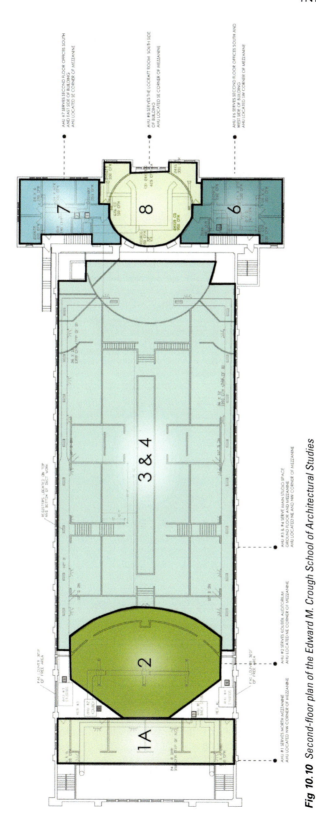

Fig 10.10 *Second-floor plan of the Edward M. Crough School of Architectural Studies*

Note: All spaces are noted with their floor number, use, and room number. AHUs are labeled on a basic floor plan of the building. This basic floor plan also recognizes the name of each space by its floor number, use, and room number

Source: *Diagrammed by Elizabeth Meyers, 2020*

INDOOR ATMOSPHERE

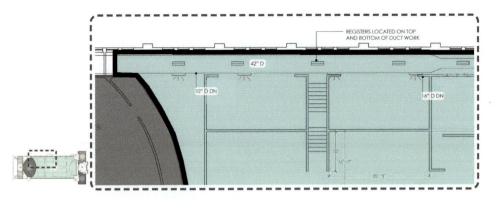

Fig 10.11 *Close-up of Figure 10.10*

Note: AHUs are labeled, major ductwork and air registers are mapped (noting size and placement) and the initial cubic feet per minute of air delivery designation found in the original 1988 document set was noted

Source: Diagrammed by Elizabeth Meyers, 2020

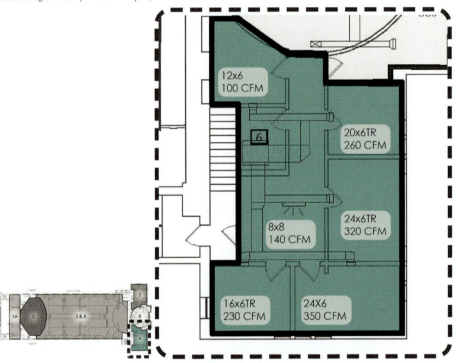

Fig 10.12 *Close-up of Figure 10.10*

Note: All rooms served by the same AHU are grouped into a single zone. AHU 6 serves five offices and one pin-up space. These six spaces comprise Zone 6

Source: Diagrammed by Elizabeth Meyers, 2020

B. ***Datatable***
- ☐ Create a datatable of information
  This should be completed by the LEED Lab student in conjunction with the facility personnel or third party consultants.
- ☐ From the previous identification gathered, generate a table that will be used to determine the path of compliance. The table logs the AHU, unit location, the area it serves, the rooms served, the use (according to ASHRAE's categories),[29] size (square feet), and occupancy (according to how ASHRAE determines occupancy) (Tables 10.1 and 10.2).

Table 10.1 AHU schedule 2013, pages 1–4

Unit location	Rooms served	Square feet	Room design CFM	Occupancy	Occupancy Category Std 62.1 def
AHU1	NW CORNER OF MEZZANINE				
	ZONE 1A GROUND FLOOR GRAD STUDIOS AND THESIS BLOCK				
	1-S-11	164.75	200	3	Art classroom
	I-S-12	162.67	200	3	Art classroom
	I-S-13	162.67	200	3	Art classroom
	I-S-14	165.2	200	3	Art classroom
	I-S-15	922.33	600(4) = 2,400	18	Art classroom
		1,577.62	3200	30	
	ZONE 1B MEZZANINE GRAD STUDIOS				
	2-S-11	93.37	300	2	Art classroom
	2-S-12	228.67	555	5	Art classroom
	2-S-13	222.83	555	5	Art classroom
	2-S-14	222.83	555	5	Art classroom
	2-S-15	228.67	555	5	Art classroom
	2-S-16	83.26	300	2	Art classroom
	2-S-17	393.62	Open against 2-S-12 to 2-S-15	8	Art classroom
		1,473.25		32	
AHU 2	NE CORNER OF MEZZANINE (SERVES KOUBEK AUDITORIUM)				
		1,279.78	1,100(6) + 1,800(3) = 12,000	228	Auditorium seats

(Continued)

INDOOR ATMOSPHERE

Table 10.1 (Continued)

Unit location	Rooms served	Square feet	Room design CFM	Occupancy	Occupancy Category Std 62.1 def
AHU 3	NE CORNER OF MEZZANINE (SERVES EAST SIDE OF LARGE STUDIO ZONE)				
	EAST GROUND STUDIOS[1]				
	Computer lab	489.13	220(2) = 440	12	Computer lab
	Computer lab	323.58	220	8	Computer lab
	l-S-4	390.55	210(2) = 420	8	Art classroom
	l-S-8	390.55	210(2) = 420	8	Art classroom
	1-S-l	470.9		9	Art classroom
	l-S-3	341.19		7	Art classroom
	l-S-7	341.19		7	Art classroom
	l-P-3	373.6		37	Multi-use assembly
	Miller East*	1,256/2	1,390 + 670 = 2,060	126/2	Multi-use assembly
		3,748.69		156	
	MEZZANINE EAST[2]				
	2-S-10	280		6	Art classroom
	2-S-7	257.5		5	Art classroom
	2-S-6	132		3	Art classroom
	2-P-3	240		24	Multi-use assembly
	2-S-l	354.3		7	Art classroom
	2-S-5	480		10	Art classroom
	2-W-l East	414.67/2		4	Art classroom
		1,743.8		59	
		East total: 5,492.5		East total: 155	

266 |

INDOOR ATMOSPHERE

AHU 4	NW CORNER OF MEZZANINE (SERVES WEST SIDE OF LARGE STUDIO ZONE)				
WEST GROUND STUDIOS[3]					
	Computer lab	490.88	220(2) = 440	12	Computer lab
	Print lab	324	220	8	Computer lab
	Servers and office	130.67	315	1	Office
	I-S-5	390.55	210(2) = 420	8	Art classroom
	I-S-9	390.55	210(2) = 420	8	Art classroom
	I-S-2	477.5		10	Art classroom
	I-S-6	341.19		7	Art classroom
	I-S-10	341.19		7	Art classroom
	I-P-4	376.2		38	Multi-use assembly
	West Miller	1,256/2	1,390 + 670 = 2,060	126/2	Multi-use assembly
		3,890.73		162	
WEST MEZZANINE STUDIOS[4]					
	2-S-2	354.8		7	Art classroom
	2-S-3	132		3	Art classroom
	2-P-4	232		23	Multi-use assembly
	2-S-4	480		10	Art classroom
	2-S-8	257.5		5	Art classroom
	2-S-9	280		6	Art classroom
	2-W-I West	414.67/2		4	Art classroom
		1,736.3		58	
	West total: 5,627.03			West total: 220	
	All studio total: 11,119.53[5]			All studio total: 375	

(Continued)

INDOOR ATMOSPHERE

Table 10.1 (Continued)

Unit location	Rooms served	Square feet	Room design CFM	Occupancy	Occupancy Category Std 62.1 def
AHU 5	SW CORNER OF MEZZANINE (SERVES GROUND FLOOR OFFICE ZONE ON SOUTH SIDE OF BUILDING)				
	1-F-1 and 1-F-2	372.4	600	2	Office space
	1-F-3	279.76	435	1	Office space
	1-F-4	298	190 + 250 = 440	2	Office space
	Lobby/hall	462	200(2) + 100 + 200 + 100 = 800	5	Main entry lobby
	1-F-5	215.22	190	1	Office space
	1-F-6	95.83	250	1	Office space
	1-F-7	131.7	300	1	Office space
	1-F-8	131.1	350	1	Office space
	1-F-9	131.1	300	1	Office space
	1-F-10	130.5	200	1	Office space
	HALL2		100		
		2,247.61	2,725	16	
AHU 6	SW CORNER OF MEZZANINE (SERVES 2ND FLOOR OFFICES ON THE WEST SIDE)				
	2-F-7	106.7	260	1	Office space
	2-F-8	154	320	1	Office space
	2-F-9	146.5	350	1	Office space
	2-F-10	112.8	230	1	Office space
	2-P-2	250	140	25	Multi-use assembly
	2-F-11	127	100	1	Office space
		897	1,400	30	

AHU 7	SE CORNER OF MEZZANINE (SERVES 2ND FLOOR OFFICES ON THE EAST SIDE)				
	2-F-1	113	240	1	Office space
	2-F-2	146.5	340	1	Office space
	2-F-3	154	20	1	Office space
	2-F-4	106.7	260	1	Office space
	Printer/copier	130			
	2-P-1	253.5	140	25	Multi-use assembly
		903.7		29	
AHU 8	SE CORNER OF MEZZANINE (SERVES LOCRAFT ROOM AND TWO OFFICES)				
	2-F-5	140	330	1	Office space
	2-F-6	140	330	1	Office space
	2-C-1 LOCRAFT	956	950(2) + 100 + 425 = 2,425	48	Conference/meeting
		1236		50	
AHU 9	BASEMENT (FRESHMAN STUDIOS)				
	Computer lab	133.78		3	Computer lab
	0-S-1	2,283.97		48	Art classroom
	Elevator mechanical	117			
	Storage	32			
	Office block entry	121		1	Main entry lobby
	O-F-1	132.14		1	Office space
	O-F-2	91.19		1	Office space
	O-F-3	115.25		1	Office space
	O-F-7	97.88		1	Office space
		3,124.21		56	

(*Continued*)

Table 10.1 (Continued)

Unit location	Rooms served	Square feet	Room design CFM	Occupancy	Occupancy Category Std 62.1 def
AHU 10	BASEMENT				
	RR women	90.5			
	RR men	90.5			
	Storage	51.13			
	Photography and resource	464.9		5	Photo studio
	0-F-4	166.1		1	Office space
	0-F-5	156.87		1	Office space
	0-F-8	105.81		1	Office space
	Entry to office block	201.67		2	Main entry lobby
	0-F-9	104.65		1	Office space
	0-C-1	705.4		25	Classroom ages 9+
		2,137.53		36	
AHU 11	BASEMENT NORTH				
	RR women	40.37	75		
	RR men	40.37	75		
	0-F-6	87	100	1	Office space
	0-W-2: wood shop	1,046.5	195(6) = 1,170	21	Wood/metal shop
	0-W-3	326.6	100	7	Wood/metal shop
	Storage	108			
	0-W-4	162.2		3	Wood/metal shop
	South hall	260			
	3D print lab	79.88	120		
		2,150.92			

AHU 12	BASEMENT		
	Paint booth	305.31	1,225

Notes:
* Miller has no ceiling and is open to above
1 1-S-l, L-S-3, L-S-7, And L-P-3 are open on east side and above to mezzanine: all sharing supply air: 1,390(7) + 670(8) = 13,030 CFM
2 All mezzanine studios are open to above and to the side: supply air is shared with 1-S-L, L-S-3, L-S-7, and L-P-3:13,030 CFM
3 L-S-2, L-S-6,3 L-S-10, and L-P-4 are open on west side and above to mezzanine: all sharing supply alr: 1,390(7) + 670(8) = 13,030 CFM
4 All mezzanine studios are open to above and to the side: supply air is shared with 1-S-L, L-S-3, L-S-7, and L-P-3:13,030 CFM
5 Large studio zone total: 440 + 220 + 420 + 420 + 2,060 + 13,030 + 440 + 220 + 420 + 420 + 315 + 2,060 + 13,030 = 33,495

Table 10.2 ASHRAE's standard 62.1 outdoor air rates, Table 6–1 for use with the table you are creating

Occupancy category	Person's outdoor air rate	
	CFM per person	*l/s per person*
Auditorium seating area Libraries Office space Places of religious worship	5	2.5
Mall common areas Museums	7.5	3.8
Classrooms Daycare General manufacturing	10	5
Health club/aerobics	20	10

Source: Redrawn by Elizabeth Meyers, 2020

C. **Testing**
- ☐ Measure of Airflow Rates for ASHRAE Compliance
  Testing is carried out at the system level; intake airflow is measured in the air-handler itself and through the building to determine if enough outside air is being introduced to the system. Exhaust system testing includes the fan speed, voltage, control sequences, and set points (if applicable). If any part of the system is not functioning properly, it should be addressed during the Performance Period and would need to be tested until proof of proper function can be provided.
  Testing may be completed by building operating staff or outside personnel with qualified expertise.
- ☐ Choose your testing method. There are three different procedures within ASHRAE 62.1 which meet airflow requirements: The Ventilation Rate Procedure (VRP), the IEQ Procedure (IEQP), and/or the Natural Ventilation Procedure (NVRP). Although the intake airflow determined using each of these approaches may differ significantly because of assumptions about the design, any of these approaches is a valid basis for design.[30] Separate exhaust ventilation applies regardless of the method chosen. The ASHRAE 62.1 standard provides detailed descriptions of the forms and resources necessary to complete each of these approaches (consult with the building operations personnel or refer to ASHRAE 62.1 Excerpts link within the Toolbox in Chapter 10).
- ☐ Measure intake airflow; the amount of outdoor air introduced to indoor spaces in cubic feet per minute (CFM). Outside air measurements need to be tested at the system level which means airflow is measured in many areas from point of origin to the destination. There are many instruments and many methods of measuring airflow which are outlined in the Tools section further on. The methods of implementing these tools include:
  a. Measurement at origin: A large grid-like measurement tool (Wilson grid) can placed against the

INDOOR ATMOSPHERE

   intake filter. This tool is attached to a handheld device (manometer) that recorded the supply airflow readings.
- ☐ Measurement through system: To quantify airflow from the exterior through the interior, measurements are taken in the supply duct. Small holes are drilled in the duct and a wand (Pitot Tube) is inserted into the duct via those holes. The wand is connected to a small handheld device (manometer) that records the airflow readings.
- ☐ Produce documentation of testing for submission. The building operating staff or outside personnel with qualified expertise will generate a detailed record of all the testing which the LEED Lab team should incorporate into the final submission.

D. **Selection**
   ☐ Select the compliance path
   The results of the testing dictate what path you will follow to accomplish the prerequisite.
   This should be completed by the Facility Personnel or external mechanical consultant in collaboration with the LEED Lab student.

   1. **Case 1 – Air Quality Meets ASHRAE**
   This can only be followed if all air-handling units in the project meet ASHRAE Standard 62.1–2010. If an air-handling unit can meet ASHRAE 62.1, then it must do so during the Performance Period. Documentation of compliance means that the testing must accompany the credit documents.
      • If all AHUs tested meet ASHRAE Standard 62.1–2010, then the project has met the requirements for Case 1. Proof of testing should be uploaded to LEED online with an appropriate project narrative.
      • If the tested AHUs are capable of meeting ASHRAE Standard 62.1, but did not, you may still obtain this credit if the systems need are balanced (Side Lesson H: Testing, Adjusting, and Balancing) and retested until every AHU becomes capable of meeting the Standard tests at the appropriate threshold. Documentation of the entire process should be uploaded to LEED online.

   2. **Case 2 – Air Quality Doesn't Meet ASHRAE**
   This is for projects employing one or more AHUs or systems with some physical limitation that would prevent the unit or system from meeting the requirements of ASHRAE 62.1. In this case, a minimum of 10 cubic feet per minute (CFM) of outside air must be provided for each person that occupies the space. Inability to comply with the ASHRAE Standard 62.1 must be documented and submitted as part of the credit, along with documentation that the minimum amount of outside air is being introduced.
      Both paths require the testing of the building's dedicated exhaust systems, such as those found in

Side Lesson H – 10.3.1: TAB Testing, Adjusting, and Balancing: In order to insure the most efficient operation of a modified or new facility mechanical system, adjustments and the balance of fluid flow distribution must be monitored closely. Before the 1950s, the installation contractor carried out all of the adjustments to HVAC fluid flows (air and fluid circulation). Eventually, buildings became more complex as designers became more interested in building performance. In order to keep up with the increasing complexity of buildings in the twenty-first century, qualified independent testing groups have emerged (see www.tabbcertified.org/).

bathrooms, kitchens, shower/locker room areas, and parking garages. The tests are run to confirm that systems are functioning properly.

If some physical constraint of an AHU or system prevents the delivery of sufficiently ventilated air, then the unit or system should be set to provide at least ten cubic feet per minute of outdoor air per person within the Perfomance Period. Other AHUs in the building's system that can meet ASHRAE Standard 62.1 must still do so.

Documented proof that the system cannot meet ASHRAE must be submitted. Proof may be provided in three different ways.
1. Design documents noting that the original design of the system was not sufficient to meet the current ASHRAE Standard.
2. Measurements taken at the system level verify that the system is not and cannot meet the current ASHRAE Standard.
3. A narrative that describes the testing methods and physical issues preventing the air-handling unit from meeting the ASHRAE Standard.

If an AHU cannot meet ASHRAE Standard 62.1, this does not mean that the project will not receive certification! USGBC simply needs proof that the system cannot meet indoor air quality standards and that the system has been set (to at least 10 CFM/ person) to provide the healthiest and most well-ventilated environment, as is currently and systemically possible.

E. **Plan**
   ☐ Perform preventative maintenance
   This may be completed by the facility personnel in collaboration with the LEED Lab Student.
   The final requirement of the prerequisite is to establish a preventative maintenance plan and document that it is being followed. However, through the accomplishment of Best Management Practices (see Chapter 8.3.1, 'Energy') such a plan should already exist or be complete prior to the end of the Performance Period. A sample of the service log that identifies when each AHU was examined, the status, and whether or not any cited improvements were made, is sufficient proof of the plan being followed.

 Tools

The tools used to complete this credit range from reference standards to physical instruments. While technicians will most likely take measurements, and engineers will seek compliance with reference standards, the LEED Lab student requires familiarity with both. Student/s however will need a thorough knowledge to use the resources to verify nonattainment areas at the inception of the project and to educate the facility personnel about the I-BEAM audit.

INDOOR ATMOSPHERE

A. ***Instruments***

Measuring airflow physically requires a range of tools depending on the type of HVAC system your facility possesses. This chart identifies the most common tools (Figure 10.13).

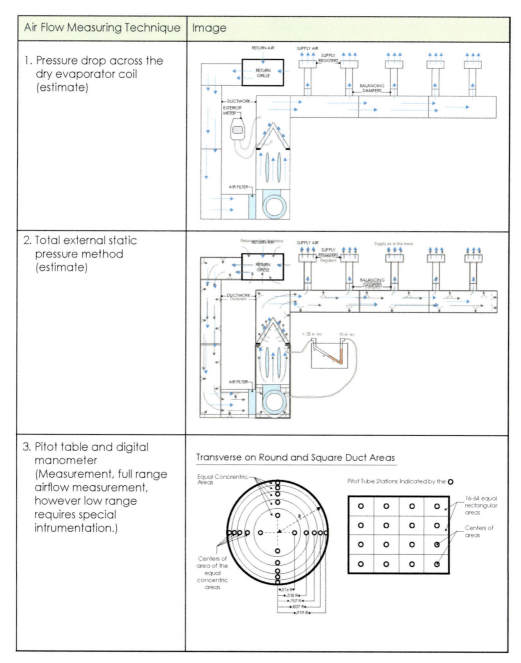

Air Flow Measuring Technique	Image
1. Pressure drop across the dry evaporator coil (estimate)	
2. Total external static pressure method (estimate)	
3. Pitot table and digital manometer (Measurement, full range airflow measurement, however low range requires special intrumentation.)	

Fig 10.13 *Measuring airflow tips and techniques chart*

Source: www.trutechtools.com/MeasuringAirflowTipsandTechniques. Diagrammed by Elizabeth Meyers, 2020

INDOOR ATMOSPHERE

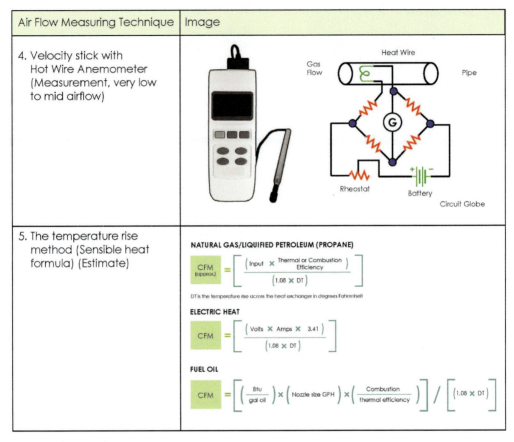

Fig 10.13 (Continued)

If your system is a standard HVAC, a pitot tube and digital manometer on the supply side and a Wilson grid on the intake are standard protocols.

B. **Standards**

ASHRAE 62.1–2010 is the primary reference standard used to achieve this prerequisite. Its purpose has been consistent since 1973 – to specify minimum ventilation rates and other measures intended to provide indoor air quality that is acceptable to human occupants and that minimizes adverse health effects (see Toolbox, Chapter 10).[31] It has since evolved through time and technology to include three main procedures for compliance (as mentioned in Tasks) in its Section 6 Procedures: The Ventilation Rate Procedure (VRP), the IEQ Procedure (IEQP), and/or the Natural Ventilation Procedure (NVRP).

- **VRP.** Calculates outdoor air intake rates based on space type, application, occupancy level, and floor area.
- **IEQP.** Calculates outdoor air intake rates based on the sources of contaminants, concentration limits and perceived air quality targets.

INDOOR ATMOSPHERE

- **NVRP.** Prescribes criteria for ventilation air provided via openings to the outdoors and may be applied in conjunction with mechanical ventilation systems.[32]

The Standard's Section 4 additionally serves as a tool for assessing outdoor air quality, but more detailed resources to determine this factor are explained below.[33]

C. **Minimum Indoor Air Quality Performance Calculator**
The Minimum Indoor Air Quality Performance Calculator can be used not only for this credit, but any project using ASHRAE 62.1. It accommodates all ventilation types from multiple zone, single-zone, 100 percent outside air in one spreadsheet.[34]

D. **Resources**
While ASHRAE 62.1–2010 serves as a reference standard, other sources below provide more detail in determining indoor and outdoor air quality thresholds necessary to – or helpful for – achieving this credit.

- **EPA Green Book.** The EPA Green Book provides the detailed information about area National Ambient Air Quality Standards (NAAQS) designations, classifications and nonattainment status[35] which ASHRAE does not, in order to determine nonattainment areas. Most specific to LEED O+M are two sections within this online guide, Particulate Matter and Ozone. If the project is in a nonattainment area for fine particulate matter (PM 2.5), filters with minimum efficiency reporting values (MERV) of 11 or higher are required. If the project is in an area where ozone exceeds the most recent three-year average in the classification, it must have air-cleaning devices for ozone.[36]
- **I-BEAM.** The IEQ Building Education and Assessment Model (I-BEAM) is a guidance tool designed for use by building professionals and others interested in indoor air quality in commercial buildings.[37] It consists of forms and calculations which help to create, audit, manage and keep IEQ practices within budget.[38]

Techniques

There are a few common unfavorable scenarios which LEED Lab teams may encounter when attempting this credit: (1) Air intakes are inaccessible or (2) HVAC systems don't supply enough outdoor air. If the outdoor air intake is not accessible, determining the airflow from the outdoors can be accomplished by using an approximation of flow rates based on temperature deltas. ASHRAE Standard 111–2008 Section 7.6.3.3 provides guidance for this procedure called the Flow Rate Approximation

INDOOR ATMOSPHERE

Side Lesson I – 10.3.1: Flow Rate Approximation by Temperature Ratio Method: Some components system airflows are virtually impossible to measure with an anemometer or pitot tube. For example, outside air measurements are affected by lack of ductwork and unpredictable turbulence (i.e., turbulence after louvers). However, this information is important in most design or TAB work. Outside airflow rate can be determined if the total supply volume from a duct traverse. The method involves temperature measurements of the outside air, the return air, and the supply air (mixed air), where…

(Outside Air) % =
(Temperature Return Air) –
(Temperature Mixed Air)
OR
(Outside Air) % =
(Temperature Return Air) –
(Temperature Outside Air)
AND
(Return Air) % =
(Temperature Outside Air) –
(Temperature Mixed Air)
OR
(Return Air) % =
(Temperature Outside Air) –
(Temperature Return Air)

This equation can be further generalized and solved such that any two volumetric components of a three-component mixed airstream can be determined if the airstreams differ in temperature and the volume of one airstream can be measured (see ASHRAE Standard: Measurement, Testing, Adjusting, and Balancing of Building HVAC Systems).

by Temperature Ratio Method (Side Lesson I: Flow Rate Approximation by Temperature Ratio Method).[39]

If the HVAC system is unable to provide an acceptable amount of outdoor air to meet ASHRAE 62.1, the system damper (Side Lesson J: Dampers) must be adjusted to admit more. The LEED Lab student in collaboration with the facility personnel must provide the initial unsuccessful testing results, then determine *and* supply the maximum possible flow that meets at least 10 CFM per person in each space to succeed in this case.

Teams may further avoid negative scenarios if they are diligent in recording the spaces which should be analyzed within the building. Hallways, lobbies and storage spaces which are either regularly or non-regularly occupied in your facility may seem irrelevant to analyze but are important to consider for the fulfillment of this prerequisite. Such spaces are listed on page 391 in the LEED O+M v4 Reference Guide.

There are also a few optimal conditions from which teams may benefit. For example, in dormitories, operable windows in each unit allow teams to avoid the mechanical ventilation required by the ASHRAE 62.1 standard. Additionally, existing VPR calculations which occurred within the past two years may be compared to outside airflow in the ASHRAE 62.1 standard. Also, referring to an accurate set of as-built mechanical drawings will help the LEED Lab student determine the units from where outside airflow measurements can be taken. Such drawings also provide equipment specifications that can inform Best Management Practices (Chapter 8.3.1).

Occupants are the best initial gauge of air quality problems within your facility. Although it's not required for this prerequisite, establishing a survey and feedback loop tracking discomfort of their air quality exposes IEQ problems before formal testing occurs. Using this strategy also synergizes with the Occupant Comfort Survey credit (Chapter 10.3.6) so two goals – or credits – are accomplished with one activity (see Toolbox, Chapter 10).

Partnering Credit

(1) Air Quality Management and (2) Enhanced Indoor Air Quality Strategies are tightly associated with this prerequisite although they are not necessarily as linked to each other as a typical Partnering Credit in this publication. The latter simply consists of an inventory of measures, while the former is associated with conducting and maintaining an air quality assessment.

Successful management of air quality should be a part of any facility's regular maintenance protocol. The Indoor Air Quality Building Education and Assessment Model (I-BEAM) is the EPA's solution for standardizing this process and facilitating a thorough assessment of your building's air quality and serves as the main requirement for the Air Quality Management credit. Released in 2002, I-BEAM is a guidance tool designed for use by building professionals and others interested in indoor air quality in commercial buildings.[40] Previously offered as an interactive CD rom, I-BEAM is now only available on the EPA's website via two modules which include the tasks of many credits in the IEQ LEED category such as installing walk-off mats as indicated in Indoor Air Quality Strategies credit, and sustainable housekeeping as indicated in the Green Cleaning credit (Chapter 10.3.3). In fact, even though it is not a prerequisite, if the I-BEAM assessment (therein the Air Quality Management credit) is pursued, many other IEQ credits will also be addressed (see Toolbox, Chapter 10 to access this efficient IEQ management tool).

If the following questions may be answered affirmatively, the Air Quality Management credit should be attempted:

- Is an Indoor Air Quality Management Program included in the O+M Plan created for the Energy Efficiency Best Management Practices Prerequisite?
- Is the Facility Personnel Staff able to conduct a full I-BEAM Audit[41] during the Performance Period and subsequently every five years?

A variety of relatively easy and seemingly unrelated measures taken to improve air quality may be accomplished to achieve the second Partnering Credit, Enhanced Air Quality Strategies. If *at least one* of the following questions may be answered affirmatively, this credit should be attempted:

- Does this facility have regularly maintained walk-off mats or permanent systems to trap incoming foot traffic debris?[42]
- Is the HVAC system in this facility equipped with an air filter with a minimum efficiency reporting value (MERV) of at least 13?
- Do the more densely populated spaces in this facility have a Carbon Monoxide (CO_2) detector? (Side Lesson K: Carbon Monoxide Detector)
- Does the facility have a direct outdoor airflow measurement device with an alarm for monitoring mechanically or naturally ventilated spaces?
- If the facility supplies natural ventilation, is there an alarm for times when windows are closed during occupied hours?

10.3.2 Smoke Control

(*Refer also to page 409 in the LEED O+M v4 Reference Guide*)

Similar to most smoking controls in every rating system and in most code-mandated buildings, avoiding smoke pollution in buildings is a requirement for LEED O+M and any other LEED certification. This prerequisite covers both commercial and residential smoking policies, however, is most frequently referenced in its commercial application on the campus. The criteria provide protection from second-hand smoke in the building by prohibiting smoking and deterring smokers from lighting up near any mechanical or stationary intakes around the building. The science underpinning the assessment provided health officials and others the evidence needed to act in protecting people from exposure to secondhand smoke. The assessment's impact

Side Lesson J – 10.3.1: Dampers: A Damper is a valve or plate that regulates air flow in air handling equipment; chimneys, ducts, air handlers, VAV boxes, and ducts. It is used for climate control and is ideal for room-by-room temperature adjustment (see https://rb.gy/fef6pi).

Side Lesson K:– 10.3.1: Carbon Monoxide Detector: A carbon monoxide detector is a device that detects carbon monoxide gas in the air. Carbon monoxide is a colorless, tasteless, and odorless gas that is unidentifiable without a proper detector (see www.bellairetx.gov/857/Why-You-Need-a-Carbon-Monoxide-Detector).

INDOOR ATMOSPHERE

has been far-reaching and has led to healthier air, particularly indoor air, for millions of people.[43] January 2018 marks the 25th anniversary of the landmark EPA health assessment of the respiratory health effects of passive smoking – the science underpinning the assessment provided health officials and others the evidence needed to act in protecting people from secondhand smoke.[44]

There should be proof that smoking is prohibited in the building. Prohibit smoking outside the building except in designated smoking areas located at least 25 feet (7.5 meters) from all entries, outdoor air intakes, and operable windows. Also prohibit smoking outside the property line in spaces used for business purposes. If the requirement to prohibit smoking within 25 feet (7.5 meters) cannot be implemented because of code, provide documentation of these regulations. Signage must be posted within 10 feet (3 meters) of all building entrances indicating the no-smoking policy.[45]

Tasks

This is a relatively simple credit to accomplish since most campuses already have provisions for no-smoking. Generally, the LEED Lab student must provide images of installed non-smoking signs, and a floor plan or otherwise indication of those locations around the facility.

A. **Location**
   ☐ Determine smoking locations
   This should be completed by the Facility Personnel in collaboration with the LEED Lab student.
   1. Obtain confirmation from the owner that smoking is prohibited inside the building. Residential projects may allow smoking in specific units, with specific requirements for ensuring that those units are adequately isolated (see *Further Explanation, Project Type Variations in the LEED O+M v4 Reference Guide*).
   2. Identify the location of building openings, including entries, outdoor air intakes, and operable windows.
   3. Identify the property line and the location of outdoor areas used for business purposes, both inside and outside the property line.
   4. Indicate these elements on a site plan, map, or sketch. Emergency exits do not qualify as building openings if the doors are alarmed, because alarmed doors will not be opened. Emergency exits without alarms qualify as building openings.
   5. Determine whether the project has or will have designated outdoor smoking areas.
   6. Locate any area designated for smoking at least 25 feet (7.5 meters) from smoke-free areas, based on the information gathered in Step 1. The 25-foot (7.5-meter) distance is a straight-line calculation (Figure 10.14).[46]

B. **Policy**
   ☐ Obtain or create rules
   This should be completed by the Facility Personnel in collaboration with the LEED Lab student.

INDOOR ATMOSPHERE

Fig 10.14 Location of designated smoking areas at The Catholic University of America
Source: Derived from The Catholic University of America Strategic Master Plan Document. Diagrammed by Elizabeth Meyers, 2020

INDOOR ATMOSPHERE

1. Obtain the campus policy for non-smoking or provide the policy for smoking mitigation activities on campus. Policies may cover university-owned and operated campus grounds, including but not limited to all outdoor common and educational areas, all university buildings, university-owned on-campus housing, campus sidewalks, campus parking lots, recreational areas, outdoor stadiums and university owned and leased vehicles.[47] The police may include enforcement. For example, individuals observed smoking on the campus will be informed and asked to stop. Organizers of public events, such as conferences, meetings, public lectures, social events and cultural events using campus facilities must advise event participants of this policy and require compliance. Violators may be provided education, offered a referral for smoking cessation and, if a student or employee breaks the rules – engaging in smoking and/or the use of smoking products in violation of this policy, there is recourse which may be recommended.

   Students may be referred to the Office of Student Conduct. Employees may be referred to their supervisor and/or appointing authority for appropriate action. Supervisors may contact the Office of Employee Relations or Human Resources for further guidance. Contractors will be referred to their respective employers for appropriate action. Visitors will be required to leave the campus if they fail to conform to the policy when advised.[48]

C. **Signage**
   - ☐ Generate and display non-smoking signs
   This should be completed by the Facility Personnel in collaboration with the LEED Lab student.
   1. Signage in campus buildings such as dormitories is required for ALL entrances, including sliding doors to dorm rooms and service entrances used only by staff.
   2. Signage must be posted within 10 feet (3 meters) of all building entrances indicating the no-smoking policy.
   3. Confirm that smoking is prohibited in non-designated areas, provide confirmation from the owner that smoking outside designated areas is prohibited in any space used by the building for business purposes, even if the space falls outside the property line. Examples of spaces used for business purposes include sidewalk seating, kiosks, and courtyards. School projects must post signage at the property line adjacent to all pedestrian and vehicular entrances indicating the no-smoking policy for the school site.
   4. Language on the signage is up to the project team.[49] The LEED O+M v4 Reference Guide doesn't mandate any particular language for signage, but it does provide some suggestions: "Smoking is allowed in designated smoking areas only" or "No smoking allowed within 25 feet"[50] (Figure 10.15).

INDOOR ATMOSPHERE

Fig 10.15 Image of example of non-smoking sign at OPUS Hall that was produced by LEED Lab students via a laser cutting machine in-house at the architecture school

Source: Photo by Patricia Andrasik

D. **Documentation**
- ☐ Generate proof of non-smoking compliance
  This should be completed by the Facility Personnel in collaboration with the LEED Lab student.

  Most states ban smoking in workplaces, including restaurants and bars. Such laws reduce exposure to secondhand smoke,[51] and increase the likelihood to quit smoking which is a clear target.[52]

  1. A description of the project's no-smoking policy, including information on how policy is communicated to building occupants and enforced is required along with a copy of no-smoking policy, signed letter from owner describing project's no-smoking policy and enforcement, or copy of any legally binding covenants or restrictions to verify status of residential units as nonsmoking (Figure 10.16).

     There are now at least 2,212 100 percent smoke-free campus sites. Of these, 1,853 are also 100 percent tobacco-free, 1,790 also prohibit e-cigarette use, 920 also prohibit hookah use, and 311 also prohibit smoking/vaping marijuana.[53] Across the US, more than 1,400 colleges ban smoking on campus, with 1,137 campuses being completely tobacco-free, according to the activist group Americans for Nonsmokers' Rights.[54]

  2. A door schedule (Side Lesson L: Door Schedules) demonstrating weather-stripping at exterior unit doors and doors leading from units to common hallways.
  3. Differential air pressure test report for units in project building.
  4. Scaled site plan or map showing location of designated outdoor smoking and no-smoking areas, location of property line, and site boundary and indicating 25-foot (7.5-meter) distance from building openings.

Side Lesson L – 10.3.1: A Door Schedules: A door schedule, in the most basic terms, is a type of list. In architectural drawing sets, a door schedule is simply a list of all the doors used in the project along with a general description. Schedules can become quite complex depending on the complexity of the project design (see www.northernarchitecture.us/building-codes/door-schedule.html).

INDOOR ATMOSPHERE

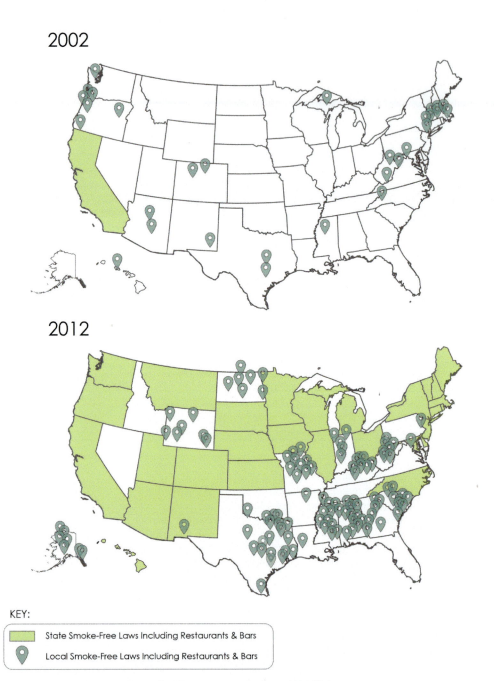

Fig 10.16 US state and local Smoke-Free Restaurant and Bar Laws, 2002–2012

Source: Derived from McGoldrick Presentation (www.ncbi.nlm.nih.gov/books/NBK206879/figure/fig_6/?report=objectonly). Redrawn by Elizabeth Meyers, 2020

INDOOR ATMOSPHERE

5. Drawings, photos, or other evidence of signage communicating no-smoking policy. Any code or landlord restrictions that prevent establishment of nonsmoking requirements.[55]

Tools

Besides the tools which are used to produce non smoking signs, anti smoking acts, laws and regulations which have been used to inform this credit are considered tools which students may glean an understanding of the universal stringency of the category. Additionally, there are resources for developing campus-wide adoption.

A. **Tobacco Control Act.** This act provides FDA with the authority to regulate the manufacture, distribution, and marketing of tobacco products to protect public health, including a broad set of sanctions for violations of the law, and the ability for FDA to contract with states to conduct retailer inspections. The act gave the Food and Drug Administration (FDA) (Side Lesson M: The Food and Drug Administration (FDA)) direct authority to regulate cigarettes, cigarette tobacco, roll-your-own tobacco, and smokeless tobacco.[56]

B. **Smoke free Campuses.** Of the roughly 20 million college and university students in the United States, more than 1 million are projected to die prematurely from cigarette smoking. While approximately 90 percent of smokers start by age 18, fully 99 percent start by age 26, underscoring the importance of supporting those in the young adult age group with more effective prevention and cessation efforts while eliminating exposure to secondhand smoke and all tobacco use in their learning environments.[57]

C. **General Smoke Control.** American Cancer Society's Center for Tobacco Control works for the adoption and implementation of policies requiring smoke- and tobacco-free in all workplaces, public places, and other important venues such as multi-unit residential settings. Additionally, it addresses major new tobacco challenges and opportunities, including taking an increasingly proactive role in addressing the changing tobacco landscape related to the rapidly emerging market for electronic smoking products, including e-cigarettes.[58]

Side Lesson M – 10.3.1: The Food and Drug Administration (FDA) is a public health organization that regulates tobacco, drugs, biological products, human and veterinary drugs, medical devices, and cosmetics for their safety, security, and efficacy (see www.fda.gov/about-fda/what-we-do).

Techniques

Projects with a property line fewer than 25 feet (7.5 meters) from the building must consider space usage when determining the outdoor smoking policy. The no-smoking requirement still applies to spaces outside the property line used for business purposes. Public sidewalks are not considered used for business purposes, but smoking must still be prohibited on sidewalks within 25 feet (7.5 meters) of openings.

A. Identify if the building designated any outdoor areas for smoking, either formally in employee manuals or site plans, or informally by providing cigarette butt receptacles, seating, or similar amenities.

B. Consider if there is any area within 25 feet of doors, air intakes, or operable windows. If so, identify if they can they be moved at a reasonable expense.
C. It is important that designated outdoor smoking areas sufficiently sheltered from the elements to ensure that occupants use them, instead of migrating to covered entrances or other locations closer to the building.
D. To this aim, the smoking policy should include this and be communicated to building users and occupants in a clear and understandable way. Are existing communication strategies effective? Does posted signage meet the prerequisite requirements? If not, what is the cost and timeline associated with installing appropriate signage?[59]

10.3.3 Green Cleaning

(*Refer also to page 419 in the LEED O+M v4 Reference Guide*)

Green cleaning means the use of those products and services that have a lesser or reduced impact on human health and the environment when compared with competing products or services that serve the same purpose. This definition comes from terms laid out in US President Barack Obama's Executive Order No. 13514.[60] It is a new interdisciplinary and systematic approach balancing multiple goals of Infection prevention, health protection, and sustainability of certain cleaning practices which may cause unintended negative effects on human health (asthma, dermatitis, etc.), environmental sustainability (pollution, ecosystem deterioration, etc.), healthcare cost, for example.[61] While simple in its approach, this definition incorporates the following three key concepts.

1. **Human health**. Of course, the principle purpose of cleaning is to protect human health so any definition of green or environmentally preferable should address human-health considerations. In the realm of green cleaning, this means we must give due deference to the health impacts cleaning has on custodial personnel and the occupants of the built environment where we are performing our cleaning activities. Special consideration should be given to more vulnerable populations, such as children, the elderly, and those with suppressed immune systems.
2. **Comparative in nature.** Note that the definition of green cleaning is comparative in nature. In other words, it does not set an absolute or final endpoint of what is environmentally preferable. Instead, it makes a comparison to competing products and services and thereby encourages continual improvement along the green spectrum.
3. **Performance.** Lastly, implicit in this definition is the concept that green products and services must perform their intended function of cleaning. It goes without saying that a cleaning product that cannot clean is a waste of resources altogether and is therefore the antithesis of environmentally preferable. More importantly, "the performance of cleaning products is critical to maintaining a safe and healthy indoor environment."[62]

INDOOR ATMOSPHERE

Tasks

This prerequisite lays the groundwork for achieving the IEQ credits for Green Cleaning and the Partnering Credits. There are two options for complying with the prerequisite. The first is to develop and implement a Green Cleaning Policy. The second is for using a certified cleaning service, which is new compliance option in LEED v4.[63] Teams can use a certified cleaning company in lieu of developing a Green Cleaning Policy. The cleaning vendor must be certified by one of the approved third-party programs (either GS-42 or CIMS-GB), and must develop goals and strategies for reducing energy, water, and toxic chemical use. Additionally, an audit of the building and/or cleaning vendor (depending on the certification) must be completed within 12 months of the end of the Performance Period.[64]

This option is attractive for projects using a cleaning vendor that is already certified, or for projects with a longer timeline that can accommodate the extra time needed to switch vendors or to allow the current vendor to obtain a third-party certification.[65]

A. **Identify**
☐ Identify the campus policy for green cleaning
This should be completed by a LEED Lab student.

There are many campuses which engage in green cleaning, and surprisingly many that may not. The increase of green cleaning regulations around the country is usually derived from a few governmental agencies – The Department of General Services, Department of Health, and Department of Education. Ten states, plus Washington, D.C., now require green cleaning in schools. Additionally, nearly 20 states have some type of policy – either a legislative initiative or an administrative rule – encouraging environmentally preferable purchasing or green cleaning in government buildings in addition to schools. These regulations vary greatly from state to state and do not necessarily include schools. For example, some states encourage or require state agencies to make environmentally preferable purchasing decisions. Others have policies or offer resources addressing green cleaning in other sectors such as restaurants or hospitals.[66] Regardless of the rule, certain facets of policy are important to include in the general Green Cleaning Policy which must be in place during a renovation or as standard upkeep in order to achieve this prerequisite.

If your institution has a policy, credit compliance will be much easier than if it doesn't. Nonetheless, there are several steps which are required to be incorporated into USGBC's interpretation of this prerequisite. If your campus possesses a policy already, the following is a checklist for conformance. If it does not, the following items B-F are required to be included in a new policy.
☐ Identify the facility personnel responsible for green cleaning
This should be completed by a LEED Lab student.

| 287

INDOOR ATMOSPHERE

B. **Renovations**
- ☐ Integrate measures for renovations

  This should be completed by the Facility Personnel in collaboration with the LEED Lab student.

  This prerequisite covers products and waste associated with periodic maintenance and renovations. Therefore, the Green Cleaning Policy must address purchasing, waste, and indoor air quality management; the project team can determine how best to allocate items among the three policies.[67] In a LEED Lab course however, a recommended approach would be to synergize the efforts of creating a separate Purchasing and Waste program (see Chapter 9, 'Materials'), and IEQ Management Program (see Chapter 10, 'Air Quality'). Additionally, the policy must include procedures for HVAC upgrades and building improvement cleaning and maintenance which typically entails significant base building alterations.[68]

C. **Products**
- ☐ List cleaning ingredients

  This should be completed by the Facility Personnel in collaboration with the LEED Lab student.

  The low or no-chemical products used for general cleaning and maintenance are required to be identified in the policy (Box 10.1).

Box 10.1 Green cleaning resources from the US Environmental Protection Agency (EPA)

Program	Resources	Website
SaferChoice Program	–	www.epa.gov/saferchoice/products#a04i000000WupwpAAB
The National Park Service, NPS	Environmentally Preferable Janitorial Products at Yellow Stone & Gran Teton National Parks	www.epa.gov/sites/production/files/2015-05/documents/cleaning.pdf
Department of Interior Headquarters:	Environmentally Preferable Janitorial Products for its headquarters	www.epa.gov/greenerproducts/department-interior-focuses-cleaning-products
US General Services Administration (GSA)	Product search	www.gsaglobalsupply.gsa.gov/advantage/ws/main/home?store=FSS
Commonwealth of Massachusetts	Environmental Preferable Product & Services Guide	www.mass.gov/handbook/environmentally-preferable-products-and-servicesguide
The City of Santa Monica, California	Case Study	www.epa.gov/sites/production/files/2015-05/documents/santa.pdf
Green Seal	Certified Products & Services	www.greenseal.org/certified-products-services
American Cleaning Institute, ACI	Understanding Products	www.cleaninginstitute.org/understanding-products

Source: www.epa.gov/greenerproducts/greening-your-purchase-cleaning-products-guide-federal-purchasers

INDOOR ATMOSPHERE

The LEED Lab student must address selection and appropriate use of disinfectants and sanitizers, develop guidelines addressing the safe handling and storage of cleaning chemicals used in the building, including a plan for managing hazardous spills and mishandling incidents and also plan for reducing the toxicity of the chemicals used for laundry, ware washing, and other cleaning activities in addition to conservation of energy, water, and chemicals used for cleaning.[69] Storage is also a significant component of the product life cycles.

D. **Equipment**
   ☐ List cleaning equipment
   This should be completed by the Facility Personnel in collaboration with the LEED Lab student.

E. **Procedures**
   ☐ Create a sequence of cleaning
   This should be completed by the Facility Personnel in collaboration with the LEED Lab student.

   The techniques of green cleaning aren't significantly different from those employed in traditional cleaning systems. However, while traditional cleaning systems tend to focus on the appearance of clean, green cleaning focuses on reducing potential negative exposures to both human health and the environment while establishing cleaning schedules and methods that yield truly cleaner buildings. Such procedures include maintaining entryways, dust mopping and even floor coatings.

F. **Policy**
   ☐ Generate a policy of green cleaning
   This should be completed by the Facility Personnel in collaboration with the LEED Lab student.

   A Green Cleaning Policy provides your team with a document of guiding principles and a single reference point for questions. It's a good idea to create your Green Cleaning Policy early in your project timeline. Working on the policy will familiarize your team with the requirements for other green cleaning credits, which will then help you decide which of those credits to pursue.[70]

   Remember that you don't have to achieve the policy targets, such as the targeted percentage of compliant cleaning products, but you do have to implement the policy to the best of your ability. The green cleaning credits reward the actual attainment of your goals. Flexibility is a plus – for example, when you address green cleaning products, list the standards that products should meet, but leave some room for discretion about exactly which products should be ordered.[71]

Tools

Although the tools for this prerequisite directly involve certain measures and equipment and products, these are identified in the policy itself. Of course, the modifiable Green Cleaning Policy template referred to from the LEED O+M v4 Reference Guide serves

| 289

as a primary tool which may be helpful when the LEED Lab student is helping to create or modify Green Cleaning Policies in conjunction with the facility personnel.[72]

A. ***Sustainability "How-To Guide."*** The International Facilities Management Association (IFMA) created an excellent resource for green cleaning which includes a guide for creating an RFP for cleaning services, and cross-references policy-making information to LEED O+M and other green building assessment systems.[73]

B. ***USDA Guidelines for Procurement.*** USDA agencies have some of the most stringent guidelines for green cleaning. With guidance for specifying, procuring, and utilizing sustainable products as required by various statutes and Executive Orders. The Sustainable Procurement Plan (SPP), formerly known as the Green Purchasing Affirmative Procurement Plan, was originally established in July 2006 under Executive Order 13101. Sustainable acquisition is defined as the purchasing and use of products, and services that contain products.[74]

 Techniques

Your facility may be managed by an outside vendor or by facility personnel. If the cleaning program is handled by an outside vendor, ensure that they have a green cleaning program that they can execute services on the site or would be willing to integrate green cleaning practices into their existing program. A company that is certified by a green program such as Green Seal's GS-42 standard provides a reliable confirmation of compliance.[75] If the cleaning is an in-house endeavor for your facility, there should be adequate staff, time and resources which would incorporate green strategies into the existing program. Cleaning supplies and equipment procurement will require specific management such as LEED-compliant options for products and a tool for product tracking (see Tools).

Training entails myriad protocols from hand-washing procedures to how spills and accidents of products are managed, including reducing toxicity of chemicals through dilution. The frequency of training and disposal of products is also important to be included (see Toolbox, Chapter 10). A part of this training should include occupant safety. If there are vulnerable building occupants such as those who have allergies or disabilities that would impede a regular cleaning cycle, consideration in the protocol must be established in the policy.

 Partnering Credit

Green Cleaning Custodial Effectiveness Assessment, Green Cleaning Products and Materials and Green Cleaning Equipment are the three Partnering Credits for Green Cleaning. Each has a dependent relationship to the prerequisite.

INDOOR ATMOSPHERE

A. **Green Cleaning Custodial Effectiveness Assessment** is achieved via an audit that can help you evaluate the quality of your cleaning services and draw your attention to areas of the building that present particular cleaning challenges. The credit can be time consuming for larger buildings and require a short duration in smaller buildings, since the amount of floor area required to audit is calculated based on the total size and the number of rooms in your building. Audit guidelines suggest a maximum time commitment of ten minutes per room.[76] If one of the following questions may be answered affirmatively, this Partnering Credit should be attempted:

- Do you have the time to perform a cleaning audit in-house with two staff members for conducting, compiling and calculating/documenting results?
- Do you have the resources to hire a cleaning auditor to perform this assessment by conducting, compiling and calculating/documenting results?

B. **Green Cleaning Products and Materials** works from the Green Cleaning Policy by maintaining a certain regulation of sustainable cleaning products.

Using environmentally friendly cleaning products is one of the easier and more effective green operations strategies to implement and can usually be achieved at no cost premium. It can be challenging, though, to get the proper product information from vendors and to determine how effective the products will be in practice. While there are plenty of green cleaning products available, the results of any given product may vary, and it may take your team time to switch to new products and assess them.[77]

If one of the following questions may be answered affirmatively, this Partnering Credit should be attempted:

- There is an inventory of products and materials which fit the criteria for non-chemical alternatives.
- These contribute towards at least 75 percent of all cleaning product purchases.

C. **Green Cleaning Equipment** works from the Green Cleaning Policy by maintaining powered cleaning equipment which is sustainably designed and operated throughout its lifecycle. "If existing equipment does not meet criteria, it is suitable to create a phase-out plan for its replacement with environmentally preferable products at the end of its useful life."[78] This credit is challenging to the LEED Lab student, particularly if your project is not currently using compliant cleaning equipment. "Teams should become familiar with the required sustainability criteria by equipment type. It's fairly common for a piece of equipment to meet some but not all of the criteria – the noise limit, for example, can be difficult to achieve."[79] If one of the following

INDOOR ATMOSPHERE

questions may be answered affirmatively, this Partnering Credit should be attempted:

- Your existing equipment is not compliant, and the facility personnel are willing to replace it with the criteria of this credit.
- Your existing equipment is obsolete, and the facility personnel are willing to replace it with the criteria of this credit.
- Your existing equipment meets the criteria of this credit.

10.3.4 Lighting

(*Refer also to page 461 in the LEED O+M v4 Reference Guide*)

A university's faculty, staff and students' productivity depends on the capacity of individual employees to work effectively. Properly designed lighting systems can and do produce measurable, long term improvements in performance, morale, reduced errors, reduced absenteeism, and higher quality products and service. Visual comfort and productivity are directly related. Visual comfort is how easily we can view tasks. More often visual comfort is discussed in the negative terms of glare (Figure 10.17). High levels of these three conditions result in lower productivity. This shouldn't be too surprising – the higher a worker's visual comfort, the higher the productivity.

Light deprivation and levels can affect natural physiological rhythms and result in dysfunctions such as seasonal affective disorder (SAD) (Side Lesson N: Seasonal Affective Disorder (SAD)) for example. The cycle of day and night, called circadian rhythm, helps regulate the hormone melatonin, and a lack of light can interfere with its production, leading to physiological imbalances. For example, indoor ceiling-mounted lighting recommended by the *Internationale de l'Eclairage* (CIE, 1986) has been found to affect positive and negative mood and cognitive function during tasks involving memory or problem solving.[80] Interestingly, the role of lighting as it affects human perceptual and circadian functions is almost completely

Side Lesson N – 10.3.4: Seasonal Affective Disorder (SAD), also known as Seasonal Depression, is a type of mood disorder related to the changes in seasons. SAD typically occurs in the winter when there is less sunlight hours and colder weather. Symptoms include fatigue, feelings of hopelessness, difficulty concentrating, insomnia, and irritation. Treatments include psychotherapy, light therapy, and medications (see www.mayoclinic.org/diseases-conditions/seasonal-affective-disorder/symptoms-causes/syc-2036465).

Fig 10.17 *Types of solar glare: disability glare and discomfort glare*

Source: Derived from Florida Solar Energy Center (www.fsec.ucf.edu/en/consumer/buildings/basics/windows/how/glare.htm). Diagrammed by Elizabeth Meyers, 2020

ignored in building codes and standards, which typically focus only on the minimal requirements for safety and function.

Three human domains of the psychological, physiological, and circadian guide lighting decisions with respect to comfort – but economy, material composition and energy efficiency also play a prime role in proposing an overall illumination strategy. As one of the most important elements in building design, lighting requires many aspects to be evaluated. Areas of the Energy, Material, and Site categories within the LEED O+M rating system include lighting optimization of all of these components, but the Indoor Environmental Quality category holds the most prescriptive requirements of how a person should comfortably function in a space.

Tasks

There are two options for achievement that require a few detailed tasks. Option 1 is a straightforward requirement of lighting controls. This is very often successfully achieved by providing task lighting, dimmers, or a more expensive solution – lighting schemes (Side Lesson O: Lighting Scheme). Option 2 illustrates a variety of strategies for achievement which range from the specifications of the lighting fixture to room reflectances (Table 10.3). However, integrating these selections synergistically with energy reduction, aesthetics and functionality requires specific training, skills and/or outside consultants. The tasks below are simplified from the LEED O+M v4 Reference Guide in helping the LEED Lab student navigate this complex topic.

Side Lesson O – 10.3.4: Lighting Schemes: A Lighting Scheme is a control setting for a series of fixtures that provides multiple options of lighting levels.

- ☐ Identify all regularly occupied spaces in the building.[81]
- ☐ Identify the following personnel:
    a. Campus architect or external consultant responsible for the lighting design commissions for the campus.
    b. The person in charge of replacing fixtures in campus facilities.
- ☐ Schedule a walk-through of the space/s with the personnel.
- ☐ Identify with the personnel which option is attainable based on existing conditions or renovations which occur during the Performance Period.

Box 10.2 Option 1: lighting control

Are there three or more lighting control levels for at least 50 percent of individual spaces/rooms and 100 percent of multi-occupant spaces/rooms?[82]

If YES, this option suffices to achieve the credit. Please provide one of the following:

1. Diagram on as-build drawings the locations of lighting controls. Note on the as-build drawings how the fixture groupings allow for lighting control.

or

2. Electrical drawings/construction documents which indicate the various lighting controls intended for the space if renovation will occur during the Performance Period.

or

3. Photos of the actual spaces with the various lighting schemes applied and the switch/panel where the lighting schemes can be controlled.

Table 10.3 Indoor Environmental Quality credit: interior lighting: strategies for lighting quality

Strategy	Scope	Exceptions/exclusions
A: Light fixture luminance	• Identify all regularly occupied spaces in the project and all light fixtures in these spaces • For the light fixtures, review luminaire cut-sheets, Illuminating Engineering Society photometric files, or other documentation to identify luminance between 45 degrees and 90 degrees from nadir and select products that meet the credit requirements. The luminance must be below 2,500 candelas per square meter	• Wallwash fixtures properly aimed at walls, as specified by manufacturer • Indirect uplighting fixtures, provided there is no view down into these uplights from a regularly occupied space above • Any other specific applications (e.g., adjustable fixtures)
B: Color Rendering Index (CRI)	• Identify all light sources used in the building	• Lamps or fixtures specifically designed to provide colored lighting for effect • Site lighting • Any other special use
C: Lamp life	• Calculate the total connected lighting load for all lighting within the building, in watts or kilowatts • 75 percent connected lighting load	
D: Direct overhead lighting	• Identify all regularly occupied spaces in the project and the total connected lighting load associated with these spaces • 25 percent connected lighting load	
E: Surface reflectance: ceilings, walls, floors	• Evaluate whether high-reflectance finish materials exist in the building as applicable to the strategy pursued: ceilings, walls, and floors for strategy E, and work surfaces and movable partitions for strategy F	
F: Surface reflectance: furnishings	• Strategy E: 90 percent of regularly occupied floor area • Strategy F: All furniture used for work surfaces	
G: Surface illuminance ration: wall to work surface	• Identify all regularly occupied spaces in the project and the associated floor area	
H: Surface illuminance ration: ceiling to work surface	• 75 percent regularly occupied floor area	

Source: LEED O+M v4 Reference Guide. Redrawn by Elizabeth Meyers, 2020

> **Box 10.3 Option 2: lighting strategies**[83]
>
> 1. Are manufacturer's specifications and cut sheets (Side Lesson P: Cut Sheet a) available for the fixtures?
>
>   If YES,[84]
>   Strategy A compliance: ____Y ____N
>   Is the fixture's luminance (Side Lesson Q: Luminance) below 232.25 candelas/sf?[85] (Side Lesson R: Candelas) (Figure 10.18)
>   Strategy B compliance: ____Y ____N
>   Is the fixture's Color Rendering Index (CRI) (Side Lesson S: Color Rendering Index (CRI)) below 80 (Figure 10.19)
>   If NO, proceed below to next question.
>
> 2. Is the total connected lighting load able to be calculated?
>
>   If YES,
>   Strategy C compliance: ____Y ____N
>   Does the total connected lighting load comprise 75 percent or more light sources that have a long lamp life?[86]
>   Strategy D compliance: ____Y ____N
>   Does the total connected lighting load comprise 25 percent or less direct-only overhead lighting?
>   If NO, proceed below to next question.
>
> 3. Are light reflectance values (LRV) (Side Lesson T: Light Reflectance Value, (LRV)) able to be identified?[87]
>
>   If YES,
>   Strategy E compliance: ____Y ____N
>   Are the weighted light reflectance average of ceilings, walls and floors high?[88]
>   Strategy F compliance: ____Y ____N
>   Is the weighted average of furnishings high?[89]
>
> 4. Is a light meter available in order to measure the footcandle (FC) (Side Lesson U: Footcandles) levels on interior surfaces?
>
>   If YES,
>   Strategy G compliance: ____Y ____N
>   Is the average illuminance ratio or less for at least 75 percent of occupied spaces[90]
>   Strategy H compliance: ____Y ____N
>   Is the average illuminance ratio of work surfaces to the ceiling 1:10 or less for at least 75 percent of occupied spaces?[91]
>   If NO, proceed with Option 1 of this credit.

Side Lesson P – 10.3.4: Cut Sheets: A cut sheet is a specification sheet from the manufacturer's original documentation or manual.

Side Lesson Q – 10.3.4: Luminance is the SI unit for luminous intensity projected on a surface from a light fixture per unit area and given direction (see https://rb.gy/jllxf1).

Side Lesson R – 10.3.5: Candelas: A Candela is the SI unit for luminance/ luminous intensity (see www.lumitex.com/ blog/light-measurement).

Side Lesson S – 10.3.5: Color Rendering Index (CRI) is the quantitative measure that indicates the color appearance of an object based on the amount and type of light it receives (see https://electrical-engineering-portal.com/ lights-up-the-facts-about-lighting).

Side Lesson T – 10.3.5: Light Reflectance Value (LRV) measures how light will reflect off a surface depending on the lightness or darkness of its color. This range goes from 0–100. Black, being the darkest, has a LRV of 0 and white, being the brightest, has an LRV of 100. The higher the LRV the lighter the color is and vice versa.

INDOOR ATMOSPHERE

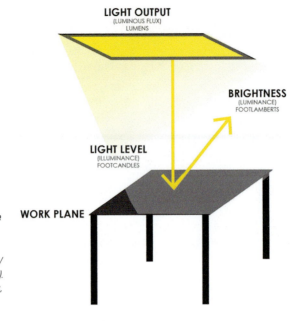

Fig 10.18 Cycle of luminance

Source: Derived from Electrical Engineering Portal (https://electrical-engineering-portal.com/lights-up-the-facts-about-lighting). Diagrammed by Elizabeth Meyers, 2020

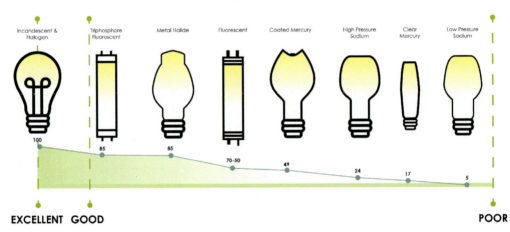

Fig 10.19 Color Rendering Index (CRI) for different types of lamps

Source: Derived from Standard Product Inc. (www.standardpro.com/colours-of-store-merchandise/). Redrawn by Elizabeth Meyers, 2020

 Tools

The few equations which are a part of the strategies in Option 2 are the most important calculation tools. However, there are physical tools which also facilitate accomplishment of some of the strategies in this option. A few of these include the following:

A. **Handheld Spectrophotometer.** Portable and handheld spectrophotometers are devices that measure the intensity of light emitted or transmitted by certain materials and surfaces and provide LRVs. This way, accurate color measurement results can be achieved in complex interiors.[92]

INDOOR ATMOSPHERE

B. **Computer or phone application.** An app which calculates contrast ratios by scanning samples of materials using the phone's camera or entering a manufacturer's LRV data may be used to identify the values of interior finishes.[93]

C. **Light Meter.** As noted in Chapter 6, 'Site', there are various sources for procuring a light meter if the facilities personnel do not have one available. This link in the endnotes provides an array of choices for procuring an ambient light meter.[94] Otherwise, searching for an 'ambient light meter' is the best way to begin procurement.

Side Lesson U – 10.3.5: Footcandles are the quantitative measurement for illuminance, which is the light falling on a surface. More specifically, it is the illuminance from a single source of light on one square foot of surface. It is the most common measurement used by designers and lighting professionals to measure light levels in spaces (see www.solardecathlon.gov/2020/assets/pdfs/sd-design-challenge-rules.pdf).

Techniques

This credit requires analyses of existing lighting systems, or an evaluation of lighting systems which may be installed if a renovation is planned during the Performance Period. It appears initially complex, and LEED Lab students may not be familiar with the terminology used in much of the credit. Following the tasks, which refer to the Reference Guide and the side lessons will help, along with these tips:

A. In addition to knowing the designated facility personnel (indicated in the task items), identify who would procure individual task lighting, if that becomes an option.
B. Identify if students will be required to procure their own task lights, or if the university provide them. If it is optional for students to use task lighting, the credit compliance may be questioned by the GBCI reviewers.
C. First investigate any complicated spaces such as multi-use flex spaces that can serve multiple purposes,[95] such as classrooms that have movable partitions or expandable spaces. These prove to be the most challenging to adhere to the credit requisites.
D. Synergize any renovations or upgrades to switches or lighting systems with reducing energy.

Partnering Credit

Daylight and Quality Views are associated with this credit, although they are not necessarily as linked as other Partnering Credits in this book. If daylighting is *sufficient* for illumination, it may displace electric lighting thus rendering a variety of interior lighting controls unnecessary. A balance must be struck between the energy efficiency, thermal comfort, visual and psychological aspects of daylighting in every project, but in particular if both Interior Lighting and Daylight and Quality View credits are to be achieved.

If the following questions in at least one of the categories below may be answered affirmatively, this Partnering Credit should be attempted:

A. **Daylighting.** At least 50 percent of the regularly occupied spaces and are accessible and are exposed to clerestories, or a high quantity of perimeter or roof glazing.[96]

| 297

INDOOR ATMOSPHERE

Side Lesson V – 10.3.5: Integrated Pest Management (IPM) is a decision-making process that uses culture, biology, and chemistry to manage the risk of pest management on health and environment. Pesticides are immediately hazardous to humans and the environment, by contributing to the cause of cancers and contamination of air, water, and soils (see https://rb.gy/s2ciul).

B. **Daylighting.** At least 50 percent of the regularly occupied spaces possess between 27.8–278.7 FC of daylighting, confirmed via the use of a light meter.
C. **Views.** At least 50 percent of the regularly occupied spaces are accessible to unobstructed vision glazing.

10.3.5 Pest Management

(*Refer also to page 517 in the LEED O+M v4 Reference Guide*)

Initially, many LEED Lab students are amused by the idea that deterring small animals in campus buildings is sustainable! Yet, rodents and insects may transport viruses and bacteria harmful to building occupants. A cycle of poor indoor air quality due to pests is further perpetuated by the damage they do to indoor materials, and the harmful chemicals used to kill them. Integrated pest management (IPM) (Side Lesson V: Integrated Pest Management (IPM)) is an approach which uses natural, pesticide-free or pesticide mitigation methods of minimizing the intrusion of pests. By engaging facility personnel in this credit, LEED Lab students may inspire a minimization of chemical applications to campus operations.

Box 10.4 Integrated pest management plan tasks[97]

- *Obtain* access to your institution's IPM Plan.
  - ☐ If this document does not exist, follow the next steps.
  - ☐ If this document exists, confirm that it includes the information below.
- *Determine* the boundary of application on the site. If the Plan pertains to the entire campus, it may be pursued as a Master Site credit (see Chapters 3, 'Platform' and 4, 'Feasibility').
- *Identify* the internal party/s and facility personnel who are or will be responsible to manage the Plan.
  - ☐ Managing: _____
  - ☐ Scheduling: _____
  - ☐ Purchasing: _____
  - ☐ Performing:[98] _____
  - ☐ Tracking (see Tools on the next page for tracking form): _____
    _____
- *Create* the IPM Plan.[99]
- *Implement* the IPM Plan.
  - ☐ Application must begin during the Performance Period unless it already exists.
  - ☐ Ensure all parties are performing their responsibilities.
  - ☐ Ensure all certifications are current.
  - ☐ Ensure that the process for notifying students, faculty and staff of emergency measures is communicated to all Plan administrators.

INDOOR ATMOSPHERE

Tools

Specific tools are critical to learn as a part of accomplishing the Tasks listed in this chapter. Although the LEED Lab student will not be administering or evaluating the Plan, they may provide the baseline Plan for their institution if it does not utilize one already. The two most important templates are the tools necessary to aid successful creating and execution of the plan:

A. Standard IPM Template[100]
B. IPM Tracking Form Template[101]

Techniques[102]

This credit requires a policy and tracking mechanism to be created. While it is quite easy to understand, there will be approvals and coordination that will take time if the institution does not currently have an IPM Plan. The LEED Lab student should factor this into their pursuit of credit compliance:

A. Include in the IPM when periodic pest population inspections will occur and by whom – an internal or external party.
B. Include the types of pests most likely to be present in the building type and geographic location (even if they are not yet a nuisance) as a preventative measure.
C. Research if existing pest management contractors/vendors provide a green focus or can alter their services to do so.

10.3.6 Occupant Comfort Survey

(Refer also to page 527 in the LEED O+M v4 Reference Guide)

This credit is intended to assess how comfortable the building's occupants are in their standard working/learning space, and taking measures to improve it; a satisfied occupant often means a successful credit! Its prime function is to survey occupants to understand their thermal comfort, space allocation, and how clean they perceive their building to be. Their opinions about acoustics, air quality, and lighting, and aspects that may disrupt the work environment are also considered and may become a catalyst used to make substantial facility improvements, particularly since students are required to pay for their learning experience, and this often occurs in their campus environments.

Although not always directly, survey results synergize with other credits which impact how people feel in their spaces, including Minimum Indoor Air Quality Performance, Thermal Comfort, Interior Lighting, Daylighting and Views, Green Cleaning – Products and Materials, Green Cleaning – Equipment, and Integrated Pest Management.

Tasks[103]

This is another straightforward credit which has a fairly easy set of steps to accomplish. Especially if the majority of occupants surveyed find their working and studying environments suitable, or there are feasible ways to improve their conditions if they don't.

| 299

INDOOR ATMOSPHERE

A survey is the primary requirement to accomplish the credit. There are initially a few ways to execute it, though the administration and development of corrective action require similar outcomes.

1. **Generation.** The first task of this credit is to create a survey; using an existing survey is the easiest route. Here are a few options:
    A. **Option 1: ARC.** Referring to Chapter 3.3, the Performance Platform called ARC rates occupant satisfaction using a scale and a smiling or frowning face. The surveys can be executed via a lobby survey, or directly emailing survey links to building occupants (see Tools on the next page). If more than one survey is launched, the platform averages them together.[104]
    B. **Option 2: Online.** Any type of third-party online canvass tool may be used to administer the survey as long as it covers the required questions in the credit (see LEED O+M v4 Reference Guide page 529), and anonymity is maintained.
    C. **Option 3: Manual.** Although less frequently selected, there may be circumstances where a paper, phone or a more traditional method of polling occurs. The same credit requirements and questions should be incorporated, and anonymity should be maintained.
2. **Administration.** Commencing the survey, communicating with the respondents, setting a deadline for responses and collecting the results are all required as the survey creation platform is decided. It is very likely that the same LEED Lab student who generated the survey may not be the same student who tallies it, nor submits its documentation towards final credit completion. As with all LEED Lab courses, the trail of what is required from to class to class and student to student should be clear (Figure 10.20)
3. **Development.** Producing a 'Corrective Action Plan' is perhaps the most extensive task of this credit, but it can be postponed until the final results reflect that over 20 percent of the occupants surveyed are not satisfied with the work/learning environments of the building being

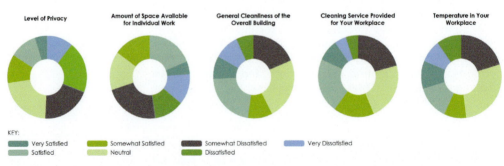

Fig 10.20 *Sample results from occupant survey for the Crough School of Architecture and Planning*
Source: Redrawn by Elizabeth Meyers, 2020

INDOOR ATMOSPHERE

analyzed. When this Plan is written, it should include two sections – one addressing no-cost solutions and one addressing capital expenditures to rectify the dissatisfaction. Only the former is required to be accomplished during the Performance Period (see Toolbox, Chapter 10 for guidance in Plan development).

Tools

The generation of the actual survey and the Corrective Action Plan, if necessary, are the primary tools needed for credit accomplishment.

    A. **ARC Human Experience Survey**[105]

This video also may be used for the Transportation Survey in Chapter 5.3.1, 'Transportation'.

    B. **Sample Occupant Survey**[106]
    C. **Corrective Action Plan**[107]

Other tools which may be used for a deep dive into analyzing thermal comfort (see the introduction to Chapter 10) include the following:

    D. **ANSI/ASHRAE Standard 55: Thermal Environmental Conditions for Human Occupancy** is an American National Standard published by ASHRAE establishes the ranges of indoor environmental conditions to achieve acceptable thermal comfort for occupants of buildings. This document is helpful to understand what is measured when considering thermal comfort.[108]
    E. **Thermal Comfort Tool** is a dynamic online platform which helps identify compliance with ASHRAE Standard 55.[109]

Techniques

The following recommendations are important to help guide the LEED Lab student in their pursuit of this credit, particularly since the results of the survey may involve a higher level of campus administration:

    A. Dissatisfied occupants should be queried for their reasons of concern. Refer to LEED O+M v4 Reference Guide page 529 to see questions which should be included in the survey as a response.
    B. Since the survey must be enacted every two years, consider a protocol that can be permanently addressed in a policy such as the Indoor Air Quality Management Policy, and facility personnel to accomplish this in their official job description.
    C. If the survey will be created by a LEED Lab student, ensure that it includes questions that cover every required occupant comfort category as specified in the templates (see Tools). Also remember to use a 7-point scale with a value of 0 as the median unbiased response.[110]

| 301

INDOOR ATMOSPHERE

D. The survey is lengthy, so the response rate may be low. In order to avoid the "quick delete" actions of many receiving an email survey, consider distributing them physically if time permits.
E. Corrective action may be as simple as adjusting the setpoints of an HVAC system, or as complex as replacing it. Remember that any changes to improve the indoor environment may be synergized with energy savings which may provide a high return-on-investment.
F. Provide accommodations in the survey for spaces with unique characteristics. Labs, dark rooms for photography, or gymnasiums may have to have a disclaimer about the activities occurring in the space which accompany the questions; occupant comfort may vary based on space function.

Partnering Credit

How students, staff and faculty experience temperature, humidity and air speed variances within the building being analyzed by LEED Lab, is related to their metabolic rate, the space function and other factors which are factors of thermal comfort. The credit Thermal Comfort is a logical partner to the Occupant Comfort Survey. If a majority of the following questions may be answered affirmatively, this Partnering Credit should be attempted:

☐ The facility being studied has a building automation system (BAS) in place already.
☐ Continuous monitoring of air temperature and humidity, and taking periodic measurements of air speed and radiant temperature are a standard protocol, or will be during and after the Performance Period.
☐ If the aforementioned statement is not true, could sensors to monitor these attributes be installed during the Performance Period in occupied spaces?
☐ Engineering experts are available to put a system of performance verification and tracking using ASHRAE 55 as the premise for thermal comfort.
☐ Operational standards of your facility include alarms to notify personnel of deviations in comfort setpoints.
☐ Building engineers and/or third-party technicians are available to perform air speed and radiant temperature testing.[111]

10.4 Case Study

The Crough Center for Architectural Studies has a unique history; the building was initially an armory upon its construction in the early 1900s. It was later converted to the University gymnasium. Finally, in 1988, the building was renovated again to become the School of Architecture. The modernization of the facility created an opportunity for students, staff and faculty to learn, study and teach architecture in a visually pleasing space with ample daylighting. However, the mechanical systems providing thermal comfort were required to be analyzed as a part of fulfilling LEED O+M certification, thus they had to be evaluated.

The first task to complete the prerequisite Minimum Air Quality Performance, was to find and identify all air-handling units in the building. Since only existing documentation for the building was the 1988 design document set, not all of the air-handling units were identified. The building had undergone a number of minor renovations, which rendered the set inaccurate and incomplete. A new and accurate set of drawings was created by a LEED Lab student. Eleven of the 12 air-handling units in the building were installed during the 1988 renovation. The 12th unit was installed in 2012, and it serves only the spray booth. The spray booth is a highly ventilated room where students work on projects that need to be painted, finished, sealed, or coated with any other high VOC finishing that is not appropriate or safe to release into the air of the studio spaces.

The next task was to identify the area, use, and occupancy of each space. After the accurate drawing set was produced, the AHUs were identified and numbered, and the major paths of ductwork were identified for addition to the set as well. Then the LEED Lab student team's next step was to determine the use, occupancy, and design flow rate for each space. Unfortunately, undocumented renovations meant that design flow rates were not available for most spaces. Use and occupancy, however, could be determined. According to the ASHRAE Table 6–1 list of uses, seven different types of spaces exist in Crough: art classrooms (architecture studios), computer labs, multi-use assembly spaces (presentation/pin-up spaces), auditorium, entry/lobby, offices, and a wood/metal shop. We debated between using actual occupancy or ASHRAE formula occupancies based on sf.

The third task was using the alternative compliance path for professional exemption. A mechanical engineer was brought on to help satisfy the prerequisite. None of the AHUs were capable of meeting the required ventilation rates and, due to budget cuts, upgrades were unlikely in the building's immediate future. All of the systems were special case scenarios and, as many LEED Lab students were tackling this sort of information for the first time, they were not comfortable or capable of managing the perquisite without professional aid.

The mechanical engineer was able to recommend a third-party testing team that came to the building to perform all AHU and exhaust testing. It was discovered that the AHUs could meet ASHRAE 62.1–2007, but some of the AHUs had been placed so that they had no access to outdoor air.

Ultimately, through the aid of the engineer and a lengthy narrative, the Crough Center was awarded the prerequisite. The prerequisite's granting hindered on proof that facilities had attempted to create the best possible environment with the building's presently installed equipment. A ten-year, budgeted maintenance and replacement plan approved by facilities was created as a result of this analysis and uploaded to the credit documentation. This plan served as proof that the school's administration was aware of the air quality problem and that the issues will be addressed as funding becomes available.

10.5 Exercises

Scenarios derived from the aforementioned case study are used as a basis for exercise questions that comprise an overview of material learned in this chapter. Actual scenarios are introduced to understand synergistic thinking. Questions testing knowledge of understanding the breadth of tools, tasks and techniques are important for LEED Lab; the investigation required in answering these exercises relates to how students should be instructed in such an action research course.

Exercise Scenario 1

What first course of action should the LEED Lab student endeavor when navigating indoor environmental qualities that have mechanical analysis as a part of their achievement?

Exercise Scenario 2

What are the pros and cons of using actual occupancies versus formula-driven occupancies based on an area's sf in achieving the Minimum Air Quality Prerequisite?

Exercise Scenario 3

Refer to the LEED O+M v4 Reference Guide to explain the alternative compliance path of a professional exemption (Licensed Professional Exemption or LPE).

Exercise Scenario 4

Besides the Occupant Comfort Survey, identify credits in a minimum of three categories (for example, Water, Energy, etc) that relate to the main credit being pursued in this case study and explain how they synergize with it.

Notes

1. Tristan Roberts, "We Spend 90% of Our Time Indoors. Says Who?" BuildingGreen, 2016. www.buildinggreen.com/blog/we-spend-90-our-time-indoors-says-who
2. Janus Welton, AIA, *The Living Elements of Building Design* (New York: iUniverse, Inc., 2007).
3. Joseph G. Allen, Piers MacNaughton, Jose Guillermo Cedeno Laurent, Skye S. Flanigan, Erika Sita Eitland and John D. Spengler, "Green Buildings and Health," *Current Environmental Health Reports* vol. 2, no. 3: 250–258.
4. "Definitions of HF/E," Human Factors and Ergonomics Society, 2020. https://rb.gy/ugmayk
5. "Facts about *Stachybotrys chartarum* and Other Molds," Centers for Disease Control and Prevention, 2017. www.cdc.gov/mold/stachy.htm
6. ASHRAE, *ANSI/ASHRAE Standard 55-2013*: *Thermal Environmental Conditions for*

Human Occupancy (Atlanta: American Society of Heating, Refrigerating and Air-Conditioning Engineers, Inc., 2013).
7 "Circadian Light for Your Health," US General Services Administration, 2018. www.gsa.gov/about-us/organization/office-of-governmentwide-policy/office-of-federal-highperformance-buildings/projects-and-research/building-research/circadian-light-for-your-health
8 Junfeng Zhang and Kirk R Smith, "Indoor Air Pollution: A Global Health Concern," British Medical Bulletin 68 (2003): 209–225.
9 "Indoor Air Pollution: National Burden of Disease Estimates," World Health Organization, 2007. www.who.int/airpollution/publications/indoor_air_national_burden_estimate_revised.pdf?ua=1
10 Green Building Institute, Inc., Green Globes Tool Overview – EB (Portland: GBI, 2015): 17. www.thegbi.org/files/training_resources/GreenGlobes-Existing_Building_Tool_Overview.pdf
11 Ibid., 2.
12 BREEAM, BREEAM In-Use Technical Manual SD221 2.0:2015 (Watford: BRE Global Ltd, 2016): 49, 205, 319. https://tools.breeam.com/filelibrary/Technical%20Manuals/SD221_BIU_International_2015_Re-issue_V2.0.pdf
13 Ibid.
14 Green Building Council of Australia, "Indoor Air Quality," "Hazardous Materials," "Lighting Comfort," "Daylight and Views," "Thermal Comfort," Acoustic Comfort" and "Occupant Comfort and Satisfaction," Green Star – Performance v1.2 – Initial Certification Submission Template r1. www.gbca.org.au/greenstar-manager/resources/?filter-rating-tool=101&_ga=2.107716033.213355384.1592333897-29415128.1591753717
15 Green Building Institute of Australia, Green Star – Performance Portfolio Certification – Release v1.0 (Green Building Council of Australia, 2015): 14. www.gbca.org.au/uploads/160/36000/Green%20Star%20Portfolio%20Certification%20Guide_160715%20Release%20v1.0.pdf; "Green Star is an Internationally Recognised Sustainability Rating System," Green Building Institute of Australia, 2018. https://new.gbca.org.au/green-star/rating-system/
16 US Green Building Council, "Indoor Environmental Quality (IEQ): Overview," Reference Guide for Building Operations and Maintenance (Washington, DC: US Green Building Council, 2013): 427–527.
17 Singapore Building and Construction Authority, BCA Green Mark GM ENRB: 2017: Technical Guide and Requirements (Singapore: Building and Construction Authority, 2017): 60.
18 BEAM Plus Existing Buildings Version 2.0 (2016.03): Comprehensive Scheme (Hong Kong: Hong Kong Green Building Council, 2016): 151. www.beamsociety.org.hk/files/download/BEAM%20Plus%20Existing%20Buildings%20v2_0_Comprehensive%20Scheme.pdf
19 Ibid.
20 Thilo Ebert et al., Green Building Certification Systems: Assessing Sustainability – International System Comparison – Economic Impact of Certifications (Detail, 2013): 60. http://ebookcentral.proquest.com/lib/cua/detail.action?docID=1075570.
21 Manuel Duarte Pinheiro, LiderA: Voluntary System for the Sustainability of Built Environments: Working Version V2.00c1 (Lisbon: Manuel Duarte Pinheiro, 2011): 20–22. http://lidera.info/resources/LiderA_English_Version_2_Presentation.pdf
22 The Pearl Rating System for ESTIDAMA Emirate of Abu Dhabi, Pearl Building Rating System: Design & Construction, Version 1.0 (Abu Dhabi: Abu Dhabi Urban Planning Council, April 2010): 75. www.upc.gov.ae/-/media/files/estidama/docs/pbrs-version-10.ashx?la=ar-ae&hash=58A67F549081968086D016E8D3757366BF29B10F
23 "Green Pyramid Rating System Levels" (Egyptian Green Building Council, 2009): 23. www.egypt-gbc.gov.eg/ratings/index.html
24 France GBC, International Environmental Certifications for the Design and Construction of Non-Residential Buildings: The Positioning of HQE Certification Relative to BREEAM and LEED (Paris: France GBC, 2015). www.behqe.com/documents/download/254
25 Dr. Karim Gazzehm and Dr Hend Ben Mahfoudh, "Green Buildings: Principles, Practices and Techniques, the French 'HQE®' Versus the American LEED®," Proceedings of the Tenth International Conference Enhanced Building Operations (Kuwait, 2010): 3.
26 Assessment Tool for the Environmental Performance of Buildings in Operation (EPB) Non Residential Buildings (Paris: Cerway, 2017). www.behqe.com/documents/download/215
27 Thilo Ebert et al. 2013, 60, op. cit.
28 US Green Building Council 2013, 389, op. cit.
29 Referring to ASHRAE 62.1 Outdoor Air Rates Table 6–1: Not all space types are listed in the ASHRAE table. The closest appropriate function should be chosen if your particular function is not listed.

30 ASHRAE, *ASHRAE Standard: Ventilation for Acceptable Indoor Air Quality* (Atlanta, GA: American Society of Heating, Refrigerating and Air-Conditioning Engineers, Inc., 2010). http://arco-hvac.ir/wp-content/uploads/2016/04/ASHRAE-62_1-2010.pdf
31 Ibid.
32 Ibid.
33 ASHRAE 62.1–2010: find a thorough explanation at www.youtube.com/watch?v=autvVa86D00
34 See website: www.usgbc.org/resources/minimum-indoor-air-quality-performance-calculator
35 "Nonattainment Areas for Criteria Pollutants," US Environmental Protection Agency, 2018. www.epa.gov/green-book
36 Particulate Matter: www.epa.gov/green-book/green-bookpm-25-2012-area-information; Ozone: www.epa.gov/green-book/green-book-8-hour-ozone-2015-area-information
37 "Indoor Air Quality Building Education and Assessment Model," US Environmental Protection Agency, 2018. www.epa.gov/indoor-air-quality-IEQ/indoor-air-quality-building-education-and-assessment-model
38 See website: https://19january2017snapshot.epa.gov/indoor-air-quality-iaq/iaq-building-education-and-assessment-model-ibeam-diagnosing-and-solving_.html
39 ASHRAE, *ASHRAE Standard: Measurement, Testing, Adjusting, and Balancing of Building HVAC Systems* (Atlanta, GA: American Society of Heating, Refrigerating and Air-Conditioning Engineers, Inc., 2008). http://spc195.ashraepcs.org/docs/Standard_111_2008.pdf
40 US Environmental Protection Agency 2018, op. cit.
41 The Audit should include an issue-resolution timeline.
42 LEED v4 requires the systems to be at least ten feet long in the direction of travel.
43 "Respiratory Health Effects of Passive Smoking: Lung Cancer and Other Disorders," US Environmental Protection Agency, 2018. www.epa.gov/indoor-air-quality-IEQ/respiratory-health-effects-passive-smoking-lung-cancer-and-other-disorders
44 Ibid.
45 US Green Building Council, "Environmental Tobacco Smoke Control," *Reference Guide for Building Operations and Maintenance* (Washington, DC: US Green Building Council, 2013): 410.
46 Ibid.
47 "No Smoking Policy FAQ," Smoke-Free Campus, University of Colorado Boulder, 2018. www.colorado.edu/smokefree/smoke-free-policy/no-smoking-policy-faq
48 Ibid.
49 US Green Building Council, "Environmental Tobacco Smoke Control" 410, op cit.
50 Trista Little, "EBOM-v4 EQp2: Environmental Tobacco Smoke Control," BuildingGreen, 2018. https://leeduser.buildinggreen.com/credit/EBOM-v4/EQp2
51 J.E. Callinan, A. Clarke, K. Doherty and C. Kelleher, "Legislative Smoking Bans for Reducing Secondhand Smoke Exposure, Smoking Prevalence and Tobacco Consumption (Review)," *Cochrane Database of Systematic Reviews* 14, no. 4 (2010).
52 J.E. Bauer, A. Hyland, Q. Li, C. Steger and K.M. Cummings, "A Longitudinal Assessment of the Impact of Smokefree Worksite Policies on Tobacco Use," *American Journal of Public Health* 95, no. 6 (2005): 1024–1029; C.M. Fichtenberg and S.A. Glantz, "Effect of Smoke-Free Workplaces on Smoking Behavior, Systematic Review," *British Medical Journal* 325, no. 7357 (2002): 188.
53 "Smokefree and Tobacco-Free U.S. and Tribal Colleges and Universities," American Nonsmokers' Rights Foundation, 2018. http://no-smoke.org/pdf/smokefreecollegesuniversities.pdf
54 Olivia Dimmer, "More Campuses have Smoking Bans – But do they Work?" *USA Today*, October 6, 2016. www.usatoday.com/story/college/2016/10/06/more-campuses-have-smoking-bans-but-do-they-work/37422275/
55 US Green Building Council, "Environmental Tobacco Smoke Control: Step-by-Step Guide" 416, op cit.
56 "Family Smoking Prevention and Tobacco Control Act – An Overview," US Food and Drug Administration, 2018. www.fda.gov/TobaccoProducts/GuidanceComplianceRegulatoryInformation/ucm246129.htm
57 "About the Initiative," American Cancer Society and Center for Tobacco Control, 2018. www.tobaccofreecampus.org/about-the-initiative/. See also Tobacco-Free Generation Campus Initiative (TFGCI) Toolkit for change at www.tobaccofreecampus.org/toolkits-guides/
58 "Our Goals," Center for Tobacco Control, 2018. www.cancer.org/health-care-professionals/center-for-tobacco-control.html
59 Trista Little 2018, op cit.
60 "Introduction to Green Cleaning," ISSA, 2018. www.issa.com/regulatory/

green-cleaning/introduction-to-green-cleaning.html
61 "Green Cleaning in Healthcare: Innovation, Implementation, and Evaluation," CleanMed 2012: Creating Healing Environments, 2012. https://noharm-uscanada.org/sites/default/files/documents-files/1083/2012-05-03_Cleanmed_quan.pdf
62 ISSA 2018, op cit.
63 Stephen Ashkin, "EBOM-v4 EQp3: Green Cleaning Policy," BuildingGreen, 2018. https://leeduser.buildinggreen.com/credit/EBOM-v4/EQp3
64 Stephen Ashkin, "EBOM-v4 EQp3: Green Cleaning Policy: Documentation Toolkit," BuildingGreen, 2018. https://leeduser.buildinggreen.com/credit/EBOM-v4/EQp3#doc
65 Ibid.
66 "Policy: Advocating for Green Clean Schools Policy," GreenCleanSchools, 2018. https://greencleanschools.org/policy/
67 US Green Building Council, "Facility Maintenance and Renovation Policy: Behind the Intent," *Reference Guide for Building Operations and Maintenance* (Washington, DC: US Green Building Council, 2013): 327.
68 Ibid.
69 Stephen Ashkin, "EBOM-v4 EQp3: Green Cleaning Policy: Credit Language," BuildingGreen, 2018. https://leeduser.buildinggreen.com/credit/EBOM-v4/EQp3#tab-credit-language
70 Stephen Ashkin, "EBOM-v4 EQp3: Green Cleaning Policy" 2018, op. cit.
71 Stephen Ashkin, "EBOM-v4 EQp3: Green Cleaning Policy: Documentation Toolkit" 2018, op. cit.
72 See website: www.usgbc.org/resources/eqp-green-cleaning-policytemplate
73 See website: http://ifmacentraloh.starchapter.com/images/downloads/Sustainability/ifma_green_cleaning_guide.pdf
74 See website: www.dm.usda.gov/emd/greening/greenpurchasing/index.htm
75. Stephen Ashkin, "EBOM-v4 EQp3: Green Cleaning Policy" 2018, op. cit.
76 Stephen Ashkin, "EBOM-v4 EQc6: Green Cleaning – Custodial Effectiveness Assessment," BuildingGreen, 2018. https://leeduser.buildinggreen.com/credit/EBOM-v4/EQc6.
77 Stephen Ashkin, "EBOM-v4 EQc6: Green cleaning – Products and Materials," BuildingGreen, 2018. https://leeduser.buildinggreen.com/credit/EBOM-v4/EQc7
78 Stephen Ashkin, "EBOM-v4 EQc8: Green Cleaning – Equipment," BuildingGreen, 2018. https://leeduser.buildinggreen.com/credit/EBOM-v4/EQc8#tab-credit-language

79 Ibid.
80 Igor Knez, "Effects of Indoor Lighting on Mood and Cognition," *Journal of Environmental Psychology* 15, no. 1 (1995): 39–51; Igor Knez and Ingela Enmarker, "Effects of Office Lighting on Mood and Cognitive Performance and a Gender Effect in Work-Related Judgment," *Environment and Behavior* 30, no. 4 (1998): 553–567.
81 "Regularly occupied spaces are areas where one or more individuals normally spend time (more than one hour per person per day on average) seated or standing as they work, study, or perform other focused activities inside a building." www.usgbc.org/leedaddenda/100001128
82 This does not include daylighting, but does include task lighting. Please see page 465 of the LEED O+M v4 Reference Guide.
83 Note that only four strategies are required to be documented for credit compliance.
84 Refer to the Reference Guide, pages 463–466 for details of credit calculations.
85 1 candela per square meter to candelas per square foot = 0.0929.
86 US Green Building Council, "Interior Lighting: Step-by-Step Guidance," *Reference Guide for Building Operations and Maintenance* (Washington, DC: US Green Building Council, 2013): 465.
87 This is able to be identified using manufacturer's cut sheets, equipment or apps. Please see tools to identify equipment or apps.
88 LRV should be at least 80 for ceilings, 50 for walls and 20 for floors per the following reference standard: David DiLaura, Kevin Houser, Richard Mistrick and Gary Steff, eds, *The Lighting Handbook,* 10th Edition (New York: Illuminating Engineering Society of North America, 2011). Also see Equation 1 on page 466 in the Reference Guide.
89 LRV should be at least 50 for furnishings. Also see Equation 1 on page 466 in the Reference Guide.
90 See Equation 2 on page 466 in the Reference Guide.
91 See Equation 3 on page 466 in the Reference Guide.
92 See website: https://measurewhatyousee.com/2015/09/03/measuring-the-light-reflectance-value-lrv-and-its-importance-in-safety-regulations/
93 See website: https://thelandofcolor.com/lrv-guru-light-reflectance-app/
94 See website: www.instrumart.com/categories/5639/light-meters
95 See website: https://leeduser.buildinggreen.com/credit/EBOM-v4/EQc4

96 See website: https://leeduser.buildinggreen.com/credit/EBOM-v4/EQc5#tab-credit-language
97 US Green Building Council, "Integrated Pest Management: Step-by-Step Guidance," *Reference Guide for Building Operations and Maintenance* (Washington, DC: US Green Building Council, 2013): 519–520.
98 Ensure that the personnel executing / performing the work of the IPM plan are licensed and/or trained with necessary credentials. Refer to www.aspcro.org/officials.html to identify officials overseeing state regulations. Vendors must be certified by either GreenPro, EcoWise, or GreenShield.
99 Refer to the LEED O+M v4 Reference Guide page 521 for IPM Plan requirements.
100 See website: www.usgbc.org/resources/v4-eqc-integrated-pest-management-plan-template
101 See website: https://leeduser.buildinggreen.com/content/ipm-tracking-tool-ipm-tracking-tool-templatexlsx
102 Trista Little, "EBOM-v4 EQc9: Integrated Pest Management," BuildingGreen, 2018. https://leeduser.buildinggreen.com/credit/EBOM-v4/EQc9
103 US Green Building Council, "Occupant Comfort Survey: Step-by-Step Guidance," *Reference Guide for Building Operations and Maintenance* (Washington, DC: US Green Building Council, 2013): 528–529.
104 "LEED Performance Path and ARC Defined + 8 Simple Steps to Earn LEED," Sustainable Investment Group, April 27, 2018. https://sigearth.com/leed-performance-path-arc/
105 See website: www.youtube.com/watch?v=rG_6QvnCJzM
106 See website: https://leeduser.buildinggreen.com/sites/default/files/credit_documentation/Occupant%20Comfort%20Survey_Sample.docx
107 See website: https://leeduser.buildinggreen.com/sites/default/files/credit_documentation/IEQc7.2%20Corrective%20Action%20Plan_Guidance%20Document.pdf
108 See website: www.researchgate.net/profile/Maged_Mikhael/post/Does_anyone_have_the_ISO_10551_and_ASHRAE_STANDARD_55-2013/attachment/5c532ccdcfe4a781a57ba5f9/AS%3A721182978473984%401548954829361/download/ASHRAE+55+%2C+17.pdf
109 See website: http://comfort.cbe.berkeley.edu/
110 Trista Little, "EBOM-v4 EQc10: Occupant Comfort Survey," BuildingGreen, 2018. https://leeduser.buildinggreen.com/credit/EBOM-v4/EQc10
111 David Scheer, "EBOM-v4 EQc3: Thermal Comfort," BuildingGreen, 2019. https://leeduser.buildinggreen.com/credit/EBOM-v4/EQc3

CHAPTER ELEVEN

PHASE 3: DOCUMENTATION

11.1 Coordination

As the Performance Period nears its end, the LEED Lab class which is delegated to undertake the final credit submission (after the Implementation Phase) is responsible for documentation. It's the most exciting time for students, faculty, staff and administrators alike. One may presume that simply ensuring tracking and setting up the credits for completion is sufficient, yet without this final phase of the tripartite LEED Lab structure, the entire effort of a few semesters or even years of carefully diagnosing a building's performance may not culminate. During the Documentation Phase, the considerable responsibility of finishing the tracking started by former students, compiling correct data or calculations (even if it means reviewing them several times), and ensuring that all of the records required for submission are complete, amounts to the gratification of pressing the 'submit' button on the LEED Online website!

The most frequently asked questions about the LEED Lab course perhaps can be answered in this final Documentation Phase, "how are students expected to complete their credit submissions when the previous semester's students were working on those credits?" or "how are the credits/prerequisites passed from class to class?" As the earlier chapters of this book recommend, there are several ways to assign credits. Yet if the correct information is not submitted to the USGBC or the governing authority over the certification, it will be questioned. Therefore the way the data from implementation is delivered to the student body submitting the final certification package is vital. Coordination is the answer and the key to success. The following subsections outline the answer to this question:

11.1.1 Recording

At some point during the Feasibility or Implementation Phases, but most importantly during the Documentation Phase (or if a different body of students is responsible for the last steps of Certification),

PHASE 3: DOCUMENTATION

Fig 11.1 LEED Online Portal login page
Source: US Green Building Council

Side Lesson A – 11.1: Interdepartmental Online Repository: A website, external data site, or any digital platform which holds all of the credit's data as a backup to LEED Online. The Catholic University uses iDOR as their Interdepartmental Online Repository (see https://sites.google.com/a/cua.edu/cua-leed-projects/).

LEED Lab students should log into LEED Online (Figure 11.1) to establish their USGBC member logins, passwords, and also to witness the registration of the project which is commonly accomplished by the course instructor. This entails the instructor 'inviting' team members (LEED Lab students and any other consultants or facility personnel) to the project during class time in order for students to see the process (Figure 11.2). The students become official members of the LEED project and may begin populating their assigned credit forms located on the LEED Online platform by uploading calculations, and any required metric or data used to achieve the credit requirements. This is considered the recording of data, but can be accomplished outside of the LEED Online platform for many credits. In fact, knowing where the credit data currently is held is important to know as a student new to LEED Lab entering a 'documentation' semester.

An assignment matrix is an in-house record of who has been assigned to which credit (Figure 11.3). It is typically located on a platform which contains all of the courses' data and is optimally accessible to staff and administrators of the university (Side Lesson A: Interdepartmental Online Repository) (Figures 11.4 and 11.5). This platform includes all previous student work, all of which are analyzed by the students in this Documentation Phase of LEED Lab. It is the Documentation Phase that necessitates LEED Online access so that students in this phase are able to upload a credit's recording requirements, and/or confirm that any existing recorded data on LEED Online are correct and complete.

11.1.2 Delegation

At the beginning of a project, the LEED Lab students who conducted Feasibility and Implementation Phases were assigned by their instructor or selected themselves to manage credit tasks, tools and techniques towards successful achievement.

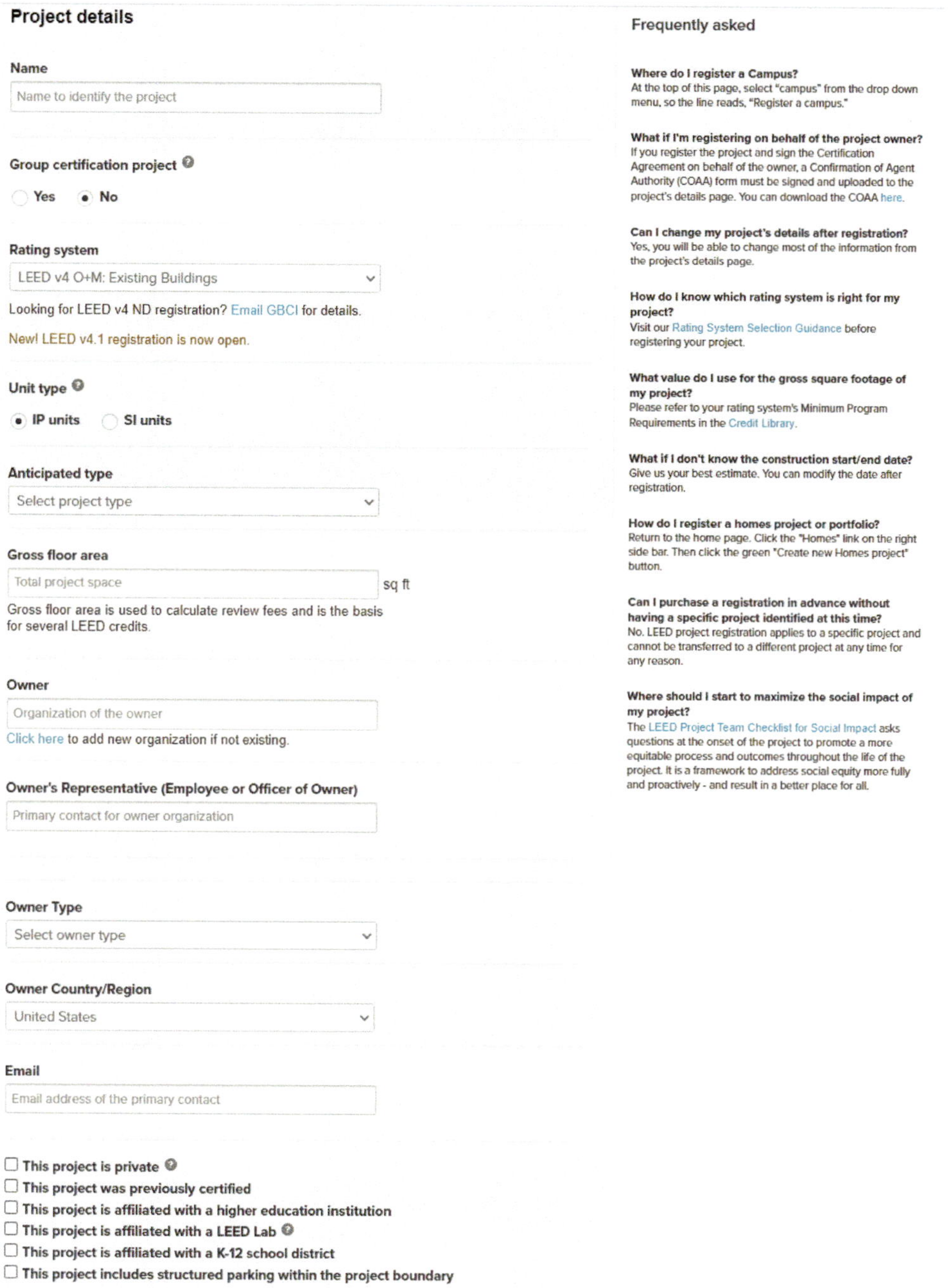

PHASE 3: DOCUMENTATION

Project details

Name

[Name to identify the project]

Group certification project
○ Yes ● No

Rating system
[LEED v4 O+M: Existing Buildings ▼]

Looking for LEED v4 ND registration? Email GBCI for details.
New! LEED v4.1 registration is now open.

Unit type
● IP units ○ SI units

Anticipated type
[Select project type ▼]

Gross floor area
[Total project space] sq ft

Gross floor area is used to calculate review fees and is the basis for several LEED credits.

Owner
[Organization of the owner]
Click here to add new organization if not existing.

Owner's Representative (Employee or Officer of Owner)
[Primary contact for owner organization]

Owner Type
[Select owner type ▼]

Owner Country/Region
[United States ▼]

Email
[Email address of the primary contact]

☐ This project is private
☐ This project was previously certified
☐ This project is affiliated with a higher education institution
☐ This project is affiliated with a LEED Lab
☐ This project is affiliated with a K-12 school district
☐ This project includes structured parking within the project boundary

Frequently asked

Where do I register a Campus?
At the top of this page, select "campus" from the drop down menu, so the line reads, "Register a campus."

What if I'm registering on behalf of the project owner?
If you register the project and sign the Certification Agreement on behalf of the owner, a Confirmation of Agent Authority (COAA) form must be signed and uploaded to the project's details page. You can download the COAA here.

Can I change my project's details after registration?
Yes, you will be able to change most of the information from the project's details page.

How do I know which rating system is right for my project?
Visit our Rating System Selection Guidance before registering your project.

What value do I use for the gross square footage of my project?
Please refer to your rating system's Minimum Program Requirements in the Credit Library.

What if I don't know the construction start/end date?
Give us your best estimate. You can modify the date after registration.

How do I register a homes project or portfolio?
Return to the home page. Click the "Homes" link on the right side bar. Then click the green "Create new Homes project" button.

Can I purchase a registration in advance without having a specific project identified at this time?
No. LEED project registration applies to a specific project and cannot be transferred to a different project at any time for any reason.

Where should I start to maximize the social impact of my project?
The LEED Project Team Checklist for Social Impact asks questions at the onset of the project to promote a more equitable process and outcomes throughout the life of the project. It is a framework to address social equity more fully and proactively - and result in a better place for all.

Fig 11.2 LEED Online Portal registration page
Note: Text continues on actual online form: www.leedonline.com/projects/register
Source: US Green Building Council

The facility personnel were partners in this task. Yet upon the final submission, their role escalates to oversee the ongoing work of the students and to ensure that the submission works with, and does not compromise, the sustainability goals of the institution. As such, the three roles which are foremost

PHASE 3: DOCUMENTATION

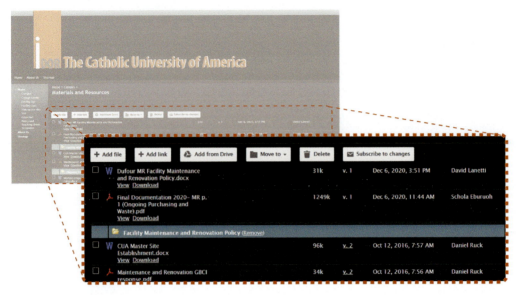

Fig 11.3 *iDOR home page*
Source: Created by LEED Lab students at CUA, 2016

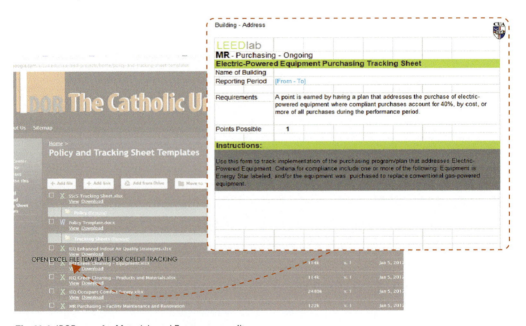

Fig 11.4 *iDOR page for Materials and Resources credits*
Source: Created by LEED Lab students at CUA, 2016

important in this category are the owner, agent and project administrator.

On a university campus, the 'owner' is the highest authority responsible for the green assessment. It can be the energy manager, a representative from the president's office, facilities department or a building manager. This individual authorizes the acceptance of the LEED O+M or any other green assessment certification agreement and ultimately has control over

PHASE 3: DOCUMENTATION

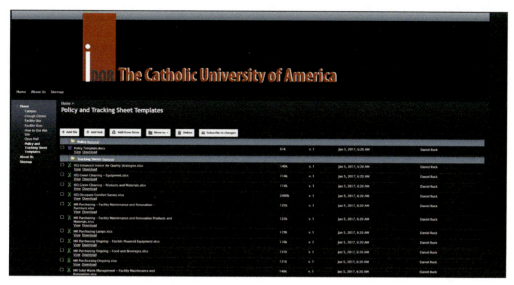

Fig 11.5 iDOR page for Policy and Tracking Sheet templates
Source: Created by LEED Lab students at CUA, 2016

the entire application.[1] It is optimal if this individual participates to some degree in each LEED Lab course, even if it is for a few single events such as a charrette or the GBCI Review. As advised in Chapters 3.1.6 and 3.1.7, the administration and staff should be involved from the onset of the project, and most often the owner is among this group of people. The 'agent' may be the same person as the owner in a LEED Lab project, or it may be any person, granted authority via the owner, to register and accept the LEED certification agreement (Side Lesson B: LEED Certification Agreement) of the project.

In a LEED Lab class, the 'project administrator' is usually the instructor of the course, thus acts as a quality manager. While students will upload all of their credit documentation to LEED Online, this individual acts as the administrator who oversees how all of this data is collected. In the Documentation Phase, this individual evaluates the LEED Lab student's work for accuracy and completion prior to submitting the entire assembly of project credits to GBCI and thereafter.

Delegation of credits among students looks similar to that of the Implementation Phase. If there is a high student-to-credit ratio during this phase, it is recommended that two or more students pair up to review and finalize the credits. For example, one student may review the previous semester's student's work and another student may review earlier work. They may split the time involved in communicating with facility personnel and uploading remaining documents. If there is a low student-to-credit ratio, doubling up on credits is the due course. This may mean postponing the final submission to the following semester. In any instance, there will be a strong possibility that the majority of credit work has already been accomplished during the first two phases by previous students. This means that this phase would

Side Lesson B – 11.2: LEED Certification Agreement: The project owner is the one who signs the LEED Certification Agreement. Once the agreement is signed then the project may be submitted to LEED Online for Preliminary Review (see https://tinyurl.com/5fzbd5sj and https://tinyurl.com/v597x7n7).

simply become a check-and-submit task. Time to revise data due to negligent work from previous semesters may warrant postponing the final submission. LEED Lab students should have the LEED O+M v4 Reference Guide at hand, carefully understanding USGBC's expectations for each credit and confirming that they have been met.

11.2 Gaps

As with any major building diagnostic task, there may be certain gaps in tracking, sometimes unnoticed until the Documentation Phase. Recognizing that systems may have a hardware or software failure is a reality to catch during the Implementation Phase, but critical to fix during Documentation. For example, during CUA's energy tracking, one of the LEED Lab students assigned to the prerequisite noticed a null register of steam power during the months of December and January – primary heating months in Washington, DC. She questioned this, and met with the primary Energy Manager. Since the heating for the Crough Center for Architectural Studies was steam and there were no lapses in heating the building that year, it was determined that our steam meter had malfunctioned. The gap in tracking caused the class to extend the Implementation Phase in order to replace the faulty meter while meeting the mandatory 12 months of energy data to accomplish the Minimum Energy Performance Prerequisite.

Outstanding credits are also expected to be completed during this phase. This requires the LEED Lab student to become a sort of detective in deciphering the trail of data left behind from former students. At times credits may be complete, but have incorrect calculations, thus not meeting the credit thresholds. In this case the instructor and the class must determine if the credit is worthwhile to pursue once it is corrected.

A common mistake made in the Documentation Phase of LEED Lab is recognizing inconsistent information. For example, students in the Feasibility Phase may record the square footage of their facility at 45,000 square feet (sf). Students in the subsequent semester of Implementation (while calculating the amount of green space within the project boundary) may arrive at an estimate of 40,000 sf from an aerial map. If students in that same class who are working on designing a water catchment device towards the water use reduction credit use the figure of 40,000 sf which they understood from their peers, the calculations will not reflect the sf recorded in the project information. Consequently, the Site Improvement Plan, Site Management Plan, and Water Use credits will be impacted. This error should be rectified by equalizing the sf in all credits before submitting the project for the GBCI preliminary review.

11.3 Submission

There are two ways in LEED Lab to succeed in certification – via initial or final certification. Initial certifications are accomplished when the class completes the credits, the instructor 'submits' them all to GBCI, and they receive approval and certification. More often, LEED Lab submissions receive an initial review, feedback from GBCI, and then an opportunity for resubmission before the project building can be certified.

The instructor sets the time frame to allow GBCI approximately two weeks to review the submission before they provide feedback.[2] The feedback is emailed to the instructor for distribution to the students. There are opportunities, if coordinated with USGBC and/or GBCI in advance, to have a live video or in-person recitation of the feedback which provides an opportunity for students to directly ask GBCI technical reviewers questions about their credits. Expect some corrections to the submitted data. Instructors should allow in the course schedule at least one full week for students to correct their mistakes. If the mistakes are significant, postponing the resubmission to another semester will be necessary. In that case, the class may decide not to pursue the credit/s in questions, or alternatively, a subsequent LEED Lab class will endeavor to complete them.

The preliminary submission should occur within two months of the end of the Performance Period, and the final submission should occur within two months after receiving preliminary review results. If these can't be met, the Performance Period should be adjusted (no more than a two-year period is allowed). This provides a great exercise of reality for the students, yet is often very time consuming to accomplish since each credit must be reevaluated.

There are many suggestions via online open source and proprietary resources for a smooth review, such as providing succinct and highlighted data relevant to the credit and neatly labeling file attachments. The best course of action specifically for a LEED Lab course however is seriously reviewing the preliminary submission feedback from GBCI. At times more information and explanations are necessary if there are unusual circumstances to the credit being pursued. For example, if an HVAC system in a dormitory is scheduled to be replaced towards the end of the Performance Period, yet energy data has been collected using the existing unit, an explanation should be provided and data for both units would be helpful to present to the reviewers. Particularly if extending the Performance Period to reflect greater energy efficiency of the newer HVAC unit would mean the difference between a higher level of certification.

For the LEED Lab student, deciding which and how much documentation to include is daunting since there are no generic submissions to follow, unless a similar building has been certified on campus. Every prerequisite and credit yields a different subset of documents for each unique building and institution. Rest assured that even professionals sometimes have a hard time determining if they are submitting too much or too little

PHASE 3: DOCUMENTATION

Side Lesson C – 11.3: Credit Appeal: After a project's final design review or final construction review any denied credits may be submitted for appeal. During the appeal process, new credits can also be attempted and submitted. After the final review has been completed click the "Appeal," button on LEED Online. Then select the "Open to Update" button, and the team will have the ability to select which credits and upload the proper documentation needed (see www.usgbc.org/help/how-can-i-appeal-denied-credit-or-prerequisite).

Side Lesson D – 11.3: Credit Interpretation Rulings (CIRs): CIRs may be sought during the implantation stage as well as documentation. They are reviewed after a 'pending' response to the initial review. The purpose of a CIR is to provide technical guidance for particular credits. The LEED review team will ensure that a team's interpretation of credits and prerequisites meet the requirements of the published rating system. Once submitting a project for review, the team must provide documentation showing CIR approvals. If a credit does not pass the CIR the team may file an appeal (see www.usgbc.org/tools/leed-certification/commercial).

information. Submit that which clearly explains the circumstance, adding photographs, diagrams, and written descriptions as needed.

11.4 Review

After the official submission of credits by the LEED Lab instructor or project manager, there is a period of respite from the type of work the class has been doing thus far. For the student it means focusing on efforts of greater campus impact such as marketing, promoting and collaborating with public relations staff and the sustainability director to prepare articles, stories and graphics demonstrating success of the class, a specific achievement or data. This is also a good time for the class to upload and organize the submission material to an internal digital repository (mentioned earlier in 11.1.1) for the campus' greater access. Often the research endeavors accomplished in LEED Lab yield information useful to campus facility personnel. Traditional quizzes, exams and ISPP submissions also are recommended to fill this class time. For the instructor, this time period means open and regular lines of communication with GBCI's technical review team.

The process of the official assessment towards certification begins immediately after the submission in what is called a 'preliminary review'. This is an analysis of data, accuracy, and completeness of the material submitted which almost always results in feedback and clarifying questions from the technical reviewer at GBCI. The class may decide to accept the achievements of this review as final despite those credits which are questioned and may not be achieved. Most often the class continues to the second step – final review.

The instructor or project manager processes GBCI's feedback from the initial review with the students so they have an opportunity to revisit their submissions, and resubmit their credit attempts – corrected and aligned to the GBCI reviewer's comments. This resubmission is called the final review and is the last opportunity, without paying additional fees, to achieve certification. The preliminary review results in credits being 'pending' or 'accepted' while the results of this final review are marked with credits either being 'denied' or 'accepted'. The credits accepted at this final review become those that comprise the level of certification.

At this point, the Project Administrator may accept the final decisions of credit achievement or denial, file a motion of credit appeal (Side Lesson C: Credit Appeal) (which is accompanied by a fee depending on the complexity of the issue and the quantity of credits being appealed) or help students to research Credit Interpretation Rulings (CIRs) (Side Lesson D: Credit Interpretation Rulings (CIRs) or LEED Interpretations (Side Lesson E: LEED Interpretations) in order to have another chance to attain credit achievement.

Any LEED O+M Master Site credits earned for the campus are applied automatically to the project during the review if the project is registered under the same campus. This is why the initial chapters of this book recommend the campus credits to be pursued prior to a specific building. Of course, if the credits are in progress, or if the campus project and the current LEED Lab project on that campus are not associated, only a USGBC LEED Lab Coach or GBCI technical reviewer can assist in linking them.

11.5 Certification

Final review results from GBCI are the pinnacle of LEED Lab! Many semesters and maybe even years of action research, learning and diagnosing a campus building's operational and physical systems have led to the hopeful outcome of LEED O+M certification. Results come in the form of a report which is required to be accepted unless an appeal is filed. The class may contest a review decision for a credit or prerequisite, and for that there is a process available by contacting the LEED Lab Coach at USGBC. The report should be carefully reviewed since once it is accepted, these actions cannot be performed.

Once certified through LEED O+M, facilities must continue to be tracked, metered, and their operations gauged in order to maintain a consistent stream of data which will provide documentation towards recertification. If measures such as those prescribed in the prerequisites and credits of the Implementation Phase are upheld by facility personnel, administration and the campus community, then future LEED Lab courses at your institution will become fluid and effective green learning platforms for future architects, building managers, engineers, contractors and tradespersons.

Side Lesson E – 11.3: LEED Interpretations are official addenda published and administered by USGBC. They are created and discussed thoroughly by LEED committees and focus on the evolution of the LEED rating system. LEED Interpretations are similar to CIRs in the sense that they also provide technical guidance for projects applying for LEED certification. However, they are different from CIRs in that they are precedent-setting, applicable to future projects. Published LEED Interpretations are accessible through USGBC's online database (see www.usgbc.org/leed-interpretations).

11.6 Closing

With the built environment growing – the US building stock increases by about three billion square feet each year – the building industry has a historic opportunity to transform its impact for the better.[3] The National Renewable Energy Laboratory calculates that adopting current best practices using energy conservation measures, facilities can achieve over a 50 percent energy reduction without incurring an additional cost.[4] Becoming aware of such simple practical measures via a performance evaluation should be learned in the foundational learning of young building professionals as a process of learning from the building beyond its final punch list. Using buildings in which they reside and occupy daily as a part of students' scholastic experience on campus while benefiting that institution begins to foster a win-win cycle of analysis, documentation and feedback that is LEED Lab.

Notes

1 "Guide to LEED Certification: Commercial" (US Green Building Council, August 15, 2020). www.usgbc.org/tools/leed-certification/commercial
2 The timeframe should be coordinated with a LEED Lab Coach at USGBC.
3 Lance Hosey, "Why Architects must Lead on Sustainable Design," GreenBiz, March 19, 2013. www.greenbiz.com/blog/2013/03/19/why-architects-must-lead-sustainable-design?page=full
4 "NREL Recommends Ways to Cut Building Energy Costs in Half," National Renewable Energy Laboratory, 2013. www.nrel.gov/docs/fy13osti/59019.pdf

INDEX

Note: Page numbers in **bold** type refer to tables.
Page numbers in *italic* type refer to figures.
Page numbers followed by 'n' refer to notes.
Page numbers followed by 'b' refer to Boxes.
Page numbers followed by 's' refer to Side Lessons.

Abu Dhabi Urban Planning Council *see* Pearl for ESTIDAMA (PORS)
Abu Dhabi Water Resources Masterplan 113
academic research 37
Accredited Professional (AP) 6–7
action: planned future 14; revised theory of 14; theory development 13
action research 10, 10s, 11–12; Action Research Cycle (Sagor) 12, *12*, 13–14, 16; criteria 11–12
adjustment factor (AF) 122s
administration 23, 313; university 22
Advanced Energy Metering Credit 172, 174, 204
agent 313
air conditioning (AC) 176; refrigerant processed in air conditioner *177*
air flow: measuring tips and techniques *275–276*; measuring tools 275, *275–276*; rates for ASHRAE Compliance 272
air pollution, indoor 245, 246–247, 252–253
air quality: doesn't meet ASHRAE 273–274; meets ASHRAE 273
Air Quality Management Strategy 278–279
Air Quality Performance prerequisite 260–279; partnering credit 278–279; standards for 276–277; tasks 260–274; techniques 277–278; tools 274–277
air temperature *248*, *249*
air-handling units (AHUs) 261–264; Crough Center *263*, *264*, 303; Schedule (2013) **265–271**; testing 273–274
AKF Group LLC 206
alterative compliance for professional exemption 303
alternative transportation 61; assessment systems 68; definition 68s; programs 74; regional factors 61–62; requirements (LEED Lab v4) 74
Alternative Transportation Credit 68–74, 77; equations *71*; Options 1, 2 and 3 69–74; strategies for achievement 74, *75*; tasks 69–70; techniques 73–74; tools 70
Alternative Transportation Plan 70–73; calculations 73, 74, 78n26; commuting 72–73b; sample campus 73
alumni 20
American Cancer Society, Center for Tobacco Control 285
American National Standards Institute (ANSI) *see* ANSI
American Society of Heating and Refrigeration Engineers (ASHRAE) *see* ASHRAE
amps 172
anemometers 14s
annual maintenance, and refrigerant cost difference equation 179–181, *180*
ANSI 28; C12.20 – Electricity Meters 172–173
ANSI/ASHRAE Standard 55 301
appeal, credit 316s
apps (applications): computer/phone 297; software 24
ARC Performance Platform 29, 29s, 30–32, *31*, 38, 300; and Alternative Transportation

Credit 69, 73–74; benefits 32; categories data 31; energy performance tracking 167; Human Experience Survey 301; Performance Certifications 32; website portal *31*
Architecture 2030 1s, 133; 2030 Challenge (2016) 1s
artificial drainage 91
artificial lighting 247
as-builds 143–144, *145*
ASHRAE 148, 260; air flow rates measurement for compliance 272; air quality meets/doesn't meet 273–274; Building Commissioning Professional (BCxP) certification 184; MERV Rating 261s; thermal comfort definition 247
ASHRAE Level I Energy Audit 22–23, 148, *149*, **149**, 174; Energy Baseline 152–154; Walkthrough **149**, 152–154, 159, 174, 210
ASHRAE Level II 22–23, 152
ASHRAE Level III 152–154
ASHRAE Standard 62.1: compliance path selection 273–274; Outdoor Air Rates Table 6-1 **272**, 303, 305n29; testing for compliance 272–273; –2007 303; –2010 273, 276–277, 278
ASHRAE Standard 111–2008 277–278
assessment: building 133; campus 3, 6, 42, 43b; certification systems 25–33; green 312–313; Green Cleaning Custodial Effectiveness 291; LEED O+M Assessment 143–148, 150–152; systems comparison 41, *41*; timeline *46*, 48–53, *48–50*
assessment phases: documentation 14; feasibility 12–13; implementation 13–14
auditing 185
audits: Capital-Intensive Modification (or "investment-grade") Audits 152, *see also* ASHRAE Level I Energy Audit

Australia: Bureau of Statistics 65; Green Building Council (GBCA) 111, 139
automobile dependency 61

Ball State University: campus greening 4; celebrate, facilitate, anticipate mantra 4; Clustered Minors in Environmentally Sustainable Practices 4–5
Barton, Jon 11
BAS 174, 185, 187, 189, 192
Base Score credits 31
BCA Green Mark 61; energy emphasis 140; green transport 66; materials and resources 227; site and sustainable impact 84; Smart and Healthy Building Category 259; Sustainable Management 66; Water Efficiency 112–113
BEAM (Building Environmental Assessment Method) 66
BEAM Plus for Existing Buildings: Building and Site Operations and Maintenance 84, 226; Energy Category 140–141; IEQ Category 258; indoor environmental issues 257–258; MAN credits 257–258; Management Category 140; materials and resources 226–227; Materials and Waste 227; site aspects 84; transportation in 66; Water Conservation 112–113; Water Management 112–113
benchmarking 2, 2s, 148; codes 7; energy 2, 134–136; Level I Energy Audit 148; profiling accounts 168; travel survey 65
benchmarks: BREEAM In-Use 28; Green Globes for Existing Buildings (EB) 28; obtaining performance 163, *165*
Best Management Practices (BMPs) prerequisite 142–160; partnering credit 160; tasks 150–155; techniques 157–159; tools 155–157
Best Management Practices for Energy Efficiency in Buildings prerequisite 218n27

INDEX

Best Practices in Commissioning Existing Buildings (BCxA) 188
bicycles 68
Biochar (Biocarbon) 127–130, 127s, *128*; innovations savings chart **130**
Biochar Curricular & Campus Integration Plan (CUA) 127, 128
Blackboard 24
bleed off 124–125
blowdown 124–125, 126s
boilers 168s
bottom-up-approach 25, 36
Bowen, Elizabeth 29
Brazil *see* HQE Exploitation
BRE Global 82
BREEAM (Building Research Establishment Assessment Method) 27
BREEAM In-Use (BIU) 27–28; alternative transportation 68; assessment system 225; Asset Performance Category 27, 64, 82, 110, 223–224, 255; benchmarks 27–28; Building Management Category 27, 82, 110, 223–224; Energy Category 138; Health and Wellness Category 255–256; Land Use and Ecology 82; Management 255; Materials and Resources Category 223–224, 225; Materials and Waste assessment 225; Occupier Management 27–28, 64, 82, 110, 223–224, 255; parts 27–28; site impact and management 82; Transport 64
Brock Center 3
building assessment 133; global systems 6; tool 6
Building Automation System (BAS) 155, *156*
building certification 25; levels 39–42
Building Commissioning Association (BCA), Existing Building Commissioning (EBCx) definition 184
Building Commissioning Professional Certification (BCxP) 184
Building Design and Construction (LEED BD+C) 25; rating system 47
Building Feasibility Checklist (LEED EB O+M) 45, 46b
Building Management System (BMS) 155, *156*
Building Operating Plan (BOP) 144, 151
building sector, energy consumption evaluation 133
building site 79–106; credits 87–98; and ecosystem services 79; rating systems comparison 80–86
Building Systems Description 144, 150–151
building walkthroughs: POE 6, *see also* ASHRAE Level I Energy Audit
Building-level Energy Metering prerequisite 134, 134s, *135*, *see also* Energy Metering prerequisite
Building-level Water Metering prerequisite 8, 120–122; partnering credits 122; tasks 120–121; techniques 122; tools 121, *121*
BuildingGreen.com 5
buildings: benchmarking 2, *2*; externally dominated 251–252; green 21, 28, 246; performance process 10; quantity registered 27; types on campus 250–252, *see also* existing buildings
Buildings Feedback Loop, Energy and Facility Management Software (EFMS) *157*

CADRE (Center for Advanced Design Research Exploration) 3
Calculated Water Use 115–116, 116–118, 116b, *117*, *118*, *119*
calendar of activities 47
calibrating, energy meters 160–161, 163, 172
campus: Alternative Transportation Plan sample 73; assessment 3, 6, 42, 43b; building types 250–252; ecological health 79; facilities as education tools 3; goals 36, 38; renovations 234; site importance 79–80; smoke-free 283, 285; Sustainability Offices

INDEX

4–5, 20, 38, *see also* Master Site credits
Campus Assessment Checklist (LEED EB O+M Handbook) 43b
Campus Implementation Workbook (USGBC) 42
Canada 3, 28
candela 295s
Canvass 24
Capital-Intensive Modification (or "investment-grade") Audits, Detailed Analysis of 152
carbon dioxide (CO_2) 133s; concentrations 32; emissions 133, 133s, *134*
carbon dioxide equivalent (CO_2e) 69, 69s
carbon monoxide detector 279s
Carbon Offsets 199–200, 202, 203; equations *202*, *see also* Renewable Energy + Carbon Offsets Credit
CASBEE EB: Building Design/Existing Building (BD/EB) energy category (LR1) 141, 227; Built Environment Efficiency (BEE) Chart 227; Built Environment Efficiency Chart (BEEC) 227; Built Environment Load (L) 227; Built Environment Quality (Q) 227; Consideration of Global Warming 66; Consideration of Local Environment 66; Indoor Environment (Q1) credit 258; Reducing Usage of Non-renewable Resources subdivision 227–228; site metrics 84–85; transportation in 66; Water Resources subcategory 113
Casey Trees 100
Cash Flow Opportunity Calculator 188
Catholic University of America (CUA): Biochar Curricular & Campus Integration Plan 127, 128; campus assessment 3, 6; Community Garden 100, 127, *129*; Department of Transportation and Parking 74, *75*; designated smoking areas *281*; energy tracking 314; Facilities 6; Facilities Maintenance and Operations Department 5, 23–24; Facilities Planning and Construction Department 23–24; Green Club 21, 127; LEED Lab EBOM Implementation Diagram *48–50*; LEED Lab unique role 36–38; Master site credits 126–128; Operating and Maintaining HVAC Systems Policy 210; Opus Hall Cooling Tower *125*; Opus Hall non-smoking signs *283*; site sustainability case study 126–128; site sustainability exercises 128–130; soil types *100*; Sustainability Plan 74, 75b, 241, *241*; Sustainability Plan missing links 76, 76b; terrain elevation map *101*; Transportation 74; vegetation on campus 98–103, *103*; water flow on impervious surfaces *102*, *see also* Edward M. Crough Center for Architectural Studies (CUA)
CBECS 167
celebrate, facilitate, anticipate mantra (Ball State University) 4
CEN (*Comité Européen de Normalisation*) International Standards 260
certification 24–33, 47; assessment systems 25–33; Building Commissioning Professional (BCxP) 184; Crough Center for Architectural Studies (CUA) 22–23; Documentation Phase (LEED Lab) 317; expedited 38; Green Building Certification Inc.™ (GBCI) 6s, 21–22, 315; Green Globes for Existing Buildings (EB) 28; initial 47, 314–315; LEED O+M 6, 7, 10, 21, 36, 39, 152; levels 39–42; Master Site 38–39, *40*; resources 32–33
Certification Agreement (LEED) 313, 313s
certification pathway: performance 29, 30–32, 38; traditional 29–30, 38
CFCs *see* chlorofluorocarbons (CFCs)
Chang, Roger 210

INDEX

chargers, quick 66, 66s
charrettes 7, 13, *13*, 13s, 15, 36, 42; PID presentation 52
Chavez, Dallas 106n37
chemical input/output, of materials 220–221
chillers 168s
China, Guangdong Province 112
chlorofluorocarbons (CFCs) 175, 176, 178; Phase-Out Plan 182
CHP 168
circadian rhythms 95, 95s, 248, 292, 293
circulating pumps 215
circulation, indoor 246
classroom scenarios 57
Clean Energy DC 74
cleaning company, certified 287, 290
cleaning products, green 288–289
Clustered Minors in Environmentally Sustainable Practices (Ball State University) 4–5
co-collaborators 19, 23–24
CO_2 *see* carbon dioxide (CO_2)
Coach, LEED Lab 22
collaboration 19
Collaborator Checklist (LEED Lab) 19
collaborators 30
college campus *see* campus
Color Rendering Index (CRI) **294**, 295s, *296*
combined fuel-end use breakdown *149*, **149**
combined heat and power (CHP) 167s
comfort: sub-topics 256, *256*; visual 292, *292*, 293; within interior environment 247–250
comfort zone, standard *250*
commercial buildings, shares of major energy sources *171*
Commercial Buildings Energy Consumption Survey (CBECS) 166, 167, 207
commissioning, new buildings 184
Commissioning (CX) Plan 187, 188, 189
Commissioning Credit Trio 160, 183–188; Auditing (Credit Option 2) 185–186; Commissioning Analysis 185; Commissioning (Credit Option 1) 185; Commissioning Implementation 186; Ongoing Commissioning 186–187; tasks 185–187; techniques 188, 292; tools 187–188
Commissioning Team (Cx) 185, 187, 188
communication protocol, energy meter data 172
Community Garden (CUA) 100, 127, *129*
commuting 61
Commuting Transportation Survey 72–73b
computer app 297
construction documents 94, 293
consultants 22–23
contaminants: indoor environment 246; stormwater 91; of water supplies 107
contractors 22–23
conversion costs 178
Cooling Tower (Opus Hall, CUA) *125*
Cooling Tower Water Use Credit 124–127; tasks 126; techniques 126–127; tools 126
cooling towers 124, 124s; water cycles analysis 126
coordination, Documentation Phase (LEED Lab) 309
Corrective Action Plan 300–301
cost/effort hierarchy, behavioural/procedural/mechanical 169–170
cradle-to-grave 220s
credit appeal 316, 316s
credit categories 7, 59; criteria aids 17
credit interpretation rulings (CIRs) 316, 316s
credits 15, 36, 59; achievement potential 47; Base Score 31; data 310; delegation 313–314; documentation 313; LEED 7–8; outstanding 314; performance periods by 47, *47*; rating system comparison 25–27, *26*; specific representatives for 22; synergizing 47
critical feedback loop 14–16, *15*

INDEX

Crough Center for Architectural Studies (CUA) *see* Edward M. Crough Center for Architectural Studies (CUA)
CUARain 99
Current Facility Requirements (CFRs) 143, 150
cut sheets 295, 295s
cycling 68

damper 278, 279s
data: ARC Performance Platform categories 31; credits 310; energy meter 163; normalization 168, 169s; recording 310; simulated energy 160
data collection: instruments; plan 13
data gathering, and dissemination 5
data loggers 14s, 156
Davin, Allison xix
Daylight and Quality Views Credit 297–298
daylighting 247–248
delegation: of credits 313–314; Documentation Phase (LEED Lab) 310–314
Demand Response (DR) 189–198; how it works *190*; tasks 189–191; techniques 192; tools 191–192
Demand Response (DR) Plan 189–191
Demand Response Quick Assessment Tool (DRQAT) 192
DeMontfort method 5–6
design 2, 3
designated smoking areas (CUA) *281*
Detailed Analysis of Capital-Intensive Modification Audits (ASHRAE Level III) 152–154
DGNB in Use 67–68; cycling 68; Ecological Quality Category 86, 142, 229–230, 259; Economic Quality Group 230, 259; energy use in credits 142; Functional Quality 259–260; Sociocultural Quality 86, 259–260; water consumption and wastewater 114

digital platform, to read energy meters 161–162, *162*
Direct Digital Control (DDC) system 185s, 204
disability glare 96s, *292*
discomfort glare 96s, *292*
District Energy System (DES) 161, 168, 168s, *169*
documentation 148, 309–317; credit 313; non-smoking compliance 283–285; ongoing 21; traditional platform 29
Documentation Phase (LEED Lab) 8, 14, 39, 148, 309–317; certification 317; coordination 309; delegation 310–314; gaps 314; recording of data 309–310; review 316–317; submission 314–316
door schedule 283–285, 283s
downstream vs. upstream 122s
Dracula of hormones 96s
drainage, artificial 91
drawings, existing buildings 143–144
dry-bulb temperature
durable goods 230s

EB O+M Handbook (LEED), Campus Assessment Checklist 43b
EB O+M (LEED): Building Feasibility Checklist 45, 46b; timeline of history 46–47, *46*
ECD Energy and Environmental Canada 28
Eco-Charrette 76
ecological health, campus 79
ecosystem: and light trespass 94–95; services 79
educational text 16
educators 19–20
Edward M. Crough Center for Architectural Studies (CUA) 5; ASHRAE Level I Walkthrough Energy Audit *149*, **149**; Campus Master Plan *100*, *101*, *102*; case study for Energy 204–215; case study for Indoor Atmosphere Credit 302–304; case study for Transportation Credit 74–77; certification 22–23; combined fuel-end use breakdown *149*,

| 323

INDEX

Edward M. (*cont.*) **149**; daily energy use 207, **208**; Energy and Atmosphere (EA) pre-requisite 206; Energy Conservation Measures **213–214**; energy metering 204–206, *205*; Energy Performance Statement *153*; exercises for Energy 215–217; history 302–303; irrigation water metering 206; lighting reduction 206; metering management system *205*; Occupant Survey *300*; Operating and Maintaining HVAC Systems Policy 210; Preventative Maintenance Schedule **211–212**; recertification challenges 240; second-floor plans *263*, *264*; Site Improvement Plan 99–103; Site Management Policy 99–103; space types 207, *209*; Statement of Energy Performance *153*; sustainable efficiency measures 99; vegetation management 99–103, *103*; water metering 204–206, *205*
effectiveness, evaluation 7
Egypt Green Building Council, Green Pyramid Rating System (GPRS) *see* Green Pyramid
electric vehicles, quick chargers for 66, 66s
electricity meters, ANSI C12.20 172–173
emergency exits 280
emissions: CO_2 133s; greenhouse gases (GHGs) 66, 133, *133*, 200, 200s
EMS 174, 185, 187, 189, 192
EN 1434 (CEN/TC 176) – Thermal Energy Meters 173
energy: benchmarking 2, 134–136; credits 142–204; and indoor air quality 248–249; savings 152, 168–169, 188, 191, **213–214**, 302; sub-meters 160–161, *161*
Energy Accounting Feedback Loop (EAFL) 148, 150, *150*, 154–155, 216; cost savings 218n33
Energy and Atmosphere (EA) pre-requisite 134, *135*;

Crough Center achievement 206–210; Minimum Energy Performance diagram *165*
energy audits *see* ASHRAE Level I Energy Audit
Energy Baseline 148–150; ASHRAE Level I Walkthrough Energy Audit 152–154
Energy Conservation Measures (ECMs) 159; Crough Center **213–214**
energy consumption, prorating 168s
energy consumption data, normalization 168, 169s
energy cost 178; savings 139, 210, 218n33
energy data: consumption 168, 169s; simulated 160
Energy Efficiency Best Management Practices Credit 22, 187
Energy End Use 174, 174s
Energy and Facility Management Software (EFMS): for buildings *157*; for Buildings Feedback Loop *157*
Energy Management System (EMS) 155–156, *157*
energy metering, Crough Center 205–206
Energy Metering prerequisite 170–174; partnering credit 172, 174; steps 170–172; tasks 170–172; techniques 173; tools 172–173
energy meters 160, 168; calibrating 160–161, 163, 172; data 163; digital platform to read 161–162, *162*, 163; location 172; procurement 171–172; tracking 155, 162, 163
energy model, facility 191
energy resources 133; ARC Performance Platform category 31; benchmarking 2; consumption 1; and indoor air quality; non-renewable 133; to treat waste water 107, 108–109
energy sources 173; shares in commercial buildings 170–171, *171*, 171b
Energy Star® 31; eligibility 166; energy target 137; label

163–166; Portfolio Manager® 159, 163, *164*, 167, *205*, 206–210; rating 159
Energy Survey and Engineering Analysis Audit (ASHRAE Level II) 152
energy tracking 148, 155, 314; system 157–159
energy use, Crough Center 207, **208**
Energy Use Intensity (EUI) 13s, 166
engagement, student 7
Engineering Analysis Audit 152
Enhanced Air Quality Strategies Credit 279
Enhanced Indoor Air Quality Strategy 278–279
Enhanced Refrigerant Management 182–183
Enthalpy Scale *250*
environment, interior 245, 247–252
environmental benefits, of green buildings 246
environmental impacts, of materials selection 220
environmental literacy 6, 36
Environmental Product Declaration (EPD) 220, 221s
Environmental Protection Agency (EPA) 175, 245; Clean Air Act (1970) 181, 182, 261s; goal to ELA studies 220; Green Book 261, 277; Green Cleaning Resources from 288b; Green Power Partnership 203; Property Types 166; Storm Water Management Model (SWMM) 93; WaterSense Budget Tool 130; WaterSense Label 115, 115s, *see also* Energy Star®
Environmentally Preferable Purchasing Policy (EPP) 231–232, *231*, 233, 240; for Facility Maintenance and Renovation *235*, *236*, 237, 239
equipment replacement or conversion, payback for 178, *180*
ergonomics 246, 246s
Eskew+Dumez+Ripple 3
ETo 122s

evaluation: facility 3; performance 3, 7; synergistic 10
evapotranspiration (ET) 122, 122s
exhaust system testing 272
Existing Building Commissioning Analysis Credit 22, 152
existing buildings: certification and precertification 32; commissioning 183–184, 188; drawings 143–144, *145*; interior assessment 245; plan *144*; recertification 30, 31; water use management importance 107, *see also* BEAM Plus for Existing Buildings; CASBEE EB; EB O+M (LEED); Green Globes for Existing Buildings (EB)
externally dominated buildings 251–252

facilities: campus 3, 45; choosing 45
Facilities Maintenance and Operations Department (CUA) 5, 23–24
Facilities Planning and Construction Department (CUA) 23–24
facility: energy model 191; evaluation 3; personnel 15, 311–312; selection 45, 46b; staff 20
Facility Maintenance and Renovation policy prerequisite 234–240; case study 240–242; exercises 23; map *235*; partnering credits 239–240; tasks 234–238; techniques 238–239
Facility Performance Evaluation (FPE) 2–3
faculty 20; full-time 20; university 20, 24
Faucet Flow Rate Conversion Equation *118*
Feasibility Stage (LEED Lab) 8, 12–13, 30, 32, 35–56, 309–310; CUARain 99; diagnostic process 12–16; Documentation Phase 8, 14, 39; goals 35–38; Implementation Phase 13–15;

INDEX

Feasibility Stage (*cont.*)
  policies 42–45; timeline 48–53, *48–50, 55*
feasibility study, for facility selection 45, 46b
feedback, submission 315
filtration 247
final review 316
Fixture Shielding 96
floor area, appropriate to rating systems 234, *234*
Flow Rate Approximation by Temperature Ratio Method 278, 278s
flush-out testing 238s
Food and Drug Administration (FDA) 285, 285s
footcandles 297s
formaldehyde 220–221, 222s
fossil fuels 61s
France, Green Building Council *see* HQE Exploitation
fresh air 260
Functional Performance Evaluation (FPE) 7; HKS 6
Functional Performance Testing (FPT) 185, 185s, 187
Fundamental Refrigerant Management 215

Gary, W.L. 22–23
German Sustainable Building Council *see* DGNB in Use
Gibney, Christine xx
glare 95–96, 96s, 247; solar types *292*
Glisic, Milan xix
global building assessment systems 6; North America and internationally based 139–140, *140*
global CO_2 emissions 133, *134*
Global Sustainable Existing Building Sustainability Assessment Tools: comparison 25, *26*; comparison for energy *137*; comparison for indoor air quality *254*; comparison for materials *224*; comparison for sites *80, 81*; comparison of transportation credits *63*; for energy *136*; for indoor air quality *253*; for materials *223*; for water efficiency *108, 109*

global warming potential (GWP) 69s
goals: campus 36, 38; LEED Lab 35–38; primary 35–36; project 38–48; secondary 36; university and course 25
green assessment 47; owner 312–313
Green Associate (GE) 6
Green Building Certification Inc.™ (GBCI) 6s, 21–22, 315
Green Building Council of Australia (GBCA) 111, 139, *see also* Green Star Performance
Green Building Initiative (GBI) 28
green buildings: environmental benefits of 246; experiences 21; productivity in 246
green cleaning, policy template 289–290
Green Cleaning Custodial Effectiveness Assessment 291
Green Cleaning prerequisite 286–292; equipment 289, 291–292; partnering credit 291–292; policy 287, 289; policy template 289–290; procedures 289; regulations 287; tasks 287–289; techniques 289, 290; tools 289–290; training 290
Green Cleaning Products and Materials 291
Green Cleaning Resources from USEPA 288b
Green Club (CUA) 21, 127
green code enforcement 133
Green Globes for Existing Buildings 28
Green Globes for Existing Buildings (EB) 28; benchmarks 28; categories 28, 254–255; certification 28; Emissions, Effluent and Pollution Control 136; Energy Category 136–138; Energy Environmental Assessment Area 62; Environmental Management assessment area 81–82; Environmental Management System Category 222–223; Indoor Environment categories 254–255; Resource Category

222; and site environmental impacts 80–82; steps 28; transportation in 62–64; updates 28; water category 109–110
Green Globes for New Buildings Canada 28
green infrastructure (GI) 92s
green power, options 201
Green Power Partnership (EPA) 203
Green Power Procurement Process (Green Power Partnership, EPA) 203
Green Purchasing Affirmative Procurement Plan 290
Green Pyramid; Credits for Building User Guide subcategory 229; Ecological Balance 86; energy criteria 141; Energy Efficiency Category 141; Indoor Environmental Quality Category 259; and site 85–86; transport in 67; Water Efficiency Category 114–115
green rating systems: comparison 61–65; LEED 16; transportation credits comparison 61–65, *62*
Green Seal, GS-42 290
Green Star Performance 27, 28–29; categories 28; Ecology and Emissions 82–83; Emissions 111; Energy Category 138–139; Fire Protection Systems Testing Credit 111; Greenhouse Gas Emissions 83, 138; Indoor Environmental Quality (IEQ) Category/sub-categories 225, 256; Indoor Environmental Quality (IEQ) Hazardous Materials Credit 225; Land Use and Ecology 82–83; Peak Electricity Demand 138–139; Potable Water Category 83, 111; site focus 82–83; Sustainable Transport Program 65; Transport Category 64–65; Transport Modes Survey 64, 65; Water Category 111
Green Tags 199
Green-e Energy Certified Resources 203

Greenfield Land 94s
greenhouse effect 133s
greenhouse gas (GHG) 133, 133s; emissions 66, 133, *133*; Scopes 1/2/3 200, 200s; use by sector 1, *1*
greywater 111, 111s
grid energy offsetting 201
groundcovers 94, 94s
groundwater 86, 91s, 109
Guangdong Province (China) 112
GWP (Global Warming Potential) 183

hardware failure 314
Harvard University Sustainability Plan **37**
Haslett, Tim 11
Haute Qualité Environnementale see HQE Exploitation
HCFCs 181
HCFC–22 refrigerant 215
health: evaluation 220–221; and green cleaning 286; impacts of interior environment 245; and light pollution 94–95
Health Product Declaration (HPD) 221–222, 223s
heat: latent *259*; sensible *259*
heat gain: latent *251*; sensible *251*; total *251*
heat island reduction 123
Heat Island Reduction Credit 90–91
heat pumps 178; refrigerant processed in *179*
heating, ventilating, air conditioning & refrigeration (HVAC&R) systems 161, 161s, 175, 178, 277–278
higher education industry 3; staffing report (2017) 4, *4*
hired vendors 240–241
hiring external party 158
HKS 3; functional performance evaluation (FPE) 6
Hong Kong/Hong Kong Green Building Council (HKGBC) *see* BEAM Plus for Existing Buildings
hospital settings 246
Hostick, Vanessa xix
HQE Exploitation: certification process areas 114; Comfort

INDEX

HQE Exploitation (*cont.*) and Health target 259; Eco-Construction Target 86; energy subcategories 142; High Environmental Quality area 86; IEQ targets 259; Sustainable Use scheme 67; transportation in 67; Waste and Maintenance targets 229; Water Management and Water Quality 115
human experience, ARC Performance Platform category 31–32
human health *see* health
humidity, relative 248
Humidity Ratio/Specific Humidity 248
HVAC&R (heating, ventilating, air conditioning & refrigeration) systems 162, 162s, 175, 178, 277–278

I-BEAM (IEQ Building Education and Assessment Model) 277, 278–279
identification, campus policy of green cleaning 287–288
IEQ Procedure (IEQP) 176
illuminance, surface **294**
impervious surfaces, CUA 102
Implementation Phase (LEED Lab) 13–15, 57–78
in-house staff 158
Independent System Operator (ISO) 189, 189s
indigenous species 124
Individual Student Progress Presentations (ISPPs) 14, 57, 58, 77; overview *58*; student examples for Light Pollution Reduction credit *59, 60*
indoor air pollution 245, 246–247, 252–253
indoor air quality, and energy 248–249
Indoor Air Quality (IAQ)/Indoor Environmental Quality (IEQ) 240; case study 302–304; comparison 252–260; credit sub-topics 246, *246*; credits 245, **246**, 252–253, 260–302; exercises 304; indoor lighting quality 293, **294**, 295–296; partnering credit 278–279; resources 277; standards 276–277; tasks 260–274; techniques 277–278; tools 274–277
Indoor Air Quality Policy (IAQP), for FMR *235*, 237–238
Indoor Atmosphere, theory 245–252
indoor environment: comfort 247–250; Health and Comfort sub-topics 256, *256*
Indoor Environmental Quality (IEQ) *see* Indoor Air Quality (IAQ)/Indoor Environmental Quality (IEQ)
Indoor Water Use Reduction Credits 115–122; partnering credits 118–119; tasks 115–116; techniques 118; tools 116–118, *117, 118*; Water Efficiency prerequisite (Option 1) *117, 118*
information: cumulative from student diagnoses 11, *11*; gathering 261; inconsistent 314; repositories of 8
initial certification 47, 314–315
Innovation Credit 77
innovations savings chart, biochar (biocarbon) **128**
Institute for Market Research 2
instructors 24, 316; part-time 20; types 20
Integrated Pest Management (IPM) 298, 298s, 299; Plan 308n93
Interdepartmental Online Repository (iDOR) 310, 310s, *312, 313*, 316
interdisciplinarity 19, 36
interdisciplinary mix 20
interior environment 245; comfort within 247–252; health impacts 246–247
interior materials 247
internal digital repository 316; iDOR 310, 310s, *312, 313*
internally dominated buildings 250
International Facilities Management Association (IFMA), *Sustainability "How-To" Guide* green cleaning resource 290

INDEX

International Living Building Institute, Living Building Challenge 3, 3s
Internationale de l'Eclairage (CIE) 292
Interpretations (LEED) 317s
invasive species 100–103
'investment grade' audit 152–154
irrigation: micro-spray 130, 130s; systems 124
irrigation water, metering (Crough Center) 206

Japan *see* CASBEE EB

K-12 building type 207
Key Performance Indicators (KPIs) 110s

Labs 21 167, 168
lamps *296*; life **294**; purchasing 233
landfill tax 234s
landscape water allowance (LWA) 122
landscape water requirement (LWR) 122–123, 122s
landscaping systems 79
latent heat *249*
lawn watering 122
LCGWP (Lifecyle Direct Global Warming Potential) 183
LCODP (Lifecycle Ozone Depletion Potential) 183
Learning Management Systems (LMSs) 24, 57
learning module icons 17, *17*
learning tool, course as
LEED Lab Timing Chart (USGBC) 47
LEEDUser 32–33, 159
Lewin, Kurt 10s, 11
LiderA: energy assessment 141; Environmental Comfort Category 258; Materials, Waste and Sustainable Use Categories 228; Resources Category 85; Site and Integration Category 85; transport in 66; Water Category 113
Life Cycle Assessment (LCA) 220, 220s; Report from Revit plug-in TALLY *221*

Life (Equipment Life) 183
Lifecycle Ozone Depletion Potential (LCODP) 183
Lifecyle Direct Global Warming Potential (LCGWP) 183
light clutter 95–96, 96s
light (lux) meters 96, 98s, 297
light pollution 94–96
Light Pollution Reduction Credit 94–98; ISPP examples *59*, *60*; Sustainable Sites Credit *97*; tasks 96; techniques 98; tools 96
light reflectance value (LRV) 295s, 307nn88&89
light trespass 94–95, 94s, *95*
lighting: artificial 247; control 293–294; day 247–248; direct overhead **294**; indoor 247–248; outdoor 94–96; reduction (Crough Center) 206; scheme 293, 293s; strategies 293, **294**, 295b
Lighting Credit 292–298; partnering credit 297–298; tasks 293–296; techniques 297; tools 296–297
Livable Building (LB), Livable Outdoors subdivision (LBo) 67
Living Building Challenge (International Living Building Institute) 3, 3s
location, smoking 280
low chemical water treatment system *125*
low impact development (LID) 92, 92s
low-hanging fruit option 124, 186, 216
LR (Refrigerant Leakage Rate) 183
luminance **294**, 295s; cycle *296*
lux (light) meters 96, 98s, 297

maintenance, annual and refrigerant cost difference equation 178–181, *180*
Maintenance/Renovation Policy 230
makeup water 126, 127s
marketing, LEED 21
Master Site credits 22, *40*, 69, 316–317; approach to achieving 38–42; CUA 126–128; LEED credits

| 329

INDEX

Master Site credits (*cont.*)
  qualifying as 39, *40*; LEED
  O+M eligible for *40*
materials: chemical input and
  output 220–221; interior 247;
  selection 220
Materials and Resources (MR)
  Category 220, 240; case study
  240–242; comparison 222–230;
  credits 230–240; exercises 242;
  IDOR page *312*; theory 220–222
melatonin 95, 96s, 292
Mella, Greg 3
mercury 231s
MERV Rating *261*; Chart *262*
Meter Certificate of Calibration,
  sample *215*
Metered Water Use 116
metering, irrigation water 206
meters: private 173; water 111, 116,
  121, *121, see also* energy meters
Meyers, Elizabeth *xiv*, xix
micro-spray irrigation 130, 130s
Middle East climate *see* Pearl
  for ESTIDAMA (PORS)
Minimum Energy Efficiency
  Performance 45b
Minimum Energy Performance
  prerequisite 160–170, 173;
  diagram **165**; partnering credit
  168–170; steps for success
  161–163; tasks 163–166;
  techniques 167–168; tools
  166–167
Minimum Indoor Air Quality
  Performance 303
Minimum Indoor Air Quality
  Performance Calculator 277
MIT Greenhouse Emissions Gas
  Inventory 36, *37*
mold 247, *247*
Montreal Protocol (1987) 175,
  181–182
moveDC 74, 74s
MR (End-of-life Refrigerant
  Loss) 183

National Ambient Air Quality
  Standards (NAAQS) 261s, 277
National Institute of Building
  Sciences 2–3
National Reference Standards 8
National Renewable Energy
  Laboratory 317

natural infiltration strategies 94
Natural Ventilation Procedure
  (NVRP) 277
nature comparison, green
  cleaning 286
navigation ease, campus 79
new buildings,
  commissioning 184
*New Construction Building
  Commissioning Best Practices*
  (BCxA) 188
New Construction (LEED NC) 45,
  234; rating system 160
noise pollution 246
non-certified buildings, initial
  certification 34n23
non-chemical cooling water
  treatments 126s
non-smoking: documentation
  283–285; policy 280–282, 285;
  signage 282–283, *283*, 286
Nonattainment Areas 261,
  261s, 277
NOOA Past Weather History 93
normalization, data 168, 169s
North Carolina State University 29

O+M Assessment (LEED)
  150–152; for best practices in
  O+M procedures 143–148
O+M (LEED): Alternative
  Transportation Category 65;
  ARC Performance Platform
  29, 29s, 300; certification 10,
  39; certification process 6, 21;
  Energy and Atmosphere (EA)
  Category 134–135, 139; Indoor
  Environmental Quality (IEQ)
  credits 256–257; launch 27;
  Master Site credits 316–317;
  Materials and Resources
  (MR) 225–226; pathways
  29–33; Rating System 29;
  Site Management Policy 83;
  Sustainable Site Category 83;
  traditional platform 29–30
O+M Plans (LEED) 144, **145–147**;
  improvement 134
O+M rating system (LEED) 7,
  29–30, 36, 39, *41*, 134;
  pathways combination 32;
  performance platform (ARC)
  29, 29s, 30–32, 38; principles
  16; on recertification 48;

release of new 30; traditional pathway 29–30, 38; Water Efficiency (WE) 108, 111–112, 114–115

O+M Reference Guide (LEED) 8, 13, 48, 123, 143, 178, 231; Assessment 143–148; credit milestones 59; energy metering prerequisite steps 170–172; energy performance benchmark *165*; Facility Maintenance and Renovation policy prerequisite steps 234–235, *235*, *236*; Master Site credits 39; Minimum Energy Performance steps 161–163; renewable energy + carbon offsets tasks 201–202; Version 4 16

Obama, Barack, Executive Order No. 13514 286

Occupant Comfort Survey Credit 278, 299–302; partnering credit 302; survey 300–301, 301–302; tasks 299–301; techniques 301–302; tools 301

Occupant Survey, Crough Center *300*

ODP (Ozone Depletion Potential) 183

off-gassing 221, 222s, 247

Ongoing Commissioning 139, 184, 186–187, 216

ongoing goods 230s

Ongoing Purchasing and Waste Policy prerequisite 230–234, 240

online platform/portal (LEED) 14, 25, 25s, 30, 38, 309–310, 313; login 309–310, *310*; registration 310, *311*, *see also* ARC Performance Platform

online *Toolbox Teaching Guide* 16, 17–18

Operations and Maintenance *see* O+M entries

Optimize Energy Performance Credit 169–170

OPUS Hall (CUA): cooling tower *125*; non-smoking signs *283*

outcomes, performance-based 47

outdoor lighting 94–96

outdoor smoking policy 285–286

Outdoor Water Use Reduction Credit 122–124; tasks 123; techniques 124; tools 123–124

outsourced analyses 158

outstanding credits 314

owner, role 312–313

Ozone 277

ozone layer 174, *175*, 175s

Paraon, Ana xix–xx

Particulate Matter 277

passive smoking 280

pathways: LEED O+M traditional platform 29–30, 38; performance *see* ARC Performance Platform

payback, for equipment replacement or conversion 178

peak energy reduction 189, 191

peak load 191

Pearl for ESTIDAMA (PORS): alternative transportation 68; Energy 141; Livable Indoors (LBi) section 258–259; Livable Outdoors (LBo) section 67; Natural Systems Category 85; Natural Systems Design and Management Category 85; Precious Water Category 85, 113; Stewardship Materials section 228; transport in 66–67; water conservation 85

performance: building process 10; evaluation 1–3, 7; green cleaning 286

performance benchmark 162; obtaining 163, *165*

Performance Certifications (ARC) 32

performance pathway 29, *see also* ARC Performance Platform

performance periods 44, 61, 83; commissioning 185–186; by credit 44, *46*; enhancing energy efficiency 169

performance platform, ARC 29, 29s, 30–32, 300

Performance Score 34n23, 38

performance-based outcomes 44

Perimeter Measurements 96; guide *97*

Perkins and Will 3

INDEX

Permanent Load Shifting (PLS) 189
personnel, facility 15, 311–312
Pest Management Credit 298–299; tasks 298b; techniques 299; tools 299
phase conversion 176, 176s
phase-out plan, refrigerants 181
phone app 297
pilot course, CUA 5, 20, 21, 22
planned future action 14
planning 19
plans/and or programs 42–45
Plant Guides 124
platforms, LMS 24
Plug Loads 174, 174s
Point Integration Diagram (PID) 13, 14s, 52; final *14*; initial *15*
policies, LEED Lab 42–45
pollutant mitigation 79
pollution: air 246–247; light 94–96; noise 246
Portfolio Manager® (Energy Star®) 159, 163, *164*, 167, *205*, 206–210
Portugal-based rating system *see* LiderA
Post Occupancy Evaluation (POE) 2–3, 5–8; DeMontfort method 5–6; Post Occupancy Review of Building Engineering (PROBE) method 5–6
potable water 84, 107, 109, 110–111, 114–115
Potomac Electric Power Company (PEPCO) 160
power meters: amps 172; single/three-phase 172
Preliminary Audit 152
preliminary review 316
prerequisites 22; LEED 7, 30, 38; rating system comparison 25–27, *26*
preventative maintenance 274
Preventative Maintenance Schedule, for Crough Center **211–212**
Preventative Management Plan (PMP) 144, 151–152
private meters 173
process water 115, 115s
Procurement and Waste Management Policy: for CUA

Sustainability Plan 241, *241*; map *231*; partnering credits 233; tasks 231–232; techniques 232–233; tools 232
productivity, in green buildings 246
products, green 288–289
professional exemption, alternative compliance path 303
professor 20
programs/and or plans 42–45
project administrator 30, 313, 316
Project Credit Interpretation Ruling (CIR) 33
project goals 36, 38; approach to realizing 38–48
prorating energy consumption 168s
Psychrometric Charts, thermal comfort zones 247, *248*, *249*, *250*, *251*, *252*
public transport 61–64, 66
Purchasing – Lamps 233
Purchasing – Ongoing 233
Purchasing Waste Policy 230; Ongoing 230
Purchasing – Facility Maintenance and Renovation Credit 239

quick chargers 66, 66s

Raingarden Alley 51, 52
raingardens 51–52
rainwater 92; collection systems 94; runoff 99
Rainwater Management Credit 51, 91–94; tasks 92–93; techniques 94; tools 93–94
rating systems 25–33; alternative 25; appropriate floor area 234, *234*; comparison 27, *27*, 41, *41*; energy categories comparison 134–142, *137*; for green transport 61–68; LEED Design and Construction 47; prerequisites and credits comparison 25–27, *26*; and site 86; site considerations comparison 80–86; water efficiency 108–115, *see also* Global Sustainable Existing

INDEX

Building Sustainability Assessment Tools; individual rating system names; O+M rating system (LEED)
RC (Refrigerant Charge) 183
recertification 25, 44–46; Crough Center 240; of existing buildings 30, *31*; O+M 30, 44
recording of data 310; in Documentation Phase 309–310
Reference Guide *see* O+M Reference Guide (LEED)
reflectance, surface **294**
refrigerant: cost and annual maintenance difference equation 178–181, *180*; processed in air conditioner *177*; processed in heat pump *179*
Refrigerant Charge (RC) 181s, 183
refrigerant cycle, physics of *177*
Refrigerant Management prerequisite 174–183; partnering credit 182–183; tasks 176–181; techniques 182; tools 181
refrigerants 175, 176s; comparison **175**; identifying 176–178; leakage minimization 182; phase-out plan 181; system analysis 178–181; use calculation 182–183
refrigeration cycle, phase conversion 176, 176s
refrigerators 178
regional factors, for alternative transportation 61–62
registration 25; O+M 30; quantity of buildings 27
Reid, Jazzmin xx
relative humidity *248*
renewable energy 217; equations *202*; sources 199; systems 199
Renewable Energy + Carbon Offsets Credit 199–204; case study 204–205; exercises 215–217; tasks 200–202; techniques 203–204; tools 202–203
renewable energy + carbon offsets equations *202*

Renewable Energy Certificates (RECs) 199, 200, *200*, 203, 204
renewable resource systems *see* green power
renovations: campus 234; green measure for products and waste 288
replacement costs 178
representatives, for credits 22
research, academic 36–38
research and engagement, post-occupancy 3
resources, LEED certification 32–33
Restore Habitat Credit 52, 83
resubmission 316
retro-commissioning 184
Return on Investment Calendar 188
review, Documentation Phase (LEED Lab) 316–317
rooms, size and space 261

Sagor, Richard, Action Research Cycle 12, *12*, 13–14, 16
saturation temperature *249*
scale 124, 126s
scholarship of sustainability 4
seasonal affective disorder (SAD)/seasonal depression 292, 292s
semester timeline *15*
sensible heat *249*
sensitivity to students and staff 79
Sequence of Operations (SOP) 144, 151, 158
setpoint 143, 151, 162, 185, 215–216, 302
sewage: municipal system options *92*; system 91
Shark Meter *162*
Sheffer, Marcus 191
sick building syndrome 246s
signage, non-smoking 282–283, *283*, 286
simulated energy data 160
Singapore-based rating system *see* BCA Green Mark
Site Assessment 47, 56, 83, 110, 148, 152, 153, 255
Site Development Credit 90
Site Development-Protect Credit 52

INDEX

Site Improvement Credit 90
Site Improvement Plan, CUA 99–103
Site Maintenance Inventory 87–88
site management best practices 89
Site Management Credit 87–98; case study 98–103; exercise 103–104; partnering credits 90–91; tasks 87–88; techniques 88; tools 88
Site Management Policy 42, 87–88; credit 42; CUA 99–103; synergistic credits to 90–91
small storm hydrology method 93, *93*
Smith, Z 3
SmithGroup 3
smoke control prerequisite 279–283; tasks 280–285; techniques 285–286; tools 285
smoke-free campuses 283, 285
smoking: outdoor 285–286; prohibited 280
Social Responsibility Report 36, 36s
software: applications 24; failure 314
soil: compaction (CUA) 99; health 127; International Year of Soils (UN, 2015) 127; turning and loosening 99; types (CUA) 99, *100*
solar glare, types *292*
Solar Reflectance Index (SRI) 91s
Solar Renewable Energy Certificates (SRECs) 199
Solid Waste Management Policy (SWMP) *231*, 232, 233, 240
Solid Waste Management – Facility Maintenance and Renovation Credit 239–240
Solid Waste Management – Ongoing 233
Space Requirements 143
space types 303; Crough Center 207, *209*, 303, 305n29
spaces, regularly occupied 307n81
spectrophotometers 296
staff 19, 313; facility 20; in-house 158; university 20, 23–24

staffing, campus sustainability 4, *4*
stakeholders 11, 36, 241
Standard Comfort Zone *250*
standards: for Air Quality Performance prerequisite 276–277; *Thermal Environmental Conditions for Human Occupancy* (ANSI/ASHRAE 55) 301
Statement of Energy Performance 148, *153*, 210
steam meter, malfunction 314
Stephens, John 11
stormwater 91, 91s, 92; management 79, 92–93; runoff 100, *101*, *102*, 123
student-to-credit ratio 313–314
students: collaboration platform 35; as collaborators 20–21, 35; engagement 7
sub-contractors 22
submission 314–316; feedback 315
support services, professional quality 23–24
surface: illuminance **294**; reflectance **294**
sustainability: campus staffing 4, *4*; driving efforts on campus 7; education 16; leaders 3; scholarship 4
Sustainability Improvement Plan 92
Sustainability Offices 4–5, 38
Sustainability Plan (CUA) 74, 75b, 241, *241*; missing links 76, 76b; Procurement and Waste Management Policy for 241, *241*
Sustainability Staffing Report, Higher Education *4*
sustainable environments, focus 4
Sustainable Existing Building Sustainability Assessment Tools *see* Global Sustainable Existing Building Sustainability Assessment Tools
sustainable facility activities 6, *7*
Sustainable Procurement Plan (SPP) 290
Sustainable Purchasing Policy 240
Sustainable Sites Credit, light pollution reduction *97*

INDEX

synergistic evaluation, of buildings 10
synergizing credits 47
synergy: diagram 55; sustainable strategies for 47, 51; water meters and documentation requirements 112
Systems Manual 187, 187s; updating 187
Systems Narrative 144, 150–151

TAB (Testing, Adjusting and Balancing) 273s
technicians 22
terrain elevation, CUA map 101
testing, air flow rates for ASHRAE Compliance 272–273
textbook, user-friendly educational 16–17
theory of action 14; revised 14
thermal comfort: ASHRAE definition 247; factors 250
Thermal Comfort credit 302
Thermal Comfort Tool 301
thermal comfort zone 247, 249s; Psychrometric Charts 247, 248, 249, 250, 251, 252
Thermal Energy Meters, EN 1434 (CEN/TC 176) 173
Thermal Environmental Conditions for Human Occupancy (ANSI/ASHRAE 55) 301
thermostats 249
timeline, LEED Lab 48–53, 48–50, 50–52, 53
tipping fee 234s
Tobacco Control Act (US, 2009) 6, 285
Toolbox Teaching Guide 16, 17–18
Torcellini, Paul 187
tracking: energy 148, 155, 157–159; energy meter data 163; energy meters 155, 162; ongoing 21
Tradable Renewable Certificates (TRCs) 199
trademark, LEED Lab 21
training, green cleaning 290
transportation 62–64; alternative 61–62, 68, 68s, 74; ARC Performance Platform category 31–32; multimodal 74; sector 61; strategies 69

Transportation Credit Category 61–77, 63; comparison 61–68; Crough Center case study 74–77; exercises 77; theory 61
Transportation Demand Management (TDM) 61, 61s
transportation survey 68–70, 74; ARC Performance Platform 69; commuting 72b; manual administration 69–70
travel surveys 65, 65s
trees 100
turfgrass 103, 123

United Arab Emirates (UAE) 141; Initial National Communication to UN on Climate Change (2006) 85, *see also* Pearl for ESTIDAMA (PORS)
United Nations (UN), International Year of Soils (2015) 127
United States of America (USA): Energy Information Administration 1, 133; Food and Drug Administration (FDA) 285, 285s; state and local smoke-free restaurant and bar laws (2002–2012) 283, 284; utility companies list **193–198**; Washington DC 74, 160, *see also* Environmental Protection Agency (EPA)
United States Department of Agriculture (USDA), *Guidelines for Procurement* green cleaning guidelines 290
United States Green Building Council (USGBC) 5, 5s, 21, 107; Campus Implementation Workbook 42; Center for Green Schools 5, 21; LEED Lab Timing Chart 47; LEED v4 Discussion Forums 33; Student Group 21
university: administration 22; faculty 20, 24; staff 20, 23–24
upstream 122s
utility: bills 133–134; companies (US) **193–198**; sub-meter system 161, 173
utility meter 160, 174; shared 173

| 335

INDEX

vegetated swales 99
vegetation management 99–103, *103*
vendors: hired 240–241; outside cleaning 290
ventilation 247
Ventilation Rate Procedure (VRP) 276
views 298
visitors 78n26
visual comfort 292, *292*, 293
volatile organic compounds (VOCs) 32, 32s, 247, 247s

walkthroughs: ASHRAE Level I Energy Audit **149**, 152–154, 159, 174, 210; POE 6
Washington DC 74; PEPCO 160
waste, ARC Performance Platform Category 31
Waste Management Policy (WMP), for FMR *235*, 237, 238
waste water 107; energy to treat 107, 108–109; reusing 107–108
water: ARC Performance Platform Category 31; building impact reduction 107–108; cooling 176–178; flush and flow summary statistics **120**; indoor and outdoor use reduction 111; makeup 125, 127s; potable 84, 107, 109, 110–111, 114–115; reuse 107–108; runoff 91, 93, 94, 98–99, 103; sub-meters 14s; supply contamination 107; waste 107, 108–109, *see also* rainwater
Water Budget Tool 123
Water Efficiency (WE) prerequisite: case study 126–128; credits 107, 115–126; exercises 128–130; Faucet Flow Rate Conversion *118*; LEED O+M 108, 111–112; rating systems comparison 108–115
water metering 111, 116; Crough Center 204–206
Water Metering Credit 120–122
water meters 111, 116, 121, *121*; stainless steel pulse output *121*; synergy with documentation requirements 112
water treatment systems: low chemical *125*; non-chemical cooling 126s
water use: calculated 115, 115–116, 116–118, 116b, *117*, *118*, *119*; and disposal 107; reduction *117*, *118*
Water Use Reduction calculation *119*
Watersense Label 115, 115s
wet-bulb temperature *249*
Wordpress 24
World Health Organization (WHO) 245; indoor air pollution causes 252–253

xeriscaping 124, 124s